BLOOMSBURY AND BEYOND

BLOOMSBURY AND BEYOND

The friends and enemies of Roy Campbell

JOSEPH PEARCE

HarperCollins*Publishers*

HarperCollins*Publishers*
77–85 Fulham Palace Road, London W6 8JB
www.**fire**and**water**.com

First published in Great Britain in 2001
by HarperCollins*Publishers*

1 3 5 7 9 10 8 6 4 2

A catalogue record for this book
is available from the British Library

ISBN 0 00 274092 3

Set in PostScript Linotype Minion
by Rowland Phototypesetting Ltd,
Bury St Edmunds, Suffolk

Printed and bound in Great Britain by
Creative Print and Design Wales, Ebbw Vale

For Ferdi McDermott

CONTENTS

PREFACE

Few writers have stirred up more controversy in their own lifetime than Roy Campbell. Loved by many, loathed by many others, Campbell was a talented but volatile character. Throughout the 1920s, following publication of his long poem *The Flaming Terrapin*, he was lauded as one of the finest young poets of the new 'Waste Land' generation. At Oxford he met and befriended T. S. Eliot and the Sitwells, Percy Wyndham Lewis and C. S. Lewis, William Walton and Peter Warlock, Augustus John and Aldous Huxley, Nancy Cunard and Nina Hamnett. Such was his reputation as a wild colonial boy, fresh from the African veld, that Marie Beerbohm dubbed him 'the Zulu', a nickname which was immortalized by Wyndham Lewis when he invented Zulu Blades, a character based on Campbell, for his novel *The Apes of God*.

Following a whirlwind romance, Campbell entered into a whirlwind marriage with Mary Garman which survived several highly charged affairs, both real and imagined. Campbell brawled publicly with Jacob Epstein following Epstein's accusations that Campbell was conducting a *ménage à trois* with Mary and her sister Kathleen, whom Epstein would later marry. Campbell would become estranged from his old friend William Plomer after Plomer alleged that Mary had made unwelcome advances in the back of a taxi. Later, Campbell would provoke widespread gossip in bohemian circles for his close friendship with Nina Hamnett. Most notorious of all the real and alleged affairs that dogged their marriage was Mary's passionate affair with Vita Sackville-West, which provoked the jealousy of Virginia Woolf. This 'Bloomsbury affair', which began when the Campbells were living on Vita Sackville-West's estate at Long Barn, would prove to be one of the most creatively catalytic love affairs in literary history, inspiring Woolf's *Orlando*, Sackville-West's *King's Daughter* and Campbell's satirical attack on the Bloomsbury set, *The Georgiad*.

In later years, Campbell would create further controversy by supporting Franco's forces during the Spanish Civil War, provoking a war of words with the left-wing poets Stephen Spender, W. H.

Auden, Cecil Day-Lewis, Louis MacNeice and Hugh MacDiarmid. This would culminate in Campbell throwing a punch at Spender during a poetry recital and becoming embroiled in a brawl with MacNeice in a London pub.

Campbell was first attacked and then befriended by C. S. Lewis, and was admired by J. R. R. Tolkien. He became an occasional member of the Inklings, the literary group centred on Lewis and Tolkien at Oxford. In later years he became both friend and mentor to Dylan Thomas, accompanying the mercurial Welsh poet on many of his drunken binges.

Against the turbulent backdrop of their life together, Roy and Mary Campbell found a degree of tranquillity in the Catholic faith. They were received into the Church in Spain in the troubled days before the outbreak of that country's fratricidal war. They almost lost their lives during the violence in Toledo in 1936, discovering with horror that the Carmelite monks, whom they had befriended and sheltered in their house, had been murdered in cold blood.

The poetry inspired by Campbell's Christianity is as paradoxically divided as his personality. From the unrelenting violence of *Flowering Rifle* to the mystical peace of his translations of St John of the Cross, Campbell's 'poetry of faith' is both perplexing and challenging – yet no more so than the poet himself, who was admired by many of his peers, including T. S. Eliot and Edith Sitwell, as one of the finest writers of verse that the twentieth century had produced.

Fine poet, beloved friend, hated enemy. Roy Campbell's reputation, a century after his birth, is in need of reappraisal. This study, looking at the man at the centre of so much love and loathing, seeks to shed light on poetry's dark horse.

ACKNOWLEDGEMENTS

This volume would scarcely have been possible without the generous assistance of Roy Campbell's daughters, Teresa and Anna, who have been unfailing in the time they have expended and the materials they have made available. I was fortunate enough to enjoy their warm hospitality during my visit to Anna's home, north-west of Lisbon, at the end of 1998. As well as providing hours of taped reminiscences about many aspects of life with their father, they made available two volumes of unpublished memoirs, hundreds of their father's unpublished letters and dozens of photographs, many of which had never previously seen the light of day. They have also corresponded regularly with me, both before and since our meeting, never failing to elucidate individual points whenever I have requested that they do so. This volume is as much a testament to their labour as to mine.

I am indebted to Rob Lyle, Campbell's closest friend during the final 10 years of his life. During our interview in Portugal and in subsequent correspondence he has offered many personal reminiscences and insights. Francesca de Carondelet, Campbell's granddaughter, has shared her own memories of Roy and Mary, as well as bestowing the warmth of her hospitality and friendship, both during and since my visit to Portugal. My gratitude is also due to Francisco Campbell Custodio, Campbell's grandson, for his continuing co-operation. The many quotations from Campbell's works are included by kind permission of Jonathan Ball Publishers, who have allowed me to quote freely from Campbell's poetry, prose and translations. Without such permission this volume would have been greatly impoverished.

Ferdi McDermott offered much encouragement during the early stages of the project, as did Father Laurie Lock who made his extensive library available to me. My father has assisted me greatly and so has Sarah Hollingsworth, who read each chapter as it was written, offering invaluable advice. A. F. W. Simmons has been unfailing in his support as ever, and Jan Mason and Iain Kidd have also been generous in offering their assistance. Finally, my enduring thanks are due to James Catford, Amy Boucher Pye, Kathy Dyke, Gina Sussens, Heather Worthy and all at Harper-Collins who work diligently to bring my work to fruition.

CHAPTER ONE

OUT OF AFRICA

> And the springbok bounced, and fluttered, and flew,
> Hooping their spines on the gaunt karroo.
> Gay zebras pranced and snorted aloud –
> With the crackle of hail their hard hoofs pelt,
> And thunder breaks from the rolling cloud
> That they raise on the dusty Veld.[1]

Roy Campbell's first visit to England was instantly forgettable. He had been taken there as a baby, but was too young to remember anything about it. His first recollection was of his native South Africa. His eight- or nine-year-old Zulu nurse-girl, Catherine Mgadi, had wheeled him further than usual on their regular morning outing. The hedge which they had been skirting suddenly stopped. They had come across an empty, railed-in site on a ridge overlooking the Indian Ocean. A horse, its head stretched over the wire fence, was startled by their arrival and reared up and turned away, 'and I, looking down the grassy slope through its legs, saw a huge living expanse of glittering azure, like a peacock's tail, electrified with winds and solar fire'.[2]

In later years, Campbell would regard his earliest memory as an almost mythic prelude to the rest of his life. 'That first remembered glimpse of the sea was symbolical of my subsequent life, since I actually saw it first *through the legs of a horse*!'[3] Horses and the sea would be permanent companions throughout Campbell's life, the marine and the equine always offering an escape from life's prosaic responsibilities and providing inspiration for his poetic imagination.

Seeing that her infant charge was visibly excited at his first sight of the ocean, Catherine told him it was *lwandhla*, the Zulu word for the sea. To the wide-eyed child the word was almost as magical as the thing it described. '*Lwandhla*,' Campbell recalled, 'which, in two syllables, Homerically expressed the pride and glory of the ocean and the plunge of its breakers, struck my mind with a force which no other word or line in prose or poetry has ever had for me since. I went on repeating the word *lwandhla* for days. It is the first word I remember *learning*.'[4]

The African roots of Campbell's childhood were culturally cross-fertilized with the Scottish ancestry of his parents. His father, Major Samuel George Campbell, known as Sam-Joj to the natives, had met a young Highlander called Dooglie during a trip to Scotland. When Sam Campbell returned to South Africa he brought Dooglie with him, and the young Scot taught the older Campbell children the bagpipes as well as Highland dancing. Roy's elder brothers, Archie and George, were soon adept at both, winning medals in the juvenile categories of the competitions organized by the Caledonian Society. 'From those times onwards, till recently,' Campbell wrote, 'I always believed we were pure Scotch Highlanders by descent. I only discovered our Irish and French ancestry by accident.'[5]

Campbell's grandfather, William Campbell, had set sail with his wife and three young children from Glasgow on 29 March 1850 on the brig *Conquering Hero*. Three months later they arrived at Port Natal. The 'harbour', a broad, shallow lagoon, was so choked with sand that the brig could not enter it. There was no jetty and the shore was a waste of sand dunes dotted with scrubby castor-oil plants and the occasional forlorn-looking palm. The only signs of human habitation were a few mud huts and a fragile-looking fort, manned by a small platoon of soldiers. Out of sight, between the lagoon and the jungle-covered hill which overlooked it, at the end of a sandy track which wound its way into the bush, was the small town for which the Campbells and the hundred or so other prospective settlers were bound. It was all a far cry from the city of Durban which would soon be rising on the site, burgeoning in size and influence until the quiet lagoon had been transformed into the greatest port in southern Africa.

Like most of the other settlers aboard the *Conquering Hero*, William Campbell had deposited his savings with Joseph Charles Byrne, the entrepreneur who had arranged the voyage. When he and the others went to reclaim their money from Byrne's agent in Port Natal, they were told that Byrne had been declared bankrupt. With horror they realized that Byrne was a confidence trickster who made his fortune from pocketing the savings of those for whom he arranged passages to the colonies. He operated under many aliases and, although bankruptcy was his favourite ploy, he was not averse to 'dying' on occasion before resurrecting himself under another name in Mauritius, Australia or some other far-flung corner of the Empire. William Campbell was saved from destitution by his wife. More cautious than her husband, she had sewn 120 gold sovereigns into the lining of her clothing before they set sail.

Apart from this faltering and naive start, William Campbell took to the colonial life with considerable success. Driven by ambition and fathomless reserves of energy, he built the breakwater that still forms the foundation of the great North Pier in Durban harbour. He was also responsible for building the first railway in Natal, a mile of wooden rails on which ran wooden, ox-drawn carriages that were used to transport the stones for the construction of the breakwater. When he was not undertaking feats of civil engineering, he was an early pioneer of large-scale sugar cane cultivation, Natal's most important crop, which would form the foundation of the Campbell family fortune.

The Campbells had six more children following their arrival in Natal. One of their sons became a chief magistrate, another became District Native Commissioner of Rhodesia, and yet another became a senator in the first Union Parliament in 1910 and a friend of the Prime Minister, Louis Botha. Sam Campbell, the son destined to become father of the poet, was born in 1861. In 1878 he went to Edinburgh to study medicine, where he took prizes for surgery, clinical surgery and botany. He graduated with honours in 1882. After completing postgraduate work at the Pasteur Institute in Paris, he went to Vienna in 1883 to specialize in the treatment of ear, nose and throat ailments. Returning to Natal, he spent three years in practice. In 1886 he travelled back to Scotland to take his MD and become a Fellow of the Royal College of Surgeons. It was during this period that he met and married Margaret Wylie Dunnachie, the daughter of James Dunnachie, a wealthy self-made businessman.

In his entertaining but highly exaggerated autobiography, *Light on a Dark Horse*, Roy Campbell decorated his family tree with several romantic embellishments. His mother's family were 'Highland Jacobites who left Scotland after 1745 but returned on the amnesty'. His maternal grandmother was 'a Gascon from Bayonne' from whom he inherited his 'love of bulls, and of Provençal, French, and Spanish poetry'. His father's family were 'descended from many generations of bog-trotting Scotch-Irish peasants who were tenants of the Kilpatricks, the squires of Carndonagh in North Donegal'. According to Campbell, family tradition held that the Campbells had fled to Ireland from Scotland after the defeat of the Earl of Argyll by Montrose in 1645. For a hundred years 'they seemed to lie very low till one of them, a "crowder" or professional fiddler, in 1750 or so, was lucky enough to catch the eye of one of the Kilpatrick girls, daughter of his landlord, while he was fiddling at a ball given by the Squire'. Warming to the romance, Campbell weaves the tale with more than a hint of Irish blarney. The furious father, discovering his daughter's affection for the fiddler, locks the lovelorn girl in an upstairs room. She escapes by throwing out her mattress and those of her sisters, and jumping down onto them. She elopes with the fiddler and there is a runaway marriage. The father pretends to disown the couple, but secretly forgives his favourite daughter. Upon his death he leaves her and her husband an equal share of his property with her sisters.

After this, they all lived happily ever after. Campbell's ancestor hung up his fiddle to become a magistrate and a colonel of the Volunteers. He married a second time, a Miss Macaulay from Derry, and divided his property into four with his sons. It was in this way, Campbell wrote, that his great-great-grandfather inherited the farm of Strathsbridge in the parish of Donagh, two miles from Carndonagh. In order to add veracity to his story he cites, somewhat surprisingly, none other than George Orwell:

> According to that valiant and fine writer, my friend, the late George Orwell, who had traced it out, I have the great honour to be related to his first wife, who was a Miss O'Shaughnessy from those parts – the heroic lady who saved his life during the massacres of International Brigaders by their fellow-Reds in Catalunya: so apparently our family tradition relating to those parts of Ireland is quite valid.[6]

Campbell also spices up the personalities of his more recent ancestors by alluding to their famous friends. His maternal grandfather, James Dunnachie, was, says Campbell, an acquaintance of both Browning and Tennyson, as well as knowing Rossetti and other Pre-Raphaelites.[7] Meanwhile, Campbell's own father was such an 'extraordinary character' that it was little wonder that he 'proved so irresistible to Mark Twain, who corresponded with him for many years and stayed at our house when passing through Durban'. Again, Campbell adds veracity to his story by adding that 'the two families remain friendly to this day'.[8]

In 1889 Sam Campbell returned with his new wife to South Africa where he established a highly successful medical practice. He was greatly loved and respected by his patients and would travel any distance, day or night, to attend the sick, treating black and white alike. This unprejudiced approach was so rare in nineteenth-century Natal that he earned the undying love of the Zulu people. The poor seldom had to pay him and his acts of generosity became legendary. He was also responsible for founding a Technical College which would later give birth to Natal University.

Sam Campbell had been back in Natal for 12 years when his third son, christened Royston Dunnachie Campbell, was born on 2 October 1901. It was, however, several days before news of his son's birth reached him. He was on active service with the Natal Volunteer Medical Corps during the final days of the Boer War, having survived the four-month siege of Ladysmith almost two years earlier. The baby was christened Royston after an uncle by marriage, Colonel 'Galloping Jack' Royston, whose legendary martial exploits were ended at around this time by his death from enteric fever. It was, however, the family name of Dunnachie which was most in his maternal grandfather's mind when he wrote from Scotland to congratulate his daughter on the christening of her latest child:

> So Royston Dunnachie Campbell has got his name at last, and I am sure from all accounts of him that have reached us that he will do honour to all three. There is something in a name, either of an individual or of a family, if the record is an honourable one. If we bear the name, it gives us an ideal and a motive to follow in the same lines, and it is ideas and ideals, not physical forces, that lie at the foundation of things, and rule the world of human effort and aspiration. May every blessing descend on little Roy.[9]

James Dunnachie's sense of family tradition was inherited by his daughter. Roy remembered long winter evenings when his mother would keep her assembled children amused by playing the piano and teaching them the old Gaelic, Highland or Border songs that she had learnt from her grandparents.[10] And then there were Dooglie's bagpipes, which infuriated the Campbells' German neighbour. In his autobiography, Roy recounted the less-than-neighbourly disputes which arose whenever the irascible German heard the sound of the pipes:

> To the compatriot of Wagner, Beethoven, and Bach, living on the other side of the corrugated iron fence which separated our two gardens, with his more exalted ideas of music, the braying of the bag-pipes (or 'pack-vives' as he called them) was an insult and a nightmare. So whenever the 'pack-vives' started up from our side of the fence, Herr Kruger, in sheer self-defence, would line up his entire staff of some dozen native servants, arm them with bricks, and get them to pound and hammer on the fence, and to yell with all their might, while two Indian waiters hammered on brass trays, as if they were trying to scare away a swarm of locusts. Then we would see Herr Kruger himself . . . waving his arms in paroxysms of fury, like the conductor of some infernal orchestra: and screeching and howling, as loud as the pipes themselves: 'Harriple pack-vives! *Harr*iple pack-vives! *Ha-a-a-rr*iple pack-vives!'[11]

Dooglie responded to this provocation by playing even louder. Soon, Campbell recalled, all the dogs, donkeys, horses and cattle in the neighbourhood would catch the excitement, adding to the cacophany. 'Our horses and the cow, Nelly, would begin to gallop wildly about under the thirty mango trees in our immense paddock – which was bad for Nelly's milk.' At first, Roy's nursemaid Catherine Mgadi would rush from the scene in panic, with Roy close behind her, and they would hide, sobbing, beneath the bed. Eventually, after the noisy disputes had recurred on several occasions, Catherine and Roy caught the excitement themselves. Thereafter, at the sound of the pipes and the din of their neighbour's response, they would experience 'a sort of awed, bewildered exhilaration . . . and would run round in circles, leaping, jumping, pulling faces, waving our arms like Herr Kruger, and imitating the noises of the pipes, the natives, and the Herr, indiscriminately, by turns'.

At this time, due to his mother's preoccupation with nursing Neil, his younger brother, Roy was very much under the benign influence of his young nursemaid, confessing that 'I got a good many of my ideas from Catherine'.[12] This cross-current of cultural influences, the flow of Gaelic tradition interacting with the perceptions of a Zulu child, coloured Roy Campbell's formative years. It produced a cultural hybrid, an Afro-Celtic chimera, which was itself a by-product of colonialism. Thus Roy and his brothers were dressed for church in Eton collars one Sunday and in kilts the next, but also, in accordance with African custom, they shot their first buck at the age of eight. Similarly, they learned Scots ballads from their parents and African folklore from the natives. At the very moment that Roy was discovering the delights of the English language in verse, he was also learning the Zulu language through his conversations with Catherine.

Yet outside the safe haven of the Campbell family home, the clash of cultures was not always so benign. In 1906, when Roy was still only four years old, his father rode off to war once again. This time it was to put down the great Zulu Rebellion which had spread throughout Natal and had resulted in the slaughtering of many white settlers. This inter-racial tension added a further dimension to Roy's childhood. He remembered the danger and friction which arose when his father was blamed by the local Zulus for causing heavy rains that damaged their crops. 'The situation was uncomfortable: it was not long since the Rebellion and we were isolated amongst a considerable population of natives who held us to blame for the floods.'[13]

The underlying tension, combined with a deep-rooted sympathy for the plight and the resentment of the Zulu people, would later find expression in 'The Zulu Girl', one of Campbell's finest and most powerful poems.

> When in the sun the hot red acres smoulder,
> Down where the sweating gang its labour plies,
> A girl flings down her hoe, and from her shoulder
> Unslings her child tormented by the flies.
>
> She takes him to a ring of shadow pooled
> By thorn-trees: purpled with the blood of ticks,
> While her sharp nails, in slow caresses ruled,
> Prowl through his hair with sharp electric clicks,

His sleepy mouth plugged by the heavy nipple,
Tugs like a puppy, grunting as it feeds:
Through his frail nerves her own deep languors ripple
Like a broad river sighing through its reeds.

Yet in that drowsy stream his flesh imbibes
An old unquenched unsmotherable heat –
The curbed ferocity of beaten tribes,
The sullen dignity of their defeat.

Her body looms above him like a hill
Within whose shade a village lies at rest,
Or the first cloud so terrible and still
That bears the coming harvest in its breast.

The smouldering, 'unsmotherable' resentment, the 'curbed ferocity' looming like a harbinger of doom . . . In the light of future events in Campbell's native country, his words conveyed more than a hint of prophecy.

For the most part, however, Roy's relations with the local people were harmonious. He played with native boys of his own age and learned a number of amusing games. One was similar to cricket, except that toy assegais were substituted for bats:

> The two sides, armed with pointed throwing sticks, formed up on each side of a mark . . . The bowler . . . bowled a huge potato-like root (whose native name I forget) the size of a melon, in a direction parallel to the line of the rival team and about three yards in front of it. The root was an irregular shape and bounced unpredictably while the 'batting side' tried to transfix it by throwing their small assegais at it . . . If the 'ball' was speared by a throw before passing the last of the file it counted to the 'batting side', if not, it counted to the 'bowling side'.[14]

During holidays in Matabeleland, Roy was much impressed by the dances and festivals held by the Mashonas. Their music was, he thought, superior and more sprightly than 'the monotonous droning of the Zulus and Matabeles, though a war-dance by the latter when in full costume, with ostrich feathers, shields, and spears, is an unforgettable sight. One feels the ground tremble beneath one's feet and gets caught up and exalted in the savage rhythm of it.'[15] Yet if the Mashonas and Matabeles were superior to the Zulus in dance, the Zulus excelled in conversation:

> The Zulus are a highly intellectual people. They have a very beautiful language, a little on the bombastic side and highly adorned. Its effect on me can be seen in *The Flaming Terrapin*. Above all, the Zulus are

great hableurs and boasters; and one thing they love is conversation. It is the only art they have, but it is a very great art . . . They take an enormous delight in conversation, analysing with the greatest subtlety and brilliance. Only our really great conversationalists equal them. They are full of Sancho-like proverbs and optimistic wisdom. And they have extremely sunny temperaments.[16]

The lasting legacy of the native African roots of Campbell's childhood was discussed by his daughter Teresa:

My father was born and bred among the natives of South Africa. He got to love their wisdom and integrity. He respected them tremendously – to him they became as brothers. He spent all his happy childhood years with them and learnt a lot about life from this close association. It was this deep sharing of life with them that gave him his clear insight to the South African problem. We were always surprised at the uncommon ease with which he could mix with any company – with peasants and fishermen. This, my mother said, came from his early mixing with the native Africans.[17]

Nonetheless, and regardless of the degree to which he imbibed African culture, Campbell's childhood was characterized overwhelmingly by his privileged position as the son of wealthy colonists. In their religious beliefs, the strict Presbyterianism of his parents belonged to a completely different world from that of their servants. Their dour puritanism was complemented by a strictly teetotal lifestyle, itself a reaction to a history of alcoholism in the family. Roy's uncle and cousin, Marshall and Colin Campbell, were both alcoholics, a grim reality which led Campbell's parents to view alcohol more as a poison than a pleasure.

Childhood Christmases were normally spent at the palatial home of Sir Marshall Campbell, and Roy retained vivid memories of the large dining room which was adorned on all sides with the heads of different stuffed animals, nailed by the scruff to wooden shields and staring blindly down from the walls.

This great dining-room . . . was for me a sort of Fairyland, especially when the Indian servants festooned it secretly on Christmas Eve as a surprise, with chains of flowers, pineapples, silver paper, and ribbons criss-crossing each other from the horns of stuffed koodoos, on one side of the room, to the tusks of elephants on the other side and back to the horns of elands, and sables, and roans, all of whom peered (together with yawning lions and leopards) with glassy eyes . . .[18]

The impression that Campbell later conveyed to his daughters was that he had enjoyed an 'idyllic childhood'.[19] Anna, the younger of the daughters, recounts how, when he was a small boy, Roy had crept into the large pantry where his mother kept all her home-made jam and, seeing a large jar, put a spoonful of its contents into his mouth. At that moment his mother came in to find her son very red-faced and with tears streaming down his cheeks. She guessed that he had mistaken mustard for jam. 'Are you enjoying yourself?' she enquired. Her son nodded violently and rushed out.[20]

The Presbyterianism of Campbell's parents did not spill over into a puritanical disdain for the arts. On the contrary, as his mother's penchant for the piano suggested, the Campbell children were given every encouragement to explore their artistic inclinations. Roy's sister Ethel followed in her mother's footsteps, learning the piano and idolizing popular pianists of the day such as Mark Hamburg, whose photograph claimed pride of place in her room. Almost half a century later, Roy met the ageing pianist, by then a septuagenarian, and informed him that he was still recognizable as the young man in his sister's photograph.[21] Roy, on the other hand, was always more interested in art and literature than music. As an infant he drew sketches of African buck and, from the age of six or seven, he was producing panoramic pictures of land and sea battles. When he was 14, he and Ethel wrote and illustrated a book for their Dunnachie grandfather. Expressing his gratitude, the old man's reply struck a prophetic note. 'Now, my dear Roy, I must thank you for your splendid letter to me; I think your literary talent is going to be equal to your artistic ability.'[22]

As he grew older, Roy's passion for literature, and particularly for poetry, eclipsed his love for art. When he was sent to the Durban Boys' High School at the age of eight, having previously attended a kindergarten run by a local spinster, he was already a voracious reader. An older brother, George, remembered him strolling along the beach, book in hand and fishing rod over his shoulder, totally oblivious of the fish he had hooked which was trailing in the sand behind him. Understandably, perhaps, considering the Jacobite romances he had learnt from his mother, Campbell's favourite poets at this time were Walter Scott and Robert Burns, both of whom were also among his father's favourite writers. A little later he developed an attachment to the Anglo-Canadian poet Robert W. Service, who was one of the first colonial poets to gain widespread popularity. Yet the child's imaginative appetite for adventure, encapsulated by the ballads of Burns and Scott and the wild colonial verse of Service, was balanced by the deeply romantic introspection which was always a crucial part of Campbell's complex personality. When he was not being whisked off to the uncharted, snow-swept north with R.W. Service, he was being wafted mystically into the Celtic dreamworld of the early W.B. Yeats, daydreaming his way to 'The Lake Isle of Innisfree'.

This verse-induced escapism was particularly in evidence in a fragment of juvenile verse in which the schoolboy, imprisoned 'in a classroom with a problem in my brain', imagines his heart set loose in the mountains and his soul 'on the ridges with the game'. Gazing at the blackboard, his mind's eye floats instead to 'some lonely, lost lagoon' where, accompanied by the sound of whispering rushes, he sees 'the virgin glory of the moon'.[23]

The boy's earnest desire to escape the confines of the classroom was due in part to the cruelty he suffered at the hands of the headmaster, A. S. Langley. Even allowing for the tendency to exaggeration which is evident elsewhere in his autobiography, Campbell's account of his schooldays is testimony to the lifelong suffering and sense of injustice which was the psychological and emotional inheritance of Langley's treatment of him. Campbell described Langley as the 'surly tutor' of his youth who despised him because he was jealous of his pupil's father. 'I was made the vehicle of the old man's envy of my father,' Campbell wrote, before proceeding to detail the various incidents of cruelty, victimization and ridicule that he suffered at the headmaster's hands.[24] Whether or not Campbell's suffering was as severe as his autobiography suggests, his daughter remains convinced that Langley's treatment of her father was largely responsible for Campbell's hostility throughout the rest of his life to what he perceived as 'Anglo-Saxon attitudes'.[25] Even if the blows were partly or even largely imagined, the scars were real.

A. S. Langley, the headmaster from hell, was the final ingredient in the potent combination of influences which were working together to forge both the man and the writer. Out of Africa came a poet quite unlike anything the literary world had seen before. In the depths of his fertile imagination there were not the hallowed halls and dreaming spires of his English contemporaries, but the exiled dreams of Jacobite émigrés, the 'curbed ferocity of beaten tribes', both Scottish and African, and the 'unquenched unsmotherable heat' of the African bush.

NOTES

1 Roy Campbell, from 'The Flaming Terrapin', *Collected Poems, Volume One*, London: The Bodley Head, 1949, p. 88.
2 Roy Campbell, *Light on a Dark Horse*, London: Hollis & Carter, 1951, pp. 27–8.
3 *Ibid.*, p. 27.
4 *Ibid.*, p. 28.
5 *Ibid.*, p. 30.
6 *Ibid.*, pp. 10–11.
7 *Ibid.*, p. 180.
8 *Ibid.*, p. 26.
9 Quoted in Ethel Campbell, *Sam Campbell: A Story of Natal*, Durban: privately printed, n.d.; reproduced in Peter Alexander, *Roy Campbell: A Critical Biography*, Oxford University Press, 1982, p. 4.
10 Roy Campbell, *Light on a Dark Horse*, p. 119.

11 *Ibid.*, p. 30.
12 *Ibid.*, p. 31.
13 *Ibid.*, p. 46.
14 *Ibid.*, pp. 93–4.
15 *Ibid.*, p. 94.
16 Roy Campbell, *Broken Record*, London: Boriswood, 1934, p. 59.
17 Teresa Campbell, unpublished memoirs, p. 96.
18 Roy Campbell, *Light on a Dark Horse*, pp. 17–18.
19 Anna Campbell Lyle and Teresa Campbell, interview with the author, Portugal, December 1998.
20 Anna Campbell Lyle, letter to the author, 15 December 1999.
21 Roy Campbell, letter to his mother, unpublished and undated, probably 1950/51.
22 Quoted in Ethel Campbell, *Sam Campbell*, p. 196; reproduced in Peter Alexander, *Roy Campbell*, p. 7.
23 Unpublished verse, reproduced in Peter Alexander, *ibid.*, p. 10.
24 Roy Campbell, *Light on a Dark Horse*, pp. 68–75.
25 Anna Campbell Lyle, conversation with the author, 14 March 2000.

CHAPTER TWO

'MISS PIGTAILS' AND 'BLACKSTOCKINGS'

> After hot loveless nights, when cold winds stream
> Sprinkling the frost and dew, before the light,
> Bored with the foolish things that girls must dream
> Because their beds are empty of delight,
>
> Two sisters rise and strip . . .[1]

In 1913, when Campbell was 11 years old, the travel writer Evelyn Wrench came to stay. Wrench was clearly impressed by Roy's knowledge of the African bush and its wildlife, and his impressions of the precocious young boy were recorded in an article for the *Daily Mail*:

> [He] entertained us the whole evening with snake and sporting stories. He is quite a naturalist and born sportsman and goes out shooting buck within a few miles of the town. The number of deadly snakes here is horrible . . . 'But you can kill any snake by putting tobacco juice on his tongue,' Roy assured us! Roy draws and keeps nature notes . . .[2]

This is an early example of Roy's abilities as a raconteur. Similar anecdotes, delivered with a brazen flourish to wide-eyed and astonished undergraduates when he arrived in Oxford a few years later, would earn him the reputation as a wild colonial boy to whom the nickname 'Zulu' was soon appended.

The anecdotal tales of Roy's African childhood, recounted with evident glee in his autobiography, are very entertaining. Perhaps the strangest of these is his description of octopus wrestling. Roy and his friends made regular excursions to seaside resorts outside Durban, where they could earn money from rich holiday-makers from Johannesburg by staging octopus fights. Having caught their octopus, the boys would join the bathers in one of the swimming pools which had been blasted out of the rock along the coast. These pools were filled and cleaned out by the high tide, but remained clear and still at low tide.

> Next, an octopus would be surreptitiously introduced into the bath and one of us would shout to the bathers: 'Hey, people, look out, there's a big kind of animal in the water there, which sucks all the blood out of your veins.' Those of us who were in the water would simulate panic (*pour encourager les autres*) and soon the pool would be empty, with an ideal circus of spectators, ready set all round for the show to begin . . .
>
> When we had got the spectators agog we would dive in, all four of us . . . Whoever caught the octopus first would let it get a grip all over him with its feelers; then rising up from the waist-deep shallow water, he would pretend to struggle, scream, and howl: 'Help, help, it is strangling me and sucking all my blood!' We would pretend to be trying to help our comrade but to be terrified and unable to save him. Then we would tug at the tentacles, trying to detach the suckers, which gave kiss-like smacking reports as they were detached, in a manner guaranteed to turn the stomachs and send a quiver up the spines of the toughest Johannesburgers. They would see the skin blistered with red sucker-marks, which were quite painless, but looked nasty enough.[3]

As the final *pièce de résistance*, a bottle of red ink, carried by the boys in their trunks, would be emptied in the vicinity of the fight, 'and we would roll about, milling and yelling in the shallow water, as if in a welter of "blood" and foam'. When the boys finally emerged triumphant from the struggle and the holiday-makers realized the joke, a hat would be passed around. It was a lucrative ruse, the boys sometimes earning as much as three pounds a day, until the fathers of Roy's three friends discovered their mercenary behaviour and put an end to it.

Although Roy evidently had several good friends of his own age, he lacked a close relationship with his older brothers. He was barely an infant when Archie and George were sent to boarding school, only seeing them during the holidays. In 1909, when Roy was still only seven, Archie departed overseas to the Ontario Agricultural College, and two years later George followed in his father's footsteps, going to Edinburgh to study medicine. In August 1914 they both volunteered at the outbreak of war and served in the Royal Flying Corps. In practical terms, Roy hardly ever saw them.

Towards the end of 1915, Roy's father, who had recently acquired a new Ford motor car, had a serious accident. Trying to avoid a dog, he swerved in front of a tram. His car was squashed between the tram and a lamppost and Dr Campbell suffered several broken ribs and concussion. It was a measure of his popularity among the natives that large crowds gathered outside the house when news of the accident spread. The Zulu newspaper *Ilanga Lase Natal* (*The Sun of Natal*), which, according to Roy, 'represented the Native opinion of the whole Province of Natal',[4] carried the following story on 4 January 1916:

> The Native People rejoice in the recovery of Dr Campbell from the effects of his serious accident. The Doctor is the most popular gentleman in Natal. His kind nature is so well known that a misfortune to him is a misfortune to the whole country. Much as his professional ability is esteemed, yet he could be of still greater use to the Union of South Africa as the Administrator of the Province of Natal.

Dr Campbell's accident did not diminish his love for the car. His son recalled that being 'driven round in these new horse-less machines was a thrill of which we never tired in those days'.[5] Roy was sitting in his father's car when he had the additional thrill of meeting the famous cricketer Jack Hobbs, who was on tour in South Africa with the MCC. Hobbs was having tea with Dr Campbell in the open-air lounge of Durban's Royal Hotel when he spotted Roy waiting outside in the car and invited him to join them. Many years later, Campbell remembered how exhilarating it was to meet the great sportsman who was, in the eyes of all his schoolfriends, 'a semi-divinity'. 'I was transported into the seventh heaven when he started giving me signed photographs of himself which of course I displayed at school, and then basked in his reflected glory for weeks.'[6]

The boy, however, was awakening to post-pubescent realities which sought their delight away from cars and cricket pitches. In his autobiography, Roy is somewhat coy about revealing the names of his adolescent loves, but his faltering attempts to impress the opposite sex are recalled with a charming blend of disarming candour and comic self-effacement. His first love, dubbed 'Miss Pigtails', was the recipient of many gifts from her young suitor, including a pair of shoes made from animal skins. Eventually, however, Miss Pigtails broke his heart by transferring her affections to an older boy 'who had more sense, time, and chivalry'. Miss Pigtails was also, Campbell adds, about three years older than he was, 'and must have laughed at my calf-love'. Unfortunately, this wisdom of hindsight was not available to the inexperienced youth, who felt both hurt and humiliated at being deserted.

> It became more than I could bear when I saw her new beau using as his wristwatch a python-skin strap I had given her, an iguana-skin belt, and a beautiful python-skin writing-case, which I had had made for her ... My humiliation was more acute when, with my usual foolhardiness, I challenged my rival ... and was hammered solidly for as long as I could stand up, and long after I could see, or remember.[7]

Although Campbell tactfully omits to identify Miss Pigtails, she was probably Daphne Henderson, the sister of his schoolfriend Ian. In a letter written to his mother in around 1950, Roy refers to Daphne, who had died of cancer several years earlier, as 'my old flame'.[8]

Miss Pigtails left him feeling very sorry for himself 'for at least four weeks', but he was soon transferring his affections to another girl whom he called 'Blackstockings', 'because they were compulsory at her school'. Blackstockings was, in fact, Joan Tatham, daughter of a local judge. Her father was overprotective and, in a manner unbecoming a member of the judiciary, he exhibited his disapproval of Campbell's attentions by threatening him with a shotgun. It was no empty threat – the judge had actually fired at another young man who had taken an interest in his other daughter. Hearing of this earlier incident, Campbell took the threat seriously and stayed well away from the house. He did not, however, stay away from the daughter. They met nearly every day, taking short train journeys together and holding hands.

Blackstockings and her sister would prove unwittingly instrumental in inspiring one of Campbell's most powerfully erotic poems. 'The Sisters', considered by Dylan Thomas to be the finest poem Campbell ever wrote, was imaginatively fertilized, according to Campbell, by the chance sight of Joan Tatham and her sister riding naked before sunrise to a cove at low tide. The excitement, accentuated by the frustration of youthful sexual fantasies, is evident in the poem's opening lines, quoted at the head of this chapter.

The poem's erotic imagery is intensified by a pent-up sense of unfulfilled passion. The girls' horses do not answer to their commands, but come in response to 'their low-whistled pleas' and 'sneeze a fiery steam about their knees'. The sisters gallop to the sleeping cove, 'their stealthy prowling hands . . . in slow caresses rove' through the manes of their mounts. Galloping 'across the milk-white sands' and wading into the quiet waters, the sisters await the climax of the dawn:

> Far out on the grey silence of the flood
> They watch the dawn in smouldering gyres expand
> Beyond them: and the day burns through their blood
> Like a white candle through a shuttered hand.[9]

Campbell's candid confession of the source of his inspiration for the poem was tempered by the defensive way in which he sought to explain how he happened to witness the episode.

> I wrote it years afterwards, when I remembered having seen the two girls just before sunrise, ride out their horses into a cove at low tide. It was a beautiful sight indeed and one for which I am very grateful, though I am no peeping Tom and had been engaged in the prosaic

> task of sitting up all night in a milkwood bough in the hope of getting a shot at some bush-pigs.[10]

Even as Roy was growing increasingly impatient with his enforced innocence in the peaceful surroundings of southern Africa, boys scarcely three years older were losing their innocence in far less idyllic circumstances in the trenches of Flanders. By the summer of 1916 the war in Europe had subsided into a sterile and muddy stalemate, entrenched in futility. Yet Roy's brothers, Archie and George, serving in the Royal Flying Corps and consequently spared the horrors of the trenches, continued to write home with optimistic accounts of the action. To those of British descent in South Africa, loyal children of the Empire, the war was still viewed through rose-coloured glasses. In a letter to his mother shortly after the outbreak of the Second World War, Campbell recalled the jingoistic fervour of South Africans during the previous conflict.

> But you always have much more *fever* out there, and the further one is from the firing line, the greater is the ferment. The stories you tell of war-fervour (or 'madness') in the family are only signs of abundant vitality, I feel sure: and they have probably subsided by now. But they make me smile. It reminds me of 1915 – the days when Mr Finney used to 'see' German aeroplanes in the sugar-cane and sit up with a shotgun among the banana-plantations with an acetylene lamp in the hopes of bagging one like a partridge. Or when Commander Lindsay mistook one of the whaling ships for a German submarine, and fired his cannon from the bluff and knocked a hole in the North Pier! And when I ran away from school to enlist. It all comes back to me in a flash.[11]

Roy's efforts to enlist, and his running away from school in order to do so, were no doubt prompted by his desperately unhappy time as the victim of Langley's cruelty. Yet the desire to escape from the headmaster's clutches must have been exacerbated by the 'war fervour' to which his later letter alluded. During 1916 the school magazine was full of stories of heroism from the front, and one of Campbell's unpublished juvenile verses sings the praises of the 'fierce legions' and 'proud platoons'. 'I must cross the sea,' the verse continues, '. . . And I must die.'[12] With such sentiments awash in his mind, Roy, at the age of 15, enlisted with the South African infantry, claiming that he was 18 years old, his name was Roy McKenzie and he came from Rhodesia. His alias might have worked if he had not been recognized. A suspicious official telephoned the Campbell family home and Ethel, Roy's sister, answered. She confirmed that Roy was only 15. 'This was the first that any of us knew of his having "run away" from school that morning and "joined up",' Ethel wrote later.[13]

Towards the end of 1917 Campbell left school with a third-class matriculation pass, the lowest possible pass mark. Any feelings of disappointment at his less than auspicious academic achievement were eclipsed by the joy of being liberated from Langley's tyranny. He registered at Natal University College to read English, Physics and Botany, but his heart was not in his studies. He was determined to join up as soon as he was old enough, intending to go to Sandhurst.

In the meantime, he was still attempting to woo Joan Tatham, with limited success. In August 1918 he wrote beseeching her to see him before he left for England. 'But you will come, won't you? I am going about the middle of the month (next) unless you can't get down till after that. But you MUST come!'[14] Whether or not Blackstockings succumbed to Campbell's desperate pleas, his letters to her in the final months of 1918 would prove to be the last passionate glow from the dying embers of their relationship. That glow would be quenched by Roy's departure for England.

NOTES

1 Roy Campbell, from 'The Sisters', *Collected Poems, Volume One*, p. 43.
2 Quoted in Peter Alexander, *Roy Campbell*, p. 10.
3 Roy Campbell, *Light on a Dark Horse*, pp. 96–8.
4 *Ibid.*, p. 37.
5 *Ibid.*
6 *Ibid.*, pp. 37–8.
7 *Ibid.*, pp. 60–61.
8 Roy Campbell, unpublished letter to his mother, *c.*1950.
9 From 'The Sisters', *Collected Poems, Volume One*, pp. 43–4.
10 Roy Campbell, *Light on a Dark Horse*, p. 67.
11 Roy Campbell, unpublished letter to his mother, 17 October 1939.
12 Quoted in Peter Alexander, *Roy Campbell*, p. 11.
13 Ethel Campbell, *The Life of Sam Campbell*, Durban: John Singleton & Williams, 1933, p. 354.
14 Peter Alexander, *Roy Campbell*, p. 16.

CHAPTER THREE

A ZULU IN OXFORD

Farewell, terrific shade! Though I go free
Still of the powers of darkness art thou Lord:
I watch the phantom sinking in the sea
Of all that I have hated or adored.

The prow glides smoothly on through seas quiescent:
But where the last point sinks into the deep,
The land lies dark beneath the rising crescent,
And Night, the Negro, murmurs in his sleep.[1]

Campbell sailed out of Durban harbour in December 1918 on the *Inkonka*, a 2,000-ton tramp steamer. Almost as soon as the ship had lost sight of the harbour, the third mate came into Roy's cabin and, taking objection to the large number of books which the 17-year-old had brought with him, promptly threw them out of the porthole into the sea. Campbell looked on in despair as his cherished volumes of Shakespeare, Milton, Keats, Dryden, Pope and Marlowe, as well as his painting and drawing materials, disappeared overboard. It was a rude awakening.

In spite of this unpromising start, Campbell was soon enjoying the voyage. Initially the weather was fine and he spent much of the time at the fo'c'sle head watching the albatrosses, sea lions, Cape hens, Cape pigeons, porpoises, 'and all those strange and beautiful creatures that inhabit the majestic southern extremity of our continent'. Going round the Cape of Good Hope, he was thrilled by the 'rugged grandeur and wildness of the scene', thoroughly exhilarated with 'a real sense of its awe and the grandeur of its stormy seas'.

> Standing up at the fo'c'sle head and ducking under the cross-plate at the vortex of the bows when the ship drove her nose into the great Cape rollers forty feet high with a quarter of a mile between their marble summits, one shouted and sang with joy and elation in the movement of the ship and in one's own immunity, as the spate of water rushed overhead and one emerged from the safety of the cross-plate to

> see the next great hill of water approaching as the ship tobogganed down the slope of the last one, to meet it.[2]

Campbell's love affair with the sea, thus far expressed only in poetically imagined theory, was consummated by the cascading waters off the Cape. Blessed with good sea legs, he never suffered seasickness, however extreme the weather, and relished the invigorating power of ocean-bound storms. He soon forgave the third mate for throwing his books out of the porthole, blessing the spare time he spent, not reading, but 'with the sun, stars, and moon, and the winds and the spray'.

> You can see the backwash of this voyage in *The Flaming Terrapin*: but of course that effort would have been impossible without all the chunks of ore stolen from Marlowe, Keats, Dryden, Pope, and Milton . . . It was only good that I was forced to concentrate on the sea while I was on it, for I loved it so much that it made me return to it.[3]

Ocean-going storms were not the only new experiences to confront the young man on his voyage to England. When the *Inkonka* landed at Dakar, he was shocked to discover (as he put it) 'whites philandering with blacks'. Most shocking of all, he was accosted by a British sailor who, begging the price of a drink, informed him that he was being kept by a Negress in the native quarter. This, of course, was unheard of in South Africa, provoking in Campbell a culturally-inherited reaction that belied his natural sympathy towards the natives.

If Campbell's racial prejudice was aroused in Dakar, his religious prejudice surfaced at the next port of call, Las Palmas in the Canary Islands. On visiting the cathedral with one of the ship's apprentices who was a Roman Catholic, he was shown some holy relics, including the heart of Bishop Juan de Frias, 'who sacrificed himself to the protection of the Guanches or natives of the Canaries'.[4] Campbell recalled that the heart was so magnified by the glass and the spirits in which it was kept that he laughed in a superior way and swore it was the heart of a rhino or a hippo. His scepticism suggests an antagonism towards Catholicism, but was also indicative of a general disillusionment with Christianity. He had moved away from a lukewarm and half-hearted acceptance of his parents' Presbyterianism towards an inarticulate agnosticism. This had found comic expression in 'The Theology of Bongwi, the Baboon', an early verse which was either written before he left South Africa or shortly after his arrival in Oxford early in 1919.

> This is the wisdom of the Ape
> Who yelps beneath the Moon –
> 'Tis God who made me in His shape

He is a Great Baboon.
'Tis He who tilts the moon askew
And fans the forest trees,
The heavens which are broad and blue
Provide Him His trapeze;
He swings with tail divinely bent
Around those azure bars
And munches to His Soul's content
The kernels of the stars;
And when I die, His loving care
Will raise me from the sod
To learn the perfect Mischief there,
The Nimbleness of God.[5]

Campbell's irreverent verse was possibly inspired by Yeats's poem 'An Indian Upon God', in which a meditative Indian hears a moorfowl declaring that God is 'an undying moorfowl' and a lotus proclaiming that 'He hangeth upon a stalk'. Yet Campbell's verse, for all its playful theological subversion, is devoid of the cynical world-weariness which is the mark of so much iconoclastic, anti-religious satire. On the contrary, it is filled with a mischievous rumbustiousness, a spiritual *joie de vivre*, which has more in common with the satirical verse of G. K. Chesterton. Indeed, if 'The Theology of Bongwi, the Baboon' is compared with 'Race Memory (by a dazed Darwinian)', a satirical poem on a similar theme by Chesterton, the deep-rooted affinity is instantly apparent.

In the middle of February 1919, during a bitterly cold English winter which was a further new experience for Campbell, the *Inkonka* slid into the Thames estuary. 'It was certainly by far the widest river I had ever seen . . . Then warehouses and other phantasmal buildings loomed through the mist on the distantly converging banks. Slowly, forests of masts and cranes began to appear, and moving almost imperceptibly we berthed in the East India Docks cracking the first film of ice I had ever seen . . .'[6] Wide-eyed with wonder, Campbell explored the streets of London, marvelling at the sight of snow and exulting at his first encounter with legendary landmarks such as Trafalgar Square. Utterly overawed by the sheer scale of England's – and the Empire's – capital city, he was too timid to call a taxi and instead hired a man with a donkey cart.

After meandering its way around most of the London sights, the donkey cart deposited the bemused colonial at Euston Station, where Campbell caught a train to Scotland to visit his Dunnachie grandfather. The old man gave his grandson £10 with which Campbell replaced the books he had lost off the coast of Africa. After a short stay he returned south, this time to

Oxford, where he hoped to learn sufficient Greek to pass Responsions (effectively an entrance examination requiring a basic grasp of classical languages) so that he could enter Merton College. His plans to go to Sandhurst had been abandoned after the ending of the war in the previous November.

When Campbell arrived in Oxford during the early spring of 1919, the city was crammed with returning servicemen. Painfully shy, he hid from this new and unfamiliar world by shutting himself away in the single attic room which he had rented in a house in Walton Street. Day after day he sat in an armchair and read voraciously. 'Never before, or since, have I done such an amount of reading as I did at Oxford,' Campbell wrote. 'Had I taken an ordinary course in English for three years, I would not have read a quarter as much.'[7]

His greatest literary passion was for the Elizabethan dramatists, particularly Marlowe who 'affected him more, in his youth, than Shakespeare'.[8] He also discovered T. S. Eliot, whose poetry was then all the rage. Clumsily, Campbell attempted to write poems in imitation of Eliot, taking as his subject the gloomy railway stations he had seen on his recent journeys to and from Scotland. Dissatisfied with the results, he threw them on the fire.[9] He also wrote in imitation of Paul Verlaine and the Sitwells, but found these equally unsatisfactory. He would later dismiss these efforts for their failure to capture his authentic voice. 'My early poems,' he said, 'were so fragile and attenuated that Verlaine is robust in comparison.'[10]

Campbell's voracious reading and imitative writing of English verse largely eclipsed his half-hearted attempts to study Greek. It was, however, at the Greek tutorials which he attended with ever-increasing reluctance that he met his first real friend at Oxford. This was the composer William Walton, who shared his enthusiasm for the poetry of Eliot and the Sitwells, and his admiration for the prose of Percy Wyndham Lewis. Campbell would later describe Walton as 'a real genius, and, at the same time, one of the very finest fellows I ever met in my life'.[11] In spite of this, the two friends seemed to have little in common. Campbell had no interest in music, or at least not in the sort of music that Walton was composing. His own preferences were for the ragtime music he could hear on the gramophone, tunes such as 'Hitchy-Koo' and the 'Grizzly Bear', or popular favourites such as 'Oh, You Beautiful Doll' and 'If You Were the Only Girl'; and of course there were the old Scottish folksongs he had learnt at his mother's knee. 'But in spite of my ear for tunes, even Willie with all his genius couldn't arouse in me the least feeling for classical music. What he did give me, even then, was a sense of vocation and how a man can live for his art.'[12]

Campbell and Walton certainly shared a loathing for Greek, preferring to neglect their studies so that they could enjoy endless nights on the town consuming large quantities of beer. They also courted two Irish waitresses at Buol's Restaurant. However, claims in a biography of Campbell by Peter Alexander that Campbell had 'at least two short-lived homosexual affairs' at this time may well be unfounded.[13] Although it is possible that Campbell went through a bisexual phase at Oxford, Alexander makes no effort to justify the claim and chooses not to name the two men alleged to have been the objects of Campbell's devotion. He merely cites Campbell's friend Rob Lyle as the source of the allegation. Lyle, however, states categorically, 'I know *nothing* of any "homosexual attachments".'[14] This being so, in the absence of any evidence to the contrary one should perhaps assume that Campbell's friendships at Oxford were platonic. There are no grounds for Alexander's claims that Campbell's 'homosexual affairs' represent 'another facet of his divided nature'.

It was through his friendship with William Walton that Campbell first met many of the leading lights of the new literature. Walton took Campbell to one of Edith Sitwell's celebrated parties at which he was introduced to T. S. Eliot, as well as to Edith's brothers Osbert and Sacheverell. Walton also introduced Campbell to Percy Wyndham Lewis, destined to become a lifelong friend, and to the composer Philip Heseltine, who wrote under the name of Peter Warlock. Heseltine, in the spirited musical periodical *The Sackbut* which he founded the following year, was one of the first people to publish Campbell's poetry, along with Russell Green who, as editor of *Coterie*, published five of Campbell's poems including 'The Theology of Bongwi, the Baboon' during 1920.

Throughout his life, Campbell would remain on friendly terms with these early Oxford acquaintances. Edith Sitwell became one of his closest friends, although he fell out for a time with all three of the Sitwell siblings after Osbert had turned him away from one of their dinner parties because he had failed to arrive in evening dress. He was never destined to be as close to Eliot, but their friendship, though distant, was both genuine and constant. Eliot remained grateful for Campbell's early outspoken enthusiasm for his verse and was always one of the most loyal defenders of Campbell's own literary reputation. For his part, Campbell declared at Oxford that Eliot was the greatest living English poet, predicting that he would soon eclipse his more popular but less gifted contemporaries. Thirty years later, after Eliot's reputation had been enhanced by publication of *The Waste Land*, *The Hollow Men* and *Four Quartets*, Campbell derived obvious pleasure from the knowledge that his prediction had proved correct. 'From then on,' he recalled in his autobiography, 'the influence of Eliot literally swallowed up many of these minor poets as a blue whale swallows mites of krill. It was as if his muse was getting its revenge on their previous derision of the dark American invader.'[15]

Looking back on these friendships, Campbell's gratitude was tinged with humility:

> To have known these six people – Eliot, [Wyndham] Lewis, Walton and the three Sitwells who have had such a tremendous influence on this age . . . makes it quite worth while having been born, even if one comes to nothing oneself. Through my love of rough company and a certain impatience of discipline, I soon forfeited these better influences and sank into that strange underworld of indigence and folly known as 'Bohemia'.[16]

Perhaps the most important formative influence upon Campbell during this time was T. W. Earp, then president of the Oxford Union, who was subsequently described by Campbell as the 'uncrowned King of Oxford'.[17] Although Earp was never to live up to the brilliant reputation he enjoyed at Oxford, his impact on the impressionable young South African was profound, as Campbell readily admitted.

> The miraculous feeling of walking into a famous University from the Bush and being accepted on a much higher level than one was accepted at home, was very exhilarating. Earp's unofficial tuition saved me years of trial and error: and it was through him that I found the French symbolists who have since influenced me most – if we discount my own basic self-immersion in the English Elizabethans and metaphysical poets.[18]

Apart from exerting a literary influence, Earp introduced his young protégé to everyone who was anyone at Oxford. In the months ahead Campbell met Robert Graves, Edmund Blunden, L. A. G. Strong, Robert Nichols, Wilfred Childe, Louis Golding, Hugo Dyson, C. S. Lewis, L. P. Hartley and Aldous Huxley. Several of these, notably Huxley, Earp and Campbell, inaugurated an informal literary club, naming it 'The Jolly Farmers' after the pub in which the meetings were held.[19] The group met every Thursday and members would read out their own verse, or recite from well-known plays by Campbell's beloved Elizabethans. In his first volume of autobiography, *Broken Record*, published in 1934, Campbell described the Jolly Farmers as 'by far the most spontaneous literary gathering I ever knew'.[20] Ten years later, towards the end of the Second World War, he would become an occasional member of the Inklings, a more famous literary gathering which met in the Eagle and Child, another Oxford pub, at which he renewed his acquaintance with C. S. Lewis and Hugo Dyson, as well as meeting writers such as J. R. R. Tolkien and Charles Williams for the first time.

In describing the 'spontaneous' meetings of the Jolly Farmers, Campbell recalled that the members 'put away quantities of beer'. This, as much as anything else, illustrated Campbell's radical change of outlook and lifestyle following his arrival in Oxford. The abstemious ways he had inherited from his teetotal parents were rejected. Instead, staggering to the opposite extreme, he lived a life of hazy hedonism, fuelled by alcohol. This would herald the beginning of his intermittent but lifelong attraction to the 'rough company' which would occasionally lead him to sink into what he called 'that strange underworld . . . known as "Bohemia"'.

Few people epitomized this underworld more evocatively and enigmatically than the artist Nina Hamnett, whom Campbell met for the first time soon after his arrival in Oxford and who would re-appear in his life at odd intervals for the next quarter of a century. Born in 1890, by the age of 21 Hamnett had already made the acquaintance of the self-styled magician and Satanist Aleister Crowley. Her own unconventional approach to morality was exhibited in the way she described the loss of her virginity to one of Crowley's entourage:

> I decided that the next man I met and whom I liked I would hand myself over to . . . One day I went to see Crowley in the Fulham Road, where I met a most beautiful creature. He had long green eyes and hands like the Angel in the National Gallery by Filippino Lippi. He seemed to like me too. He took two rooms near Fitzroy Square; one night I arranged to see him at 10.30. I arrived and he said, 'Will you take your clothes off?' So I did and the deed was done. I did not think very much of it, but the next morning I had a sense of spiritual freedom and that something important had been accomplished.[21]

Tiring of life in Chelsea, where she had befriended Arthur Ransome, Walter Sickert and Roger Fry, Hamnett decamped to Paris in 1913 where she lived the life of Montparnasse, drinking heavily with Modigliani and other Parisian artists. Returning to England, she tried marriage, but, bored with the experience, was relieved when her husband was deported. At the time of her first meeting with Campbell, she was on the fringes of the Bloomsbury group, working with Vanessa Bell, Roger Fry and Duncan Grant. By 1920, a year after making Campbell's acquaintance, she was back in Paris where her circle of friends widened to include Picasso, Ford Madox Ford, Jean Cocteau and James Joyce.

Nina Hamnett's first impressions of the young South African, whom she met in the company of T. W. Earp and Aldous Huxley, were entirely favourable. 'Roy Campbell was about seventeen and very beautiful indeed. He had the most wonderful grey eyes with long black eyelashes. He spoke with an odd gruff voice and a funny accent.'[22] Roy presented her with a volume of Arthur Rimbaud's poems and kept her amused by singing 'Kaffir songs'.

Hamnett had travelled to Oxford with Marie Beerbohm, who seems to have been equally impressed by the beautiful young colonial boy. It was Marie who first gave Roy the nickname 'Zulu', an appendage which stuck fast and inspired Wyndham Lewis to invent the character of Zulu Blades for his novel *The Apes of God*:

> Blades was the 'black beast', an evil neighbour: what with his upstart disrespect as well for his metropolitan betters, since he had brought the hearty habits of the African out-stations into their midst, here. His skill with women was natural, it was true he roped them in like steers, he must be working off ten years' solitary confinement in the Veldt.[23]

Even allowing for Lewis's liberal use of artistic licence, his description of Zulu Blades must present a fairly accurate, if impressionistic, picture of the way Campbell was perceived by his refined Oxford contemporaries. Such a picture is highlighted by the memories of Nancy Cunard, who – in common with her friend Nina Hamnett, to whom she often donated her cast-off evening dresses – was equally at home with the aristocratic high-life and the Bohemian low-life of London and Paris. Like Hamnett, she had first met Campbell shortly after his arrival at Oxford.

> It was with T. W. Earp, the poet who had talked so much of 'the Zulu', a strange, young, new figure who had recently appeared: about him Earp managed to set a certain amount of mystery, possibly because he was so very much impressed by him. To Earp he was clearly a prodigy. I puzzled over the term 'zulu': a swarthy South African perhaps? Why I did not ask Earp to which race he belonged I cannot imagine and rather expected to see a South African Negro.[24]

Instead, when they met in the Brasserie of the Café Royal, she was confronted with a 'tall, adolescent, strong, loose limbed youth with dark hair and red cheeks . . . now and again his eyes would flash, he was vivacious yet seemed a little shy, or reserved'. In appearance, he contrasted greatly with Earp who was 'fair haired, precise, high voiced' and 'English'. Cunard recalled that Earp 'radiated admiration for Roy's poetry', predicting confidently that he had a great future ahead of him. After this initial meeting, Cunard met Campbell on several occasions at the small, intimate parties held by the barrister Montague Shearman,

> where various intellectuals sat enjoying his generous drinks, gazing at a beautiful Matisse, the first that the barrister had brought back from Paris and which, to some people, was controversial . . . By then Roy Campbell knew many people in London and if he had been looked

> upon at first as rather a *rare avis* or something of a rough diamond, he was by now quite at home in England.[25]

Nancy Cunard was wrong. Campbell's beer-emboldened surface may have been 'at home', but the rest of him, the poetic soul, was increasingly alienated. 'The old colleges . . . seemed to resist me and push me out, as someone born under corrugated iron,' he wrote.[26] The initial sweetness of Oxford had been soured by the realization that neither he nor Walton were going to pass their exams. Writing to his father, Roy attempted to put on a brave face, concealing both his disappointment and the reasons for his failure.

> With regard to a degree, I find that Oxford with its lectures, etc, interferes very much with my work. I cannot conscientiously apply valuable time to such a subject, for instance as Anglo-Saxon. If I were to take a degree and become a schoolmaster, or a professor, could you imagine me in that kind of a job? First of all there would be my fellow professors – could you imagine my giving out dogmas to a crowd of gaping students, hour after hour, day after day? Could you imagine my being friendly with the type of person that does that kind of thing? I would be half-way across the Pacific after two months of it. As far as money goes, I am very sorry to be so expensive. It is unnecessary to tell you how grateful I am to you. I will try to reward your kindness by making my future as great as your past.[27]

In the light of Campbell's later life, it is indeed difficult to imagine him as a schoolmaster or a professor. At the time, however, if his own words on the subject are to be believed, he harboured a real ambition to become an academic, in which case his failure in Responsions must have been particularly devastating. Compare, for instance, the dismissive tone of the letter to his father with the wistful regrets expressed 15 years later:

> My one ambition was to be a Don and live in a mouldy old tower with a salary, so that I should never have to do any uncongenial work. I wanted to read and write in front of a big fire with good college beer to drink. But the great barrier of Greek intervened, and I could only be my own private Don in a back-street.
>
> Whenever I think of Oxford it is with regret . . .[28]

Once Oxford's dreaming spires had become a distant and unreachable mirage, the whole edifice of England seemed to dissolve around them. Campbell began to feel nostalgic for Africa and its innocence, and dismissive of England's charms. 'English scenery to me is like those pictures one sees on chocolate boxes,' he would later write to his mother. 'I would sooner see one sakaboola rising in the wind than have a thousand nightingales sitting on my chimney top and singing for all they are worth.'[29]

Disillusioned and deeply disappointed, he left Oxford and moved to London, where he shared a flat in Regent Square with Earp, Huxley and Russell Green. Yet even his old Oxford friendships seemed sullied by his change of circumstances and the change of heart that accompanied it. He was irritated by Earp's cultivated precision of speech and irked by Huxley, whom he described as 'this pedant who leeringly gloated over his knowledge of how crayfish copulated . . . but could never have caught or cooked one'.[30]

The artist Augustus John, who had first met Campbell early in 1920, believed that Campbell took to drink 'as a means of counteracting the almost pathological condition of moral discomfort' which he felt in Oxford.[31] More prosaically, Campbell himself explained the discomfort in terms of 'over-domestication',[32] but perhaps Lawrence Durrell came closest to a true understanding of the roots of Campbell's disillusionment and his feelings of dejection. Campbell's poetry, Durrell wrote, 'booms and roars and surges like the ocean breaking on the long empty beaches of his native Africa. After all, he was a colonial, as I am; and I feel that I can understand his cast of mind . . .' With a penetrating combination of empathy and sympathy, Durrell projects himself into Campbell's predicament and provides some telling insights into England's impact on a colonial 'Zulu':

> 'What do they know of England?' What indeed? A colonial poet grows up with the clan spirit, the clan mentality, a sense of family loyalty which derives from the mystique of his race. Like Kipling, Roy was abruptly wakened from the gallant dream of his childhood, full as it was of ideals and traditional valour, when compelled to compare it to the reality – a little stuffy parochial island, indifferent to its legendary heritage! The innocent illusion! . . . A colonial is terribly much at a disadvantage, like a country boy, his head full of dreams, thrust into the *sly* world of a big city!
>
> And then there is the purely physical aspect of the business: the feverish impatience which grips a colonial in England! At twelve years of age you had your own horse and outside your window was the veldt or the Himalayas. Your physical life was magical and resolute, springing directly from the natural world . . . It is a pretty poor consolation to stroll in Hyde Park with a bowler hat on your head waiting for the pubs to open.[33]

Roy Campbell, still only 18 years old, had no intention of accepting such poor consolation. With feverish impatience, he was already planning his escape.

NOTES

1 Roy Campbell, from 'Rounding the Cape', *Collected Poems, Volume One*, p. 27.
2 Roy Campbell, *Light on a Dark Horse*, pp. 174–5.
3 *Ibid.*, p. 175.
4 *Ibid.*, p. 177.
5 *Collected Poems, Volume One*, p. 17.
6 Roy Campbell, *Light on a Dark Horse*, p. 178.
7 Roy Campbell, *Broken Record*, p. 38.
8 Anna Campbell Lyle, *Son of Valour*, unpublished memoir, p. 8.
9 Peter Alexander, *Roy Campbell*, p. 20.
10 Anna Campbell Lyle, *Son of Valour*, p. 8.
11 Roy Campbell, *Light on a Dark Horse*, p. 181.
12 *Ibid.*
13 Peter Alexander, *Roy Campbell*, p. 21.
14 Rob Lyle, written reply to the author, February 2000.
15 Roy Campbell, *Light on a Dark Horse*, p. 225.
16 *Ibid.*
17 *Ibid.*, p. 183.
18 *Ibid.*
19 Sybille Bedford, *Aldous Huxley: A Biography, Volume One, 1894–1939*, London: Chatto & Windus, 1973, p. 59; Peter Alexander, *Roy Campbell*, p. 23.
20 Roy Campbell, *Broken Record*, p. 37.
21 Nina Hamnett, *Laughing Torso*, London: Virago, 1984, p. 44.
22 *Ibid.*, p. 107.
23 Percy Wyndham Lewis, *The Apes of God*, Part II, London: The Arthur Press, 1930, p. 78.
24 Hugh Ford (ed.), *Nancy Cunard: Brave Poet, Indomitable Rebel 1896–1965*, Philadelphia: Chilton Book Company, 1968, p. 353.
25 *Ibid.*
26 Roy Campbell, *Broken Record*, p. 39.
27 Ethel Campbell, *The Life of Sam Campbell*, p. 355.
28 Roy Campbell, *Broken Record*, p. 39.
29 Ethel Campbell, *The Life of Sam Campbell*, p. 356.
30 Roy Campbell, *Light on a Dark Horse*, p. 184.
31 *Sunday Times*, 12 October 1958.
32 Roy Campbell, *Light on a Dark Horse*, p. 184.
33 Alister Kershaw (ed.), *Salute to Roy Campbell*, Francestown, New Hampshire: Typographeum, 1984, pp. 24–5.

CHAPTER FOUR

WHIRLWIND

My stiff quills made the hurricane their lyre
Where, pronged with azure flame, the black rain streams:
Huge brindled shadows barred with gloomy fire
Prowling the red horizon of my dreams,

Thick storm-clouds threatened me with dense eclipse,
The wind made whirling rowels of the stars –
Over black waves where sky-careering ships
Gibbet the moon upon their crazy spars,

From bow-bent wings I shot my white resilience
Grazing the tempest like a shaft of light,
Till with the sunrise, shivering into trillions
Of winged fish, I saw the wave ignite.[1]

Campbell's arrival in England had unleashed a whirlwind of conflicting influences which the naive 17-year-old had struggled to assimilate. Politically, his antagonism towards Anglo-Saxondom found a natural outlet in his support for the Irish republican movement Sinn Féin. In a letter to his mother, he wrote enthusiastically about a speech given to the Oxford Union by Esmond, 'the youngest and most brilliant of the Sinn Féin leaders'.

> He had the house in tears of laughter over the British policy towards Ireland. It was very courageous of him to speak in the way he did in a hostile country. I was surprised to find that Sinn Féin won in the voting. It would have won at Cambridge; but Oxford is so narrow-minded and Imperialistic that I didn't expect it. Esmond says he can give me a job for the vacation, i.e., to deposit a bomb under Lord French's bed. I wouldn't mind the job, but I firmly object to the penalties that might come. But he says that if I succeeded he would have me canonized as a Saint of the Catholic Church, which they are

> going to do to all the Irish martyrs. It would be a joke to be St Campbell after being a dirty little undergrad at Oxford![2]

Yet it was the endeavour to get to grips with the latest developments in philosophy, art and science that had really set his head whirling. Writing to his father, Campbell boasted that he had read most of the works of Darwin and Freud, much of the work of Thomas Huxley, and seven volumes of Nietzsche while at Oxford. He and his friends were also reading the French symbolists, the modern futurists, the Elizabethans, the modern scientists, the Roman poets, 'and as much as we can of the Greeks'. The overall effect of this rush of influences on Campbell's circle of friends was highly contagious. A sort of intellectual influenza was spread, creating an enthusiastic uniformity of belief in those who caught it. Another effect was a degree of affectation in its adherents, as Campbell's letter illustrates.

> We have passed the ages of Romanticism, Parnassianism and Symbolism. We have come to the age of psycho-analysis – futurism. Art is not developed by a lot of long-haired fools in velvet jackets. It develops itself and pulls those fools wherever it wants them to go . . . Futurism is the reaction caused by the faintness, the morbid wistfulness of the symbolists. It is hard, cruel and glaring, but always robust and healthy. It is Art pulling itself together for another tremendous fight against annihilation. It is wild, distorted, and ugly, like a wrestler coming back for a last tussle against his opponent. The muscles are contorted and rugged, the eyes bulge, and the legs stagger. But there it is, and it has won the victory.[3]

This is art seen through the prism of Freud, Darwin and Nietzsche. It is progressive, in the sense that the present and the future are always perceived implicitly as being superior to the past. It is deterministic, in the sense that art 'develops itself' and pulls the helpless minions of humanity 'wherever it wants them to go'. It is Darwinian, in the sense that art behaves in parallel with those biological imperatives that demand the survival of the fittest. The selfish muse, like the selfish gene, is 'hard, cruel and glaring, but always robust and healthy'. It is Nietzschean, in the sense that art is progressing, striving, struggling to become 'super-art'. It pulls itself together for a 'tremendous fight against annihilation', wrestling with its enemies for superiority.

The ideas propagated in this letter are crucial to a true understanding of Campbell's predicament as he first embraced and then rejected the allure of literary England. He had taken on these new and exciting ideas in much the same way as he had taken on the new and exciting friendships which post-war Oxford and London had to offer. Whereas he retained many of the friendships, however, he would come to reject most of the ideas. The plethora of progressive 'isms' which he adopted as a result of the endless reading and discussions during his first year in England led to an information overload where conflicting concepts, imbibed thirstily but largely undigested, fought for supremacy. The contradictions and mental contortions created doubts which set in motion further contradictions and contortions. A vicious circle of self-questioning and self-doubt was set in motion. Having become drunk with new ideas, he now faced the hangover of their rejection. He needed an escape from the intellectual atmosphere as much as from the cultural atmosphere in which, increasingly claustrophobically, he found himself.

Apart from the intellectual and cultural estrangement, the third factor which served to complete the unhealthy trinity was Campbell's growing moral alienation. His increasingly troubled conscience had already prompted Augustus John's remark that he had taken to drink 'as a means of counteracting the almost pathological condition of moral discomfort' which he felt at this time. This discomfort, or rather the uncomfortable memory of it, surfaced many years later when Campbell confessed to his daughter that he had been 'stricken with remorse' at Oxford for cutting a barmaid with whom he had previously had an affair because he happened to be in the company of a snobbish homosexual.

> He was haunted by this, to him, inexcusable behaviour for a long time and kept performing acts of Quixotic reparation. For instance, when dining at the Tom Burnses one night, the maid tripped on entering the dining-room with a plate of red mullet. Roy immediately got down on all fours and started to throw the fish on to the table, so that in the general mêlée, the maid would be able to get over her embarrassment.[4]

This episode could, of course, add weight to the suggestion that Campbell went through a bisexual phase at Oxford – which, if so, would have added to his moral dilemma. Yet having homosexual friends does not automatically imply sexual relations and, in any case, Campbell's deep sense of remorse is not related to his being with the homosexual but with his inexcusable cutting of the barmaid. It is not his sexuality but his snobbery which is at issue, and it is the latter which requires 'acts of Quixotic reparation'. If anything, the episode illustrates Campbell's intensely tuned conscience and his uneasiness with the pretentiousness and the air of social elitism which he was beginning to adopt. This finely tuned conscience, informed by the belief that a soul's nobility is tainted by corruption, emerged with eloquence two years later in four lines from *The Flaming Terrapin*:

> So dread Corruption, over human shoals,
> Instead of pearls, comes groping after souls,
> And the pure pearl of many a noble life
> Falls to the scraping of his rusty knife.[5]

Aware of his new friend's condition of discomfort, Augustus John sought to interest Campbell in the beauties of Provence. Campbell, encouraged by the artist's seductive descriptions of the Provençal landscape, decided to make his escape, travelling to the south of France in 1920 in the company of another artist, Geoffrey Nelson. After the 'chocolate box' drabness of England, the sunshine and sparseness of Provence delighted him. 'I was ravished by the beauty of the country,' he wrote; 'my eyes were able to rest on sober dry colours and drink real sunlight once more.'[6] Like a caged animal released back into the wild, Campbell rejoiced in the space and the freedom which he had not experienced since leaving South Africa.

Parting company with Geoffrey Nelson at Cassis, Campbell renewed his love affair with the sea by finding employment on an Italian three-masted barque, the *Santa Maria*, which plied between Marseilles and Naples, with occasional trans-Mediterranean detours to Algiers. It was while working on the *Santa Maria* that he fell from a gangplank into shallow water, receiving injuries that kept him from work for several weeks, during which time he relied on the charity of friends. Some time later he received a more serious injury while working on a smaller, single-masted vessel. A blow from a block in the rigging caused a slight fracture in one of the vertebrae in his neck. It seemed to heal fairly well at the time, but would return with a vengeance in later years.

Between voyages, Campbell helped with the grape harvest, sleeping alfresco in the mild weather which preceded the arrival of the mistral. During the harvest he had as his 'partner' a gipsy girl called Imperio, a 17-year-old widow. In the weeks that followed, he and Imperio appear to have had a close but casual relationship. Campbell described her as 'beautiful but innocent'. She also seemed to be both hot blooded and sharp tongued, because Campbell claimed that she was unsurpassed in 'the art of the Unspeakable Word', being able to swear fluently in five languages, Catalan, Valencian, Provençal, French and Spanish.[7]

Throughout this period Campbell was still trying to write verse, yet his authentic voice remained elusive and he almost invariably destroyed his efforts. It was, however, during his first visit to Martigues in 1920 that he began work on one of his most enigmatic and endearing poems, 'St Peter of the Three Canals', subtitled 'The Fisher's Prayer'. In a general sense the poem reflects the poet's experience as a fisherman, coupled with a confused but embryonic search for religious belief. More specifically, it exhibits a deep love for the simple faith of the fishing folk and peasants of Provence, fused with remnants of his own agnosticism. The agnostic mocks the simple superstitions of the fishermen, but always good-humouredly, and there is a creeping sense that, whereas the fishermen are enriched by their rudimentary faith, the poet is impoverished by his doubt and faithless sophistry.

The poem's puzzle, its enigma, is rooted in the fact that Campbell did not complete it until 10 years later. In 1930, when he was once more back in Martigues, he came across the early fragmentary verses scribbled on the flyleaf of one of his books.[8] As such, 'St Peter of the Three Canals' offers a telescopic reflection of Campbell's spiritual development over the intervening decade. In the early verses, presumably drafted, if not necessarily polished, in 1920, the statue of St Peter is 'an old green idol' and the saint himself is seen as a superstitious blending of pagan and Christian tradition:

Saint Peter-Neptune fronts the wind,
In whose Protean role combined
All deities and creeds are One.

Three verses later the cross-mixing of pagan and Christian re-emerges with a further allusion to the Saint Peter-Neptune hybrid:

Oh, strong is he when winds are strident
To tame the water with his trident . . .

By the later verses, presumably written 10 years afterwards, St Peter is seen far more in his orthodox role as the first and greatest of the Popes, and as the eternal guardian of the Gates of Heaven:

Arch-patriarch of Navigation,
He bears the lifebuoy of Salvation
To souls that flounder in the lurch:
With God he walks the azure decks,
Great Quartermaster-Pontifex
Whose vessel is the Holy Church.

The poem moves towards its final *coup de grâce* when the Fisherman-Poet beseeches the Fisherman-Saint to remember him. In a sublime paradox, since Campbell was not a Catholic in 1930 any more than he had been 10 years previously, it culminates in a cry of faith without its acceptance. Faith is not affirmed, but it is longed for:

O Captain of the Saint-filled Ark,
Ere loaded to the Plimsoll mark
Your saintly cargo put to sea,
And we attend the Great Inspection,
The Roll-call of the Resurrection,
The pay-day of Eternity –

Remember in your high promotion
How once, poor flotsam of the Ocean,
You followed such a trade as mine.

The winter nights, have you forgotten,
When hauling on a seine as rotten
You cracked your knuckles on the line?

Have you forgot the cramp that clinches
Your shoulder, turning at the winches –
And not a mullet in the mesh?
Have you forgotten Galilee –
The night you floundered in the sea
Because your faith was in your flesh?[9]

When he was not at sea, or fishing, or composing verse, or grape-picking, or gallivanting with gipsies, the shabby-looking 19-year-old dabbled at painting. He also met several English artists, though it is surely unlikely, contrary to Campbell's claims in his autobiography, that one of these was Winston Churchill. At that time, Churchill was secretary of state for war and deeply involved in trying to put down the unrest in Ireland. Whoever these artists were, Campbell seems to have disliked most of them and, in a letter to his mother, voiced his festering aversion to Anglo-Saxon gentility.

> There are some English painters here, very rich and stuck up, staying at the big hotel here. One of them came up to me and asked if I would sit for him and he would pay me two francs per hour. He thought I was an ordinary Provençal fisherman. He spoke atrocious French, so I had no difficulty in keeping up the bluff. An Englishman out of his own country is a funny specimen! They never seem to be able to change their habits according to their environment . . .[10]

In spite of his ambivalence towards England, after 18 months in Provence punctuated by only the occasional trip to London, Campbell decided that he would return there. By late September 1921 he was back in England's capital city.

If the months in Provence had been a welcome and much needed diversion, the following months in London would herald a deviation which, dervish-like, would whirl Campbell off his feet and send his life spinning in an entirely new direction. In October, within weeks of his return, he met Mary Garman. He had just turned 20; she was 23. It was chemistry, if not necessarily love, at first sight. When he first set eyes on her, he was confronted with 'the most beautiful woman I have ever seen'.[11]

Mary Garman was the eldest of nine children (seven daughters and two sons) of Dr Walter Garman, a wealthy doctor from Wednesbury in the West Midlands. According to Mary's own account, her mother was the illegitimate daughter of Lord Grey of Falloden by his Irish housekeeper.[12] Yet mystery surrounds the source of her strikingly Latin beauty, which seems neither English nor Irish. Her pale skin, offset by dark eyes and thick black hair, resemble the classic characteristics of Spain or Portugal rather than the features normally associated with the English aristocracy, legitimate or otherwise, or the daughters of a doctor from the Midlands. The mystery is accentuated by the present interpretation of the Garman family tree, exhibited in a singularly confused fashion, by Mary's daughters, Teresa and Anna:

TERESA: My mother was English, pure English . . .
ANNA: You think the Garmans are English? I thought they were Irish.
TERESA: No. I mean, Grandfather was supposed to be a Welshman.
ANNA: They're supposed to be gipsies by one lot. The only thing I know is that everybody thinks they're Jewish. My cousin had the family tree drawn up and they can't find a Jew anywhere, so I don't know.[13]

Her mysterious inheritance aside, Mary was brought up in the security and stability of a respectable and wealthy family residing at Oakswell Hall, a stately Elizabethan manor house, with the full retinue of governesses, nannies, parlour maids and gardeners. She had a devoutly Anglican upbringing and in her early teens fell hopelessly in love with the local priest. Later, at 17, she fell in love with the art mistress at the fashionable boarding school to which she had been sent, the earliest indication of her latent bisexuality.[14] At around this time she read a life of that most mystical and passionate of saints, Teresa of Avila, who would exert an enduring influence on her subsequent life.

In 1916, when she was 18, Mary learned to drive and began to chauffeur her father on his medical rounds. She took art and music lessons in neighbouring Birmingham and played golf and tennis. Yet in spite of these recreations she began to feel restless in Wednesbury. The newspapers were full of the war across the Channel and a number of her friends and cousins were among the lengthening list of casualties. Compared with the drama being played out in the trenches, the humdrum routines and comforts of life in the Midlands seemed stultifying, particularly to someone of Mary's passionate temperament and adventurous spirit. 'It was altogether a gloomy time,' says her daughter, 'and Mary longed to get away from home . . . She used to tell me how the eternally grey skies of the Midlands, and the smog from factories and coal fires, which turned even the roses in the garden black by evening, used to oppress her spirits.'[15]

Having failed to obtain her father's consent to go to London, she simply ran away, taking her younger sister Kathleen with her. (Coincidentally, at around the same time Roy was also running away, in his fruitless effort to enlist with the South African infantry.) Arriving penniless in London, Mary found employment driving a van for Lyon's Corner Houses. Liberated from the constraints of provincial life, the sisters began to enjoy the city's cultural delights. Mary attended classes at the Slade School of Art and concerts at the Queen's Hall, while Kathleen studied music and became a model for several sculptors, including Jacob Epstein, who, according to Mary's daughter Anna, was 'much taken with her unusual face with its very high cheekbones and long, green slanting eyes'. Mary said her sister Kathleen 'looked rather like an Egyptian princess'.[16]

Kathleen became Epstein's mistress. They had three children, eventually married, and, when her husband was knighted, Kathleen became Lady Epstein. The artistic legacy of their relationship is still visible in several parts of London, where Epstein immortalized his love for Kathleen in prominent sculptures. Years later, Anna was driving near Hyde Park with some foreign friends. They were caught in a traffic jam right beside one of Epstein's sculptures. Kathleen was portrayed in it, racing naked with a greyhound, and Anna could not resist pointing out that the model for the statue was her aunt.[17]

Mary also had her admirers. Her drawing master at the Slade had painted her portrait, and the composer and conductor Bernard van Dieren had fallen in love with her. Van Dieren, middle-aged and married, followed Mary relentlessly for over a year, sending her letters beginning, '*Dolcissima, carissima* Maria . . .' No doubt flattered by the incessant but devoted attention, she eventually invited him back to the rented studio room in Regent Square that she shared with Kathleen. He was soon a regular visitor, cooking the sisters wonderful meals on their gas stove and composing several songs for Mary which she sang for him at Kathleen's piano.

Apart from regular visits from Jacob Epstein and Bernard van Dieren, the sisters paid court to other young artists and musicians, hosting bohemian parties. Having no concept of housekeeping, Mary and Kathleen lit their room with naked flames during these parties, oblivious of the dangers of their failure to put mantles on the gas jets. At one such gathering this nearly had disastrous consequences. Kathleen noticed with horror that the tall Jewish artist Jacob Kramer's long hair was alight. 'Kramer, you're on fire!' she shrieked across the room. Kramer's initial amusement at what he took to be a joke was soon transformed into panic as he patted his head frantically to put out the flames.[18]

Since Mary and Roy were moving in similar circles, it was perhaps inevitable that their paths would cross eventually. In fact, Mary had spotted Campbell from a distance a couple of weeks before their first meeting. She recounts her first impressions of him in the only page of memoirs she ever wrote:

> My sister Kathleen ... and I were riding on the top of a bus in Tottenham Court Road ... when we saw Roy for the first time. He got off the bus when we did and made for the Eiffel Tower Restaurant in Charlotte Street. We were quite intrigued, he was so good-looking, so foreign, who could he be? Once inside the restaurant he went straight to a table where a golden haired girl, Iris Tree, was sitting alone, evidently waiting for him ...[19]

Mary's instant attraction to the tall, exotic stranger was reciprocated a short while later by Roy's bewitchment at the first sight of her dark and equally exotic beauty. Uninhibited by questions of morality, Mary and Kathleen invited Roy, who claimed to be homeless, to come and stay with them. 'Anyway Roy came back with us and quite a lot of interesting things happened at Regent Square in the next few months.'[20] The three would lie arm in arm in front of the fire, and Roy would read fragments of his own verse to his new-found admirers, or else he would entertain them with stories of Provence or the African bush. These early, heady days were recalled by Mary:

> I suppose it was my love of poetry that was the main cause of our marriage, the marriage of Roy and myself. At twelve years old I was in love with poetry. I remember reading Blake and Shelley with the greatest delight. When I met Roy he seemed to me the personification of poetry and when he recited couplets from *The Flaming Terrapin* which he had just begun to write I realized that I had met a poet in flesh and blood.[21]

Not surprisingly, the unorthodox *ménage à trois* led to the unfounded rumour that Roy had become the lover of both sisters. This sparked tremendous jealousy in the girls' admirers. Van Dieren would arrive on his regular visits, dressed in his perfectly cut suits, to find himself displaced in Mary's affections by a bedraggled and bearded beggar. He would sit upright in a chair and stare disapprovingly at Roy squatting in front of the fire. 'You don't wear shoes, Campbell,' he would observe coldly. 'You prefer to go barefoot.'[22] Eventually, van Dieren had little option but to acknowledge defeat, bowing out gracefully. Epstein, however, having serious designs on Kathleen, remained violently jealous of the strange intimacy between Campbell and the two sisters.

Regardless of Epstein's understandable suspicions, the only deep intimacy was between Roy and Mary, who had fallen passionately in love. It was, in the classic sense, a whirlwind romance. Within two months of their first meeting, Roy was being introduced to Mary's parents. Two months later they were married. Many must have feared that such haste heralded disaster, but although their marriage was often turbulent, it would survive, weathering several storms along the way.

'Two such explosive and arrogant temperaments might have been mutually destructive,' wrote Rob Lyle, who knew the couple better than almost anyone. 'In fact they have thrived on clashes and collisions which would have shattered lesser personalities into a thousand fragments, or sent them spinning in opposite directions.'[23] In the years ahead, the volatile love of Roy and Mary Campbell would sometimes hurl them apart, but would always drag them back together. In the tempest of their passion for each other, peace could only be found in the eye of the storm.

NOTES

1 Roy Campbell, from 'The Albatross', *Collected Poems, Volume One*, p. 35.
2 Ethel Campbell, *The Life of Sam Campbell*, p. 354.
3 *Ibid.*, p. 355.
4 Anna Campbell Lyle, *Son of Valour*, p. 7.
5 *Collected Poems, Volume One*, pp. 75–6.
6 Roy Campbell, *Broken Record*, p. 129.
7 Roy Campbell, *Light on a Dark Horse*, pp. 194 and 214–15.
8 Unpublished note from Campbell, 21 May 1947, cited in Peter Alexander, *Roy Campbell*, p. 106.
9 *Collected Poems, Volume One*, pp. 182–5.
10 Ethel Campbell, *The Life of Sam Campbell*, p. 356.
11 Roy Campbell, *Light on a Dark Horse*, p. 238.
12 Peter Alexander, *Roy Campbell*, p. 28.
13 Anna Campbell Lyle and Teresa Campbell, interview with the author, Portugal, December 1998.
14 Anna Campbell Lyle, *Son of Valour*, p. 12.
15 *Ibid.*
16 Quoted in Teresa Campbell, unpublished memoirs, p. 3.
17 Anna Campbell Lyle, *Son of Valour*, p. 12.
18 Peter Alexander, *Roy Campbell*, p. 29.
19 Quoted in Teresa Campbell, unpublished memoirs, pp. 3–4.
20 *Ibid.*, p. 4.
21 *Ibid.*
22 Peter Alexander, *Roy Campbell*, p. 29.
23 Rob Lyle, quoted in Anna Campbell Lyle's introduction to Roy's letters to Mary, unpublished.

CHAPTER FIVE

A STABLE RELATIONSHIP

But when the Muse or some as lovely sprite,
Friend, lover, wife, in such a form as thine,
Thrilling a mortal frame with half her light
And choosing for her guise such eyes and hair
As scarcely veil the subterfuge divine,
Descends with him his lonely fight to share . . .[1]

'My parents had come together in London after the Great War,' writes Teresa Campbell. 'They were both searching for something. They were both runaways. My father abandoned his studies at Oxford and my mother had run away from home with a younger sister. In their different ways they were trying to escape convention. As my mother was always saying when she was about eighty – "Roy and I were the first Hippies" and she seemed very proud of the fact.'[2]

Roy and Mary were clearly moving in the best bohemian circles at the time they met. At the Eiffel Tower Restaurant, as Roy recalls in his autobiography, they rubbed shoulders with the 'very beautiful' Iris Tree and Dorothy Warren, Raquel Meller, the Asquiths, Augustus John, Maurice Baring, Philip Heseltine, Wyndham Lewis, Cecil Gray, Nina Hamnett, who was 'a fine trooper', and last but not least 'the whole Bloomsbury contingent'.[3] In many respects, Roy was lionized in these circles and was afforded a certain celebrity status. Still known as 'Zulu', his wild reputation had been further enhanced by the exaggerated stories of his adventures with the fishermen and gipsies of Provence. His legendary prowess with women achieved near-mythic status through the rumours arising from his presumed *ménage à trois* with Mary and Kathleen. Basking in the reflected glory of these cultural and carnal conquests, both real and imagined, Roy was, temporarily and on the surface at least, fully at home and at ease in London's Bohemia.

He was, however, neither at home nor at ease when he accompanied Mary and Kathleen to Oakswell Hall for the family Christmas at the end of 1921. His discomfort was heightened immediately upon their arrival by the tactless candour of Kathleen's introduction. 'Father,' she announced stoutly, 'this is Roy, who's going to marry Mary.' Shocked by the bluntness of the statement, the old man looked the tall visitor up and down. 'My eldest daughter?' he mumbled doubtfully. 'To a complete stranger?'[4] The unpromising start must have added to Roy's unease. He later confessed that he had felt completely overwhelmed in the presence of Mary's parents, and all eight of her brothers and sisters, during his first meal with the family. He was acutely aware that he was being stared at and could feel almost physically the curious eyes examining him.[5] At first, anxious to impress, he refused all wine during meals, but he was soon seeking to escape the intensity of the situation by frequenting the local pub, occasionally taking Mary's young sister Helen with him. Dr Garman observed this behaviour disapprovingly, warning Mary that she was 'marrying a dipsomaniac'.[6]

Mary was oblivious of her father's cautionary words. She was well aware of Roy's excessive drinking and was an enthusiastic accomplice, however much she abstained in the presence of her parents. Painfully aware that they were powerless to thwart their daughter's determination to marry the jobless poet, Mary's parents reluctantly gave way to the inevitable. 'All their good sense was useless,' wrote Anna Campbell Lyle. 'My parents already considered themselves eternal partners.' Years later, when Anna asked her mother how Roy had proposed to her, Mary replied with great indignation that he had never proposed. 'We took it for granted that we would marry when we first spoke to each other!'[7]

Having gained the less than enthusiastic acquiescence of Dr and Mrs Garman, there still remained Dr and Mrs Campbell, Roy's parents in South Africa. Fearing their opposition, Roy decided to overcome this particular obstacle by the simple expedient of avoiding it. He chose not to tell them. It was a cowardly but effective option.

> My father heard of our marriage too late to stop it; he was naturally hurt that, being a minor, I had not consulted him about it, since he had always been so good to me and had always sent me any money I asked for when I was hard up. My excuse was, and still is, that I was taking absolutely no risks at all of not getting married to this girl.[8]

Relieved to escape from Oakswell Hall shortly after Christmas, Roy took his fiancée to stay with Augustus John and his young family at Alderney Manor in Dorset. During the visit one of John's other guests suggested that they organize some play-acting to amuse the children. This took the form of a masquerade designed to celebrate the engagement of Roy and Mary. One of the guests took the role of the priest, while T. W. Earp was a choirboy and Augustus John an acolyte. 'It was good fun,' wrote John, 'and I thought wanted very little to make it a true and valid ceremony. As a matter of fact, there could have existed no closer union in the world than that of Roy and Mary Campbell.'[9]

After this light-hearted interlude, Roy and Mary returned to Oakswell Hall where, on 11 February 1922, they were married in the local Anglican church. The bridegroom, possessing nothing suitable of his own, arrived from London in a shiny, second-hand suit, purchased at the last minute for the princely sum of 12 shillings, and an old-fashioned frock coat borrowed from a waiter at the Eiffel Tower Restaurant. The overall effect, especially when combined with Roy's efforts to tame his unkempt appearance by plastering down his hair, made the groom look not dissimilar to a Victorian undertaker at Lord Palmerston's funeral. Mary was horrified when she saw him and insisted that he change into his old suit. For her part, Mary wore a long black dress and a golden veil, not to be eccentric but simply because she had nothing else. The whole shabby affair was completed when Roy knelt at the altar and exposed the holes in the soles of his shoes to the assembled guests. It was all too much for Ada, Mary's one-time nanny. 'Oh dear, I always thought Miss Mary would marry a gentleman with a park!' she exclaimed.[10]

After a sedate wedding breakfast, Roy and Mary returned to London, barely four months after they had first met, as Mr and Mrs Campbell. A wild party ensued at the Harlequin Restaurant in Beak Street. Roy's elder brother George, who had just completed his medical studies at Edinburgh, arrived unexpectedly and gazed in respectable wonderment at 'the howling dervishes of London Bohemia'.[11] At the height of the festivities the newlyweds retired to the room upstairs which they were now renting, having just moved from the studio room on Regent Square. Wyndham Lewis was among the guests and, characteristically, created a legend out of Campbell's exploits by providing a graphic account of the proceedings:

> The marriage-feast was a distinguished gathering, if you are prepared to admit distinction to the Bohemian, for it was almost gipsy in its freedom from the conventional restraints ... In the middle of it Campbell and his bride retired. The guests then became quarrelsome.
>
> Jacob Kramer and Augustus John were neighbours at table and I noticed that they were bickering ...
>
> At this moment Roy Campbell entered in his pyjamas. There was a horrid hush. Someone had slipped out to acquaint Campbell with the fact of the threat to the peace. In a dead silence the bridegroom, with catlike steps, approached the back of Kramer's chair ...
>
> 'What's this, Kramer?' barked Roy, fierce and thick, in his best back-veldt. 'What are you doing Kramer!' Roy Campbell pointed his

> hand at his guest and began wagging it about in a suggestive way as if he might box his ears or chop him in the neck with it.
>
> 'Nothing, Roy! I'm not doing anything, Roy!' the guest answered, in a tone of surprise and injured innocence . . .
>
> 'Look. Could I throw you out of that window if I wanted to Jacob?'
>
> 'I know you could, Roy.' Kramer nodded his head, his eyes screwed up.
>
> 'Well then let my guests alone, Jacob. You let my guests alone. Don't let me hear you've interfered with John again. Mind I'm only just upstairs, Jacob. I'll come down to you!'
>
> A strangled protest and assent at once came from Kramer; and stiffly and slowly, his shoulders drawn up, his head thrust out, in apache bellicosity, Campbell withdrew, all of us completely silent.[12]

In changing Campbell from a 'Zulu' to an 'apache' brave, Lewis had surpassed himself. Embellishment aside, however, the story appears to be substantially true. In *Light on a Dark Horse* Campbell alluded to Lewis's 'comical account of the fun' and confirmed its basis in fact. At the same time he sought to play down the 'apache bellicosity'. Jacob Kramer was 'that lovable Jewish Giant' who was 'a good boxer'. Kramer and Campbell, though friends, had a healthy respect for the other's physical reputation, to the extent that Campbell confessed that they were slightly afraid of each other. It was, therefore, 'a piece of bluff and bravado on the simple-minded Jacob' which Campbell only performed 'out of gratitude to Augustus John', adding that 'for few others would I have risked so much'.[13]

The Campbells' married life began turbulently. Roy's father, infuriated at the underhand way in which the marriage had been arranged, stopped his son's allowance. This exacerbated the young couple's already tenuous financial position, forcing them to pawn their wedding presents. Added to these problems were the strains caused by Epstein's continuing jealousy. He was still convinced, mistakenly, that Campbell was the lover of both sisters. Driven to desperate measures by his desire for Kathleen and his distrust of Roy, Epstein enlisted the help of the waiters at the Harlequin Restaurant to gather evidence of the orgies he believed were taking place in the room upstairs. Roy was understandably furious when he discovered that he and his wife were being spied on by the waiters, and was apoplectic when he realized that they were acting on Epstein's behalf.

One evening when Kathleen and Epstein were dining at the Harlequin, Campbell sent Mary out with Augustus John before asking a waiter to deliver a message to Epstein's table: 'Mr Campbell would like a word upstairs with Mr Epstein.' Most of the other diners in the small restaurant were well aware of the rumours surrounding Campbell's relationship with Kathleen and Epstein's jealousy, and the whole place fell silent as Epstein rose from the table and went upstairs. There was a seemingly eternal and foreboding silence, during which all eyes rested furtively on Kathleen, now seated alone and feeling decidedly awkward. Suddenly there was a thunderous hammering on the ceiling as the two men began to fight upstairs.

Kathleen rushed up to Campbell's room. Flinging open the door, she was confronted by the sight of her brother-in-law and her future husband rolling about on the floor in the midst of upturned furniture. 'Stop it! *Stop* it!' she screamed. 'You're behaving like animals – you *can't* behave like that here!'[14] The two men rose to their feet and Campbell, without a word, went out to find Mary and John. He told them of his victory and claimed, if the version he later told is anything to go by, that the slight scratch on his forehead was caused by the buttons on Epstein's waistcoat as he threw him over his head.[15]

Since this 'epic battle' between Epstein and Campbell had been witnessed at first hand by half of Bohemia, or had at least been heard by it through the floorboards, it did not take long for the grapevine to start working. Stories surrounding the Campbells intensified and it was soon rumoured that Roy was complaisantly allowing Mary to conduct an affair with van Dieren.

Feeling increasingly uncomfortable with the notoriety of their public reputation, Roy and Mary sought to escape to somewhere quieter. They chose a remote corner of Wales which Mary knew well from family holidays. With a gift of five pounds from Mary's old nurse, they travelled to the isolated coastal village of Aberdaron. They camped out for a time, then stayed in two cottages before finally renting a converted but somewhat dilapidated stable, Ty Corn, situated about three miles out of the village. Augustus John's son Romilly was staying with them at the time, having run away from home, and he later recalled his dismal first impressions of Ty Corn:

> The floor was earth stamped unevenly down, and in some places the mud had fallen from between the rocks of which the walls were built, so that the wind came whistling in. Mary and I both fell prey to unspeakable gloom . . . But it was astonishing how quickly we cheered up under the influence of Roy's indomitable spirit. I really think it had never crossed his mind that the cottage in any way fell short of a desirable country residence; nor did it, when the holes had been stuffed up and a great fire was roaring up the chimney.[16]

Roy's 'indomitable spirit' was no doubt fuelled, as it had been upon his arrival in Provence two years earlier, by a sense of liberation from the artificiality and claustrophobia of life in London. It is almost as though he could only keep up the pretence of the macho persona, which the contrived 'Zulu' reputation demanded of him, for short, intense periods of time, egged on by alcohol. Eventually, an escape became necessary so that the real, pre-Oxford Roy could re-emerge. It was, as Lawrence Durrell implied, the call of the wild colonial boy from within the walls of aesthetic affectation. Alluding to this aspect of her father's personality, Anna spoke of his childhood when 'everything was beautiful, and like paradise', comparing it with his arrival in 'this funny little country full of fog, with no wild animals, very little sun and no mountains – he had a really mystical feeling about mountains . . . So he got a funny thing about England. I think he was terribly anti-Anglo-Saxon. He had a passion for Celts.'[17] It is easy to imagine Roy's spirits lifting as he beheld for the first time the mountains of Snowdonia as he and his new bride passed through the valleys *en route* to their Celtic haven.

Campbell's antagonism towards Anglo-Saxondom, particularly in its modern manifestation, was expressed both bluntly and amusingly in *Broken Record*: 'My ancestors cleared out of Britain at the first whiff of the nineteenth and twentieth centuries, and I only came back to see what made them clear off in such a hurry, which I soon found out.'[18] This terse sentence expresses Roy's ambivalence towards many aspects of modern life and his intermittent longing to escape from it, and there is clearly a sense that on this occasion he was following in the ancestral footsteps by 'clearing off' in such a hurry from London. He even uses the same language, explaining that he and Mary had 'cleared off, as we were sick of city life, to a corner of Wales, of which my wife was very fond'.[19]

Roy and Mary stayed at Ty Corn for more than a year, living on a diet of home-grown vegetables, seabirds' eggs collected from the nearby cliffs, and rabbits and pheasants poached by Roy with a small shotgun. There were also fish, lobsters and crabs obtained from the local fishermen, who called Roy 'Africa'. For fuel to keep their fire blazing through the long winter, Roy had to carry a hundredweight of coal every week from the road two miles away.

Roy befriended many of the local inhabitants, and was particularly fascinated by the small offshore community on Bardsey Island. The fishermen on the island 'were almost savages and wore ear-rings and beards' and 'few of them could speak a word of English'.[20] Roy was proud that he and Mary had been accepted by the islanders, who did not normally take kindly to 'foreigners'. Yet if Roy and Mary were fascinated by the natives, the natives were more than fascinated by their exotic neighbours. They were still remembered more than half a century later by elderly villagers who spoke of the notoriety that 'Africa' and his wife had gained in the neighbourhood. They wore flowing, brightly coloured clothes and Roy's hair was far longer than local custom dictated. They also inflamed local gossip by regularly making love on the cliff-tops in broad daylight. Locals who visited Ty Corn returned to the village with reports that Roy and Mary had covered the walls of their converted stable with charcoal sketches of each other in the nude. On one occasion a local man, arriving at Ty Corn on some sort of business, was confronted at the door by Mary and her sister, both naked. In bashful confusion, he forgot what he was going to ask and went away in a state of shock.[21]

In many respects, life at Ty Corn was one extended honeymoon. Apart from the seemingly insatiable delight in each other's bodies, Roy and Mary rejoiced in the unencumbered tranquillity of their surroundings. Mary stumbled across some foxes dancing in the moonlight, and when she and Roy bathed in the sea a small seal regularly kept them company.[22] In the autumn, as the weather deteriorated, they would huddle in front of the blazing fire drinking the beer which Roy had carried up from the village in a gallon jar. They spent the evenings reading poetry to each other by firelight – Dante, Pope's Homer, Dryden's Virgil, Milton, Donne, Mickle's Camoëns, Cervantes, Rabelais, Marlowe, Shakespeare and many of the Elizabethans. They were living, Campbell wrote, 'under the continual intoxication of poetry'.[23]

In the midst of this idyll, their first daughter, Teresa, was born in far from ideal circumstances, in the middle of the night during a violent midwinter storm on 26 November 1922, almost nine months to the day after their wedding. 'I have not seen anything to equal the extraordinary courage of my wife in fighting through this fearful night, when the wind blew the tiles off our roof and the rain and wind rushed in headlong,' wrote Roy.[24] Mary was helped through the ordeal by a young Welsh midwife, who delivered the baby girl by the light of a single oil lamp that swung wildly from the rafters in the wind. The nervous husband weathered the storm in a completely different way. Unable to be present, he sheltered behind a piece of corrugated iron on the beach, suffering fearful sympathetic pain. At dawn, as the storm abated, he shot a snipe and grilled it on a spit for Mary's breakfast, placing it on a tray with a bunch of flowers.[25]

Years later, when the painful memories, like the storm, had abated, Mary and Roy could look back on the terrible night with a nostalgic fondness born out of the anaesthesia of romance. As for Teresa, although she never tired of telling her friends that she had been born in a stable, she never forgot to emphasize the painful aspects of her birth. 'I weighed ten pounds, my mother nearly died having me, I was so big.'[26]

The 'continual intoxication of poetry' at Ty Corn was not confined to the verse of others. In the long summer months of Mary's pregnancy, Roy was going through a period of unprecedented inspiration, writing – with the exception of a few fragments composed during his wanderings in Provence – the whole of *The Flaming Terrapin*, the long, vibrant poem which would establish his reputation. Night after night, while Mary slept below, he wrote lying on his back on a mattress, a notebook propped on his knees, in a tiny loft with the rafters just above his head and two or three candles flickering in a saucer by his side. He would emerge in the morning to read what he had written to the newly awakened Mary and then would crawl into the bed she had recently vacated, sleeping for the remainder of the morning.

By the beginning of September 1922, the poem was completed. Laboriously, he made several handwritten copies and sent them to his closest friends. Edgell Rickword, a friend from his Oxford days who was destined to become the editor of *Left Review*, was the first to respond.

> I have waited three days and three nights to be able to tell you quite coolly that the poem is magnificent. One doesn't often find anything to overwhelm one's expectations but this did completely . . . I know of *no-one living* who could write in such a sustained and intense poetical manner . . . Lots of things might have weighed against my liking it (particularly your philosophy of sweat) but the sheer fecundity of images ravished my lady-like prejudices . . . Good luck and ten thousand thanks for such a poem.[27]

Campbell's ecstatic reaction to Rickword's praise was expressed in a letter to his mother. 'He is the one man among the younger poets whose opinion I revere at all and I only expected rather a cold-blooded criticism from him. I simply fell down on my bed and howled like a baby when I got it.'[28]

Roy was still only 20 years old in September 1922, but it must have seemed, as he read his friend's eulogistic letter, that his life was complete. He had found the inspiration to write 'magnificent' verse, he was contented in his daily life, he was soon to be a father and, most of all, he was married to the woman who had made it all possible. After the inner turmoil which had whisked him away to Provence, and the whirlwind romance that had swept him off his feet, Campbell began to perceive in his wife a peacefulness which could calm his warring spirits. More than that, she had unloosed his tongue. Through her, his poetic vocation had found its voice. The long search for that authentic voice, as beguiling and elusive as a shadow, had somehow been made complete by his marriage.

NOTES

1 Roy Campbell, from 'Dedication to Mary Campbell', *Collected Poems, Volume One*, p. 16.
2 Teresa Campbell, unpublished memoirs, p. 3.
3 Roy Campbell, *Light on a Dark Horse*, pp. 230 and 244.

4 Peter Alexander, *Roy Campbell*, p. 30.
5 Anna Campbell Lyle, *Son of Valour*, p. 14.
6 Peter Alexander, *Roy Campbell*, p. 30.
7 Anna Campbell Lyle, *Son of Valour*, p. 15.
8 Roy Campbell, *Light on a Dark Horse*, p. 246.
9 Augustus John, *Autobiography*, London: Jonathan Cape, 1975, pp. 414–15.
10 Anna Campbell Lyle, *Son of Valour*, p. 15.
11 Roy Campbell, *Light on a Dark Horse*, p. 247.
12 Percy Wyndham Lewis, *Blasting and Bombardiering*, London: Calder & Boyars Ltd, 1967 edition, pp. 221–3.
13 Roy Campbell, *Light on a Dark Horse*, p. 247.
14 Peter Alexander, *Roy Campbell*, p. 32.
15 Roy Campbell, *Light on a Dark Horse*, p. 251.
16 Romilly John, *The Seventh Child*, London: Heinemann, 1932, pp. 211–13.
17 Anna Campbell Lyle, interview with the author, Portugal, December 1998.
18 Roy Campbell, *Broken Record*, p. 155.
19 *Ibid.*, p. 168.
20 *Ibid.*, p. 169; and *Light on a Dark Horse*, p. 254.
21 Peter Alexander, *Roy Campbell*, p. 33.
22 Anna Campbell Lyle, *Son of Valour*, p. 15.
23 Roy Campbell, *Broken Record*, p. 169.
24 *Ibid.*, pp. 170–71.
25 Peter Alexander, *Roy Campbell*, p. 34; and Anna Campbell Lyle, *Son of Valour*, p. 17.
26 Teresa Campbell, unpublished memoirs, p. 2.
27 Peter Alexander, *Roy Campbell*, p. 34.
28 *Ibid.*

CHAPTER SIX

THE MUSE AFLAME

Now the Earth meets the Sun: through nerve and limb
Trembling she feels his fiery manhood swim:
Huge spasms rend her, as in red desire
He leaps and fills her gushing womb with fire:
And as he labours, sounding through the skies,
The thunders of their merriment arise![1]

The other friends to whom Campbell sent his handwritten copies of *The Flaming Terrapin*, apart from Edgell Rickword, were Philip Heseltine and Augustus John. Heseltine wrote of the immense 'buoyancy and exhilaration of the whole thing', adding that it was 'practically unique . . . in this dispirited and half-hearted generation that knows not youth. Bravo!'[2] Augustus John thought it 'a most remarkable work, in spite of its unflagging and, to me, rather exhausting grandiloquence'.[3] John showed it to T. E. Lawrence who, 'much excited', took it to Jonathan Cape. 'Normally rhetoric so bombastic would have sickened me,' Lawrence wrote. 'But what originality, what energy, what freshness and enthusiasm, and what a riot of glorious imagery and colour! Magnificent I call it!'[4] Cape shared the excitement and decided to publish the work.[5] Meanwhile, Rickword enthused about the poem to Desmond MacCarthy, literary editor of the *New Statesman*, who was so impressed by it that he took the unusual step of deciding to review it before learning of its acceptance by a publisher.

It was not long before the waves of enthusiasm broke on the reclusive shores of the Campbells' Welsh retreat, restoring the couple's appetite for literary London. Increasingly, as news of *The Flaming Terrapin* spread, their friends began to plead with them to return. 'We were urged to abandon the backveld and to come into the limelight,' wrote Campbell.[6]

In the late spring of 1923, Roy and Mary moved back to London, taking a room at 90 Charlotte Street. Soon after their arrival, Jonathan Cape arranged a meeting with Roy at which the publisher expressed his delight with the poem and gave the overwhelmed young poet an immediate advance of £10.

After the months of silence and seclusion in Wales, Roy took to the glamour and clamour of Bohemia like a fish returned to water. He was soon frequenting all the old haunts and renewing all the old acquaintances. Nina Hamnett recalled that Roy accompanied her, along with about 15 other people, to a seedy boxing match in Camden Town. Her lurid description of drunken revellers amidst limbless boxers is reminiscent of one of Otto Dix's graphic post-war depictions of humiliated and mutilated ex-servicemen.

> Roy brought a bottle of whisky and we borrowed a tumbler from the boxers' dressing-room. One of the boxers who was fighting got very badly bashed about and Roy handed a glass to his seconds to revive him. The person who drank most of the whisky was sitting at the end of the row. He seized a one-armed boxer and roared advice on boxing to him. The one-armed man had been a very good Army boxer before he lost his right arm ... He would take on a much younger man who had also lost his arm and occasionally they would appear in the ring and fight. It really was a shock to me the first time I saw them. I don't think anyone else liked it very much, except the one-armed boxers themselves. They made very good use of their respective arms and got in some terrific punches. At the end of the fight they were both announced as winners, which delighted them and made them laugh.[7]

Hamnett recalls other trips to the boxing bouts in Camden Town, salivating over Italian boxers who 'had apparently trained on spaghetti and were very fat indeed', and on their followers who arrived 'complete with concertinas and razors'. On one such occasion, which Hamnett recounts with evident relish, a fight broke out between Italian and English fight-goers over the merits or otherwise of Mussolini, who had established himself as Italy's fascist dictator in October 1922. 'The police force was called in and the audience with some difficulty was disentangled. Quite a lot were discovered fighting under the ring itself.'[8] Hamnett does not record that Campbell was present on this occasion, but Roy's daughter Anna writes that '"Chile" Guevara, a south American, was a boxer much liked by the literary set in London. I don't know why except that everything "tough" was in vogue in the twenties.'[9] It is perhaps not surprising that Anna adds that her mother 'certainly did not approve of Nina'.

Roy's occasional drunken neglect of his wife and child was evident in March 1924, when Mary returned one evening to Charlotte Street to discover that her husband had locked up and gone off to a pub. It was a cold, snowy night and Mary sat for hours on the doorstep, trying to comfort the crying baby, until Roy returned, drunk and contrite. For the first time, she was reminded of her father's cautionary words and wondered whether he had been right to disapprove of her marriage to a 'dipsomaniac'.[10] For the most part, however, Roy was a caring and considerate husband and father. In order to give Mary a break from looking after Tess, he would strap the baby to his back in a blanket, Zulu-style, and, donning a wide-brimmed straw hat and a scarlet bandanna, he would walk with her for hours through the streets and crowds of London.

Roy's love for Mary was evident in a letter he wrote to his mother early in 1924. 'I am awfully pleased that you appreciate and understand how much she is to me; our life together, in spite of its ups and downs, has been almost like a dream. In these days when girls are, as you say, rather selfish and are brought up to keep an eye on their own comfort, she seems all the more wonderful.'[11] In a postscript to another letter to his parents, Roy offers a picture of family life when he explains that 'Tess has been shaking my pad most of the time' and that 'Mary is just getting her bath ready'.[12]

Roy sent a handwritten copy of *The Flaming Terrapin* to his parents some months prior to its publication, and was at pains to elucidate both its moral and its meaning to them. Aware that they were somewhat puzzled by the poem, he wrote apologetically that 'its moral is rather too deeply embedded in the symbolism'.

> However, I'll try to explain. The whole moral of the poem is contained in Christ's words, 'Every tree that bringeth not forth good fruit is hewn down and cast into the fire,' and again in His words, 'Ye are the salt of the earth but if that salt shall have lost its savour it shall be scattered abroad and trodden under the feet of men' (I have probably misquoted it). Christ was one of the first to proclaim the doctrine of heredity and the survival of the fittest. Nietzsche was too dull to understand the aristocratic outlook of Christ, he slangs Him for inventing a religion for the weak and wretched. But in this he was wrong for Christ in his gospels is continually emphasising how hard it is to get into the Kingdom of Heaven . . . Christ who was really the first philosopher, and possibly the last to be gifted with ordinary commonsense together with intuitive vision, has been borne out in almost everything he ever said, by Darwin and Einstein and there is nearly always some deep scientific meaning in his sayings.
>
> However, to continue my explanation: in a world suffering from shell-shock, with most of its finest breeding-stock lost, and the rest rather demoralised, it is interesting to conjecture whether a portion of the race may not have become sufficiently ennobled by its sufferings to reinstate and even improve on the pre-war standard, and in the

> end to supplant the descendants of those who have become demoralised and stagnant, like the Russians for instance. I have taken this more cheerful view, as I would much sooner feel that I was a Simian in the state of evolution into something higher, than a fallen angel in a state of decline. So, with the deluge as symbolising the war and its subsequent hopelessness, I have represented in the Noah family, the survival of the fittest, and tried to describe the manner in which they won through the terrors of the storm and eventually colonised the earth.[13]

This short exposition throws as much light on the poet as it does on the poem. A confused Christianity, no doubt accentuated in order to placate his parents' puritanical sensibilities, is added to the confusion of influences which had dominated at Oxford. Whereas the letter to his parents four years earlier had looked at art through the prism of Nietzsche, Darwin and Freud, this letter looks at theology and politics through a similar prism, although Einstein appears to have replaced Freud in his affections. There is evidence of a more questioning approach to Nietzsche, but the idealization of the Nietzschean 'strong' and the Darwinian 'fittest' remains. The first tangible evidence of Campbell's aversion to communism emerges in his view of the Bolshevik revolution as being the product of post-war demoralization and stagnation; and there is the first indication of a kind of proto-fascism in his hope that communism could be supplanted by those who refuse to become demoralized or stagnant, but instead are 'ennobled' by the sufferings of the war. Beneath the surface, submerged but omnipotent like the Terrapin itself, is the hidden influence of T. S. Eliot's *The Waste Land*, published 18 months earlier, with its post-war angst and superficial cynicism pointing towards possible resurrection.

For Campbell, the forces of resurrection, in the form of creation – or re-creation – are symbolized by the Terrapin of the poem's title. In Eastern tradition, he informed his parents, the tortoise was 'the talisman which represents strength, longevity, endurance and courage'. It was also the symbol of the universe, 'the dome representing the heavens and the body of the earth'.[14] Thus the Terrapin's progress is accompanied by a joyful and fertile song of creation:

> The Flaming Terrapin that towed the Ark
> Rears up his hump of thunder on the dark,
> And like a mountain, seamed with rocky scars,
> Tufted with forests, barnacled with stars,
> Crinkles white rings, as from its ancient sleep
> Into a foam of life he wakes the Deep.

And again,

> Freed from the age-long agonies of birth
> This living galleon oars himself along
> And roars his triumph over all the earth
> Until the sullen hills burst into song.
> His beauty makes a summer through the land,
> And where he crawls upon the solid ground,
> Gigantic flowers, exploding from the sand,
> Spread fans of blinding colour all around.
> His voice has roused the amorphous mud to life –
> Dust thinks: and tired of spinning in the wind,
> Stands up to be a man and feel the strife
> Of brute-thoughts in the jungle of his mind.

Yet the Terrapin, Campbell informed his parents, is also 'the symbol of masculine energy'.[15] Campbell's poem, like his daughter, was conceived during the protracted honeymoon, and the whole work burns with the afterglow of one alive and aflame with the physical delights of the marriage bed. The feminine Earth feels the Sun's 'fiery manhood swim' through trembling nerve and limb:

> Huge spasms rend her, as in red desire
> He leaps and fills her gushing womb with fire . . .

It was written during his wife's pregnancy, in the weeks and months when the child in the womb was beginning to assert itself, kicking and protruding ever more obviously. It is little wonder that Campbell's fertile imagination found poetic expression in a joyous fertility rite. *The Flaming Terrapin* is a hymn to life transfused with mystic symbolism. The Rainbow, the symbol of the fruitful union of the Earth and the Sun, is a 'blaze of watery fire'.

At its deepest, *The Flaming Terrapin* conveys a promise, at this stage both inarticulate and unfulfilled, of the poet's emerging mysticism and spirituality. It offers a premonition of Campbell's own future, a prophecy of a paganism christened, fertilized by faith and reborn. In the early part of the poem there is a profound insight into the spiritual basis of all matter which is reminiscent of Christian philosophers such as Duns Scotus and Christian poets such as Gerard Manley Hopkins and G. K. Chesterton. In spite of Campbell's later satirical lampoons of Hopkins, there is more than a trace of the Jesuit poet's concept of 'inscape' and Chesterton's philosophy of gratitude in the following passage from *The Flaming Terrapin*:

> Action and flesh cohere in one clean fusion
> Of force with form: the very ethers breed
> Wild harmonies of song: the frailest reed

Holds shackled thunder in its heart's seclusion.
And every stone that lines my lonely way,
Sad tongueless nightingale without a wing,
Seems on the point of rising up to sing
And donning scarlet for its dusty grey!

The Flaming Terrapin was published in Britain and America, almost simultaneously, in May 1924. For the most part it was received warmly by the critics, who seemed to be swept along by its verve and vigour. It was, wrote a reviewer in the *Spectator*, 'like a breath of new youth, like a love-affair to a lady in her fifties'.[16] It was also, to many reviewers, a breath of fresh air which blew away both the banal rustications of the Georgians and the stale nihilism of the new generation of pseudo-sceptics. A review in the *New Statesman* was typical:

> We wanted air: and here is a south-wester straight from the sea. So, it appears, many have felt in the last few weeks; it is excellent that such a work should win its recognition; but it throws also a strong light on the shabby gentility of modern poetry as a whole, that this book should have been at once so feverishly praised and overpraised. Yet it is natural that this should happen; we are so tired of the confessions of second-rate sensitive minds with nothing to confess and no gift for confessing it; with lyrically bleeding hearts on every sleeve, the poor daws can scarcely summon the appetite to go on pecking.[17]

These sentiments were echoed by a review in the *Dial*:

> . . . in this extraordinary poem we are far from the mimble-mamble of the slim-volumed Georgians, as far too from the elegant nervosities of pseudo-Eliots and pseudo-Cocteaus. Full circle! We have spun back . . . back to an exuberant relish of the sheer sonority and clangour of words, words enjoyed for their own gust, and flung down to fit each other with an easy rapture of phrase.[18]

In similar vein, George Russell in the *Irish Statesman* hailed Campbell as a newly emergent giant of literature:

> Among a crowd of poets writing delicate verses he moves like a mastodon with shaggy sides pushing through a herd of lightfoot antelopes . . . No poet I have read for many years excites me to more speculation about his future, for I do not know of any new poet who has such a savage splendour of epithet or who can marry the wild word so fittingly to the wild thought.[19]

Years later, the South African poet David Wright sought to put the exuberance of the critical response to Campbell's first major poem into historical context.

> It was the energy and flamboyance of *The Flaming Terrapin* that surprised everyone. Its verve and extravagance burst like a bomb in the middle of the faded prettiness of the 'Georgian' poetry then in vogue. Written in conventionally rhyming iambic pentameters, it was obviously not 'modernist' in the manner of Pound, Eliot or the Sitwells, yet in everything else appeared far removed from the fatigued 'traditionalism' of the 'Georgians' . . . Campbell's flamboyant imagery, drawn from his memories of the spectacular and bizarre vegetation and fauna of his native Africa, exploded with an almost surrealist proliferation of exoticism. Today, it is not easy to appreciate the impact made by this long and rambling poem, which at one stroke established Campbell . . . as a poet of achievement rather than promise.[20]

Almost overnight, Roy Campbell, still only 22 years old, found himself rocketed into the ranks of the illustrissimi of English letters. His work, which previously had been completely unknown except among a handful of friends, was suddenly being discussed in the same breath as that of Eliot and the Sitwells. It was a far cry from the long nights in a converted stable in a bleak corner of Wales when the unknown poet, alone in a loft by candlelight, had given birth to his art.

NOTES

1 Roy Campbell, from 'The Flaming Terrapin', *Collected Poems, Volume One*, pp. 88–9.
2 Quoted in Peter Alexander, *Roy Campbell*, p. 37.
3 Augustus John, *Autobiography*, p. 90.
4 Quoted in Roy Campbell, *Light on a Dark Horse*, p. 255.
5 Augustus John, *Autobiography*, p. 90.
6 Roy Campbell, *Light on a Dark Horse*, p. 254.
7 Nina Hamnett, *Is She a Lady? A Problem in Autobiography*, London: Allan Wingate, 1955, pp. 54–5.
8 *Ibid.*, p. 55.
9 Anna Campbell Lyle, letter to the author, February 2000.
10 Peter Alexander, *Roy Campbell*, p. 41.
11 Ethel Campbell, *The Life of Sam Campbell*, p. 357.
12 *Ibid.*
13 *Ibid.*, pp. 356–7.
14 *Ibid.*, p. 357.
15 *Ibid.*
16 *Spectator*, 23 August 1924.
17 Quoted in Rowland Smith, *Lyric and Polemic: The Literary Personality of Roy Campbell*, Montreal and London: McGill–Queen's University Press, 1972, pp. 16–17.
18 *Dial*, November 1924.
19 Quoted in Peter Alexander, *Roy Campbell*, p. 37.
20 David Wright, *Roy Campbell*, London: Longmans, Green & Co., 1961, pp. 10–11.

CHAPTER SEVEN

WHIPLASH

His humble townsfolk sicken to behold
This monstrous changeling whom they schooled in vain,
Who brings no increase to their hoard of gold,
Who lives by sterner laws than they have known
And worships, even where their idols reign,
A god superbly stronger than their own.[1]

In spite of the critical acclaim that greeted the publication of *The Flaming Terrapin*, Roy and Mary were still struggling to survive financially. This material uncertainty, coupled with the re-emergence of Roy's restless discomfort at living in London, led the poet once again to seek an escape. This time he planned a return to South Africa.

The need to escape, the necessity of providing for his wife and child, and the desire to see his parents and relatives after a separation of more than five years, were tempered by the prospect of being separated from Mary and Tess. 'I will hate leaving my two girls,' he wrote to his mother in spring 1924, 'but I think that a trip home will set me up again. Mary will have Tess for company while I am away and she insists on my going. So in spite of the fact that we will feel rather lost without each other, I am looking forward "with a long stretched neck" to seeing you all again. After all Mary and I have years to be together so we will not grudge the few months that I spend with you.'[2]

Leaving Mary and Tess with his mother-in-law, Roy set sail in May 1924 on the SS *Umtata*. The letters he wrote to Mary *en route* are full of hopes for the future and a deep sense of longing for the wife and child he had left behind. 'How I long for you!' he wrote, as the ship headed for its first port of call at Las Palmas.

> We have just passed through all the filthy weather of the Bay of Biscay and have come out into wonderful calm weather. There has been a very good omen today!! As I was looking over the side of the ship suddenly I saw something like a piece of floating rubbish and lo and

> behold, it was a huge Terrapin covered with barnacles: it just swam slowly on without worrying about the ship . . . How I wished you had been there to see it with me. I'm sure you would have felt it meant good luck.[3]

Roy wrote that he was enjoying the trip more than he had expected, but that he dare not think of Mary and Tess all the time 'as I would go mad'. Mary's reaction to his absence can be gauged by Roy's efforts to reassure her.

> Darling, you are of a slightly brooding Nature: for God's sake don't make yourself sad. If you are sad, tell me – but do fight against it. I don't want you to pretend anything to me: tell me if you are worried but try to keep your mind off things. Don't read gloomy books: just drug yourself with unconsciousness as I am doing till I see you again. You must only think of me in the happy way, as being your lover and Tessie's father. When I think of you and her I feel that I am a king in spite of my temporary abdication. I feel no interest in the success of the *Terrapin* or anything else, except that I am the lover of Mary Margaret, the 'Zulu-haired' Mary with a heart like a mountain boulder and a spirit like a ship in full sail.[4]

He kept a photograph of Mary with him, and a lock of her hair, but he never felt the need to look at them. 'I could have done just as well without them. You are too real to me to make them necessary.'

Roy was helped by the distraction of socializing with the other passengers. Most of the passengers were young men, predominantly Scots, with whom he sat and sang every night. 'I always sing the songs that remind me of you,' he wrote to Mary, 'like the "Landlubbers" and "A-Roving", as we always sang them together down at Aberdaron.' He also sought consolation in the vastness of the ocean, staring for hours at the surf and rejoicing whenever he caught sight of whales, sharks or flying fish.

When the *Umtata* finally sailed into Durban harbour in June 1924, Campbell's new-found celebrity status was evident in the way his arrival was greeted in the South African newspapers. On 14 June, the *Natal Advertiser* heralded his arrival with the headline, 'A South African Poet: Author Visits His Home at Durban'. Other newspapers in Johannesburg and Cape Town followed suit, taking the success of *The Flaming Terrapin* in England as the starting point for local-boy-makes-good potted biographies of questionable accuracy. 'It is wonderful, kid, the way they are fussing about me here,' Roy wrote to Mary. 'The *Johannesburg Star* had a huge notice and in the *Durban Advertiser*, when the news came about the *Manchester Guardian* review, they put it in the headlines of the paper, before the political news.'[5]

Such news was of little consolation to Mary, who was frantic at Roy's failure to send her a telegram on his arrival. Receiving her 'sad little wire', Roy could only apologize pathetically, blaming his father for refusing to provide the money to send a telegram. To add insult to injury, Roy had been away on a whaler when Mary's wire had arrived, so his mother had replied to her in his absence. Yet in the following weeks his letters to her from South Africa must have reassured her of his continuing love, and their candour provides a valuable insight into Mary's profound influence on him.

> I am sick of hanging about without you and Tessy. All the lovely things I see are only half as lovely as they would be if you were here to share them. You have taught me to look at things in the same way as you do and I *do* miss half their beauty when you're not there. D'you remember when I used to laugh at you for raving about sunsets etc. I always had the logic on my side but you had something stronger. What an awful stupid intellectual bore I must have been in those days. You wonderfully natural creature, it nearly breaks my heart with shame that I ever poo-pooed your ideas. You are far above me in most things. You are a kind of mixture of Sappho and Saint Teresa . . .
>
> Oh my Mary how I bless the day when I first set eyes on you! I love you more deeply than I ever thought it possible for a human being to love another. Darling how sorry I am now for getting annoyed with you for being sad. I must have been inconsiderate and I'll never be like that again – but all the time I loved you sweetheart more deeply than I can say: You would understand how I love you if you could see me now. I am crying like a baby and I must be writing an awfully bad letter. Sometimes I become almost delirious about you and have to ride away alone for miles and miles. I often talk silly love-gibberish to you when I get out into the country alone. I sit on the roof for hours and hours and try to call back every little line of your eyes and face, and think of how we used to lie through the long evenings drowsing together and me kissing you on the back of your darling curly head and the side of your neck, and one arm folded round your beautiful tender breast: and little Tess snorting in her cot . . .
>
> With fifty thousand *real* kisses to you and twenty five thousand fatherly ones to Tess,
>
> Your boy,
> Roy[6]

When he was not moping over Mary's absence, or exercising his adventurous spirit on the whalers, Roy passed the time by riding and shooting. At first, he was tolerably happy and appeared to be on good terms with his father, whose health was in steady decline. Later, their relationship became increasingly strained. As the weeks and then the months passed, Roy became more and more frustrated at the continued separation from Mary and Tess. 'I can't be anything without you my precious. You must be near me all my life. I am afraid of being without you. It is Hell to me,' he wrote. In her absence, he watched the sunsets alone, seeking to share them with her in his letters, describing the 'pale green' sky 'covered with tiny little downy pink cloudlets', looking 'lovely behind the blackness of the gumtrees'.[7] It is not clear exactly how long Roy initially intended to stay in South Africa, but it seems that some time after his arrival he decided to settle more or less permanently, necessitating arrangements being made for Mary and Tess to join him.

Mary's own frustration is evident in Roy's constant urging of her to be patient and his efforts to reassure her about the future.

> You said in one letter that you just wanted to live with me away in the forest, and that will soon come true. Mother says that if I only wait, things will be all right. But oh how sick and tired I am of it all. I just mope round the house – waiting, waiting, waiting. It just seems as if my whole life has stopped like a clock.
>
> Sweetheart Mary, be patient darling, I implore you. It is the first time our love has been tested . . .
>
> I am sick of waiting. But oh darling what joy it'll be to catch a glimpse of your bonny faces again. How I look forward to our first kiss. I can hardly contain myself when I think of our house in the bush where we will be all alone, away from our relations, away from everything but love and work – the only two things that matter at all in life.
>
> We shall be as comfortable as kings in the place I have chosen . . .
>
> I *adore* those two photos. They are not up to you, but in this loneliness they almost speak to me. O if I only had you here beside me as I shall soon. I will make you so happy beloved and I shall be the happiest man on earth.[8]

In the event, seven months elapsed before they were finally reunited, in December 1924, when Mary and Tess came out to join him in South Africa. Early in 1925 they moved out of his parents' home on Musgrave Road to the appropriately named Peace Cottage, a bungalow to the north of the Umthlanga Lagoon where Roy had spent idyllic holidays as a boy. Situated about 30 yards from the beach, the house was connected to the lagoon by two buck paths and an unmetalled road. 'At night it was lit up by a sort of Morse code of electric blue thunderflashes from the inrolling breakers which shook the house and made the candles tremble with every crash, as they cascaded with phosphorescence, illuminating the twisted boughs of a giant milkwood tree which over-arched the house.'[9]

Within weeks, however, they had moved again, this time to a seaside bungalow at Sezela on the Umdoni Park estate which was owned by Lewis Reynolds, son of a local sugar baron. Reynolds, who had left Oxford shortly before Campbell had arrived there, was a generous patron of the arts and a great admirer of *The Flaming Terrapin*. His offer of accommodation was accepted eagerly by Campbell, who was desperate to attain a degree of independence from his parents.

If Mary had just wanted to live 'away in the forest' with Campbell, she must soon have thought that she had got more than she had bargained for. Set in thick bush by the edge of the sea, the bungalow's situation was romantically wild, but dangerously so also. Soon after their arrival they killed a cobra on the path near the house, and they later killed a deadly mamba just as it was going in through the front door. On another occasion Mary was chased by a large and threatening baboon.[10]

Throughout 1925 Campbell wrote for various South African newspapers and also gave several lectures. The extent to which he was lauded by his compatriots was evident from the fact that the *Natal Witness* reprinted the text of one of Campbell's lectures in instalments over five weeks from 19 March to 23 April. In this lecture, delivered at the Technical College founded by his father, the young poet set out his views on modern poetry. He condemned the Victorians for failing to appreciate Blake and Shelley, who were 'still the great energisers of modern thought'.

> Surely there must be something very wrong with an age in which Shelley was considered an ineffectual angel, and Blake a mere literary curiosity, and in which multitudes were affected to tears by the poetical liver-attacks of Byron? The fact is that the presiding deity of the Victorian era was the goddess of Reason. Their poetry is the poetry of reason, their poetry is a paradox.[11]

Campbell's incoherence was exposed by his condemnation of the Victorians for submitting everything to the test of reason, while at the same time he praised John Davidson as 'one of the few poets who grappled with the Darwinian idea of evolution instead of taking refuge with the old religion'.[12] Within moments of making this statement he seemed to contradict himself again by praising 'the deeply religious poetry of Sassoon and Wilfred Owen', adding that 'these two poets upheld the golden heresy of truth, and fought for the ideals of Christianity' when the world's scientists and politicians during the war 'were carried away by sentimental hysteria'.

Yet amidst this mish-mash of self-contradiction, the lecture contains the occasional diamond-edged, crystal-clear criticism:

> Owen was killed while he was still in his early twenties. Many speculations have been made as to what he would have done if he had survived the war. But from reading his work one gets the idea that his mind could never have survived the experience. It seems almost as if every bullet that maimed and killed the young men round him passed through his very soul.[13]

The figure of Nietzsche looms as large as ever throughout the lecture, but Campbell was becoming more discriminating in his approach. He attacked Nietzsche's misogynism, but praised his call to self-renunciation:

> Nietzsche has sharpened our insight into many social wrongs; he has shown the meanness of the tendency of modern democracy. For its 'I want more' he has substituted his own 'I want to give', for its 'I want to rise' he has substituted his own 'I renounce myself'. The doctrine of the renunciation of Self is one of his merits.[14]

Also emergent during this lecture was Campbell's neo-Luddite approach to new technology and his desire for a simplified and less artificial world. 'Our progress in mechanical science during the last century has so far outpaced the development of our intellectual and moral faculties that we have suddenly lost ourselves. All those useful mechanical toys which man primarily invented for his own convenience have begun to tyrannise every moment of his life . . .'[15] These sentiments would find expression in July of the following year in Campbell's sonnet 'The Serf', in which the 'patient hooves' of the oxen complement the unhurried ploughman, the 'slow somnambulist'.

> But as the turf divides
> I see in the slow progress of his strides
> Over the toppled clods and falling flowers,
> The timeless, surly patience of the serf
> That moves the nearest to the naked earth
> And ploughs down palaces, and thrones, and towers.[16]

The seemingly powerless ploughman is as potentially powerful in his 'somnambulism' as is the apparently sleeping sea which 'growls and tosses' before the impending storm in *The Flaming Terrapin*. The serf and the surf represent timeless verities beyond the reach of 'progress'. An obvious affinity exists between this poem and Thomas Hardy's 'In Time of the Breaking of Nations', in which the Wessex ploughman 'will go onward the same, Though Dynasties pass'. Yet Campbell's 'Serf' is not an English peasant but a subdued Zulu warrior. As in the sonnet 'The Zulu Girl', which Campbell wrote at around the same time, there is the brooding resentment of a conquered people. Whereas the Zulu girl's child imbibes the 'curbed ferocity of beaten tribes' and the 'sullen dignity of their defeat', the Zulu serf suffers in his 'insult torn' heart 'more deeply than he wounds the plain'.

The creative tension in both these poems sprang from Campbell's fear of native insurrection combined with feelings of compassion for the injustices suffered by the dispossessed natives. The same tension animated a letter he wrote in November 1925 to the writer and critic Edward Garnett:

> The government is going to segregate the natives as much as possible – that is all right, provided they give them fertile areas and so on. But they have denied them any power of voting whatsoever. This is only procrastinating trouble, instead of settling it . . . It is obvious to everybody that the population will eventually be a coloured one . . . If we take it on ourselves to be their lords and masters because they are less civilized, we have no right to oppose their aspirations towards our civilization.[17]

These were remarkably liberal views for a white South African to hold in 1925. To a degree he had inherited them from his family. His father was known as a supporter of the Zulus and the Zulu newspaper *Ilanga Lase Natal* often paid him tribute as a friend of the African. Campbell's uncle William was even more of a maverick, disappearing into the wilds of Zululand for weeks on end to live among the tribesmen. He was one of very few white men to be accorded the honour of becoming a Chief of the Zulus, and when he became ill he would call in a witch doctor.[18] Campbell was also steeped in native culture. He spoke Zulu fluently, which enabled him to empathize as well as sympathize with the plight and aspirations of the natives. Yet his views, however acceptable they may have been within the confines of his family, were anathema to the vast majority of white South Africans. It was only a matter of time before Campbell's views would clash acrimoniously with those of his compatriots.

The vehicle with which Campbell would crash his way through the prejudiced sensibilities of his fellow countrymen was a literary journal, financed by Lewis Reynolds, entitled *Voorslag* – 'Whiplash'. Campbell had thought of the title, intending to use the journal to lash out at many aspects of South African colonial society. In June 1925, while preparations for the new magazine were being set in motion, Campbell met William Plomer for the first time. Plomer had just finished writing his first novel, *Turbott Wolfe*, which would be published in London in March of the following year. Its theme, the taboo subject of inter-racial love and marriage, was bound to be received with hostility in South Africa. During their first meeting, at Twine's Hotel in Durban, Plomer told Campbell about his novel and Campbell, suitably impressed, informed Plomer of the plans for the literary magazine, inviting Plomer to help with it, which he 'gladly agreed to do'.[19] Campbell also recruited the painter Edward Roworth as *Voorslag*'s principal art critic.

Towards the end of the year, after Plomer had introduced them, Campbell invited Laurens van der Post to become Afrikaans editor of *Voorslag*. This was itself a radical step which would make *Voorslag* one of the first bilingual literary journals in South Africa. Yet such a step paled into insignificance beside the journal's stance on the race issue. Campbell made his own position clear in September 1925 in a letter to Edward Garnett. 'I don't expect very much of my poetry for some time yet . . . I would far sooner, even at the risk of ruining any artistic qualities that I possess, load my work with some moral purpose and direct all the knowledge I possess towards counteracting the evils of race-hatred and colour-hatred that cause so much misery out here.'[20]

The extent to which Campbell's views were at odds with the prevailing mood among white South Africans was illustrated by the hostile response which greeted the publication of *Turbott Wolfe*. On 19 March 1926 the *Natal Advertiser* carried a review of Plomer's novel under the headline, 'A Nasty Book on a Nasty Subject'. The editorial in the same edition of the paper echoed the disgust of the reviewer:

> From first to last the book pictures rottenness; starting from the point where the white stranger with artistic leanings outrages the sentiments of his neighbours by filling his studio with native 'models', and treating them as though they were white people, and ending with the marriage of the royally beautiful Mabel van der Horst to the full-blooded native Zachary.

Campbell's forthright response to such criticism appeared three months later in the first issue of *Voorslag*. In a review of Plomer's novel entitled 'The Significance of Turbott Wolfe', Campbell castigated the critics, but also questioned Plomer's motives in writing the book. He sensed that his friend's presentation of 'the great antagonistic race-forces' was marred by 'a very strong bias against the white colonists'.

> . . . it is this bias that detracts more considerably from *Turbott Wolfe* than anything else. Everything Mr Plomer records is just and true; but he takes a too malicious delight in recording it. He is not content with having produced a large and lively skeleton from our cupboard but he must needs pipe to it and make it dance in front of us . . . but if one regrets this, one can at least be grateful that Mr Plomer's biting

> satire has administered an excellent tonic to our self-satisfaction. For as a race we are easily satisfied with ourselves . . .
>
> Mr Plomer has shown his white characters when acting under the influence of race-feeling, behaving with typical ferocity and injustice. But he fails to let them relax often enough into their individual and comparative decency. He keeps pointing at them all the time and nudging the reader. I have known many farmers who capable of the most callous and criminal behaviour to the blacks, were guileless sons of the soil, as innocent as sleeping babes, with devout souls and sky-blue eyes. Their cruelty and impulsiveness was not even remembered when they relapsed again into their individual rationality. This type is far more normal than the bloodthirsty type described by Mr Plomer and it confronts one with a far more terrible enigma. If Mr Plomer had realised this his satire would have been more devastatingly complete and he might have achieved a masterpiece.[21]

The measured tone adopted by Campbell in this review was well and truly dropped elsewhere in the same issue of *Voorslag*, in which Campbell attacked colonial South Africa with unrestrained venom. The assumption of the white man's superiority was dismissed as 'a superstition which was exploded by science ten years ago and by Christianity two thousand years before'. As a nation, South Africa was 'three hundred years behind modern Europe and five hundred years behind modern art and science'. Furthermore, white South Africa was little more than a nation of parasites:

> We have no excuse for our parasitism on the native and the sooner we realise it the safer for our own future. We are as a race without thinkers, without leaders, without even a physical aristocracy working on the land.
>
> The study of modern anthropology should be encouraged as it would give us a better sense of our position in the family tree of Homo-Sapiens – which is among the lower branches: and it might even rouse us to assert ourselves in some less ignoble way than reclining blissfully in a grocer's paradise and feeding on the labour of the natives.[22]

From the outset, Campbell and Plomer had intended that *Voorslag* should live up to its name – that it should 'sting . . . the mental hindquarters . . . of the bovine citizenry of the Union'.[23] Inevitably, however, the whiplash also provoked a backlash. Lewis Reynolds, who had already invested £1,000 in the magazine, was alarmed at the provocative line. He was known to be *Voorslag*'s wealthy proprietor and was fearful that the public hostility which the magazine was attracting could adversely affect his ambitions to enter

Parliament. In July 1926 Reynolds told Campbell that he wanted to remove some of the poet's editorial control over the content of *Voorslag*. Campbell was indignant at the very suggestion. He refused, his voice quivering with rage, and tendered his immediate resignation. He had only been editor for two issues. The third issue carried the terse note: 'I have much pleasure in announcing my resignation from "Voorslag". Roy Campbell.'

Campbell's anger over the *Voorslag* episode would ripen into the bitter fruit of satire. For the first time he vented his spleen and took his revenge by launching a satirical attack on his enemies, demonstrating the sadistic streak which was the least pleasant aspect of his character. His targets in *The Wayzgoose*, which he wrote in 48 ire-filled hours and which would cause a storm of protest when it was finally published two years later, were those associated with *Voorslag*, with the exception of Plomer and van der Post. Yet he also poured scorn on colonial South Africa in general, and Durbanites in particular, repeating in poetry the accusations he had made in prose.

> Alas, poor Durbanites, which will you choose,
> Which of the dread alternatives refuse,
> This is the ultimatum that you shirk,
> The awful question – Poverty or Work?
> Work, that can turn a draper to a Man
> And give a human accident a plan.
> Work, that could make the sugar-planting race
> Stand up and look a black man in the face!
> Is it the sign of a 'superior race'
> To whine to have 'the nigger kept in place'?[24]

NOTES

1 Roy Campbell, from 'Dedication to Mary Campbell', *Collected Poems, Volume One*, p. 15.
2 Ethel Campbell, *The Life of Sam Campbell*, p. 357.
3 Roy Campbell, unpublished letter to Mary Campbell, May 1924.
4 *Ibid.*
5 Roy Campbell, unpublished letter to Mary Campbell, June 1924.
6 *Ibid.*
7 Roy Campbell, unpublished letter to Mary Campbell.
8 *Ibid.*
9 Roy Campbell, *Light on a Dark Horse*, p. 101.
10 Peter Alexander, *Roy Campbell*, p. 45.
11 Peter Alexander, Michael Chapman, Marcia Leveson (eds), Roy Campbell, *Collected Works IV: Prose*, Craighall, South Africa: A. D. Donker, 1988, pp. 173–4.
12 *Ibid.*, pp. 175–6.
13 *Ibid.*, p. 176.
14 *Ibid.*, p. 179.
15 *Ibid.*, p. 184.
16 *Collected Poems, Volume One*, p. 30.
17 Quoted in Peter Alexander, *Roy Campbell*, p. 65.

18 *Ibid.*, p. 66.
19 William Plomer, *The Autobiography of William Plomer*, London: Jonathan Cape, 1975, p. 168.
20 Quoted in Peter Alexander, *Roy Campbell*, p. 49.
21 *Voorslag*, Vol. 1, No. 1 (June 1926), published in Campbell, *Collected Works IV: Prose*, pp. 195–6.
22 *Ibid.*, pp. 202–3.
23 Quoted in Peter Alexander, *Roy Campbell*, p. 52.
24 *Collected Poems, Volume One*, p. 253.

CHAPTER EIGHT

BOMBAST AND FIRE

Exiled like you and severed from my race
By the cold ocean of my own disdain,
Do I not freeze in such a wintry space,
Do I not travel through a storm as vast
And rise at times, victorious from the main,
To fly the sunrise at my shattered mast?[1]

Before the outbreak of the *Voorslag* controversy, Campbell appeared to be enjoying life in South Africa. He and Mary travelled to Durban to attend a performance of George Bernard Shaw's *Man and Superman*, which he described in a letter to the South African artist Edward Roworth as 'great fun'.[2] In fact, since *Man and Superman* was the most overtly Nietzschean of Shaw's plays, it is safe to assume that Campbell wholeheartedly approved of the philosophical comedy. At this time, Roy was a great admirer of Shaw, lauding him in his lecture at the Technical College as 'a less cynical, and far more human, Solomon'.[3]

Campbell would later drastically revise his opinion of Shaw, coming to believe that Shaw had lied deliberately about the terrible famine brought on by Stalin's persecution of the peasants, or *kulaki*, in the Soviet Union. Echoing her father's opinions, Anna Campbell Lyle explained Roy's change of perspective:

> Shaw was responsible for much of the world's blindness vis-a-vis the Soviet Union. When people get an *idée fixe* about their favourite obsessions they would rather lie (even when it means the mass murder of millions) than face the facts. British socialists were so certain that they had found, at last, the solution to injustice in the world that they became unable to face the facts as they were. For Roy this meant that they had sold their souls in order to retain their beliefs in utopias, and this filled him with dismay and later with scorn.[4]

During their excursion to Durban, Roy and Mary had taken the opportunity to obtain 'a pile of Elizabethan Dramatists' from the library. Returning to their bungalow in the bush, they enjoyed 'a pleasant week reading them aloud to one another'.[5] Roy's love for the Elizabethans was undiminished and his comments to Roworth about their renewed impact during the week in which he and Mary read them aloud throw an invaluable light on their continuing and powerful influence on his own work.

> By Jove they are marvellous poets: we have been reading Dekker's 'Old Fortunatus' which is full of enough poetry to set up half a dozen modern poets, although the play itself is a disjointed sort of affair.
>
> I think after having a really good Wallow in Chapman, Peele, Dekker and company, my poetry will go up fifty per cent. I have not read them since before I wrote the *Terrapin*: but they give me a breath of new life. I don't know why I didn't go back to them sooner. Their poetry is so living and fresh it makes even the greatest work of Keats and Shelley seem just a little bit artificial – though one acknowledges their superiority.
>
> When you come back you'll find us ranting long passages of bombast and fire.
>
> 'See, a diamond, that would have brought Lollia Paulina
> When she came in like starlight, hid with jewels!'
>
> That's the stuff to give them. I am absolutely drunk with these fellows. They wrote poetry just as a machine-gun fires off bullets. They couldn't stop writing it. They don't even stop to get their breath. They go thundering on until you forget everything about the sense and . . . end up in a positive debauch of thunder and splendour and music.
>
> Everything that disparaging critics say about the Elizabethans may be true. They are raw, careless, headstrong, coarse, brutal. But how vivid they are, how intoxicated with their own imagination and their sudden newly-found mastery over a yet unexploited language. For three years I have been reading the Russians hard and the modern French but this is like having a wild Saturday night after a week of Sundays.[6]

In this intoxicated and intoxicating letter, Campbell has unwittingly described many of the characteristics of his own work. The flamboyance of the Elizabethans had coloured the imagery in *The Flaming Terrapin* with a vivid sharpness which distinguished it from most other contemporary verse, in much the same way as the vivid sharpness of the Pre-Raphaelites had stood out from the monochrome subtleties of Impressionism. Yet there was also something prophetic in Campbell's words. In describing the 'bombast and fire', the writing of poetry 'just as a machine-gun fires off bullets', the failure to stop to catch one's breath, Campbell was describing his own satires, still to be written. These too would be 'raw, careless, headstrong, coarse, brutal' and would be written in a breathless stream of invective, in stark contrast to the care he took with his lyrical verse.

In spite of the glorious weeks alone with Roy, when they would read aloud to each other as they had done in Wales, Mary was finding life very difficult in South Africa. Roy's father, in rapidly deteriorating health, was increasingly irritable, taking out his frustration on his daughter-in-law. 'When little Tess and Mary turned up in Durban,' explains Anna, 'Grandfather Campbell was torn between adoration of his first grandchild and indignation with Mary. He reduced this woman who so seldom wept, to sobs . . . Poor Mary must have wondered what on earth she had got herself into. Coming from a free and easy family, she was ill-prepared to deal with her very strict in-laws and the stultifying society of 1920s South Africa.'[7]

In later years, when Anna asked her mother what it had been like, Mary replied that she had been 'rather surprised that your dynamic father came from such rigid surroundings'. Roy's father was, Mary recalled, 'an irritable little man, though great in his own way', and his mother was amiable 'despite her severity'. Mary's only close friends in Durban were William Plomer, Laurens van der Post, and Paul and Anna von Schubert. She also said that Roy's brother George was 'always kind – but on the whole the whites paled into insignificance beside the novelty of the country, the picturesqueness of the Africans . . . and the wild beauty of the animals which was overwhelming.'[8]

The picturesqueness imprinted itself upon the three-year-old Tess also. Her earliest memory was akin to that of her father, although it was the sound rather than the sight of the Indian Ocean that initially impressed her. She recalled 'a mysterious, thundering, nostalgic vibration' and then, presumably held aloft by one of her parents, she saw the seething motion of the sea and the spray-covered waves crashing on the beach. 'All this must have been after a heavy storm because the sea was savage and the sounds booming.' During another storm in the summer of 1926, the infant Tess stared in wonder as her father became wild and intent, his spirits as turbulent as the weather, his face pale and dripping with sweat. With unbridled passion, he was pacing to and fro reciting lines from Goethe:

Und Stürme brausen um die Wette
Von Meer aus Land, von Land aus Meer
Und bilder Wütend eine Kette.
Der tiefsten Wirkung rings umber
Da Flammt ein blitzendes Verbeeren
Dem pfade von Donnerschlags.

'He emphasized the words *blitzendes* and *Donnerschlags*, repeating the lines over and over again, as he leapt into bed and out, his resounding voice accompanying the flashes and blasts – the strange German words, mixed with his fantastic behaviour were like an echo of the tumultuous goings on outside ... To me it was all uproarious ... and in spirit we all joined in with the mood of high exultation.'

Tess remembered being placed in her cot on the verandah in the evenings to be lulled to sleep by the strange sounds of the wildlife in the bush beyond. By day she played and bathed in rock pools, and gorged herself on mangoes, pawpaws, guavas, lychees, grenadillas, avocado pears, bananas, tangerines and other local fruit. 'My love for South African fruit was such that I was constantly found up the guava trees and had to be spanked before I gave up.' Apart from the sounds of the bush and the tastes of exotic fruits, the child's earliest sensory perceptions were enhanced by the strong smells of Indian spices wafting from the kitchen as the Campbells' Hindu cook prepared meals.

The three-year-old was struck with fear, however, at the sight of the Hindu ritual dances which occurred at regular intervals at Sezela.

> Tall dancers came towards the house in slow motion, with crowns and clanking metals, feathers and jewellery all over their naked bodies, their faces painted white. They danced and leapt to the sound of the drums. It wasn't the dancers themselves that frightened me, it was more the spirit of the thing – there was an air of cold detachment from anything or anyone around. Even the far off sight of them sent me into hysterics and I would shoot off and hide my face in our black nurse's lap.[9]

Tess's younger sister Anna was born at Sezela on 1 February 1926. On the day before she gave birth, Mary had taken one of her regular walks into the bush, where she had stumbled across a large, old baboon who threw stones at her and gave chase. Mary, heavily pregnant, was forced to run for her life. There is no suggestion that this 'rather frightening' experience induced the labour, but Anna emerged into the world at half-past eight on the following morning.[10]

The joy of their second child's birth was followed, six weeks later, by sorrow. On 12 March, Roy's father died while on a fishing holiday on the Little Mooi River. He had been suffering for some time from trypanosomiasis, or 'sleeping sickness', and had sunk into a coma from which he did not recover. The funeral was one of the largest ever seen in Durban, with about 30,000 people, mostly Zulus, thronging the streets. Roy was grief-stricken at his father's passing and was filled with remorse for his failure to heal the estrangement which had arisen between them since his return to Africa. There were several reasons for Roy's alienation from his father, ranging from straightforward youthful rebelliousness to a difference in their respective approaches to the race issue. Dr Campbell believed that the white man's role in Africa was one of paternalistic benevolence, whereas his son believed in the nobility and integrity of the indigenous African cultures.[11] Whatever the reason, Roy's remorse would remain for the rest of his life. 'He had a terrible quarrel with his father,' says Anna. 'He regretted it all his life, terribly – so much so that it used to worry me.'[12]

Campbell smothered his remorse with his work as editor of *Voorslag*, but his untimely departure in July created a whole new set of problems. His resignation, however much it had been rooted in principle, removed his only source of regular income and plunged his family into penury. He had little option but to write a begging letter to C. J. Sibbett, a wealthy Cape Town advertising executive who was a great admirer of his verse:

> I have had a violent row with Roworth and *Voorslag*. Myself and family are completely stranded and I have neither employment, health nor money.
>
> For political reasons, because Plomer and I are negrophilists, the founders of *Voorslag*, including Roworth, have intrigued to get me to resign . . .
>
> Mary is trying to find work as a lady-help and I have a very bad lesion in my spine which I can only get cured in England. Therefore I am asking you to send me fifty pounds. I shall never be able to repay it. I am asking it as a gift. You are about the only person in the country I have not made enemies with. My mother is in England and I am without any resources whatever. I am too ill to work. We are going to put our children in a creche and wait till I can get money to go to England, where we have friends. None of my relations will look at me because of the opinions I have expressed in *Voorslag*.[13]

Campbell's desperation was evident from the pathetic pleading of the postscript: 'Please answer me at once whether you can help me or not, I am absolutely on tenterhooks.'

Sibbett replied on 31 July, enclosing a cheque for £25 and promising to send the other £25 a month later if it was still required. 'This terrible upheaval in your friendships is very sad,' he wrote, 'and I hope that the storm will be as brief as it has been violent.'[14] The upheaval had certainly taken its toll because Roy, suffering from depression as well as a recurrence of the spinal injury he had received in Provence five years earlier, was too ill to reply. Mary wrote to Sibbett on 4 August, describing the cheque as 'a godsend' because they were 'practically penniless' and explaining that Roy would reply in person 'directly he feels well enough'. Her husband had been ill for a long time now, she explained, 'and all this worry has made him much worse'.[15]

Apart from being practically penniless, the Campbells were also practically homeless. Their bungalow at Sezela was owned by Lewis Reynolds who clearly, in the light of the acrimonious breach in their relationship over the running of *Voorslag*, wanted them to vacate the premises as soon as possible. They stayed on at the bungalow, along with Plomer, who was living with them at the time, until the end of August, when they returned reluctantly to the Campbell family home in Durban. In the weeks before leaving Sezela, Campbell triumphed artistically over adversity by writing some of his finest poems. In a burst of creativity he wrote 'The Serf', 'The Zulu Girl', 'To a Pet Cobra', 'The Making of a Poet' and 'Tristan da Cunha'.

The last of these, considered by many as his greatest achievement, was completed on 14 August. That evening Campbell and Laurens van der Post carried Anna, who was now six months old and teething, along the beach so that Mary could get some rest. Unable to stop the baby from crying, they decided to build a fire to distract her. The fire quickly burned out of control in the high winds and threatened to spread to the acres of sugar cane skirting the beach. Frantically, the two writers struggled to beat it down. When their exertions had proved successful, Campbell, exhilarated and panting, informed van der Post that he had completed his poem on Tristan da Cunha. He began to recite it, his voice competing with the roaring wind and crashing waves:

> Turn to the night; these flames are not for you
> Whose steeple for the thunder swings its bells;
> Grey Memnon, to the tempest only true,
> Turn to the night, turn to the shadowing foam,
> And let your voice, the saddest of farewells,
> With sullen curfew toll the grey wings home.

Van der Post listened as Campbell recited the poem through to the end. As he did so he watched the dying embers of the fire being swept along the beach in the wind. The poet was at one with the elements. Anna, lulled by the rhythm of her father's words, had stopped crying, while van der Post, aroused by the sea, the stars and the wind, and by the bombast and fire of the words, was moved to tears.[16]

There is evidence in the poems written during this emotionally turbulent month that Campbell was, in the very act of their composition, exorcizing his haunting depression. Certainly they contain many allusions to the *Voorslag* episode and illustrate his efforts to put his feelings into perspective. 'The Serf' and 'The Zulu Girl' are spectral representations of the race issue, while 'Tristan da Cunha', 'The Making of a Poet' and 'To a Pet Cobra' allow the poet to make sense of his predicament. 'Tristan da Cunha' has the poet exiled like his subject, 'severed from my race / By the cold ocean of my own disdain', where he battles 'like a rock, aloof and friendless'. Similarly, in 'The Making of a Poet' he is a restive steer,

> Who leaps the cows and heads each hot stampede,
> Till the old bulls unite in jealous fear
> To hunt him from the pastures where they feed.

'To a Pet Cobra' presents the poet in the role of hero, one of the 'sons of strife' who thrive on self-sacrifice:

> There shines upon the topmost peak of peril
> A throne for spirits that abound in life:
> There is no joy like theirs who fight alone,
> Whom lust or gluttony have never tied,
> Who in their purity have built a throne,
> And in their solitude a tower of pride.

By early September Campbell could write to Sibbett, who had further alleviated his financial problems by sending another cheque for £25, in a much more settled frame of mind.

> I am really thankful to have finished with *Voorslag* and to be able to attend to my 'dynamo' which is working again beautifully. It was a great mistake on my part to have had anything to do with *Voorslag*. My mind is only built for my own work and since I have been able to turn to it again I have been so happy that I would not care much if the roof were to fall in on top of me.[17]

Sibbett's generosity towards Campbell was not restricted to financial support. On 6 September he wrote to Desmond Young, editor of the *Natal Witness*, in support of both Campbell and Plomer. 'I am very glad to hear where your sympathies lie in the "Voorslag" controversy. Roy and Plomer were like thoroughbreds pitted against pack-mules. Natal seems to me to be Wesleyan-ridden with a strong dash of Calvinism thrown in and it is astonishing how these two Cuckoo eggs came to be hatched here.'[18]

Campbell also stepped back into the fray, firing off letters of scorn about his former colleagues on *Voorslag* to various South African papers. Typical of these was a letter he wrote to the *Cape Argus* in which his denial of feeling embittered by the controversy is negated by a transparently shallow and self-defeating rancour.

> How then, O myriascopic Argus, should I be embittered by their attacks, which are so rapidly helping me regain my self respect. My rumoured excursion to Europe was contemplated as the result of a

> medical consultation and had nothing to do with embitterment. Both Plomer and myself find the proximity of the South African public very soothing: the stillness of the mental atmosphere out here is restful to the strained nerves of a hardworking artist. What the South African journalists or public think about us has little, if anything, to do with us. Both of us are extremely meek and humble and I personally am quite content with the opinions of the leading critics in France, Russia, England, Germany and Italy without wishing to extend my reputation to a country where my only concern is the study of the native and Asiatic questions . . . I survey the panic which was caused by my temporary aberration into local literature with the same innocent bewilderment as yourself. You wrongly accuse me of taking part in the battle which was waged over the corpse of *Voorslag*, my resignation was due largely to the fact that I had more important work to do; when one is occupied with a dynamo one cannot be expected to get excited when the tea-kettle, stranded on the stove, begins letting off steam.[19]

Campbell's envenomed satire, inspired by a scarcely concealed contempt for the narrow-minded provincialism of the South African public in general and its journalists in particular, would find a poetic outlet a few weeks later when he sat for 48 revenge-filled hours writing *The Wayzgoose.* The poem was provoked in part by the refusal of many South African newspapers to publish his letters on the *Voorslag* affair, but the bitterness which was its principal motivation was already apparent in the poems he had written in August, particularly in 'To a Pet Cobra', in which he wrote that 'the hate of men' had 'sharpened us to sting':

> Sired by starvation, suckled by neglect,
> Hate was the surly tutor of our youth:
> I too can hiss the hair of men erect
> Because my lips are venomous with truth.

The fact that *The Wayzgoose* was the product of an uninterrupted stream of vitriol was confessed by Campbell within days of its completion in late November 1926. 'Funnily enough it is the first bit of "inspired" writing I have ever done,' he wrote in a letter to Sibbett.

> The words and phrases formed themselves automatically and only 48 hours elapsed between its start and its finish. My best poetry generally takes me a year and the poems grow only by means of assiduous cultivation. But this stuff just gurgled out like water through a plug-hole. However on re-reading it, I find it has a certain amount of kick in it and I shall make alterations and polish it up.[20]

It is perhaps appropriate that Campbell should have used the imagery of water gurgling down a drain in describing the flow of 'inspiration' behind his first verse satire. In this and later satires he all too often allowed the beauty of his muse to be disfigured by the ugliness of his anger. The result, inevitably, is that the quality of the satirical poetry seldom lives up to the standard set by his lyrical verse. At best, in his hastily composed satires, he casts his poetic pearls before swine; at worst, he becomes a swine himself in the haste of their composition and the uncharitable nature of his attacks.

A year later, looking at *The Wayzgoose* through more dispassionate eyes, he was noticeably more dismissive of its merits. 'It is only a farce,' he wrote. 'It is a satire in doggerel heroic couplets making fun of South Africa and my fellow colonials . . . But it is not very ambitious *as poetry*. It is utterly grotesque: and it is slightly modelled on Churchill's Prophecy of Famine and Marvell's Satire against the Dutch.'[21]

Just days after *The Wayzgoose* was finished, there was a sudden change of circumstances which would abruptly end the Campbells' sojourn in South Africa. Roy explained the new developments in a hastily appended note at the end of his letter to Sibbett. 'Since writing this letter all my plans have changed. I shall be leaving at once for England – in about 3 weeks. I have had a bad time with my neck again and the only thing is to go and see Sir Herbert Barker. If we pass Capetown I shall call and see you. R.C.'[22]

Roy, Mary and their two daughters sailed out of Durban on the *Themistocles* on 22 December. Having made his mark in his native land principally by making powerful enemies, Campbell was seen off at the harbour by C. J. Sibbett, one of the few friends on whose loyalty and support he could still depend. And so, in far less heroic circumstances than had surrounded his arrival two and a half years earlier, the poet bid an embittered farewell to the land of his birth.

NOTES

1 Roy Campbell, from 'Tristan da Cunha', *Collected Poems, Volume One*, p. 42.
2 Roy Campbell, unpublished letter to Edward Roworth.
3 Roy Campbell, *Collected Works IV: Prose*, p. 185.
4 Anna Campbell Lyle, *Son of Valour*, p. 31.
5 Roy Campbell, unpublished letter to Edward Roworth.
6 *Ibid.*
7 Anna Campbell Lyle, *Son of Valour*, p. 20.
8 *Ibid.*
9 Teresa Campbell, unpublished memoirs, pp. 6–7.
10 *Ibid.*, p. 8; and Anna Campbell Lyle, *Son of Valour*, p. 20.
11 Anna Campbell Lyle, interview with the author, December 1998.
12 *Ibid.*
13 Roy Campbell, unpublished letter to C. J. Sibbett, July 1926.
14 C. J. Sibbett, unpublished letter to Roy Campbell, 31 July 1926.

15 Mary Campbell, unpublished letter to C. J. Sibbett, 4 August 1926.
16 Peter Alexander, *Roy Campbell*, p. 64.
17 Roy Campbell, unpublished letter to C. J. Sibbett, early September 1926.
18 C. J. Sibbett, unpublished letter to Desmond Young, 6 September 1926.
19 Roy Campbell, letter to the *Cape Argus*, 1926, in the author's possession.
20 Roy Campbell, unpublished letter to C. J. Sibbett, late November or early December 1926.
21 Roy Campbell to Herbert Palmer, *c.* October 1927; quoted in Peter Alexander, *Roy Campbell*, p. 69.
22 Roy Campbell, unpublished letter to C. J. Sibbett, late November or early December 1926.

CHAPTER NINE

A BLOOMSBURY AFFAIR

Then – with the worst
Accepted, best to trust –
Only can burst
This passion so divine
As blackens all the shine
Of wealth, the lust of wine,
The wine of lust.[1]

The voyage to England was far from pleasurable. It was a very rough crossing, the boat being battered by one tropical storm after another. One of these storms was so violent that an Irish stewardess rounded up all the terrified third-class passengers, assembled them together on deck, and led them in the rosary to stave off disaster.[2]

Mary suffered from seasickness for much of the trip, trying at the same time to cope with two small children in the claustrophobic confines of a third-class cabin. Roy, who never suffered from seasickness, spent much of the time drinking heavily with two Jewish cardsharps he had befriended. On one occasion Mary was horrified to find that Roy had strapped Anna's pram to the mast with his belt while he went off for a beer. Years later, Anna could find her father's neglect amusing. 'I, the baby, cried without ceasing. Roy would strap my pram to the mast so that my howls were buffeted into outer space.'[3]

Disaster struck when Roy left the porthole open and a huge wave flooded the cabin. Many of the family's possessions were ruined and several of Roy's manuscripts were lost, most notably his only copy of 'The Golden Shower', a long love poem on which he had expended much effort over many months. Years later, with C. J. Sibbett's help, he recovered a small section of this poem which had been printed in South Africa, publishing it with minor amendments as a 'Fragment from "The Golden Shower"' in the second volume of his collected verse. Campbell dedicated the surviving fragment to Mary and it is clear from the section that remains that the lost poem was intended as a permanent and monumental celebration of their love.

And while my words in many a burning gyre
Fume on the breeze and set the winds on fire
Like pollen in the spring: your soul shall seem
A glittering bee that travels to and fro
Loaded with all the wealth that I can dream
And all that I can realize and show.

The whole poem is a passionate hymn of praise to the woman who was the incarnation of his muse, as well as being a confession of his complete dependence on her.

And our clear sprites, whom rays and showers begem,
Burn through each other as the world through them.

Roy had expressed his dependence on Mary more prosaically only three weeks before they set sail for England. In the letter to Sibbett informing him of their imminent departure, he wrote that Mary's help was 'invaluable' to his work. 'I should never be half the writer I am, I'm afraid, if it weren't for her. She positively keeps me alive. She is the perfect model of what an artist's wife should be. But I get all the damned credit for it.'[4]

Considering the disastrous nature of the voyage, the arrival of the *Themistocles* at Southampton must have come as a great relief to all concerned. 'Thank God! At last I'm home!' Mary exclaimed as they disembarked.[5] Roy's feelings, tinged with the bitterness of his rejection at 'home' (Anna recalls that her father always referred to South Africa as 'home'),[6] were not as straightforward. It was snowing when they arrived,[7] and Roy must have been reminded of his first arrival in an ice-bound England eight years earlier. On that occasion he had been filled with all the hopes and dreams of youth. Now, as he surveyed the drab dock and the bleak English weather, his future was filled with nothing but uncertainty.

They were met on the quay by Mary's former governess, Elizabeth Thomas, described by Anna as 'a diminutive spinster, with the face of a dove and the heart of a lion, who was always coming to the rescue in our much tribulated lives'. Known as 'Tony' to the growing flock of Garman cousins, she was 'a great crisis resolver'.[8]

After spending a fortnight in London, during which he presumably saw Sir Herbert Barker about the recurrence of his spinal injury, and a few weeks at the home of Mary's now-widowed mother at King's Pyon, near Leominster, the Campbells moved to the village of Sevenoaks Weald in Kent. They were surviving financially with the help of £20 a month that Roy now received from his father's estate, supplemented by the £100 a year that Mary received from her own father's estate and the money earned from reviews and occasional poems published in magazines.

One morning in May 1927 they met Vita Sackville-West, daughter of the third Baron Sackville, in the village post office. She had just returned from Teheran where her husband, Harold Nicolson, had been on diplomatic service. Vita, a well-known poet in her own right, had read *The Flaming Terrapin* the previous year with mixed emotions. Sending it to Virginia Woolf, she called it 'a wild uneven thing, almost ridiculous in parts, almost magnificent in others'.[9] For their part, Roy and Mary would have been aware of Sackville-West's poetry, not least because her long poem, *The Land*, had just been awarded the Hawthornden Prize.

Discovering that they were neighbours, Vita invited the Campbells to dinner on 23 May at Long Barn, her beautiful half-timbered house. The evening must have have gone well because the Campbells were soon regular guests, although Harold Nicolson's first impressions of Roy were not entirely favourable. In his diary, he wrote that Roy was 'an ugly and uncouth creature with fine eyes and brow and a certain charm'.[10] Their relationship warmed, however, and a couple of weeks later, in early June, Nicolson found himself both entertained and amused by Roy's accounts of his adventures in Africa and Provence, describing the poet-adventurer in his diary as 'another Rimbaud'.[11]

If Nicolson's attitude to Campbell contained an element of ambivalence, Roy's attitude towards his new-found friends was also less than entirely uncritical. 'Roy never liked Harold though he found Vita tolerable,' recalls his daughter.[12] He certainly did not like Vita's poetry, although for the time being he was careful to remain tactful in the name of friendship. In a letter to Sibbett, he was dismissive of *The Land* but full of affection for its author: 'It isn't much of a poem but she is very nice, and has a wonderful library.'[13]

On 16 June Vita and Harold, accompanied by Leonard and Virginia Woolf, travelled to London for the official presentation of the Hawthornden Prize. John Drinkwater, presenting it to Vita, declared that her poem contained some of the loveliest verse written that century, a judgement endorsed by many other critics. Despite winning the coveted award, however, *The Land* was not without critics who shared Campbell's low opinion of it, the most vocal of whom was Edith Sitwell. For six months, Sitwell had written scathing attacks on *The Land* in publications such as the *Weekly Despatch*, *T.P.'s Weekly* and the *Daily Mirror*, deriding it as 'poetry in gumboots', which would 'be of great use to prospective farmers, for it is one long catalogue of agricultural implements'.[14]

'Your friend Edith Sitwell seems to be entering upon a regular campaign,' Vita had complained to Virginia Woolf. 'Whichever way I turn, that Gorgon's head springs up on my path . . . she says it's "the worst poem in the English language"; now I'm *not* vain, as you know, but I'm hanged if it's as bad as all that!'[15] Virginia replied on 24 June that Vita needed to realize how difficult it was for Sitwell, a 'natural innovator', to appreciate the work of a 'natural traditionalist'.[16]

For Campbell, as for Sitwell, *The Land* represented all that was wrong with the Georgian poets. Sackville-West's rural idyll was rooted in a patronizing and paternalistic idealization of a romantic peasantry seen through the leisurely eyes of the gentry. It was an unreal rustic vision, perpetuating the myth of the 'chocolate box' England that Campbell so despised. 'Georgian Spring', one of Campbell's more subtle satirical verses written a couple of years later, is an acerbic and incisive attack on *The Land* in which he mocks the triteness of Vita's imagery and the unimaginative shallowness of her vision.

> We know, we know, that 'silver is the Moon',
> That 'skies are blue' was always our belief:
> That 'grass is green' there can be no denying . . .
> As for the streams, why, any carp or tench
> Could tell you that they 'sparkle on their way'.
> Now for the millionth time the 'country wench'
> Has lost her reputation 'in the hay' . . .
> For who would frown when all the world rejoices,
> And who would contradict when, in the spring,
> The English Muse her annual theme rehearses
> To tell us birds are singing in the sky?
> Only the poet slams the door and curses,
> And all the little sparrows wonder why!

Roy's uneasiness in his new 'chocolate box' surroundings stood in marked contrast to Mary's delight at her return to the heart of Anglo-Saxondom. 'The English countryside is too gorgeously lovely,' she eulogized in a letter to William Plomer soon after their arrival in Kent. 'We are in a most English village – the sort I used to imagine I couldn't stand . . .'[17] She also informed Plomer of the interesting people she was beginning to meet at Long Barn.

> When I was talking to Harold . . . Vita Nicolson appeared & in her wake, Virginia Woolf, Richard Aldington and Leonard Woolf. They looked to me rather like intellectual Wolves in sheep's clothing. Virginia's hand felt like the claw of a hawk. She has black eyes, light hair & very pale face. He [Leonard] is weary and slightly distinguished. They are not very human.[18]

Plomer would have been suitably impressed by Mary's name-dropping. It had been he, almost exactly a year earlier, who had urged Roy to let him send copies of 'The Serf' and 'The Zulu Girl' to Leonard Woolf, 'so that they could become known in London as soon as possible'.[19] His efforts bore fruit, and Woolf arranged for the poems to be printed in the *New Statesman* and the *Nation.*

Apart from regular visits from the Woolfs, a whole host of leading literary figures passed through Long Barn, which was one of the hubs around which the Bloomsbury group spun. In June, Roy and Mary were again invited to dinner, to find that David Garnett and Eddy Sackville-West were fellow guests. Like Vita, Garnett had won the Hawthornden Prize and had several successful novels to his name. Eddy Sackville-West, Vita's cousin, was also a published novelist and, at the time of his first meeting with Campbell, was working for the *New Statesman* as assistant to the literary editor, Desmond MacCarthy. At another dinner party hosted by Harold and Vita, this time in the Great Hall at Knole, the huge Elizabethan house two miles from Long Barn which was Vita's ancestral home, MacCarthy and Eddy Sackville-West were present, along with Roy, Mary, Raymond Mortimer and Clive Bell. For the most part, Roy was uncomfortable at such gatherings. The Bloomsburys, ultra-refined and cosseted, were simply not his type. He formulated his awkwardness into an epigram entitled 'Home Thoughts in Bloomsbury':

> Of all the clever people round me here
> I most delight in Me –
> Mine is the only voice I care to hear,
> And mine the only face I like to see.[20]

The full extent of Campbell's alienation from the milieu in which he found himself was expressed with more eloquence a couple of years later in his verse satire, *The Georgiad*:

> Dinner, most ancient of the Georgian rites,
> The noisy prelude of loquacious nights,
> At the mere sound of whose unholy gong
> The wagging tongue feels resolute and strong,
> Senate of bores and parliament of fools,
> Where gossip in her native empire rules;
> What doleful memories the word suggests –
> When I have sat like Job among the guests,
> Sandwiched between two bores, a hapless prey,
> Chained to my chair, and cannot get away,
> Longing, without the appetite to eat,
> To fill my ears, more than my mouth, with meat,
> And stuff my eardrums full of fish and bread
> Against the din to wad my dizzy head:
> When I have watched each mouthful that they poke

> Between their jaws, and praying they might choke,
> Found the descending lump but cleared the way
> For further anecdotes and more to say.
> O Dinners! take my curse upon you all,
> But literary dinners most of all . . .

Roy's alienation from Vita's literary set coincided with Mary's growing attraction to it. This inevitably put a strain on their relationship. Anna Campbell Lyle sought to explain her parents' differing attitudes.

> Roy literally never noticed discomfort, he seemed to revel in it, but Mary had a sensual nature and sometimes found the spartan way of life she had to lead with her husband very hard . . . By the time we arrived at Weald, Mary had been living for six years without a home of her own. She now had two young children to look after . . . She felt strained and very tired.[21]

It was, therefore, hardly surprising that she accepted the comfort of Vita's friendship with relief. Soon, however, the friendship took on a physical dimension which would threaten to wreck the Campbells' marriage.

Teresa Campbell insists that her mother told her 'definitely' that Vita was initially attracted to Roy and was disappointed when her overtures were rejected because 'my father was not so enthusiastic'.[22] The assertion seems to tie in with a line in *The Georgiad* in which Campbell complains of being 'ogled by some frowsy poetess' at one of Vita's dinner parties. Since Vita is the only poetess who springs to mind among Campbell's acquaintances at Long Barn, she would seem to be the 'ogler' in question. Yet if this is the case, and bearing in mind that some form of physical attraction between Vita and Mary seems to have existed as early as July or August 1927, the only logical deduction is that Vita was simultaneously trying to seduce both husband and wife.

Vita had been an active lesbian since before her marriage to Harold in 1913 and she was certainly promiscuous. At the end of June she had spent the night with another Mary at her London home on Ebury Street. This was Mary Hutchinson, a friend of the art critic Clive Bell. A few days later she went to Haworth in the heart of Brontë country with Dorothy Wellesley, an excursion which aroused the jealousy of Vita's most famous lover, Virginia Woolf. Referring to herself as 'poor Billy', Virginia wrote that she 'isn't one thing or the other, not a man nor a woman, so what's he to do?'[23]

Possibly in an attempt to provoke the same degree of jealousy in Vita that she was herself feeling, Virginia wrote at the beginning of August that a male friend had renewed his advances to her: 'I am loved, by a man; a man with an aquiline nose, a nice property, a wife of title and furniture to suit. The proposal was made the day before I left, and I have a letter now confirming it. What do you wish me to do? I was so overcome I blushed like a girl of 15 . . .'[24]

If Virginia's intention had been to arouse Vita's jealousy, she was undoubtedly successful. Vita had flushed with rage as she read the letter.

> I didn't know I was so jealous of you. *Who* is your damned man with the aquiline nose? Look here, I really mind. But if it comes to that, I have on my table a letter of the same sort, – which I haven't answered. What sort of answer I send, depends on you. I really am not joking. If you are not careful, you will involve me in an affair which will bore me horribly. If you are nice, on the other hand, I'll send my correspondent packing. But I won't be trifled with. I really mean this.[25]

It is likely that the letter on Vita's table was from Mary and the 'affair', far from boring her horribly, would in fact become, for a time at least, an all-consuming passion. Their relationship began in earnest on 2 September when Mary sent for Vita. When Vita arrived and asked why she had been sent for, Mary's reply was brazen. 'Because I wanted you so. There is nothing else to say.'[26] Thereafter, they met almost every day, usually in the evening, and walked in the lanes and woods.

It was easy for Mary to keep the affair a secret from Roy. He was seldom at home. Increasingly unhappy with life in Kent, he had taken to escaping from their strained relationship by going on drinking binges in London with old friends such as Augustus John and Philip Heseltine, finding them more convivial company than the visiting Bloomsburys at Long Barn. Neglected by her husband, Mary sought the solace which Roy was finding in the bottle in the welcoming arms of her new lover. From the start, Mary was far more dependent on Vita than Vita was on her. She saw in the blue-blooded poetess, who at 35 was six years older than her, a maternal figure who could be both a mother and a lover. Vita possessed 'everything in women that I most need and love'. 'You are sometimes like a mother to me. No one can imagine the tenderness of a lover suddenly descending to being maternal. It is a lovely moment when the mother's voice and hands turns into the lover's.'[27]

Vita's attitude to the relationship was far less complex. The physical embrace of a woman still in her twenties was a pleasant change from the embraces of Virginia Woolf who was in her mid-forties, 10 years older than Vita and 16 years older than Mary. In the first weeks of the affair Vita took Mary to Knole, where they read Shakespeare's sonnets together in her old sitting room and kissed in her old bedroom. At Long Barn she made love to Mary on the same sofa where Virginia had made her first definitive 'little move' towards her. Finally she took Mary up to her own bedroom and, at considerable risk, slept with her while Nigel, her 10-year-old son, feverish with flu, was asleep in a small adjoining room.

In mid-September, a couple of weeks after the relationship had begun, Vita made it easier for them to meet by suggesting that Roy and Mary move into 'the gardener's cottage' in the grounds of Long Barn. Also known as 'the babies' cottage' because it normally housed the Nicolsons' two children and their nanny, it had become vacant when the boys had returned to school. Oblivious of his wife's affair, Roy was initially delighted at the suggestion. The cottage, which was being offered rent-free, would help to alleviate the family's precarious finances. 'We have had a certain amount of luck since we arrived here,' he wrote to Sibbett in October. 'We have been given a nice house free of rent and for about the first time in our lives we have really settled down.' Campbell's letter to Sibbett conveys nothing of the underlying tensions. Instead, he paints a romanticized picture of life at Long Barn.

> We are on the estate of Knole Palace; and we have the run of Knole Park which is a fine big forest full of deer. The Hon. Mrs Nicolson who has fixed us up here is Vita Sackville-West . . . She is the daughter of Lord Sackville who owns Knole. At Knole is the place where Dryden, Pope, Otway and many of my favourite authors used to spend most of their time. It is full of Reynoldses and Gainsboroughs and it is a magnificent building dating from the fourteenth century. It has nearly 400 rooms and the biggest private library I have ever seen. We are in a house that used to be for the servants. Vita Nicolson's house is next to ours. It is also an interesting place. Caxton was born there and it is as old if not older than Knole itself.[28]

Campbell's tone of optimism suggests that he was trying to fall in line with his wife's evident happiness. Yet in doing so he was fooling himself, forcing his head to govern his heart for her sake. Certainly this bland and sugary eulogizing of life with Vita and Harold bears no resemblance to the later bitterness of his satire on the Bloomsbury set. A few weeks after the apparently carefree letter to Sibbett was written, he would make the devastating discovery which would sour the sweetness of Bloomsbury and leave only the bitter aftertaste which would prompt him to describe life at Long Barn in drastically different terms:

> Hither flock all the crowd whom love has wrecked
> Of intellectuals without intellect
> And sexless folk whose sexes intersect . . .

NOTES

1 Roy Campbell, from 'Faith', *Collected Poems, Volume One*, p. 139.
2 Peter Alexander, *Roy Campbell*, p. 76.
3 Anna Campbell Lyle, *Son of Valour*, p. 35.

4 Roy Campbell, unpublished letter to C. J. Sibbett, late November or early December 1926.
5 Peter Alexander, *Roy Campbell*, p. 77.
6 Anna Campbell Lyle, interview with the author, December 1998.
7 Anna Campbell Lyle, *Son of Valour*, p. 35.
8 *Ibid.*
9 Victoria Glendinning, *Vita: The Life of V. Sackville-West*, London: Weidenfeld & Nicolson, 1983, p. 175.
10 Peter Alexander, *Roy Campbell*, p. 78.
11 *Ibid.*
12 Anna Campbell Lyle, *Son of Valour*, p. 37.
13 Roy Campbell, unpublished letter to C. J. Sibbett, *c.* October 1927.
14 Vita Sackville-West, *The Land* and *The Garden*, Exeter, Devon: Webb & Bower, 1989, p. 10.
15 Louise DeSalvo and Mitchell A. Leaska (eds), *The Letters of Vita Sackville-West to Virginia Woolf*, London: Hutchinson, 1984, p. 232.
16 *Ibid.*, p. 233.
17 Peter Alexander, *Roy Campbell*, p. 80.
18 *Ibid.*
19 Alister Kershaw (ed.), *Salute to Roy Campbell*, p. 105.
20 *Collected Poems, Volume One*, p. 196.
21 Anna Campbell Lyle, *Son of Valour*, pp. 36–7.
22 Teresa Campbell, letter to the author, 21 March 2000.
23 Victoria Glendinning, *Vita: The Life of V. Sackville-West*, pp. 178–9; and DeSalvo and Leaska (eds), *The Letters of Vita Sackville-West to Virginia Woolf*, p. 233.
24 DeSalvo and Leaska (eds), *ibid.*, p. 242.
25 *Ibid.*
26 Victoria Glendinning, *Vita: The Life of V. Sackville-West*, p. 179.
27 *Ibid.*, p. 180.
28 Roy Campbell, unpublished letter to C. J. Sibbett, late October 1927.

CHAPTER TEN

ABSOLUTE HELL

Out of his pain, perhaps, some god-like thing,
Is born. A god has touched him, though with whips:
We only know that, hooted from our walls,
He hurtles on his way, he reels, he falls . . .[1]

In his effusive letter to Sibbett, written shortly after he and Mary had moved into the gardener's cottage, Campbell enthused about all the writers who regularly visited Long Barn, informing his friend that 'we have got to know dozens of interesting people'. He had made up his quarrel with the Sitwells, he said, 'and now we are all good friends'. Osbert Sitwell had written in the *Morning Post* that Roy was 'one of the three poets who had done anything since the War', a compliment that had 'flattered my vanity'.[2]

Through his acquaintance with Desmond MacCarthy and Eddy Sackville-West, Roy had been given the opportunity to write regularly for the *New Statesman*. Consequently, he was the beneficiary of the sort of Bloomsbury patronage which he would later condemn as being incestuously masonic in its mutual back-scratching. Yet, as his letter to Sibbett conveys, he was already out of step with the ideological sensibilities of the set of which he was part: '. . . it is a mildly socialistic paper and I get up the backs of the readers fairly often. But so far I have always managed to have the last word. I am always having shots at vegetarianism, "liberty" and Fabianism. Of course as my reviews come under the literary section, I am able to say what I like.'

Campbell's negative attitude towards the 'mildly socialistic' readers of the *New Statesman* suggests a radical shift in his outlook, particularly with regard to Bernard Shaw. Since Shaw was the most famous advocate of both Fabianism and vegetarianism, Campbell's attacks would have been seen as an implicit attack on Shaw himself. This was a far cry from the near hero worship which Campbell had afforded Shaw during his South African lectures and suggests a major watershed in his political philosophy since his return to England. In part, his new-found aversion to some aspects of Shavianism could have been prompted by a simple knee-jerk reaction to the sort of talk which dominated the literary dinner parties he so disliked. It may also have been influenced by his renewed friendship with Wyndham Lewis, who despised the prevailing ethos of the Bloomsbury group. No doubt, in their correspondence and during their occasional meetings in London, Lewis would have expressed his contempt for Campbell's new friends and Campbell, increasingly irritated by the set-up in Kent, may have found in Lewis a sounding board for his own frustrations.

Yet Lewis's role in Campbell's change of heart should not be overstated. His influence was not as pronounced in 1927 as it would become later, and Campbell's highly critical review of Lewis's *Time and Western Man*, published in the *New Statesman* on 3 December, illustrates clearly that he was no mere disciple of Lewis at this time. Describing *Time and Western Man* as a 'disappointment', Campbell berates Lewis for preferring to use 'picturesque epithets ... instead of arguments'. Moreover, Lewis 'is more obsessed by the Time-obsession' he criticizes 'than his Time-obsessed victims are with Time itself'. Lewis 'reminds one of a medical specialist who diagnoses the same disease and prescribes the same medicine for all his patients'. Lewis's failure to distinguish the physical from the metaphysical, particularly in his discussion of Einstein's theories, is exposed as a serious flaw in his reasoning: '... since his incursion into physics is purely *meta*physical he leaves Einstein untouched. It is only when he starts swinging Einstein's metaphysical and philosophical kittens by the tail that he becomes effective.' In spite of several redeeming features, such as Lewis's effective demolition of Spengler's 'chronological fatalism', Campbell's overall disappointment at the 'inconsistencies and obvious weaknesses' of *Time and Western Man* is unequivocal.

Political and philosophical differences aside, Campbell was being lauded by all and sundry in the autumn of 1927. On 22 October the *New Statesman* published a letter from T.S. Eliot in which Eliot praised the quality of Campbell's work in general and his poem 'Tristan da Cunha' in particular. Clearly excited by Eliot's praise, Campbell wrote to Sibbett that 'Tristan da Cunha' 'has made quite a stir'. Eliot was 'the best critic in England ... He says my control of metre is remarkable and that I am stronger and less flamboyant than ever before.'[3] At a party at the home of Augustus John everyone was praising 'Tristan' and Sacheverell Sitwell echoed his brother's admiration for Campbell by stating that 'he would sooner have written the hundred odd lines of Tristan than the whole of the Terrapin'.[4]

As Roy basked in the glory of his expanding reputation, he remained in blissful ignorance of his wife's affair with his hostess at Long Barn. Yet while Mary was finding little difficulty in keeping her clandestine union a secret from her husband, Vita was having much greater difficulty keeping it a secret from Virginia Woolf. On 9 October Woolf wrote plaintively to Vita, her suspicions of Mary implicit in the terse references to 'Campbell'.

> Look, dearest what a lovely page this is, and think how, were it not for the screen and the Campbell, it might all be filled to the brim with lovemaking unbelievable: indiscretions incredible: instead of which, nothing shall be said but what a Campbell behind the screen might hear . . .
>
> Yesterday morning I was in despair . . . I couldn't screw a word from me; and at last dropped my head in my hands: dipped my pen in my ink, and wrote these words, as if automatically, on a clean sheet: Orlando: A Biography. No sooner had I done this than my body was flooded with rapture and my brain with ideas. I wrote rapidly till 12 . . . But listen; suppose Orlando turns out to be Vita; and it's all about you and the lusts of your flesh and the lure of your mind (heart you have none, who go gallivanting down the lanes with Campbell) . . . Shall you mind? Say yes, or No . . .[5]

Nigel Nicolson, Vita's son, wrote in his memoirs that this letter confirms that jealousy was the 'secret motive' for Woolf's writing of *Orlando*. 'She would reclaim Vita from Mary Campbell by writing her a love letter, so long, so fantastic, so flattering, that it would be irresistible.'[6]

Vita was delighted at the prospect of being both the subject and the inspiration for Woolf's next novel. 'My God, Virginia, if ever I was thrilled and terrified it is at the prospect of being projected into the shape of Orlando. What fun for you; what fun for me.' She added that her letter was 'lovely . . . Campbell or no Campbell'. Mary, she thought, would be 'flattered' to think that she had been the cause, through the jealousy she had provoked, of Woolf's next book – 'if she knew. But she doesn't and shan't.'

If Virginia's intention in telling Vita of her plans for the novel had been to woo her back from Mary's clutches, she was clearly having some success. Vita assured her that she had been right to force herself on Virginia at Richmond in January 1923, 'and so lay the train for the explosion which happened on the sofa in my room here when you behaved so disgracefully and acquired me for ever'. She omitted to mention that the same sofa had served a similar function for herself and Mary more recently. She also assured Virginia that, even though the previous night was 'the most beautiful misty moonlight night I ever saw in my life . . . No, I did *not* go down the lanes [with Mary]'.[7]

A few days later, Virginia's proposed novel had ceased to be an object with which to woo her lover, but had become a weapon with which to cajole her into submission. 'If you've given yourself to Campbell, I'll have no more to do with you, and so it shall be written, plainly, for all the world to read in Orlando . . .'[8]

If Mary was the unwitting inspiration for Woolf's *Orlando*, she was also the source for a series of sonnets which Vita would later daringly publish against the embarrassed advice of her husband. *King's Daughter*, the title Vita gave to the volume, is obviously both a pun on Roy's name and an allusion to the mother-daughter aspect of Mary's desire for Vita. She is Roy's, but she is also Vita's – the wife of the former, the 'daughter' of the latter, and the lover of both.

In the first of the poems, Mary is described, somewhat coyly, as 'a changeling soul', suggestive of the bisexuality beneath the conventional surface. In the second, she is depicted being pursued by Vita 'barefoot through daisied grasses', an evocation of their secret evening walks through the country lanes near Long Barn. In an ironic parallel with the imagery employed in Campbell's 'The Sisters', Mary is set astride 'a raven horse' which has broken free of its harness. She is placed in various Pre-Raphaelite poses, playing her harp by the lake, singing 'in the reeds' and gliding away 'into the fir-trees' night'. She is wild, romantic, nomadic, alone. The sonnet sequence becomes progressively erotic. She stands by candlelight before her looking-glass, 'slips her shift, and dreams'. Her 'young and lovely throat' is whiter than candle wax, whiter than the rose. There is an element of voyeurism, with Vita requesting a 'spy' to penetrate the lady's room where 'no one dare to pry'.

Vita wrote 11 of these sonnets in the throes of a creative obsession in just one evening on 1 December 1927. Two more were written the following morning and another three on 5 December, a day that Mary had spent with her. She described her writing of these 'as a sort of catharsis to a great many pent-up feelings'.[9] By this time Roy knew about the whole affair, not through his own discovery but from Mary's open confession.

In early November, now deeply in love with Vita, Mary decided to tell her husband everything. Perhaps she hoped to give some permanence to her relationship with Vita by forcing Roy to come to terms with it. Perhaps she hoped that he could be persuaded to be as complaisant towards her affair as Harold Nicolson was towards Vita's lesbian relationships. Nicolson, however, was himself a homosexual with little physical interest in his wife, although they were certainly in love, whereas the relationship between Roy and Mary seems always to have existed on the sexual level. In the marriage of Harold and Vita it was simply a question of each partner looking for gratification elsewhere; with the Campbells any extramarital affair would inevitably involve the complexities of the eternal triangle. It is also possible that Mary's desire to confess was less rationally motivated. Perhaps she was simply finding the burden of duplicity too much to bear. Still in love with her husband, she may have felt unable to continue the deception, unable to live the lie.

As she braced herself to tell Roy everything, Mary must have been uncertain of his response. On the one hand, they had always been both frank and liberal-minded about their previous love affairs. She knew of his, and he of hers. There was little of the prude in either of them. Mary had told him of her bisexuality and he seems to have been entirely unconcerned. Indeed, a letter he wrote to Mary soon after his arrival in South Africa in June 1924 suggests that he could make light of it. Roy had acted as gun-bearer to 'a great Society beauty' on a hunt in the bush, he explains, adding that 'everyone raves about her'.

> I had to help the young lady on to her horse every time so I got a good view of her legs etc. She tries to make impressions on people in an innocent way, but I have my own idol: I made my whole conversation about you and showed her your photo. She says she wants to meet you in England. I hope she's not a Lesb.[10]

On the other hand, Mary was all too well aware that Roy was capable of violent jealousy. She told Vita that soon after their marriage, Roy had hung her out of their bedroom window over a busy London street after she had reminisced about the beauty of an earlier woman lover. Roy recounted the episode in his autobiography, stating that his action had been provoked by 'some quarrels'. In fact, as Mary confirmed to Peter Alexander, he had rushed at her in a fury, crying, 'Don't you *ever* say that again!' The incident fired Vita's imagination to such an extent that she wrote an unpublished poem entitled 'Interior' about it, noting beneath, 'This was the story Mary Campbell told me about Roy.'[11]

Mary made her confession on Sunday 6 November. On the previous day, Roy had disappeared on one of his regular 'escapes' to London. Meanwhile, Mary had gone for a walk with Vita in the morning and had spent much of the rest of the day with her. In the evening she played the gramophone while Vita wrote a paper to be given at St Hugh's College, Oxford. Roy telephoned to say that he had met up with Augustus John and would be staying in London overnight. As Mary dined with Vita, she was, in Vita's words, 'in rather a fuss about Roy' because meeting John 'always means that he will get drunk, and then he will be ill for a fortnight'.[12]

The next day Vita and Mary met Roy from the train. When Roy and Mary were finally left alone at the gardener's cottage, with Roy presumably ill with a hangover, Mary told him about Vita. He listened in silence and then questioned her about the extent of the affair. Mary kept little back. He was stunned by the news, but remained pensively silent. Observing him anxiously, Mary looked for signs of passive acceptance or suppressed fury. At first she must have been hopeful. There were no outward signs of anger and at dusk they went to see Vita. All three discussed the matter in Vita's sitting room and Roy claimed that he was himself sleeping with Dorothy Warren, a bisexual friend of Vita's. 'He went off quite amicable,' wrote Vita, 'then Mary came back and said he had changed completely.'[13]

The volcano of Roy's anger, apparently passive when Mary had first told him, had only been sleeping. Bewildered and hurt, and unable to bottle up his emotions any longer, he flew off in a rage and caught the train to London. There, in a pub, he met C. S. Lewis, whom he knew slightly from his Oxford days. At this time Lewis was a young don, a fellow of Magdalen College, who was almost entirely unknown outside Oxford. Lewis still nurtured hopes of being recognized as a poet, having met with a small degree of success the previous year with the publication of *Dymer*, a long allegorical poem which received favourable reviews in the *Sunday Times* and the *Spectator* but precious little else. Campbell was one of Lewis's favourite contemporary poets, in fact one of the few 'moderns', apart from Charles Williams and Kathleen Raine, for whom he had any respect. As such, the young don would have been pleasantly surprised to have met the young poet, treating him with considerable deference.

After the ale had flowed in sufficient quantity, Campbell took Lewis into his inebriated confidence and poured forth the whole story of his wife's affair with Vita. Lewis, wide-eyed with wonder, listened in fascinated silence until Roy had finished and then sat back ruminatively. 'Fancy being cuckolded by a woman!' he mused.[14] The remark, intended harmlessly, was incredibly tactless. Roy dashed out of the pub, his hurt and his anger intensified, and returned in a violent temper to Weald.

That night he erupted in fury, storming around the cottage for the whole night, threatening both murder and suicide, demanding a divorce and, at one stage, chasing Mary with a kitchen knife. Tess, who was then approaching her fifth birthday, woke up to find that she and her sister were alone in the house, presumably after Mary had fled with her husband in hot pursuit.

> I remember waking up about four in the morning and crying out for Mother and for Father, there was no answer and the house looked as if a wild wind had passed through it. I remember the dread feeling, with my sister standing up in her cot and yelling her head off. It was dreadful to us both because nothing like that had ever happened to us . . . I don't know how long this suspense lasted but by next day we were all reunited . . . the disappearance left a bad taste . . . but it was gradually forgotten with the flow of events.[15]

Seen through adult eyes, the 'bad taste' which remained the following morning was recorded in Vita's diary. It was, she wrote, 'a dreadful day'. She had tried 'miserably' to continue with her Oxford paper amid Mary's 'constant incursions' to tell her of Roy's changing moods. In the cold, hard light of day, as the dreadful reality dawned on him, Roy alternated between sullen silence, seeming acceptance, confused exasperation and renewed anger. In a 'rainy dusk', Vita walked up to the village with Mary to get beer for him. After dinner, 'unable to bear things any longer', Vita went to the cottage to talk with Roy. When she arrived, Mary, 'poor child', was 'quite numbed and dead tired'. Returning home, Vita rang a friend 'in sheer misery'.[16]

Two days later Roy informed Vita that he and Mary were to get divorced, to which Vita replied that he was being 'silly'. Vita found Roy calmer when she visited the cottage later on the same day. They talked for a while and after Mary had joined them they made what Vita cryptically called 'certain arrangements' which left her 'feeling much happier'. Roy's calmer, if still confused, state of mind was clear from a generously worded letter to Vita, scribbled on a torn-out leaf from an exercise book.

> I am tired of trying to hate you and I realize that there is no way in which I could harm you (as I would have liked to) without equally harming us all. I do not dislike any of your personal characteristics and I liked you very much before I knew anything. All this acrimony on my part is due rather to our respective positions in the tangle. I am much more angry with M.

He hoped that he and Vita might 'both reach a state of mind when we realize that we have not done each other any *lasting* harm: and I want to reach that state of mind as quickly as possible because this is absolute Hell.'[17]

Vita felt a genuine sympathy for Roy, which she expressed in one of the sequence of sonnets composed about three weeks later. The sonnet speaks of both of them enjoying Mary's beauty and her passion 'as a shared and secret thing'. They had both tapped her 'passion at its spring'. Yet, regretting the division this had caused, Vita hopes through the words of the sonnet, rather naively, that they should meet 'more truly' in their common love for Mary and find a new, deeper bond with her as its source.

Naiveté aside, Vita was also suffering the emotional pain of her own particular love triangle. On the day after she had sought to console Roy and had made the 'certain arrangements' which made her feel happier, she had broken down in tears when making her own confession to Virginia about the affair with Mary. Although Virginia was certainly suspicious of Vita's relationship with Mary, as her correspondence had indicated, it appears that Vita had concealed the full extent of the affair. Virginia was angry, as Roy had been, but was ultimately less passionate and more controlled in her response. 'I have been so really wretched since last night,' Vita wrote to her the following morning. 'I felt suddenly that the whole of my life was a failure, in so far as I seemed incapable of creating one single perfect relationship – What shall I do about it, Virginia? . . . My darling, I'm grateful to you; you were quite right to say what you did; it has given me a pull-up; I drift too easily.'

She sought to reassure Virginia that her love was 'absolutely vital' and, no doubt fearful of Virginia's threats to end their relationship, declared that she did not know what she would do if the threat were carried out. 'You disturbed me a good deal by what you said . . . Surely you can't mean anything serious? Oh no, that's too unthinkable.' She ended with a plea for forgiveness. 'Darling forgive me my faults. I hate them in myself, and I know you are right. But they are silly surface things. My love for you is absolutely true, vivid, and unalterable.' Placated by Vita's contrition, Virginia wrote a conciliatory reply regretting her anger and the harsh tone of her voice, and sympathizing that Vita could not help 'attracting the flounderers'.[18]

There is no doubt that Mary felt very much the flounder as Vita's growing coolness left her high and dry. She clearly needed Vita more than she needed Roy at this time, sending her flowers and desperate love notes pleading for a renewal of their relationship. 'Is the night never coming again when I can spend hours in your arms, when I can realize your big sort of protectiveness all round me, and be quite naked except for a covering of your rose-leaf kisses?' Vita, unmoved, told her that the price of their love was too high. For Mary there was no price too high: 'Darling is it very often that we get weeks of such amazing happiness . . . and I *don't regret it at any time*, even when I suffer most it becomes more worthwhile.' When Vita still refused to resume the affair, Mary began to point the finger of blame. Vita was 'guilty' while she was 'a weak fool to be led away by you'.[19] As she grew increasingly irritated, Vita's sonnets took on a sardonic tone. Mary became 'a scurrying mouse' between two poets whose interest was 'perverse'.

On 14 December Vita departed for Berlin to spend a week with her husband, who had been posted there since October as Counsellor to the British Embassy. Even during her week away, Mary's pursuit was relentless. Letters arrived to 'my rose, my darling mother' in which Mary told of her desolation and of a recent quarrel while driving in London with Roy and Dorothy Warren which had reduced her to tears. 'You should have seen me sitting in your motor in Piccadilly Circus crying quite helplessly,' she wrote. For Mary, as much as for Roy, the first year back in England was ending in 'absolute Hell'.

NOTES

1 Roy Campbell, from 'Mazeppa', *Collected Poems, Volume One*, p. 22.
2 Roy Campbell, unpublished letter to C. J. Sibbett, late October 1927.
3 *Ibid.*
4 *Ibid.*
5 DeSalvo and Leaska (eds), *The Letters of Vita Sackville-West to Virginia Woolf*, pp. 251–2.
6 Nigel Nicolson, *Long Life: Memoirs*, London: Weidenfeld & Nicolson, 1997, p. 41.
7 DeSalvo and Leaska (eds), *The Letters of Vita Sackville-West to Virginia Woolf*, p. 252.
8 *Ibid.*, p. 255.
9 Victoria Glendinning, *Vita: The Life of V. Sackville-West*, p. 186.
10 Roy Campbell, unpublished letter to Mary Campbell, *c.* June 1924.
11 Victoria Glendinning, *Vita: The Life of V. Sackville-West*, p. 180; Roy Campbell, *Light on a Dark Horse*, p. 248; Peter Alexander, *Roy Campbell*, p. 32.
12 Victoria Glendinning, *Vita: The Life of V. Sackville-West*, p. 182.
13 *Ibid.*, p. 183.
14 Rob Lyle, letter to the author, February 2000, confirming that Roy had told him of the meeting with Lewis as reported in Peter Alexander, *Roy Campbell*, p. 83.
15 Teresa Campbell, unpublished memoirs, p. 9.
16 Victoria Glendinning, *Vita: The Life of V. Sackville-West*, p. 183.
17 *Ibid.*
18 DeSalvo and Leaska (eds), *The Letters of Vita Sackville-West to Virginia Woolf*, pp. 256–7.
19 Victoria Glendinning, *Vita: The Life of V. Sackville-West*, p. 184.

CHAPTER ELEVEN

BREAKING WITH BLOOMSBURY

Too sensitively nerved to bear
Domestication, O my friends
On a perpetual change of air
Whose sole stability depends,

By what phenomenal emotion,
Alas, is each of us obsessed
That travel, flight, and ceaseless motion
Must keep us in a state of rest?[1]

At the beginning of 1928 Roy became very ill with appendicitis and in early February he was taken to hospital for an operation. During his subsequent convalescence he was frequently left to fend for himself at the gardener's cottage while Mary spent days and nights with Vita, who, allowing their affair to resume after all, had written Mary four more sonnets.

Mary's neglect of Roy, and Roy's self-neglect, were both in evidence when Laurens van der Post came to visit shortly after Roy's discharge from hospital. Mary took immediate advantage of his arrival by absenting herself even more than usual. Van der Post was horrified by his friend's emaciation, by his disinclination to stir from his bed, and by the squalor in which he was living. He wrote later that he could hardly believe that the 'thin, shivering hulk of a human being in torn and tattered clothes' could be the same person who, only 18 months earlier, had recited 'Tristan da Cunha' 'with the voice of a prophet' on a beach in South Africa.[2]

Roy spent his days in bed, half-dressed, drinking heavily and continuously – mostly gin and cider because of their cheapness, and reading back numbers of the German magazine *Der Querschnitt*. Van der Post sensed, although Roy did not confide in him, that his friend's dramatic decline had something to do with problems in his marriage. At night, van der Post found it difficult to sleep because there were very few blankets in the house and the cottage was cold. On several occasions he awoke to find that Roy had covered him during the night with his own blanket, an act of charity carried out in the depths of misery which van der Post found astonishing.

Eventually, van der Post managed to persuade Roy to travel with him to London to meet the South African journalist and painter Enslin du Plessis. It was a bitterly cold winter's day, but Roy wore neither an overcoat nor a tie. Instead he clasped a thin jacket over grey flannel trousers so torn that the skin of his buttocks was clearly visible. He was unwashed and unshaven. The meal of sausage and bacon they had at a coffee house on Fleet Street was, according to van der Post, the first that Roy had eaten for days. Years later, van der Post told Peter Alexander that 'cold though that winter was, Campbell's spirit was bleaker still'.[3]

At the end of February Vita went to stay with her husband in Berlin, where, in early March, she enjoyed a passionate fling with Margaret Voigt, the wife of one of Harold's friends. With Vita out of the country, Mary reluctantly returned to her own dishevelled husband. She wrote to Vita every day and, in spite of the distractions of her affair with Voigt, Vita found time to reply to each of her letters. Wretchedly lost without her, Mary had sought to spend a morning in Vita's sitting room, in an effort to feel closer to Vita and possibly to escape for a while from Roy. Yet in spite of her request for access to Long Barn during Vita's absence, she was firmly frozen out by Vita's French maid Louise Genoux.

Mary and Roy were now so miserable in each other's company that they had reached the brink of a trial separation. It was, therefore, with considerable relief that Mary arranged to spend the first night of Vita's return with her in London. 'My own I still feel warm from your arms,' Mary wrote to her on 2 April. 'I still burn with last night's love.'[4]

Meanwhile, the looming separation from Mary had also brought Roy to the brink of a final break with Bloomsbury. He was growing increasingly embittered and vitriolic towards all its aspects, particularly those he had witnessed at Long Barn. He no longer sought to conceal his contempt in the name of real or feigned friendship, as the following conversation with Lytton Strachey, recorded by Roy in the margin of *The Georgiad*, demonstrates.

STRACHEY: Some people find expression like you, Roy, in poetry, others in good works, others in heroism. But I look in a higher direction altogether and find it in detachment.
CAMPBELL: Strachey you are about as *detached* morally, physically and intellectually as the animal you most resemble.
STRACHEY: What is that?
CAMPBELL: A tapeworm.[5]

It is, of course, possible that these words were never actually uttered and are only an expression in hindsight of what Roy would have liked to have said to Strachey. Nonetheless, they illustrate his growing sense of anger and his resentment of the whole 'parasitic' set in which he increasingly felt himself trapped by circumstances.

His contempt for Strachey's supercilious attitude towards the Victorians was evident in a review of Evelyn Waugh's life of Dante Gabriel Rossetti.

> When the next generation comes to revalue the standards of the present one, it is possible that they will react against us as violently as we have reacted against the Victorians. As we ridicule the Victorians for their prudishness and hypocrisy, so our children may come to regard our ostentations of frankness as a rather feeble apology for our flabby sensuality, and ourselves as a generation of harmlessly undiscriminating old fogeys who were about as sheepish about our few virtues and enthusiasms as the Victorians were about their vices . . . In comparing our promiscuity and frankness with that of the eighteenth century they will not fail to notice the peculiar absence of zest or enjoyment in its pleasures, and the lack of intellectual and physical vitality, which distinguish the present generation . . . All this should be borne in mind in dealing with such a figure as Rossetti – a subject so dangerously well-suited to the traditions of modern biography, especially in its attitude to Victorians. The tradition of modern biography is to search for incompatibilities: to adopt a tone of indulgent irony towards one's subject: and to rely on a slick, slightly epigrammatical, journalistic style to carry it off. At its supreme moments it provokes one to a mischievous titter at the absurdity of some great man like Wordsworth or Goethe. It is the most perfect instrument that has yet been invented to enable the mediocre to patronize the great.
>
> . . . Mr Waugh has achieved a rare distinction for a contemporary biographer – he has succeeded in not patronizing his subject, though he makes no attempt to whitewash him. He is fully alive to the comic aspects of his subject, but does not make this a pretext for adopting a superior tone. The result is that . . . he has produced a life of Rossetti which is both lively and reliable.[6]

There is little doubt that Campbell used Waugh's book as a stick with which to beat Strachey. The repeated reference to modern biography and its iconoclastic and patronizing attitude towards the Victorians was clearly intended to be seen as a sideswipe at the sort of biography which Strachey had made popular with the publication of his *Eminent Victorians* in 1918 and his *Queen Victoria* in 1921. The former was all the rage with undergraduates while Campbell was at Oxford in 1919 and it is inconceivable that he would not have read it, imbibing its cynicism as he did so. Indeed, Strachey's influence was apparent in Campbell's own supercilious tone towards the Victorians in the lectures he gave in South Africa, implying that Strachey, like Shaw, had been knocked off his pedestal as Roy increasingly came to reject the idols of his youth.

Since Waugh's *Rossetti* was published in April 1928, it is likely that Campbell's review would have been written during the previous month, at the very height of his personal misery. As such, the barbed references in the review to the 'sex-socialism of this period, with its genteel and fashionable ramifications of inversion' carry a particular resonance.

Campbell's explicit praise for Waugh and implicit derision of Strachey is suggestive of the cultural and spiritual direction in which he was beginning to travel. Campbell and Waugh were not quite contemporaries, Waugh being almost exactly two years younger, but their lives had run along similar lines. Like Campbell, Waugh had become intoxicated both physically and metaphysically by Oxford, imbibing the aesthetic pleasures of the new literature and the anaesthetic pleasures of drunken hedonism. Like Campbell, Waugh had come under the sway of a literary mentor at Oxford whose influence would be of pivotal importance to his subsequent development. Harold Acton was to Evelyn Waugh what T. W. Earp had been to Campbell. Acton introduced Waugh to the new poets, particularly to the works of T. S. Eliot, and took him to one of the Sitwells' literary gatherings where he made the acquaintance of Strachey, Clive Bell and Oscar Wilde's ageing 'sphinx', Ada Leverson. Like Campbell, Waugh's over-riding preference for beer and Bohemia adversely affected his studies and he left Oxford without a degree.

Clearly their paths appeared to be converging, even if they had not yet crossed. Consequently, and with the advantage of hindsight, Campbell's review of Waugh's first book displays a prescience towards the then unknown writer which indicates the recognition of a kindred spirit. In the following years, Waugh would break with the 'bright young things' in much the same way as Campbell was now breaking with Bloomsbury – lampooning and lambasting in his satirical novels the same vacuous hedonism that Campbell would target in his satirical verse.

A similar prescience was operating in Campbell's attitude towards D. B. Wyndham Lewis, who, as Campbell himself emphasized in a review published in the *New Statesman* on 24 March, 'must not be confused with his less disarming namesake'.[7] The 'less disarming' but better known namesake was, of course, Campbell's friend Percy Wyndham Lewis, whose *Time and Western Man* Roy had criticized in a largely negative review three months earlier. In contrast, D. B. Wyndham Lewis's study of François Villon was greeted with a largely positive response. The lesser known Lewis was 'a conscientious and earnest scholar' with 'a real knowledge of the Middle Ages' who 'above all ... has a genuine feeling for Villon's poetry'. Clearly aware that D. B. Wyndham Lewis was better known as a newspaper satirist, particularly as the originator of the highly popular 'Beachcomber' column in the *Daily Express*, it seems Campbell was also aware that he was both a Catholic convert and a fervent disciple of Belloc and Chesterton.

> ... his style reminds us of the feverish and desperate gaiety with which we have been familiarised in the daily press ... For the rest, Mr Lewis endears himself to us by means of the same genial caprices as those by which Mr Belloc and Mr Chesterton endeared themselves to our fathers. He belongs belatedly to that school of literature which for some years rotated round the incongruous poles of the public house and the Catholic church, with the former as its spiritual home and the latter as its official headquarters.

Bearing in mind Campbell's awareness of D. B. Wyndham Lewis's religious sensibilities, it is perhaps surprising that his most serious criticism of Lewis's study of Villon is its failure to address the intricacies and implications of the French poet's faith.

> The moral and religious aspects of Villon's life present a difficult problem to biographers and critics. In the particular case of Villon, the noncommittal, disinterested attitude which we demand from most biographers leads to a certain amount of banality. Villon was a rogue. It would be priggish to deal with him from the standpoint of the heavy moralist. His biographer is therefore left with no other alternative than rather lovingly to patronise and chuckle over the rogueries of his hero – an attitude which wavers precariously between impertinence and tiresomeness. Villon was a believing Christian; it is possible that he is best dealt with from that point of view. His rogueries to him were serious responsibilities which endangered not only his neck, but his future existence. Mr Lewis does not underrate this fact, but he does not really sympathise with it. *The Judgment of François Villon*, a play by Herbert Palmer, which is written from a highly religious point of view, though it differs both in scope and aim from Mr Lewis's book, seems to present a far more lively portrait of Villon, simply because the author, evidently a fervent believer in Christianity, has actually lived through, or at any rate imaginatively experienced, the various religious emotions which made Villon's life such a difficult, complicated and terrifying affair.[8]

Apart from fathoming depths of discernment previously unplumbed in Campbell's literary criticism, this particular review also displays a greater ability to empathize and sympathize with orthodox religious experience. It appears to herald a change of heart as much as a change of mind. Furthermore, his belief that the moral and religious aspects of a subject's life are possibly best dealt with from a specifically religious perspective places him at loggerheads with the Strachey school of biography, with its lack of sympathy and its reliance on pseudo-Freudian constructs.

Early in 1928, Campbell used an essay on contemporary poetry, published in *Scrutinies by Various Writers* edited by his old friend Edgell Rickword, to signal yet another conscious distancing of himself from the mindset centred on Shaw, Wells, Fabianism and the 'sex-socialist' moralizing of the Bloomsburys. More significantly, the whole essay is awash with thinly veiled attacks on Vita Sackville-West. This is most evident in the criticisms levelled at Walter de la Mare and Robert Graves, which are transparently intended as a gibe at the Georgian poets in general and Vita's *The Land* in particular.

> This type of poetry, which we might term the 'Merrie England' school of poetry, concerns itself largely with mere quaintness: it revives curious words such as 'hey-nony-no' and 'Derry down derry' from the child-lore of the past. It relishes archaisms such as 'marmosite' and 'manticor', and it is not above using quaint repetitions of words and phrases in order to heighten the effect of jollity or irresponsibility.[9]

The allusion to *The Land* could scarcely be more obvious, especially as Vita's poem had previously been criticized for being little more than a long list of quaint archaisms. There is also more than a faint glimmer of resentment at the surfeit of luxury at Long Barn in Campbell's attack on 'Domestic Comfort'.

> Our age is dominated by the prophets of Domestic Comfort, Shaw, Wells, and Bennett – two of whom have shown in their Utopias that they would be prepared to sell the experience of the human race – youth, pain, passion, courage and danger – for the hygiene of a few patent bath-taps or the moral serenity of meandering about in a sort of universal Fabian summer-school with a few fellow-vegetarians, in a state of almost maudlin contentment; and the last of whom quite openly admits, in the *Evening Standard*, in his weekly tips to young poets, that he places his insurance policy, his clothes, and his belly a long way before his brains: and that he considers it a far greater privilege to be Mr Bennett – and pay his grocer's bills – than to be Homer, and die in poverty.[10]

In spite of the obvious negative references to the prevailing ethos of Bloomsbury, it would be a gross error of judgement to perceive that Campbell's feelings of discomfort were due simply to his unhappy sojourn at Long Barn, or to suggest that they were merely the result of his resentment of the sort of life that Vita and Mary were enjoying while he languished in wretchedness. It would be truer to say that his bitter experiences in Kent, both before and after his discovery of Mary's affair with Vita, only served to confirm those self-sacrificial instincts which were well embedded long beforehand. When Campbell, in the same essay, expressed contempt for the 'philosophy of almost every modern writer . . . dictated by his fear of discomfort, excitement or pain than by his love of life', he was expressing a truth at the very heart of his own psyche. The need for an element of hardship, adventure and suffering was always central to Campbell's love of life. Too much comfort always made him uncomfortable.

Roy's increasingly vociferous attacks did not prevent him being regarded favourably by some of those associated with the Bloomsbury group. Dora Carrington wrote to Gerald Brennan on 6 April recommending Roy's essay in *Scrutinies by Various Writers*. 'Roy Campbell has a review of poetry that is good and Lawrence is amusing with his tirades against Galsworthy.'[11]

It was not until Roy's anti-Bloomsbury satire, *The Georgiad*, was published in 1931 that the leading lights in the Bloomsbury group began their undeclared war of attrition against him. This was continued until well after Roy's death, not least by Leonard Woolf who, in his autobiography published in 1967, painted a picture of Roy as a demented, paranoid and comical eccentric.

> One afternoon there walked into my room at the *Nation*, Roy Campbell, whose poetry at that time was creating something of a stir. I knew him only slightly. He was dressed in or swathed in one of those great black cloaks which conspirators wear in operas and melodramas and he had a large black sombrero. He sat down, scowled at me, and then said in the peculiar voice which the villain always used in old-fashioned melodramas: 'I want to ask you whether you think I ought to challenge Robert Graves to a duel'. Experience as editor or publisher soon teaches one that authors, like Habbakuk, are capable of anything, but I was so astonished by what I heard that I could only gasp: 'But why?' 'Why?' he said, 'Why? Don't you remember the review he wrote of my book, the review you yourself published two weeks ago?' It was true that Robert had reviewed Campbell's book, but it had never struck me that there was anything in it to drive the most hypersensitive writer into lunacy. For the next quarter of an hour I had a lunatic conversation persuading Campbell that the laws of honour and chivalry obtaining in Great James Street in 1926 [*sic*] did not require him to fight Robert Graves.[12]

There is more than a hint of malice in Woolf's words, even if mitigated by motives of revenge, and they were clearly intended to show his adversary in the worst possible light. Yet Woolf's account of this whole episode may be little more than a work of fiction, only told after the one person able to verify or deny it, i.e. Campbell himself, had died. It is likely, in fact, that the story arose from a titbit of gossip appended at the end of a letter from Vita Sackville-West to Virginia Woolf in April 1928.

> Tell Leonard that Roy has written to Graves, challenging him to a duel, and saying that he shall say exactly what he likes about him and all the pipsqueaks of his sort; but tell Leonard not to repeat this, as Roy may change his mind – and we mustn't make bad blood between the poets. I oughtn't to say it but it will amuse Leonard. It's the rudest letter I ever read![13]

Virginia chose not to comment on whether Campbell's rude letter had amused her husband. Instead, she replied to Vita the next day on a more pressing matter. 'I rang you up just now, to find you were gone nutting in the woods with Mary Campbell . . . but not me – damn you . . .'[14]

It was now more than five months since Mary had made her confession to Roy about her affair with Vita. The agony unleashed on that November day had dragged on relentlessly ever since. Roy, unable to bear the burden any longer, was ready to break away. Having severed his last remaining intellectual links with Bloomsbury by declaring his independence in a succession of articles and reviews, he was now about to break with it physically.

In *Light on a Dark Horse* Roy referred to life at Long Barn as 'something between a psychiatry clinic and a posh brothel'.[15] This general impression was borne out by a story he would later tell his daughter. 'What put the finishing touches to his malaise at Long Barn,' remembers Anna, 'was coming across Virginia Woolf, crawling about under the bushes. She raised to his a face so ravaged by madness that he fled to London and thence to Provence, like Tam O'Shanter pursued by the witches.'[16] Whether this story is strictly true, or whether it should be taken as purely apocryphal, it demonstrates graphically Campbell's growing unease at the whole Bloomsbury set-up. As Virginia, real or imagined, raised her face to his, he saw the whole unsettling face of Bloomsbury staring up at him. In her was the mirror of his own malediction.

In April 1928, unable to bear the impotence of his position any longer, he departed, deprived of both wife and children, for Provence, the same refuge he had sought eight years earlier. In fleeing from Bloomsbury, from Long Barn, from Mary's affair with Vita, he was ultimately fleeing from himself – yet in doing so he would also find himself. His daughter believed that the 'deep psychological disturbances engendered in his unconscious by Mary's revelations made him grow up . . . it was a salutary shock'.[17] It was, therefore, a more mature, though shell-shocked, poet who arrived in the Provençal town of Martigues towards the end of April 1928, in search of a fresh start and a new life.

NOTES

1 Roy Campbell, from 'The Festivals of Flight', *Collected Poems, Volume One*, p. 37.
2 Laurens van der Post, letter in *Contrast* 38, January 1976, Vol. 10, No. 2, p. 75; quoted in Peter Alexander, *Roy Campbell*, p. 85.
3 Peter Alexander, *ibid.*
4 Victoria Glendinning, *Vita: The Life of V. Sackville-West*, p. 192.
5 Anna Campbell Lyle, *Son of Valour*, pp. 38–9.
6 Roy Campbell, review of *Rossetti: His Life and Work* by Evelyn Waugh, published in *The Nation and Athenaeum*, 19 May 1928.
7 Roy Campbell, review of *François Villon: A Documental Survey* by D. B. Wyndham Lewis, published in the *New Statesman*, 24 March 1928.
8 *Ibid.*
9 Roy Campbell, 'Contemporary Poetry', first published in Edgell Rickword (ed.), *Scrutinies by Various Writers*, London: Wishart, 1928; reprinted in Roy Campbell, *Collected Works IV: Prose*, p. 246.
10 *Ibid.*, p. 247.
11 David Garnett (ed.), *Carrington: Letters and Extracts from her Diaries*, London: Jonathan Cape, 1970, p. 390.
12 Leonard Woolf, *Downhill All the Way: An Autobiography of the Years 1919–1939*, London: Hogarth Press, 1967, pp. 132–3.
13 DeSalvo and Leaska (eds), *The Letters of Vita Sackville-West to Virginia Woolf*, p. 285.
14 *Ibid.*, p. 286.
15 Roy Campbell, *Light on a Dark Horse*, p. 256.
16 Anna Campbell Lyle, *Son of Valour*, p. 40.
17 *Ibid.*

CHAPTER TWELVE

VITA NUOVA

Rest under my branches, breathe deep of my balm
From the hushed avalanches of fragrance and calm,
For suave is the silence that poises the palm.
The wings of the egrets are silken and fine,
But hushed with the secrets of Eden are mine:
Your spirit that grieves like the wind in my leaves
Shall be robbed of its care by those whispering thieves
To study my patience and hear, the day long,
The soft foliations of sand into song.[1]

Roy arrived in Provence with nothing. He appeared to have lost his family and he lacked both material and spiritual comforts. In 'The Festivals of Flight', he looked with wistful humour at the consolations which eluded him.

Yet I could wish, before I perish,
To make my peace with God above
Or, like a millionaire, to cherish
My purse with soft marsupial love . . .

His destiny was to spurn the comforts of domesticated poets, to resist 'riding an arm-chair for my steed'. He was running away, taking flight, which was 'home of the homeless', 'the last hosanna of routed angels' and the 'sword that fights the coward free', the 'rough first-aid for Cupid's darts . . . and ambulance of broken hearts'.

Although he was desperately unhappy, sending Mary pleading letters full of contrition for his previous neglect of her, Roy found a degree of consolation in the people and culture of Martigues, the same Provençal town that had soothed his troubled spirits when he had last taken refuge there. His love of Provence – its people, customs, landscape, wildlife and climate – would breathe life into many of his finest poems. 'Mass at Dawn', 'Horses on the Camargue', 'Choosing a Mast' and 'St Peter of the Three Canals' vibrate with the poet's love for his adoptive land.

Taking a room in Pascal's Restaurant, Roy befriended the local fishermen and townsfolk, exhibiting the genuine democratic delight in the company of ordinary people which was apparent wherever he lived. The contrast between the simple, unaffected people of Provence and the pretensions and class-consciousness of the literary set at Long Barn and Sissinghurst could not have been more striking. Compare, for instance, Roy's delight in the company of fishermen with Vita's disgust at the craftsmen who had installed central heating at Long Barn in the previous December. 'And my God how workmen smell,' she wrote to her husband. 'The whole house stinks of them. How I hate the proletariat.'[2] This stark declaration of the social elitism prevalent at Long Barn is an example of the ethos that Roy found so unsettling. The 'sex-socialism' he so derided was an egalitarianism of licence, not love.

On 12 May 1928, only a few weeks after Roy's arrival in Martigues, Mary travelled to the French fishing town to discuss a reconciliation. She was alone, having left their two daughters in the charge of a woman in Weald village. The reasons for Mary's apparently sudden change of heart are shrouded in mystery. Anna believes that her mother returned to Roy 'because he wrote her such pathetic letters that she realised they could not live without each other'.[3] This may be an oversimplification. It is probable that Mary's return had more to do with being pushed away from Long Barn than with any pull to Provence through Roy's pleading letters.

Vita liked her affairs to be uncomplicated. Unfortunately, Roy's sudden departure had complicated matters considerably – uncomfortably so. Vita did not mind 'sharing' Mary with Roy, but she did not want the responsibility of having her to herself. Mary's place in Vita's life was always conveniently on the side. With Roy's departure, it is likely that Vita resented the added intensity of Mary's attentions and sought an escape in a conscious cooling off, if not necessarily a calling off, of their relationship. Unwilling and unable to meet Mary's emotional demands, she may even have mooted the suggestion that Mary return to Roy. She had, in any case, renewed her affair with Margaret Voigt, inviting her to Long Barn on the weekend that she had persuaded Mary to leave. On the day that Mary left for Martigues, Vita took her to the station, saw her off on the train for London and then met Margaret off another train and brought her back to Long Barn. 'I forget about people very quickly when I am away from them,' she wrote dismissively to her husband.[4]

Whatever the reason for Mary's return, Roy was overjoyed at her arrival. In June she returned to Kent to collect the children, and brought them back to Martigues. Two-year-old Anna remembered being taken up to a room where her 'very thin' father was lying in bed. 'He was shaking with excitement and hugged us all.'[5] They found a small, cheaply priced house at 3 Rue

St Mitre, where they rented the ground floor and began once again to live as a family. For the children, that first summer in Provence was full of the delights of carefree innocence. One of Anna's earliest memories comes from this time. She was in her cot with the sun trying to burst through the closed shutters of her bedroom window. 'I remember the gold and silver motes dancing in the rays of the sun. Roy, very tall, was leaning over my cot and a little flaxen-haired girl, my sister Tess, was looking at me through its bars.'[6] For Tess, now five years old, the family's arrival in Provence was the moment when 'one of the happiest childhoods imaginable started for me'.

> . . . all those years between five and ten were lived in the most peaceful, idyllic surroundings and circumstances . . . There was something about that first blazing Provençal summer when we arrived, that was inspiring and inviting, everything about it was hot and welcoming. The people were so warm hearted and interested in the right things – at least the things which seemed the most important to me and we soon got on well with them.[7]

These rose-tinted memories were shared by Anna: 'Our childhood in Provence was a happy one. I saw my parents as giants who only had to appear for life to become full of extraordinary events.'[8]

Life was not so rosy for the girls' parents, who were finding it difficult to pick up the pieces of a marriage which had, until recently, seemed shattered beyond repair. Matters were made more difficult by Mary's continuing love for Vita, to whom she still wrote regularly, going to elaborate lengths to keep her correspondence a secret from Roy. The depths of her feelings were evident in October 1928 when she wrote to Vita after reading Virginia Woolf's recently published *Orlando*. Even if she remained ignorant of the fact that she had been the unwitting instigation of Virginia's writing of the novel, the fact that Vita was its inspiration was beyond doubt:

> I hate the idea that you who are so hidden and secret and proud even with people you know best, should be suddenly presented so nakedly for anyone to read about . . . Vita darling you have been so much Orlando to me that how can I help absolutely understanding and *loving* the book . . . Through all the slight mockery which is always in the tone of Virginia's voice, and the analysis etc, *Orlando* is written by someone who loves you so obviously . . . Don't you remember when we imagined you as the young Orlando?

Mary's principal objection to Virginia's novel was that 'Orlando is too safe, too sexless and too easy-going to be really like you. But then I am thinking of him as he appears to *me*, he is something so different to Virginia. Ah! an entire book about Orlando with no mention of her deep fiery sensuality –

that strange mixture of fire and gloom and heat and cold – seems to *me* slightly pale.'[9] There is something almost pitiful in Mary's desperate emphasizing of '*me*', as though her own knowledge of the real and intimate Vita was superior to that enjoyed by Virginia. Her words are a defiant but ultimately futile effort to convince herself, and perchance Vita also, that she, Mary Campbell, was Vita's one true love.

In November, a few weeks after these words were written, Mary endeavoured to convince Vita in person of her undiminished and unrelenting love when she went to stay with her at Long Barn. She met with a cool rebuttal of her advances. Vita's affections had meandered in other directions and she had no desire for a renewal of their intimacy. It was a crestfallen Mary who wrote to Vita from Paris on her way back to Roy in Provence. 'Virginia is right, darling. I wish she weren't, but you have never lost yourself in love.'[10] Her words were meant as a sad rebuke; they were probably taken as a compliment.

Back in Martigues, the Campbells' marriage staggered on uncertainly. In December, possibly as a result of rows over Mary's recent visit to Long Barn, their relationship appeared once more to be stumbling to an acrimonious end. Mary wrote to Vita that she despaired of being able to live with her husband and spoke of separating from him and living alone. This, however, was the low point of their reconciled life together. The New Year brought new hope and new happiness. There was a sense of a new beginning, new horizons, a new life. The most striking evidence of this change for the better in their relationship was Roy's 'Dedication to Mary Campbell', written in January 1929, which celebrates his love for Mary and his joy in their reunion. Mary was his muse, his 'friend, lover, wife', who 'descends with him his lonely fight to share'.

> He knows his gods have watched him from afar,
> And he may take her beauty for a sign
> That victory attends him as a star.
> Shaped like a Valkyrie for his delight
> In lovely changes through the day to shine
> And be the glory of the long blue night.

Alluding to the previous year's despair, the poem speaks of the poet's 'spent heart' which 'had drummed its own retreat' before Mary had 'rallied the red squadron of my dreams', protecting them from 'a night of spectres foul and grim'.

> Sweet sister; through all earthly treasons true,
> My life has been the enemy of slumber:
> Bleak are the waves that lash it, but for you

And your clear faith, I am a locked lagoon
That circles with its jagged reef of thunder
The calm blue mirror of the stars and moon.

In some respects the poem is more than a celebration of Roy's love for his wife. It can also be seen as a baptism signifying a real and symbolic rebirth of their marriage. In this 'Dedication' Roy was sacramentally offering his love and sacrificially offering himself to it; and not only himself but his art also. Since Mary was his muse, he was laying this and the other poems in *Adamastor*, a volume of verse dedicated to Mary which would be published the following year, at her feet. Having no earthly possessions, he was offering her literally everything he had – himself and his art. This, of course, was all that Roy had to offer when they had first met and Mary, it seems, was now ready to respond once again as she had done then. She would once more become the wife of a poet, sacrificing herself and the promise of worldly comforts for a life of hardship and uncertainty.

The renewal of their love sparked a revival of Roy's creativity. He had written no poetry for almost a year when he picked up his pen to write the 'Dedication'. Thereafter, throughout 1929, he would write some of his finest verse. Apart from the emotional stability engendered by the reconciliation and the solid foundation it provided, this new period of creativity was fired by Roy's love for the local Provençal culture with which he was endeavouring to saturate himself.

Life in Martigues for Roy, Mary and the children could fairly be described as approaching idyllic in 1929. The steady income of £20 a month which Roy had received since the death of his father was more than enough for the family to live comfortably in France. They moved from their ground-floor apartment in the house on Rue St Mitre to a small farmhouse shaded by giant umbrella pines at Tour de Vallier, about two miles out of town. In front of the house there stretched a wide terrace and beneath this were two fields of olive trees 'that shivered into silver in the mistral'.[11] Among the olives grew slim almond trees that burst into bloom each year, splashing the landscape with pink. Beneath them, each spring, scarlet tulips added a deeper shade of red. Anna described the scene:

> Behind our house, a meandering path led down through the woods, to the Etang de Berre – not a lake at all but a miniature sea connected to the Mediterranean by four canals. In our day, before it was polluted by factory waste, it teemed with marine life . . . We would find rust-red, sage-green and ink-blue urchins, every colour of seaweed, shoals of darting fish and a small, solitary fish with the brilliant hues of a

> kingfisher. The lake was our paradise and we would spend whole days there.[12]

Tess recalled being awakened by a heated row between her parents soon after they had moved to Tour de Vallier. It had been caused by Mary's opposition to Roy's heavy drinking. 'This rather disturbing incident was still an aftermath of the English influence, it took time to pass and then the Latin sway took over and an idyllic life began for us all – sadness and mysteries were washed away and life changed and put on a new meaning.'[13]

> All our life in Provence, especially for me, was spent in imbibing creation to the fullest . . . the sun, the shade, the woods, the lake, the fruit, the seafood, the wine, the moonlight, the stars, our games, our friends and nature as a whole were the source of all our inspiration and happiness . . . But above all we were free! Very free to enjoy all these things to the utmost. Our time passed so pleasurably and harmoniously – we welcomed each booming day with its freedom, adventures and contrasts.[14]

Part of this unusual degree of freedom was due to the fact that Tess did not attend school. Instead, her parents gave her lessons at home. Roy taught her maths, struggling in vain to interest the six-year-old in the fascination of square-root equations. He also bought an atlas, laying it in front of his daughters as the basis for lessons in geography. 'He also taught us astronomy from this book and sometimes gave us lessons of this with the night sky spread above us.' These impromptu astronomy lessons were sometimes given on cold evenings when the family was walking home from Martigues, 'when the icy mistral in our faces made the tears come to our eyes so that they magnified the stars, then my father would point out to us all the different constellations and planets.' Mary took on the responsibility of teaching the girls English and history, and she led them in half an hour's gymnastic exercise in a clearing near the woods. 'We learnt a lot about literature from our parents' conversation and general knowledge we learnt every day, as my father was an ambulating encyclopedia; we assimilated most of this because it was so interesting.' Roy also taught them how to fish, row and swim.[15]

At harvest time, Tess and Anna would join their friends in the fields, playing round the threshing machines which would do the rounds of all the neighbouring farms. They would slide in the straw and make houses and tunnels with the bundles. In the evenings, accompanied by their parents, they would join the harvest festivities:

> . . . the children of the farms were our friends and we used to join them, their families and harvesters in all their customs, festivities and dancing and meals, laid on long tables, in the shade of the plane trees

> and eat their carefully prepared food. There was plenty of red wine and everyone was very merry and for dessert they would bring out the melons and watermelons and slice them up.[16]

Mary's new-found peace of mind was evident in the fact that she resumed painting for the first time in seven years. A portrait of a suntanned Tess earned the praise of Augustus John, who urged Mary to continue painting. In the evenings she would play the guitar on the terrace, accompanying Roy and their friends as they sang. She also resumed the partial practice of the Anglo-Catholic faith of her youth, teaching Tess and Anna the 'Our Father' and 'Hail Mary' and saying prayers with them at night.[17]

Apart from his poetry, Roy found a great deal of peace and fulfilment in his friendship with the local fishermen. He would spend nights seining in the Mediterranean with them, or on the Etang spearing mullet by the flare of an acetylene torch. One of the fishermen he befriended was a tall, blond youth named Marius Polge, whom everyone called 'Grandpère'. They decided to go into partnership, buying a 10-foot boat named *La Clemence*, and later a second which Campbell called the *Teresa and Anna* after his daughters. On summer evenings the Campbell family and their friends would go out into the middle of the lake aboard the *Teresa and Anna* and bathe until the moon rose and the dusk descended. Roy and Grandpère would dive for mussels, bringing them up in handfuls which Roy would cook after the party had returned to shore. Grandpère's relationship with the Campbells became even closer when Helen, Mary's sister, visited Martigues and became Grandpère's mistress and subsequently his wife. (The couple's daughter would later marry the author Laurie Lee.)

Under Grandpère's guidance, Roy took up the Provençal sport of water-jousting. In this dangerous sport each jouster, balanced on a small, raised platform mounted on the back of a boat, protected by a wooden shield on his chest and armed with a heavy lance, attempts to knock his opponent into the water as their respective boats pass. Roy, being powerfully built, excelled at this test of courage, strength and skill and soon became a valued member of 'La Joyeuse Lance Martegale', one of the most successful teams on the Mediterranean coast. He sported the team's green beret with pride and waxed lyrical about *les joutes nautiques* in his autobiography, *Light on a Dark Horse*, in which he claimed that the jousts descended from the old *naumachia* of the ancient Greeks in the Isthmian Games and had come to Provence via the Roman arena:

> When, under Constantine, the gladiatorial combats were abolished, they were relegated, in a modified form, to the sea-port. Here they became a necessary part of marine war-training until spikes and spears

> were replaced by fire-arms ... In those days the collision was precipitated by the force of the oars but in our time it reached its climax through the use of fast motors, so we were meeting at a greater speed than the mediaeval knights on their horses, and with less protection.[18]

In October 1929, Roy wrote to Wyndham Lewis boasting of his conquests with the other members of La Joyeuse Lance Martegale. 'Martigue beat all the other teams including Marseilles and we shall soon be dividing the prize money. So I shall be all right for a long time now ... We have had a great time this summer and financially I am well off now.'[19]

At the end of their second summer in Provence, Roy, Mary and their two girls were more contented than ever. They had settled into a new life, worlds away from the cares and upheavals of their former turbulent existence. Many years later, Roy would still look back on this time with a lasting sense of nostalgia.

> That sacrament of friendship, a good Provençal meal, which even on Fridays is better than the best Northern meal, whether it be *bouillabaisse* or a *roti*, is best honoured in the open air, and best of all in the evening, with the limitless sweep of the Crua, the Camargue and the sea, under a crimson and violet sky with the stars coming out and the crickets relieving the cicadas. A few bottles of Chateauneuf from whose black columns the setting sun strikes one or two Aldebaran-like ruby sparks: green olives from one's own vat scented with fennel after each one has been lovingly bruised between two stones: black olives in their own oil: silver bread like the nimbus of the cloud at noon over the Ventour: a pourtague of the negre or black mullet cured by ourselves from our own fishing, which has been pressed between rocks and out-savours the finest roe of the sturgeon: and then the gigot or haunch of a lamb which in all its life never ate anything but the thyme, the rosemary, and the fennel of the Crau ...
>
> If you, my reader, at any future date find yourself sitting there with your arm round some beautiful living torso, and as you drink your wine looking down over the Camargue and the Crau from the old ruins of Fos ... say a Grace for me and my beloved and my friends, for we also knew what you know,
>
> 'Yet, though knowing naught,
> Transcended knowledge with our thought.'[20]

The 'sacrament of friendship' that Roy recalled so evocatively was remembered with equal poignancy by some of those who shared it with him. One of these was the painter Tristram Hillier, who wrote in his autobiography of the idyllic evenings on the terrace at Tour de Vallier.

> Roy Campbell . . . and his wife and their two small daughters had a house in the pine woods quite near to ours, and some of the best evenings of my life were spent there; in summer, upon their terrace – the air heavy with the scent of resin and the pungent night odour of aromatic herbs, the staccato croak of bullfrogs serving an orchestration to our voices and to the guitar that Mary, his wife, gently strummed; or in winter, crowded round a blazing fire of pine logs when Roy, in gravely measured tones, would recite to us his verse. A big wicker-covered jar of wine stood always in a corner of the room, and as the night advanced and discussion became more wild and violent, so the jar would be brought more frequently to fill the jug on the table, until in the pale light of dawn, I would return through the still, scented woods to my home . . .[21]

Echoes of these Arcadian evenings would resonate across the years, so that a long time later Campbell could propose a toast:

> To the guitar that thrilled and bounded,
> With female torso on one's thigh –
> Valhallan healths and songs resounded,
> Till morning, when the tun ran dry.[22]

NOTES

1 Roy Campbell, from 'The Palm', *Collected Poems, Volume One*, p. 50.
2 Victoria Glendinning, *Vita: The Life of V. Sackville-West*, p. 186.
3 Anna Campbell Lyle, letter to the author, 2 April 2000.
4 Victoria Glendinning, *Vita: The Life of V. Sackville-West*, p. 195.
5 Anna Campbell Lyle, letter to the author, 2 April 2000.
6 Anna Campbell Lyle, *Son of Valour*, p. 46.
7 Teresa Campbell, unpublished memoirs, pp. 10–11.
8 Anna Campbell Lyle, *Son of Valour*, p. 46.
9 Victoria Glendinning, *Vita: The Life of V. Sackville-West*, pp. 205–6.
10 *Ibid.*, p. 206.
11 Anna Campbell Lyle, *Son of Valour*, p. 46.
12 *Ibid.*
13 Teresa Campbell, unpublished memoirs, p. 12.
14 *Ibid.*, pp. 12–13.
15 *Ibid.*, p. 13.
16 *Ibid.*
17 *Ibid.*, p. 12; and Teresa Campbell, letter to the author, 21 March 2000.
18 Roy Campbell, *Light on a Dark Horse*, p. 263.
19 Roy Campbell, unpublished letter to Percy Wyndham Lewis, October 1929.
20 Roy Campbell, *Light on a Dark Horse*, pp. 208–9.
21 Quoted in Anna Campbell Lyle, *Son of Valour*, pp. 55–6.
22 Roy Campbell, from 'The Moon of Short Rations', *Collected Poems, Volume Two*, London: The Bodley Head, 1957, p. 74.

CHAPTER THIRTEEN

VITA BREVIS, ARS LONGA

> I love to see, when leaves depart.
> The clear anatomy arrive,
> Winter, the paragon of art,
> That kills all forms of life and feeling
> Save what is pure and will survive.[1]

In early summer 1929 Mary visited friends and family in England, leaving Roy in charge of Tess and Anna. Roy's dependence on her is evident from the nature of his letters during her absence. He wrote every day, beseeching her to do likewise.

> My girl, think about me – I long to have your sweet face lying on my chest. I long to kiss you and drink out of your lovely eyes . . . I adore you and I am in a rage of impatience to see you . . . Kisses everywhere – all over you: 200,000 of them . . . My little baby girl dream about me – I love you and I want to kiss you a thousand times.[2]

Shortly after her return, Mary wrote to William Plomer of her love for Provence and its people.

> The day after I arrived there was a great feast at our house. Five jouters, fishermen, invited themselves to a bouillebasse [*sic*] which they brought caught and cooked themselves. They made a large fire in the open air and all helped with this sacred rite! One felt they were the remote descendants of the men the gods [loved?]. I don't love them; as soon as I had eaten & drunk with them I hid myself in my room – but I must say I have more respect for them than many rooms full of the London Paris New York intelligentsia. I believe there is a quality in this air & soil & sea to be found nowhere else in the world.[3]

Even though there is an element of ambivalence towards its more robustly masculine aspects, Mary's preference for the company of fishermen to that of cosmopolitan intellectuals illustrates that she had come to share her husband's distaste for the latter. However much she still missed Vita's company, she clearly felt little remorse for the loss of her friendship with the rest of the Bloomsbury group.

Roy's love for Provence was as strong as Mary's. Tess remembered how his *joie de vivre* was infectious, affecting the rest of the family.

> Wherever my father was he got mixed up with the local people. Here at Martigues he had a spontaneous, exuberant zest for life. He seemed to be inebriated with the love of it, this of course affected us all. He joined up with the fishermen of Martigues; he used to go out with them whole nights, fishing for sardines and tunny fish and came back and slept all day. Sometimes he would bring the fishermen back to the house and cook an outdoor 'bouillabaisse' with them under the pine trees. He also got mixed up with the bullfighting of Provence. He did some amateurish part, like taking the cocarde off the bull's horns. He was very healthy and strong and this outdoor life made him even more so.[4]

The 'amateurish part' that Roy played in the bullring gave him the ambition to be as successful at bullfighting as he had become at water-jousting. If he was an 'amateur', he was an amateur with professional pretensions, as this letter to his South African friend C. J. Sibbett, written in June 1929, illustrates.

> If I take off another cocade [*sic*] I will be given a trial at the mise à mort with the sword which has always been my ambition. For a cocade one gets 500 francs for a mise à mort 1000 frs after that you can become an entrant for being a matador. If I could get that job I would sell my boats at once . . . I would give anything to become absolutely good at it.[5]

Any hopes of becoming a matador were abandoned two months later following two humiliations in the arena at Istres when the bull caught him, trod on his foot and tossed him. Chastened by his experience, he wrote to Wyndham Lewis that he had 'given up all thought of bullfighting in an expert way – the last affair was a fiasco & I feel a fool for having written about it in such a confident way. It will take far too long for me to learn anything but cocarde snatching.'[6]

Inevitably, Roy's humiliation in the bullring, which stood in marked contrast to his conspicuous success in the water-jousting, gave rise to a number of legends. Stories soon abounded of his less than heroic escapades. Typical of these was the story told by a friend of Laurens van der Post. According to this particular account, Roy was at a bullfight one afternoon in Arles when he jumped into the arena intent on snatching the cocarde from between the bull's horns. Unfortunately, having had too much to drink, he promptly fell sprawling in the middle of the arena. At this point, to the great amusement of the crowd, the bull came over and licked his cheek.[7] A similarly amusing account of Roy's bullfighting career was given by Augustus John. 'At Martigues . . . he had indulged in the local sport of cow-baiting, and was, I believe, once knocked over by an irate milker whose new-born calf he was unsuccessfully attempting to skewer . . .'[8]

There was, however, a serious side to Roy's love for tauromachy which was undiminished by his failures in the arena. In *Taurine Provence*, written two years after his own misadventures and published in 1932, he provides a romanticized evocation of the bullfighter's art and the culture that surrounds it.

> Athletes, the poets of action, are inspired equally, as poets are, by an inward necessity to surpass, and to perform feats of excellence and skill: and like poets the greater that necessity is, the more they will undertake. A poet of limited ambition, like Tennyson, remains in the precincts of the croquet lawn: but a great poet like Shakespeare will wrestle with the phantoms of terror, fear, jealousy, hatred, madness and death imposing the laws of his own victorious imagination upon them. So men in whom the heroic principle works will be driven by their very excess of vitality to flaunt their defiance in the face of death or danger, as in the modern arena.[9]

Roy's unusual pairing of the athletic with the aesthetic has its roots in his admiration for classical antiquity. He was impressed by the fact that the bullring existed in Crete 5,000 years ago, emphasizing that tauromachy, like water-jousting, had its antecedents in ancient Greece. 'Many of the customs of the Greek arena are . . . preserved intact in the modern bull-fight, as the ancient "Naumachia" is preserved in the *joutes nautiques*.'[10]

By 1930 Roy's philosophy had matured into a fusion of Provençal romanticism and Graeco-Roman classicism. He was a great admirer of Caesar, along with the martial spirit of ancient Rome and the stoicism with which it was underpinned. In defending the self-sacrificial spirit which unites the poets and the toreadors he was affirming Martial's epigram, *vita non est vivere sed valere vita est* ('life is more than merely staying alive'), and also the Hippocratic aphorism, *vita brevis, ars longa* ('life is short, art is long').

The importance of this change of heart and mind needs to be stressed. It explains Campbell's contempt for those such as H. G. Wells, whose utopian visions gave precedence to worldly comforts over spiritual realities. It explains his attack on Arnold Bennett's assumption that the desire for material security comes before an artist's duty to his art. Perhaps most importantly, it indicates that Campbell's distaste for Bloomsbury went much deeper than any question of personalities. The dilettante dabbling of the Bloomsbury group and the self-gratifying principles they espoused were alien to him. He was searching for meaning beyond meanness. Whether or not he believed in God, he certainly believed in gods greater than himself, even if they were merely the muses of the ancient Greeks. *Vita brevis, ars longa*. Life without art is worthless.

The extent to which Roy's philosophy placed him at loggerheads with the prevailing ethos of Bloomsbury was illustrated in his defence of bullfighting in the face of what he perceived as hypocritical Anglo-Saxon objections to it.

> Bull-fighting is the only sport which is at the same time a great art and in which the man opposes a terrific adversary with inferior weapons. It is the only sport which has inspired great painters and poets.
>
> It always surprises me to hear English people decrying the bull-fight as being cruel, when they hunt defenceless foxes with packs of dogs, buffaloes and lions with rifles, pheasants with shot-guns, and trout with fish-hooks. They eat cutlets, poultry, venison, pheasants, and partridges, all of which have been killed at no personal risk.
>
> Any pot-bellied draper who has made a fortune, can arm himself with a rifle (an invincible weapon against any animal) and go out and 'bag' his elephant, lion, tiger, rhino, then he returns as a hero with a few paragraphs in the gossip-column. I have never yet heard of one of these heroes trying to win distinction inside the barricades. That may be the reason why the corridas are so hated and decried by this type of Tartarin. Lord Dash and Lady Blank can go off and wound fifty antelopes which, escaping, die in agony after several days. But the priests of Mithras, who are forced to put their victims to death from the most perilous position . . . with the horns of the bull an inch off their entrails, are considered to be cruel and barbarous . . .[11]

Campbell's ostentatious defence of tauromachy and his broadside at Anglo-Saxon hypocrisy represent a deliberate distancing of himself from the 'chocolate box' culture from which he had recently escaped. He was well aware that the bullfight was the one facet of Mediterranean life which was guaranteed to raise the hackles of those in England whom he had come to despise. In choosing to champion it so vehemently, he was thumbing his nose at Bloomsbury and the literary set on the *New Statesman*. His beliefs were clearly intended to shock what he had once called the 'mildly socialistic' sensibilities of the *New Statesman*'s readers. It was not so much a case of wildly waving a red rag in front of the bull as waving the bull in front of the 'mildly' red rag.

It would, however, be an oversimplification to dismiss Campbell's defence of bullfighting as nothing more than a knee-jerk reaction to his literary enemies in England. It was much more than that. The rituals of the arena, rooted in antiquity and bequeathed by tradition to each generation, represented a quasi-religious response and a countercultural riposte to the ethical uncertainties of a rapidly changing world. Provence, its people and its place in the pattern of life, represented a permanence amidst the shifting sands of secular relativism and modern technology. This notion was clear in Campbell's defence of Provençal culture against the encroachments of science-worship in *Taurine Provence*. He was particularly scathing in his attacks on the prominent biologist J. B. S. Haldane.

> Modern science, the slave of puritanism, has a horror of the physical. Mr Haldane shudders at the indecency of milking cows. He might prefer to prepare the maternal fluid by means of test-tubes, etc (and would probably prefer synthetic sirloins to the real article): whereas I would sooner take a bucket (unsterilized) and go into the field and milk the bloody thing myself and, as for sirloins, they suit me all right.[12]

For Campbell, life in Provence represented true reality as opposed to the virtual reality that the prophets of 'progress' offered as an artificial alternative. At the deepest level of his being he was more at home with the simplicities of Martigues than with the complexities of cosmopolitanism. Fishermen were simple because they were real. Their lives were an engagement with Life. Provence represented for Campbell a purification, a stripping away of artificial accretions. In *Taurine Provence* he sees the bitter winds of the mistral as the symbolic means by which Provence keeps itself pure from the encroachments of an unwanted modernity.

> Nobody who has not participated as one of the people themselves, as one of the actors, can fully appreciate the fun of a Provençal fête in those towns as yet unspoilt by tourists, Montparnassians, and Bloomsburies as are all those stuffy little haunts of gossip and boredom such as Sanary, Bandol, St. Tropez, Cagnes, etc., that lie to west of Marseilles. At the sight of a tourist or a bad painter, the mistral, the guardian bull of the true Provence, will lash its sides, paw the ground, and with a single snort of its nostrils, fill his eyes and mouth with grit, balloon his plus-fours like a couple of zeppelins, scatter his easel and paints, and send him coughing and grumbling back to the Riviera.[13]

This sense of purification is particularly evident in 'Autumn', a poem which Campbell wrote late in 1929. The falling of the leaves exposes the 'clear anatomy' of the trees, stripping everything from them except the bare, life-giving essentials. He describes the purity and simplicity of winter as 'the paragon of art',

TOP LEFT Mrs Sam Campbell with Roy, aged six months, in April 1902.

ABOVE Roy, aged five or six, with an unidentified servant.

LEFT Roy in his last year at Durban Boys High School.

ABOVE Roy and Mary in 1921, the year in which they met.

RIGHT Roy (centre) with William Plomer and Mary, pregnant with Anna, in South Africa in early 1926.

Laurie Lee, Mary and Roy on the roof of the Campbells' first house in Toledo, with the towers of the Alcazar in the background.

RIGHT Roy's favourite photograph of his wife – Mary, aged forty, in Rome, 1939.

BELOW Anna, Tess, Roy's mother, Roy and Mary surrounded by pigeons in St Mark's Square, Venice, 1939.

ABOVE Tess Campbell, aged sixteen, Lisbon, 1937.

RIGHT Anna Campbell, aged eighteen, London 1944.

Father Gregorio, parish priest of Altea, who received the Campbells into the Church in 1935 and was murdered by Republican militiamen from Alicante in the following year.

Roy with his mother at Altea in 1935.

BELOW From left: Roy's mother, Roy, Mary, Tess and Anna on a donkey. Uys Krige's friend Emelia is in the foreground.

RIGHT Reunited: Roy and Mary in Provence, 1929.

BELOW Roy, Mary, Anna and Tess in the pine woods near Martigues, circa 1930, in a photograph taken by the poet, Hart Crane.

TOP RIGHT Mary Campbell in 1927, the year in which she met Vita Sackville-West.

ABOVE Vita Sackville-West. ©*Hulton Deutsch Collection*

RIGHT Virginia Woolf. © *Hulton Getty*

ABOVE LEFT Roy in the uniform of the King's African Rifles, Nairobi, 1944.

ABOVE Mary, circa 1944, London.

LEFT Roy, London, 1950.

ABOVE Roy, with hat and stick (second left), at the Catherine Wheel with friends in 1951.

LEFT Tess's wedding party at Bochechos, 7 August 1954. From left: Anna, Rob Lyle, Mary, Tess, Ignatius Custodio. At Tess's feet, unidentified, and Anna's daughter, Francesca.

BELOW Mary's last portrait of Roy, three months before his death in 1957.

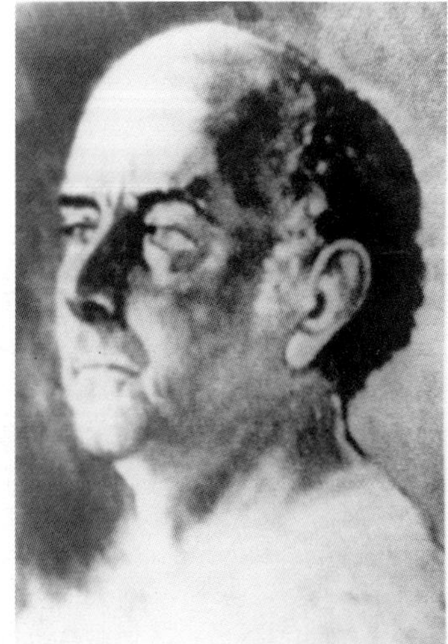

That kills all forms of life and feeling
Save what is pure and will survive.

The purifying impact of Provence is apparent in the other poems written at this time which would be included in *Adamastor*, a volume of his verse published in 1930. 'Horses on the Camargue' is a celebration of the primitive equine breed, 'the original wild mustangs of Europe',[14] who still roam wild in the Camargue national park. They are 'Sons of the Mistral . . . whose strong gusts they love to flee'. Mystically united to the surf, the 'great white breakers gave them birth' and they are 'plumed . . . with the snortings of the sea'. Ever wild and never enslaved, they represent a desire for freedom and disdain for domestication.

For when for years a slave,
A horse on the Camargue, in alien lands,
Should catch some far-off fragrance of the wave
Carried far inland from his native sands,
Many have told the tale
Of how in fury, foaming at the rein,
He hurls his rider; and with lifted tail,
With coal-red eyes and cataracting mane,
Heading his course for home,
Though sixty foreign leagues before him sweep,
Will never rest until he breathes the foam
And hears the native thunder of the deep.

Freedom, however, comes at a price. For the wild horses of the Camargue and the tempestuous poet alike, freedom is only earned through the sacrifice of comfort.

Still out of hardship bred,
Spirits of power and beauty and delight
Have ever on such frugal pastures fed
And loved to course with tempests through the night.

'Horses on the Camargue' affirms one of life's eternal paradoxes, that the sacrifice of comfort leads to the comfort of sacrifice. Freedom is ample reward for the loss of comfort it entails. Similarly, 'Mass at Dawn', one of the finest of Campbell's Provençal poems, affirms the related paradox, that the enjoyment of consolation is only possible after the endurance of desolation. This short poem encapsulates the sense of serenity which Roy and Mary had found since their arrival in Provence. On the surface it depicts Roy's return to harbour after a night's fishing at sea where he is met by his daughters on the quayside. More profoundly it depicts the lagoon-like peace which Roy and Mary had rediscovered after weathering their own particular storm.

> My arms were tired and I was heavy-eyed,
> But when with food and drink, at morning-light,
> The children met me at the water-side,
> Never was wine so red or bread so white.

NOTES

1 Roy Campbell, from 'Autumn', *Collected Poems, Volume One*, p. 52.
2 Roy Campbell, unpublished letter to Mary Campbell, May 1929.
3 Mary Campbell, unpublished letter to William Plomer, June 1929; quoted in Peter Alexander, *Roy Campbell*, pp. 107–8.
4 Teresa Campbell, unpublished memoirs, p. 17.
5 Roy Campbell, letter to C. J. Sibbett, June 1929; quoted in Peter Alexander, *Roy Campbell*, p. 115.
6 Roy Campbell, postcard to Percy Wyndham Lewis, August 1929; quoted in Peter Alexander, *ibid.*, pp. 115–16.
7 Anna Campbell Lyle, letter to the author, 20 January 1999.
8 Augustus John, *Autobiography*, p. 415.
9 Roy Campbell, *Taurine Provence*, Paris/London: Alyscamps Press edition, 1994, pp. 11–12.
10 *Ibid.*, p. 12.
11 *Ibid.*, pp. 14–15.
12 *Ibid.*, p. 49.
13 *Ibid.*, p. 32.
14 *Ibid.*, p. 50.

CHAPTER FOURTEEN

THE APES OF WRATH

And when I hate, my hate shall bare a spike
Clear in intention, though it fail to strike –
Not like your own that dribbles, week by week,
Like lukewarm bilge out of a running leak,
Scented with lavender and stale cologne
Lest by its true effluvium should be known
The stagnant depth of envy that you swim in,
Who hate like gigolos and fight like women . . .[1]

Shortly after Mary's return to Provence following her visit to England in the summer of 1929, the Campbells were visited in Martigues by Nancy Cunard. The purpose of her visit was to discuss the publication of a volume of Campbell's verse for her Hours Press in Paris. Their discussions came to fruition during the following year when Campbell's *Poems* were published in the same tall, slim format as that chosen for the poems of Robert Graves, Harold Acton and others.

Cunard arrived in Martigues with her African-American lover, the pianist Henry Crowder. Fearing 'the general reaction of many South Africans towards people of colour', she was worried that Campbell would greet them frostily but was relieved to find that they received 'a beautiful, friendly welcome'.[2] The vivid impression that Cunard's visit made on the Campbell children is clear from Anna's memoirs. She remembered her arriving 'in a large car driven by a very big and jovial black chauffeur whom she called "Darling"'. Anna found her 'fascinating, with bracelets from wrist to shoulder'. She spread around her 'a strong aroma of scent and dry martinis' and was like 'a beautiful, but over stimulated, snake'.[3]

Apart from these occasional, one-off visits from old friends, Roy and Mary received regular visits from Tristram Hillier, Augustus John and Aldous Huxley, all of whom lived locally. Anna also recalled visits from the Irish writer Liam O'Flaherty, who was 'a bit too wild even for Roy',[4] and the American poet Hart Crane, who 'looked more like a bank clerk than a poet'.[5]

Hart Crane, who stayed for a week in June 1929 at Roy's invitation, wrote his verse directly onto a typewriter, much to Roy's surprise. In spite of this unorthodox method of composition, Roy expressed his admiration for the American's poetry. The two men formed an instant friendship. 'Once,' Anna recalled, 'walking back from the lake in the evening, Roy threw himself on some tufts of thyme in a field near our house. Hart Crane immediately followed suit and so did we children. The scent from all that crushed thyme was heavenly. Roy called this "getting scented before dinner".'[6] These happy memories were shared by Tess, who remembered Crane as having a 'very generous and expansive nature'.[7]

Within a few days of his arrival, however, Crane's public indiscretions and his alcohol-induced mood swings were causing his hosts considerable embarrassment. On one occasion Roy had to restrain him from throwing himself off the bridge in a fit of depression, and a little later he had to rescue him from an angry sailor to whom he had made homosexual advances. 'He was an extraordinary, tragic creature,' Roy wrote in *Light on a Dark Horse*, 'who appeared in those classical surroundings like a mad howling dervish, always weeping, or exalting beyond himself.'

> He could neither hold his drink nor control his abnormal 'queer' nymphomania: he made himself a public laughing-stock everywhere among the sailors and fishermen, by making advances to them, so that we had to send him away. He was charming when sober, which was seldom: he read his wonderful poems like an angel, and we were very fond of him, but he needed a keeper. He had only one religion, the Almighty power of the U.S.A. – he believed in Whitman's vision of it, altogether. When drunk, this puny, flatfooted fellow would boast for hours about how with seventy American marines he could conquer Europe . . . He was forever comparing poverty-stricken Martigues with the glory of his native skyscrapers and Brooklyn bridge.[8]

'He is a good poet . . . but he went off his rocker completely,' Campbell wrote to his South African friend Enslin du Plessis shortly after Crane's departure.

> We had to get him to go away but we parted good friends . . . We found him at 12 at night in the middle of the road with his typewriter on one side of him and his portmanteau on the other crying like a baby. Then he tried to jump off the bridge. I think it was dope. I managed to get him back to his own people.[9]

A very different account of Crane's visit was given by Campbell in a letter to Wyndham Lewis, written at around the same time. According to this version of events, Campbell had leapt to Lewis's defence when Crane had criticized *The Enemy*, Lewis's magazine.

> We had some very strong wine on the table to which he helped himself with a sort of Frenzy. I started pumping him about the *Enemy*: he became almost inarticulate and seized upon one very small self-contradiction of yours in *Time and Western Man* . . . He started banging the table and shouting so I made him shut up. Then I threw a bucket of water on him to make him perfectly sober . . . He then wept, and said he was coming over to Europe with a Brigade of Americans to shoot every European. Then I thought it was about time to show him what he would get if he did. His chief quarrel against Europe it seems was that the sailors and fishermen were not pederasts. I chucked him out of the house when he became so truculent. He was so worked up, he was crying like a big fat baby and said he couldn't walk through the forest at night. I said he'd have to or the wolves and wild boars would bite him and he believed it. I put his typewriter into one of his hands and the valise in the other and gave him a kick behind to get him moving.
>
> After this humiliating treatment he has written a long whining letter 4 pages long asking me to forgive and forget him . . . The garde champetre found him sitting in the middle of the main road with his typewriter and valise, howling and howling. So the garde . . . looked at his papers and gave him another kick to move him along. I don't know how he got away from Martigues.

Campbell ended this unpleasant letter by levelling a string of personal insults at 'the American poet', describing him as 'a disgrace both intellectually and morally, a howling, ugly looking, lachrymose devil, like nothing I have ever seen before . . . I have never seen such a preposterous mixture of a swash-buckler and a whining coward.'[10]

There is clearly a chasm of divergence between this account of Crane's sojourn with the Campbells and all the others. The pleasant memories recounted by Anna and Tess are supplanted, in the letter to Lewis, by their father's concentration on one nasty and possibly largely fictional encounter. The account given to Lewis, in which Campbell casts himself in the role of a ruthless persecutor, obviously contradicts the letter written to du Plessis, in which Roy presents himself as Crane's paternalistic protector who sought always to save the mercurial poet from himself and others. Since Roy's memories of the visit recounted in his autobiography 20 years later conform with the charitable approach expressed in his letter to du Plessis, and with the pleasant memories recalled by his daughters, it has to be assumed that the tone and content of his letter to Lewis were – for whatever reason – little more than a calculated pose.

There was to be an unsavoury and prophetic postscript to this episode. A few weeks after the first letter to Lewis, Campbell wrote again, still gloating over his ill-treatment of Crane. 'My wife had a postcard from Hart Crane from Brooklyn still begging our pardon!! He said when he got back he was going to "hurl" himself off Brooklyn bridge: but the silly ass seems to have forgotten to do so.'[11] When, three years later, Hart Crane committed suicide by throwing himself off the very same bridge, Campbell's heartless words came back to haunt him. Anna remembers that he was 'terribly upset' when he heard of the suicide. 'When he stayed with us Roy loved him, I think, like a brother.' Referring to the cruel letter he had written to Lewis, she lamented Lewis's 'ghastly influence' on her father. 'It maddens me!'[12]

If the Hart Crane affair, in its real and fanciful manifestations, exposes a Jekyll and Hyde split in Campbell's character, it also exposes Wyndham Lewis as the catalyst that brought out Roy's darker side. The power of Lewis's negative influence still puzzles Campbell's daughters. Anna remembers Lewis, who made occasional visits to Provence to see Roy, as 'that cold man who used to come to Martigues and stay with us and never seemed to smile or laugh . . . but for some reason my father absolutely worshipped him . . . It is extraordinary that he should feel such love for this man who seemed to have such a cold heart. I don't know. We'll never know. He made him laugh, really and truly . . . Every time a book came from Lewis – they were very witty but very cruel – my father used to burst into laughter.'[13] Anna conjectures that the affinity between her father and Lewis may have had its roots in a shared antagonism towards the English aristocracy.

Tess believes that Lewis exerted 'a dominating effect' on her father which sprang from Roy's appreciation of Lewis's satire. 'My father found a kindred spirit. To find just one kindred spirit in the world, you cling to it.'[14] A similar view was held by Rob Lyle, Roy's friend and confidant during the last years of his life. In Lyle's view, Lewis was 'the only person who, intellectually, dominated him so that he wanted to imitate him. He very rarely came up against the kind of intellect he wanted, except for Lewis who happened to have views he was ready to adopt. He wanted an intellectual framework and he found it in Lewis and became very dependent. People do get influenced by other people. Every artist in his formation is influenced by somebody. Then they grow out of it and become themselves, but they have used this material to help them develop.'[15]

Yet if Campbell, by the summer of 1929, was dominated by Lewis and had accepted the ready-made 'intellectual framework' which Lewis had provided, what had happened in the 18 months since his highly critical review of Lewis's *Time and Western Man* had appeared in the *New Statesman*? How and why had the discerning critic become an uncritical disciple in such a short time? Was Lewis's intellectual dominance so powerful that Campbell found himself unquestioningly accepting everything he said?

Campbell had admired Lewis's writing since his days at Oxford. In *Light on a Dark Horse* he wrote that *The Caliph's Design*, published in 1919, had 'put me under the spell of Lewis and I gradually came more and more under his influence till I started generating ideas of my own'.[16] In making such a sweeping statement, Campbell does himself an injustice and at the same time overemphasizes the importance of Lewis's ideas. Contrary to his own self-effacement, by the end of the 1920s Campbell had generated many ideas which were in obvious conflict with those espoused by Lewis. A comparison between Campbell's views and those that Lewis advanced in the books he published in the twenties, such as *The Art of Being Ruled*, *The Lion and the Fox*, *Time and Western Man* and *Paleface*, will indicate their fundamental differences.

Lewis's belief in the desirability of a cosmopolitan world order in which unique local cultures would be swallowed up in a global monoculture, presided over by a world state 'with a recognised central world-control',[17] is diametrically at odds with Campbell's love for Provence and its local traditions and customs. Lewis's misanthropy, evident throughout his work in his contempt for the ordinary ranks of humanity who were only fit to be manipulated by elites, is strikingly at variance with Campbell's love for fishermen and peasants and his defence of their indigenous cultures against the encroachments of modernity. Lewis's opposition to Christianity, which he considered to have had a detrimental impact on history, is contradicted by Campbell's increasing attraction to Christian tradition. Clearly, at the most basic and radical level, real differences existed between Campbell and Lewis which placed a metaphysical gulf between them. This being so, their evident sense of affinity becomes even more mysterious. What was it that bridged the abyss?

The key to their apparent unity is to be found in a shared love of satire as a form of expression, and in their shared use of it against a common enemy. Lewis had always opposed the power exerted by literary cliques and he vented his spleen with particular virulence against the Bloomsbury group. In 1927 he founded an almost one-man magazine entitled *The Enemy*. In the editorial to the first of the three issues that appeared, he boasted that there was no '"movement" gathered here (thank heaven!), merely a person; a solitary outlaw and not a gang'.[18] Lewis, as a self-appointed 'solitary outlaw' and 'the Enemy' of Bloomsbury, was bound to find an ally in Campbell, who was increasingly seeing himself in the same role.

The publication of Lewis's *The Apes of God* in 1930, with its satirical broadsides against the Bloomsburys, would have confirmed Campbell in his belief that he had found in Lewis a kindred spirit and a powerful ally. In its assault on the 'select and snobbish club' which is Bloomsbury, *The Apes of God* combines facetious farce with serious conceptual analysis. Lewis disguises his characters just enough to avoid being libellous, without hampering their identification with the individuals he is targeting. The sexual ambiguity of Matthew Plunkett is suggestive of Strachey, for example, whereas Dan Boleyn's acceptance as a genius is a clear allusion to the 'invention' of Duncan Grant by Bloomsbury. Amidst the satire, Lewis injects sober analysis to reinforce his arguments.

> It is to what I have called the Apes of God that I am drawing your attention – *those prosperous mountebanks who alternately imitate and mock at and traduce those figures they at once admire and hate* . . . In *Bloomsbury* it takes the form of a select and snobbish club. Its foundation-members consisted of monied middleclass descendants of victorian literary splendour. Where they approximate to the citizens of this new cosmopolitan Bohemia is in their substitution of money for talent as a qualification for membership. Private means is the almost invariable rule . . . All are 'geniuses', before whose creations the other members of the Club in an invariable ritual, must swoon with appreciation . . . They yield to none, however . . . in their organized hatred of *living* 'genius'.[19]

The Apes of God provoked an uproar. Newspaper gossip columns had a field day in their efforts to identify the originals of the 'apes'. Montague Slater, writing in the *Daily Telegraph*, reported Osbert Sitwell's anger and added that 'Aldous Huxley and Norman Douglas have armed themselves with whips and scorpions'. The character of Jimjulius Ratner, the second-rate writer with the 'epiphany' style, was generally thought to refer to James Joyce. Others mentioned in connection with the novel included Richard Wyndham, Sydney Schiff, Edwin Muir, Lytton Strachey and almost anyone remotely associated with Bloomsbury.[20] With evident satisfaction, Lewis wrote to Richard Aldington that the 'agony column of *The Times* has echoed the rage of people who considered themselves attacked in the Apes'.[21]

Not surprisingly, Campbell was delighted with Lewis's attack on Bloomsbury and wrote to congratulate him.

> The *Apes of God* is great . . . I think it is the most important thing you've done. Read it in 3 days first, only stopping to eat and sleep, am now rereading it more carefully . . . My review will give you everything I

> think of the *Apes* which is magnificent, a modern prose – *Valpone* & *Alchemist* in one. I laughed over it like anything.[22]

The review to which Campbell referred was intended for the *New Statesman*, but was rejected for being 'too favourable'. This served to confirm Campbell's and Lewis's assumption that the power of Bloomsbury had been brought to bear to suppress any positive criticism of the book. Campbell wrote a furious letter to the *New Statesman*'s editor, reinforcing Lewis's view of him as his literary bodyguard. 'Campbell is a very fine fellow *and* a great bull-fighter,' he wrote to Augustus John.

> He was quite right to make a fuss. What happened in the offices of the *New Statesman* happened (no doubt) in at least half-a-dozen other editorial offices. *The Times, Spectator* & *Nation* all had disgraceful notices. Something had to be done about it and it was a good thing that I had a pugnacious matador (a credit to the Camargue) to take up the banderillo for me! Vive le Roy![23]

The Apes of God inspired Roy to resume work on his own verse satire of Bloomsbury. In the spring of 1931 he informed Lewis that he was 'just finishing a long satire, the *Georgiad*'.[24] A week or so later, *The Georgiad* having been finished, Roy wrote to Lewis again, explaining that it 'answers, explains and completely shatters anything written in this Bloomsbury manner: it punches hard and fast especially at the end'. Following its publication in the autumn, Roy was 'delighted' that Lewis approved of it and wrote gloatingly to him of its impact.

> I have no reviews from the Bloomsbury press – perhaps it is another boycott. But the '*G*' has had more publicity even than *Adamastor* . . . [J. B. Priestley] wrote 2 columns of newspaper to prove it wasn't worth writing about while for 4 other books (all according to him first rate and *worth* writing about) he only reserved two short paragraphs. Swinnerton, *Everyman, Saturday Review,* and (I believe) Rebecca West (*Telegraph*) all boosted it sky-high in long reviews. Good old Rebecca! (She hates V. Sackville West and must have enjoyed the *Georgiad*).[25]

In similar triumphalist vein, Campbell boasted in a letter to another friend that he did not think 'anything so scurrilous has appeared in England for about 150 years. Nearly everyone is mentioned by name.'[26] In many respects, however, his triumphalism was misplaced. The very nature of *The Georgiad*'s attack was its greatest weakness. It was so lacking in charity and so full of vindictiveness that its victories were pyrrhic and those it targeted were vindicated as the hapless victims of unjust persecution. In a grim and ironic reversal of the poem's intended purpose, it had succeeded in gaining for Bloomsbury the status of underdog.

Bloomsbury's revenge was more subtle than Roy's – and more effective. Rumours were circulated that *The Georgiad* was written because of Roy's sense of inferiority in the presence of his intellectual betters at Long Barn. As Harold Nicolson explained,

> The current legend is that out of charity we lent him the gardener's cottage at our home at Long Barn, Sevenoaks Weald. That we there introduced him to several of our literary friends who came down to dine or sleep or to stay from Saturday to Monday. That some of these friends, notably Raymond Mortimer and Edward Sackville-West (my wife's cousin) did not play sufficient attention to the Campbells and in fact talked about people whom they did not know or books in French and German which they had not read. That Roy Campbell was incensed by this behaviour and acquired angered feelings of inferiority. That he therefore quitted the house and thereafter revenged himself on all of us in 'The Georgiad'.[27]

The very suggestion that Roy would have felt inferior, either intellectually or artistically, to such as Mortimer or Edward Sackville-West is patently absurd, as is the inference that 'books in French and German' were beyond his reach; and, of course, the claim that Vita had suggested that the Campbells move into the gardener's cottage 'out of charity' was considerably less than entirely honest. Indeed, Nicolson admitted that the 'legend' was a distortion of the truth, though only in a private letter. Publicly, the legend was allowed to go unrebutted and was generally believed to be a true explanation of Roy's motive for writing *The Georgiad*. In a classic display of the supercilious dishonesty that Roy so despised, Bloomsbury had gained its revenge. Needless to say, once rumours of Mary's affair with Vita began to leak out, Roy's motives were perceived as being even more base.

The difference of approach between Roy's attack and Bloomsbury's riposte was exemplified in four candid lines in *The Georgiad* itself:

> And when I hate, my hate shall bare a spike
> Clear in intention, though it fail to strike –
> Not like your own that dribbles, week by week,
> Like lukewarm bilge out of a running leak . . .

In the event, the 'running leak' proved far more effective than Campbell's stream of invective. His guns had been spiked by his hate's own 'spike'.

Unfortunately, *The Georgiad*'s weaknesses have obscured the more serious points it sought to make. Embedded between the vitriolic attacks on Vita Sackville-West, Virginia Woolf and the rest are classically refined objections to the prevailing philosophy of the Bloomsbury group, mounted like pearls of wisdom in the basest of metal.

> Nor knew the Greeks, save in the laughing page,
> The philosophic emblem of our age,
> Whose Hoof is stamped on all, whose voice is law
> Whom every poet serves with reverent awe,
> And makes his voice one deafening he-haw,
> One loud complaint of devastating griefs
> Against his life, his loves, and his beliefs,
> Still in his tender disillusion sore
> Because, ten years ago, there was a war,
> Seeing in all things woes to wound his nerves
> Save in the damp philosophy he serves,
> Which is the fountain-source of all his woes,
> And yet to which the fool for healing goes,
> And wonders why he should return all damp
> In spirit, with a belly-ful of cramp.

In this rejection of post-war pessimism and its nihilistic ramifications, Campbell was siding with others, such as T. S. Eliot and Evelyn Waugh, who were similarly seeking glimmers of philosophical light amidst the prevailing gloom. In his affirmation of classical philosophy and its conscious objectivity, Campbell rejected Freudianism with its shift towards subconscious subjectivity.

> But down below, invisible and dim,
> The complexes in soft inertia swim,
> Huge useless squids that out of shame or fright
> Have sunk insulted from the conscious light –
> To these their zigzag courses are related,
> By these each ship of fools is navigated:
> None with his quadrant ever deigns to sight,
> The intellect, that sun of fire and light;
> And when the ship's piled up, the labour lost,
> And all the cargo to the tempest tossed,
> They'll blame all things in the revolving year
> Save the philosophy by which they steer,
> By which they'll prove you, with a final air,
> The rock they've split on shouldn't have been there,
> And that the world's all wrong whose winds and tides
> Don't tally with the tables and the guides . . .

Related to Campbell's rejection of the fundamental tenets of Freudianism is his rejection of those who seek to make 'happiness' or sex a servile subject of psychology. He snorts contempt at those who study Bertrand Russell's 'melancholy recipes for "happiness"':

> All who in Russell's burly frame admire
> The 'lineaments of gratified desire' . . .
> All who of 'Happiness' have learned the ropes
> From Bertrand Russell or from Marie Stopes.

In subjecting sex to the presuppositions of psychology or psychoanalysis, self-appointed 'experts' were stripping it of its joy, its beauty, its meaning – and ultimately even the pleasure it has to offer.

> He roars with agony at Venus' thrill
> And takes his pleasures as a bitter pill
> Or social duty, much against his will;
> And when he leaps enthroned in stallion state,
> Less with hot flame, than pedantry, elate,
> Ponders the physiology of birth,
> And strives, of sex, 'the meaning' to unearth:
> And, if he found it, would not stop to breathe
> But straight the sex of meaning would unsheathe,
> And, even that discovered, would not wait,
> But work out its relation to 'the State' . . .

Campbell believed that sex should not be a subject of morbid fascination but a glorious mystery to be enjoyed in the purity of passion: when attempts are made to strip it of its mystery it is simultaneously stripped of its higher meaning, leaving nothing but a gaudy and sterile remnant. Sex, as preached and practised in Bloomsbury, was the omnipotence of impotence. This is the *leit-motif* which predominates in *The Georgiad*. Androgyno, Campbell's hero, is so shocking to the puritanical prurience of Bloomsbury because he mocks their furtiveness in an unrestrained fertility rite. Androgyno is the shamelessly potent vanquisher of psychosexual impotence.

Androgyno may have vanquished Bloomsbury, but its creator failed singularly in his efforts to do likewise. The gems of philosophical insight in *The Georgiad* were overlooked in the rush of recriminations which followed its publication. Vitriolic abuse had muddied the clarity of its message, and it was difficult to see the sense amidst the scandal. As with so many of Lewis's satires, Campbell's *The Georgiad* was the victim of its own vendetta. This time the apes of God had escaped the clutches of the apes of wrath.

It would be easy to blame Lewis's malign influence for the excesses of *The Georgiad* and his shadow certainly lurks over many of its maledictory lines. Yet, as Campbell's earlier writing of the equally spiteful satire *The Wayzgoose* shows, he shared with Lewis a malevolent streak which their friendship merely served to exaggerate. There is no doubt that the two men liked and respected each other. They found themselves on the same battlefield fighting the same enemy at the same time – yet, like ships in the night, they would never be as close again as they were during this period. The 'kindred spirits' were already drifting apart. As the years unravelled, Campbell would come to realize that his enemies' enemy was not necessarily his friend.

NOTES

1 Roy Campbell, from 'The Georgiad', *Collected Poems, Volume One*, p. 220.
2 Hugh Ford (ed.), *Nancy Cunard*, p. 354.
3 Anna Campbell Lyle, *Son of Valour*, p. 55.
4 *Ibid.*
5 *Ibid.*, p. 54.
6 *Ibid.*, pp. 54–5.
7 Teresa Campbell, unpublished memoirs, p. 23.
8 Roy Campbell, *Light on a Dark Horse*, pp. 311–12.
9 Quoted in Peter Alexander, *Roy Campbell*, p. 111.
10 Roy Campbell, unpublished letter to Percy Wyndham Lewis, June or July 1929.
11 Roy Campbell, unpublished letter to Percy Wyndham Lewis, July or August 1929.
12 Anna Campbell Lyle, interview with the author, Portugal, December 1998.
13 *Ibid.*
14 Teresa Campbell, interview with the author, Portugal, December 1998.
15 Rob Lyle, interview with the author, Portugal, December 1998.
16 Roy Campbell, *Light on a Dark Horse*, p. 224.
17 Julian Symons (ed.), *The Essential Wyndham Lewis*, London: Vintage, 1991, pp. 6–7.
18 *Ibid.*, p. 5.
19 Percy Wyndham Lewis, *The Apes of God*, London: The Arthur Press, 1930, pp. 131–2.
20 Robert T. Chapman, *Wyndham Lewis: Fictions and Satires*, London: Vision Press, 1973, p. 102.
21 W. K. Rose (ed.), *The Letters of Wyndham Lewis*, London: Methuen & Co. Ltd, 1963, p. 190.
22 Roy Campbell, unpublished letter to Percy Wyndham Lewis, 1930.
23 W. K. Rose (ed.), *The Letters of Wyndham Lewis*, p. 194.
24 Roy Campbell, unpublished letter to Percy Wyndham Lewis, March? 1931.
25 Roy Campbell, unpublished letter to Percy Wyndham Lewis, late 1931.
26 Roy Campbell, letter to Herbert Palmer, June 1931; quoted in Peter Alexander, *Roy Campbell*, p. 98.
27 Harold Nicolson, unpublished letter to W. H. Gardner, 27 March 1958; quoted in Peter Alexander, *ibid.*, p. 99.

CHAPTER FIFTEEN

FRIENDS AND ENEMIES

> Under a pine, when summer days were deep,
> We loved the most to lie in love or sleep:
> And when in long hexameters the west
> Rolled his grey surge, the forest for his lyre,
> It was the pines that sang us to our rest,
> Loud in the wind and fragrant in the fire,
> With legioned voices swelling all night long,
> From Pelion to Provence, their storms of song.[1]

Life in Provence prior to the furore over *The Georgiad* could be likened to the calm before the storm. Roy's peace of mind in the spring of 1931, and his love for his adoptive home, were evident in a letter to his South African friend, C. J. Sibbett. His evocative description of the pine forest surrounding Tour de Vallier resonates with the imagery of 'Choosing a Mast', one of the most powerful of his Provençal verse, which he was in the midst of writing.

> These pines, that grow all over Provence, are magnificent trees ... They move in the wind like huge waves. There is something liquid and fluid in their motion and in their eternal roaring and thundering, which never ceases day and night. The mistral is a glorious wind, a dry wind, as cold as ice but full of the fragrance of pine, thyme, fennel and rosemary with which the million rocky hills of Provence are covered from base to summit. The mistral blows away all the cobwebs of the mind. It is cold, yet sunny: and at night there is nothing I like better than to hear it plunging in the pines outside while one sits in front of a log-fire. I have a fragmentary verse about it ...
>
> – and when in long hexameters the West
> Rolled their grey surge, the forest for its lyre,
> It was the pines that sang us to our rest
> Loud in the wind, and fragrant in the fire.[2]

The letter to Sibbett abounds with high-spirited *joie de vivre*. He praised the 'very blackest and richest of old red Provençal wine' which tasted 'as if God were walking down one's gullet in velvet slippers'. He reported happily that his family 'flourishes ... and we all enjoy excellent health'. His daughters were 'fine strapping wenches' and Mary was 'in the bloom of her womanhood, healthy, strong, cheerful and capable – an invaluable person in every way'. Beyond Provence, *Adamastor*, his latest volume of verse, was enjoying 'terrific success in America'.

Adamastor had also been terrifically successful in England when it was published the previous year. The volume contained all Roy's shorter verse, from the earliest South African poems such as 'The Theology of Bongwi, the Baboon' through to his more recent Provençal verse, such as 'Mass at Dawn' and 'Horses on the Camargue'. It was received with almost universal praise and sold in sufficient quantities to earn him more money in a lump sum than he had ever received before. 'I understand from Faber that the 3rd edition of *Adamastor* is just coming out – not bad in one month!' he wrote jubilantly to Enslin du Plessis.[3]

T. S. Eliot had liked the poems sufficiently to publish them with the coveted Faber imprint and wrote a very appreciative letter to Campbell, praising his work. Roy, who had always admired Eliot, was overwhelmed. 'Few things have given me more pleasure and confidence than your last letter. A word of encouragement from you is worth far more to me as a poet than any other sort of notice I could get. I shall do my best to live up to it and I am very grateful indeed.'[4]

Most critics shared Eliot's enthusiasm, including many who would shortly be satirized by Campbell in *The Georgiad*. Desmond MacCarthy, in a long review in the *Sunday Times*, professed himself 'embarrassed' to assist at the birth of a book destined to be famous.[5] Arnold Bennett proclaimed Campbell to be 'a master of words' and was grandiloquent in his praise. 'Mr Campbell is quite outrageously a poet. He has plenary inspiration. Emotions, crude and primeval, surge out of him in terrific waves ... He rides on words as on horses, loving them as violently as he whips them. His is indeed the grand manner.'[6] There was even praise from Harold Nicolson and Vita Sackville-West, in the *Daily Express* and the *Fortnightly Review* respectively, both of whom were blissfully oblivious of the bombshell which Campbell was about to drop on them. Equally oblivious, Virginia Woolf wrote to Julian Bell urging him to read *Adamastor* and offering to send him a copy if he had not obtained one.[7]

C. Henry Warren, writing in *The Bookman*, struck a prophetic note in his expression of regret that Campbell's passion too often became envenomed, poisoning itself in the process:

> There is still in fact too much venom in the man. It gives his fierce epithets an occasionally fictitious strength. Only when the venom is washed away by an intense sympathy of understanding, leaving the old power of words and the old stupendous imagery, does he achieve the fine quality of which one knows him to be capable . . .
>
> Proof enough is in this book then that Mr Campbell has 'arrived'. His note is as individual as anyone's now singing. Purged of some unnecessary rancour, he may one day give us really peerless poetry; for he has an intensity of vision that often reaches white heat.[8]

Roy, basking in the success of *Adamastor*, shared his renewed sense of contentment with his friends and family. Augustus John (who nicknamed Mary 'Little Lord Fondleroy') was a regular visitor. Without knowing of Roy's work on *The Georgiad*, John was nonetheless aware of his friend's distaste for Bloomsbury. 'Though never stirring from the district,' John wrote of Roy in his autobiography, 'he always seemed somehow to keep in spiritual touch with Bloomsbury, of which cultural centre he always spoke in terms of familiarity and loathing.'[9]

Aldous Huxley was another frequent visitor to Tour de Vallier. Anna recalls that Huxley made 'a profound impression on my youthful mind . . . His high-pitched, rather affected voice, his lanky and disjointed body, the thick glasses he wore because of his near blindness, all fascinated me.'[10] She remembered an amusing incident during one of Huxley's regular weekend visits.

> Once after our usual bathe in the lake, Mother and I were left behind. Aldous also, because of his sight, was lingering and Mary was having difficulty doing up the countless little buttons on the back of her dress. I tried to help her but my small hands were ineffectual (I was five at the time), so that Aldous came over to see whether he could manage. He peered at the buttons for a long time and then started to do them up, saying, 'I hope I'm getting this right. If I get one wrong I shall have to start again and we shall be here all night!'[11]

Roy's friendship with both John and Huxley was jeopardized by his public support of Percy Wyndham Lewis and would be damaged almost beyond repair by the publication of *The Georgiad*. Campbell confessed to Sibbett that the part he had played 'in sticking up for Wyndham Lewis' had 'embroiled' him with Huxley, 'with Plomer, and several of my old friends'.[12] In the acrimonious aftermath of Roy's broadside against Bloomsbury, John terminated his frequent visits and Huxley no longer came for weekends. Yet such was Roy's love for Lewis at this time that he seemed to believe that the loss of other friendships was relatively unimportant.

Lewis's infrequent visits to Tour de Vallier impressed themselves upon Anna's mind as vividly as had the visits of Huxley. 'Long into the night they talked, laughed, sang and drank in Homeric feasts of wit.' Anna and Tess would drift off to sleep to the sound of their animated conversation, which, though muffled by their bedroom walls, was still discernible as their father's voice 'competed with the mistral in relentlessness'. In the evenings, Roy, Mary and Lewis would walk down to the lake, where, as often as not, Tess and Anna were already playing. 'All three swam so far out into the lake that their heads looked like tiny dots bobbing about in the distant water,' remembers Anna. After their swim, Roy would grill fish over a fire of dried fennel as the moon rose over the water. Then Mary would pick up her guitar and strum while all three sang 'Nita Juanita' and other songs tinged with melancholy. As Anna grew tired, she would be picked up and rocked to sleep by either Lewis or Roy, 'and I would wake up the next morning safe in bed, with the reassuring sun trying to burst through the shutters'.[13]

The political drift of the conversation centred on the Soviet Union. Rumours were beginning to emerge of Stalin's extermination of the peasant proprietors, or *kulaks*, who had stubbornly resisted the enforced collectivization of their farms. There was also much talk of Dostoevsky, whose sufferings as a prisoner in Siberia foreshadowed those of the new generation of political prisoners in Stalin's 'brave new world'. 'I remember how excited both men became whenever the strange new words "kulak" and "Dostoevsky" were mentioned,' says Anna. In fact, the five-year-old Anna heard the name 'Dostoevsky' so often that she called one of her kittens 'Dr Evsky', much to Roy's amusement.[14]

Lewis's visits also made a lasting impression on the nine-year-old Tess. 'Of all these people Wyndham Lewis left the clearest memories, perhaps because he was the most striking. He shed a mysterious aura about him. His dark appearance and black hat accentuated this.'[15] Lewis's 'mysterious aura' was also accentuated by his secretive manner and his paranoid sense of being persecuted. This aspect of his eccentric personality was captured succinctly by Augustus John, who alluded to one of Lewis's visits to Roy with characteristic wit in his autobiography: 'I was absent when Wyndham Lewis paid him a brief visit . . . The two seem to have passed a few hours in secret session, after which, his mission accomplished, Lewis, heavily disguised, caught his train back to Paris.'[16]

Lewis celebrated his visits to Roy in his novel *Snooty Baronet*, published in 1932, in which Roy appears as 'Rob McPhail'. Lewis wrote in this novel of the deep feelings of affinity which he shared with Roy, stating that 'the likeness of our respective ways of feeling (on a number of points) is exceedingly marked. I am astonished at the likeness. I feel towards him as I should towards a brother.'[17] On 6 April 1932, Lewis expressed a profound debt of gratitude towards his friend in the wake of the furore over *The Apes of God.*

> Lastly, always remember this. At a point in my career when many people were combining to defeat me (namely upon the publication of *The Apes of God*) you came forward and with the most disinterested nobleness placed yourself at my side, and defended my book in public in a manner that I believe no other work has ever been defended. And you can accept it as the most hundred per cent true statement that I would consider myself as the last of the ruffians, and the most ungrateful, if I ever by act or word did anything to harm or offend you.[18]

For his part, Campbell was engaged during 1931 in the writing of a monograph on Lewis, commissioned by Chatto on Lewis's recommendation that Campbell was 'the only person'[19] capable of writing it. The book would eventually be withdrawn before publication for 'contractual' reasons, but not before Roy had spent several weeks during the spring and summer of 1931 soaking himself in his friend's works, after which he expended several further weeks writing a piece of eulogistic praise. In his apparent eagerness to please his friend, he seems to have glossed over his earlier objections to aspects of Lewis's *Time and Western Man* and *Paleface*, expressed in reviews in the *New Statesman* in 1927 and 1929 respectively. The emphatic endorsement of Lewis's work given by Campbell in the unpublished monograph was clear from a letter he wrote to Sibbett while he was in the midst of researching it.

> I am convinced that Lewis is a writer of the stature of Swift; and certainly a very great thinker in deed. *The Art of Being Ruled*, *Time and Western Man*, *Paleface* and *The Diabolical Principle* are epoch-making works. Lewis sees clean through most of the cheap revolutionary machinery which predominates in all modern art and philosophy. He is a fiery fighter and a terrible antagonist – in no way inferior to Nietzsche as a polemicist. As a great comic satirical writer in his novels he is in the same class with Swift, Cervantes and Rabelais: but for the moment he is the most hated man in England. He must not be confused with his namesake D. B. Wyndham Lewis (the funny man on the Daily papers). This Lewis is a very different type – I shall send you his 'Apes of God' as soon as the new edition appears. It is the most uproarious and heroic jest – it reminds me of the Alchemist and Volpone.[20]

Roy's decision to align himself so vociferously with the 'most hated man in England' resulted inevitably in the estrangement of even more friends. Apart from Huxley, John and Plomer, the last of whom Roy had derided in a letter to Lewis as 'a proper Bloomsbury',[21] Campbell's friendship with Lewis had alienated him from the Sitwells. Edith Sitwell, in a provocative and unpublished essay on Lewis which she wrote in Paris in 1931, lamented that Lewis could invoke the 'aid and admiration' of 'noisy frothing little Mr Roy Campbell (that typhoon in a beer bottle) . . .'[22]

The collective anger of the literary establishment was exemplified by the response of the *New Statesman* to the publication of *The Georgiad*. In marked contrast to the long and laudatory reviews it had published of *The Flaming Terrapin* and *Adamastor*, *The Georgiad* warranted only two terse sentences in its column 'Brevities on Books' on 14 November 1931. Commenting on *The Georgiad* and the literati's reaction to it, a reviewer in the *Times Literary Supplement*, writing almost two decades later, could survey the scandal more dispassionately: 'It was unpardonable; but it was also undeniably funny. And what was the immediate response? From the public, laughter, mingled with some indignation: from the victims, a conspiracy of silence, a stiffening of the upper literary lip. On behalf of literary gaiety one could wish that it had been otherwise . . .'[23]

In a general sense, the reviewer in the *TLS* was right. It would have been better if *The Georgiad* had been discussed openly, whether with hostility or with the magnanimity and charity which the poem itself lacked. Perhaps, however, the 'stiffening of the upper literary lip' was sometimes justified. Vita Sackville-West suffered more than anyone from *The Georgiad*'s sneering barbs. Her poetry, particularly *The Land*, was cruelly criticized – albeit in lines which were 'undeniably funny'.

> Write with your spade, and garden with your pen,
> Shovel your couplets to their long repose
> And type your turnips down the field in rows.

Her physical appearance also came under Campbell's sadistic scrutiny, in terms almost too nasty to be humorous.

> Her gruff moustaches dropping from her mouth,
> One to the North, the other to the South,
> Seemed more the whiskers of some brine-wet seal
> Than of a priestess of the High Ideal . . .

Vita, to her credit, decided not to respond publicly. With restrained dignity she replied to a private enquiry that *The Georgiad* was 'a painful and complicated subject'. She continued with what appeared to be genuine magnanimity:

> I admire Roy's poetry enormously, and have reviewed it in the most enthusiastic terms whenever I got the chance – and so has my husband. I am afraid that there is no doubt that the whole poem is the most

> violent and muddled attack on us both – our house, our garden, our friends, and even our dogs!
>
> ... It is only fair to Roy to say that he and I did have a frightful row, and that therefore I suppose he was justified in attacking me, but he had no grievance against Harold ...
>
> However, I know he is a very queer character and I don't really bear him any grudge, and I shall continue to think of him as a very fine poet. I detest literary rows and will never be drawn into them.[24]

Vita's dismissal of *The Georgiad* as a 'violent and muddled' personal attack was evidence that Roy's deeper intentions had been lost in his vitriol. Most people saw only the spiteful abuse of his former friends, not the underlying attack on the self-gratifying philosophy of Bloomsbury or the prurience of the sex-psychology which the poem's hero, Androgyno, was sent to conquer. *The Georgiad* should have shown a mind that had gone beyond Bloomsbury; instead it merely illustrated a bitterness that had sunk beneath it.

Roy himself described *The Georgiad* as the slaying of 'a sort of psychic miasma'.[25] This has been mistakenly interpreted in Freudian terms to suggest that Roy wrote the satire as a form of self-therapy, as a means of exorcizing the 'psychic miasma' from himself. This, however, is to miss the point of the poem. Worse than that, it is to judge it by the very criteria it explicitly rejects. Contrary to such assertions, *The Georgiad* battles with the psychic miasma with which Roy believed Bloomsbury to be afflicted. It is Bloomsbury and the egocentric relativism it represents which Roy endeavours to defeat – the miasma without, not the miasma within. In the event, *The Georgiad* failed in its purpose because it spent too much time trying to assassinate individual characters. Instead of hating the sin and loving the sinner, it hated the sinner so much that it forgot all about the sin.

In the long term, the most serious wounds which resulted from *The Georgiad*'s publication were self-inflicted. Such was the shrillness of Roy's satirical voice, and such was the enmity it provoked, that his reputation never fully recovered from the damage the poem had caused. *The Georgiad*, and the persistence of the grudge which many people bore, would hang round Roy's neck like a millstone. In fact, two lines from a shorter satirical verse entitled 'The Prodigal', which Roy wrote a couple of years later, strike an aptly prophetic chord:

> The Pen is mightier than the Sword,
> But slower than the Clock.

Vita took refuge from *The Georgiad*'s fallout by indulging her increasingly reclusive tendencies. She sought solace in the gardens of Long Barn and Sissinghurst as well as in the latest of her affairs – with Evelyn Irons, the 30-year-old

Women's Page editor of the *Daily Mail.* In one of her 'diary poems' she confessed a view of pain and suffering, so apparently absent during her affair with Mary, with which Roy would have sympathized wholeheartedly – had he known. Without 'the sting of pain, of sensation', she wrote, there is nothing but a comfortable numbness, akin to nothingness. Therefore, she welcomed 'the familiar turmoil, the stinging'. She welcomed it, feared it, and welcomed her own fear of it. During the comfortable numbness, she could only conceive of 'wars, hatreds, envy' from a position of patronizing superiority. Only with the 'sudden springing and stinging of pain' could these passions become intelligible again to a soul which had previously become passionless:

> The desert of my heart has flowered again, become alive.
> I suffer, but I am glad to discover in myself that I still have the capacity to suffer.[26]

Perhaps it was from the wells of this rediscovered wisdom that Vita drew the grace to greet Roy's attack upon her with such magnanimity. Perhaps, if Roy had known that she shared his suspicions of 'Domestic Comfort' and his belief in the need for suffering, he would not have made the attack upon her in the first place. Perhaps, on the other hand, he was far too passionate ever to have made such a dispassionate judgement. Hypotheses aside, Vita's words indicate that she was well aware of the 'psychic miasma' of which she stood accused. Possibly she was in the process of slaying it herself.

Roy sought shelter from the post-Bloomsbury fallout in the place where he had always sought it – in his beloved Provence. He escaped from the sophistries and the internecine quarrels of the English literary world into the simplicity and camaraderie of his life with the fishermen of Martigues. The water-jousting team won the championship for the second successive year in 1932, and he still relished the timelessly somnambulant rituals of Provençal life. During the quiet evenings with Mary he found peace in the eternal 'storm of song' as the mistral whistled through the pine forest, or, when the wind was still, in the warm calmness of the shores by the lake where they lay together watching the moon and stars reflected in the water. The poems inspired by such moments convey the peace of mind which is so lacking in his satires.

> The night ran like a river deep and blue:
> The reeds of thought, with humming silver wands,
> Brushed by the silence like a fleet of swans,
> Sang to the passing wave their faint adieu.
> Stars in that current quenched their dying flame
> Like folding flowers: till down the silent streams,
> Swan-drawn among the lilies, slumber came,
> Veiling with rosy hand the lamp of dreams.[27]

NOTES

1 Roy Campbell, from 'Choosing a Mast', *Collected Poems, Volume One*, pp. 104–5.
2 Roy Campbell, unpublished letter to C. J. Sibbett, spring 1931.
3 Roy Campbell, letter to Enslin du Plessis; quoted in Peter Alexander, *Roy Campbell*, p. 117.
4 Roy Campbell, letter to T. S. Eliot; quoted in Peter Alexander, *ibid.*
5 *Sunday Times*, 20 April 1930.
6 *Evening Standard*, 24 April 1930.
7 Nigel Nicolson (ed.), *A Reflection of the Other Person: The Letters of Virginia Woolf, Volume IV: 1929–1931*, London: The Hogarth Press, 1978, p. 169.
8 *The Bookman*, October 1930.
9 Augustus John, *Autobiography*, p. 129.
10 Anna Campbell Lyle, *Son of Valour*, p. 54.
11 *Ibid.*
12 Roy Campbell, unpublished letter to C. J. Sibbett, spring 1931.
13 Anna Campbell Lyle, *Son of Valour*, p. 58.
14 *Ibid.*, p. 59.
15 Teresa Campbell, unpublished memoirs, p. 23.
16 Augustus John, *Autobiography*, p. 129.
17 Percy Wyndham Lewis, *Snooty Baronet*, London: Cassell & Co. Ltd, 1932, p. 182.
18 W. K. Rose (ed.), *The Letters of Wyndham Lewis*, p. 206.
19 *Ibid.*, p. 198.
20 Roy Campbell, unpublished letter to C. J. Sibbett, spring 1931.
21 Roy Campbell, unpublished letter to Percy Wyndham Lewis, late 1930.
22 Victoria Glendinning, *Edith Sitwell: A Unicorn Among Lions*, London: Weidenfeld & Nicolson, 1981, p. 83.
23 *Times Literary Supplement*, 24 March 1950.
24 Victoria Glendinning, *Vita: The Life of Vita Sackville-West*, p. 240.
25 Roy Campbell, *Light on a Dark Horse*, p. 186.
26 Victoria Glendinning, *Vita: The Life of Vita Sackville-West*, p. 238.
27 From 'Swans', *Collected Poems, Volume One*, p. 101.

CHAPTER SIXTEEN

FAMILY AFFAIRS

When sick of self my moods rebel,
The demon from his secret hell,
The eagle from his cage of brass,
They have been lent such scented wings
Over the wreck of earthly things
In silence with the sun to pass.[1]

Campbell's sense of isolation in the wake of the bitter controversy surrounding *The Georgiad* led to periodic bouts of melancholy. During these periods he did little or no work, choosing instead to spend his waking hours drinking wine with his friends in Martigues. He was in the midst of such a period when Wyndham Lewis paid one of his visits. Some time afterwards, Roy wrote apologetically to Lewis, informing him that he had made up his mind 'to stop boozing and loafing'. 'This has had a very good effect on my morale – you will find me much more alert, and ready for anything, than when you last came here. I was tired and vacillating then. It was a sort of "period" which lasted a year – I don't know if it happens with everybody (but I feel quite different now).'[2]

These 'periods', which would recur throughout his life, enabled Roy to sympathize with those of his friends who struggled with depression. In 1932 the news of Hart Crane's suicide left Roy feeling 'terribly upset' and haunted by the ghosts of guilt. He was also shocked to learn that his old friend from Oxford, Philip Heseltine, had committed suicide, and expressed his grief in a letter to Sibbett.

> I lost one of my best and oldest friends the other day in Philip Heseltine (Peter Warlock) the musician – one of the most witty, brilliant, manly, and carefree people it has ever been my luck to know. He went and put his head in the gas oven for no reason at all and committed suicide. It is the most inexplicable thing that ever happened. He was blind

> drunk at the time, which seems to me to be the only reason for his doing such a thing.[3]

Even in his deepest periods of melancholy, Roy never appears to have become suicidal. His zest for life always transcended his introspection, keeping the worst excesses of depression at bay. Indeed, in spite of his 'boozing and loafing', life in Martigues during 1932 was apparently carefree, especially when perceived through the eyes of his daughters, then aged nine and six. Tess remembers the changing seasons enjoyed in the open air. In the spring, after the winter rains, 'the earth oozed water' and the woods were full of 'crystalline pools, so clear'. Near the house were 'lush emerald cornfields' full of poppies and tulips. 'As spring advanced and the days grew hotter, some giant bushes of broom turned into a mass of burning flowers and, as one passed, the heady scent nearly made one swoon', and every year the pomegranate flowers 'burst flame-red' against the sky.

> At the end of the summer there were the 'vendanges', the picking of grapes for the wine making. Then we just picked grapes all day – bunch after bunch of golden and black grapes and put more into our tummies than into the baskets. We spent our time swallowing grapes until we felt satisfied. For about three days we ate nothing else, then we would go back to our normal diet again. Some years we joined in the wine making and drank the grape juice in handfuls from the gutters where it flowed. We always got fat in the summer because of the grapes.[4]

In the winter the Campbells would go *en famille* to Martigues, usually to a café. Roy would join in the games of lotto which the men played, usually for the game they had brought back from the hunt, and Tess recalls her father winning a large pheasant on one of these occasions. On Sunday evenings they would sometimes go to the cinema. As this was on the far side of Martigues, it entailed a long walk through three districts of the town as well as the three kilometres on the country road from Martigues to Tour de Vallier. After these family outings they would trail home with a howling and bitterly cold wind against them.[5]

'Both my parents were continually seeing beauty and pointing it out to each other and to their children,' remembers Anna. 'It was in this way that they taught us to see life and it has certainly enriched our existence to an enormous degree.'[6]

Roy's deep discomfort in the presence of too much 'Domestic Comfort' was exemplified in his attitude to Lorna Wishart, Mary's sister, who came to stay at Tour de Vallier with her wealthy husband. After they had left, Roy remarked, 'Did you notice? They never mentioned the beauty of Provence or the Etang de Berre. All they did was complain about the inadequacy of the plumbing!'[7] There is much in this seemingly insignificant incident that offers real insight into Roy's character and the key to his creativity. His impatience with those who are blinded by comfort and convenience and his yearning for a life lived in its fullness through the apprehension of beauty and the acceptance of suffering are central to any understanding of his complex character. This facet of her father's psyche is emphasized by Anna.

> Most of the great lyrics written in Provence sprang from Roy's delight in life, even those that hold an undercurrent of suffering. In modern times suffering has become something to be avoided at all costs, and yet without that good soil much beauty is lost, for beauty takes root in suffering. Perhaps that is why so much contemporary art is ugly. The 'suffering' and tortured verse of modern times results not from real suffering which is an heroic destiny, but from a denial of suffering: hence its self-pity and abject poverty. Roy had an Homeric capacity for suffering physically and spiritually, not by an anguished nihilism, but by a shining strength. Materialism rejects the concept of suffering since this is a spiritual concept. Roy was never a materialist – the very thought makes me smile.[8]

Anna believes that Roy found 'great harmony' in Provence, adding that 'its life, customs, traditions and poetry were exactly what he needed'. Provence 'contained a mixture of pagan and Christian, classical and romantic, which was so much part of Roy's personality'.[9]

When he was not working or drinking with friends in Martigues, Roy continued to spend much of his time instructing Tess and Anna in the wonders of the world. 'He gave us his own deep love for almost everything under the sun,' says Anna. 'Sometimes when he was describing to us something he loved or admired he would tremble with excitement.' Imparting to them his own contagious zest for life, he talked of birds, fish, flowers, trees, stars, constellations, clouds, races, civilizations, Greek and Latin, French and English literature.

> He never tired of recounting to us the stories he adapted from Homer, Chaucer, Rabelais and the anonymous Zulu servants of his youth . . . It was he, also, who told us about the Courts of Love and the beautiful Queen Jeanne. He told us how the great Provençal poet, Mistral, had been born at Les Beaux, among the ruins and the goats and how when he grew up, he got the French government to re-house the peasants there, so that it became once more a place of pilgrimage.

He told them of Julius Caesar, one of his great heroes, telling them that the great Roman Emperor had once lived in Provence. It thrilled him to think that Caesar had listened to the mistral, 'and he wondered whether Caesar had loved its wildness as he did'.[10]

Finding their unorthodox education so engrossing and enjoyable, Tess and Anna were always disappointed when their father began to write. They would sense an approaching spell of inspiration because he would become distracted and nervy. Then he would disappear altogether, writing all night and sleeping during the day for anything from two to six weeks at a time. 'We hardly saw him during that time since he seemed to live entirely on cigarettes and coffee. Only occasionally he would wander in to a meal, his eyes bulging with concentration, stuff a few grapes into his mouth and wander out again.'[11]

As he had done in Wales 10 years earlier when he was writing *The Flaming Terrapin*, Roy worked in a tiny attic. It was a few stairs up from the children's bedroom and Anna often woke in the middle of the night to hear her father murmuring to himself as he read out what he had just written.

> One night, when I had been frightened by the intensity of the mistral which was howling round the house and shaking the pines out of their orbits, I crept to his door and looked in. He was lying on the floor on a mattress, propped against the wall by several pillows, his pad on his bent knees, a couple of candles flickering in the draught on a chair by his head and his pen scratching away. There were books everywhere and spilt ink bottles and mountains of scribbled papers. He would write a line of a poem and then turn the page and start again until whole pads or exercise books would have one or two lines on each page, gradually lengthening to whole poems. The only material luxury he fussed about was having the correct paper, ink and special pen nibs.[12]

Anna and Tess would also know when one of these bouts of artistic absorption were coming to an end, because their father would emerge in the morning, singing cheerfully. He would hang a looking-glass on a nail outside the front door, into which he peered as he shaved off several weeks' growth of beard, singing as he did so. He was often singing, from a repertoire which included Scots and English ballads, French sailing songs, of which Anna recalls that 'the ones from Brittany were especially moving', American ragtime and popular songs from the First World War, of which 'Pack Up Your Troubles' was a great favourite.

Having missed their father during his protracted absence, Anna and Tess relished having him back. Anna recalled idyllic summer mornings, when the shadows were long on the terrace and her mother would appear at her bedroom window immediately above the front door and send a shopping list fluttering down to Roy. Then, laden with baskets and a *bonbonne* for wine, Roy, Anna and Tess would set off for Martigues to do the shopping – in a leisurely fashion. At the fish market, where all the fish were still alive and writhing in the baskets, they would select the ingredients for a *bouillabaisse*. Then, armed with fresh saffron, vegetables, fruit and wine, they would stop at Pouzol's for Roy's glass of *gros rouge* and for the children's lemonade, which they called 'pins and needles'. While Roy immersed himself in animated conversation with half a dozen friends, Tess and Anna would play round the fountain in the square, shadowed with plane trees. When they became bored of their games, they would draw Roy's attention to the time. Reluctantly, he would gather up the baskets, the mail and the wine and they would set off for home.

Much of the cooking at Tour de Vallier was done by Roy. *Bouillabaisse* was a speciality, as were *boboches*, herb-scented fish cakes and salt cod. The *boboches* were cooked on an open fire in the garden and the *bouillabaisse*, a great favourite with guests, was always tinged with garlic and hot chilli sauce called *rouille*. After eating one of these meals full of the fire of the *rouille*, Roy would joke that he could get a job as a plumber's mate because he would only have to breathe on the pipes to melt them.

Roy sometimes took Anna and Tess fishing with him in one or other of his two boats. They would set off before dawn and return with buckets and baskets full of fish, mussels and sea urchins. The sea urchins were full of golden eggs which were spread on bread and butter with lemon juice and pepper as an *hors d'oeuvre*. He also took them hunting for wild asparagus, mushrooms, dandelion leaves and pine cones, the kernels of which were used by Mary in her cakes.

While Roy took the children off on these various expeditions, Mary painted landscapes and portraits of all the family. 'Mary's ideas of motherhood were very vague,' says Anna. 'She was rather like a careless lioness. She never seemed to notice where Tess and I were, what we were doing, or whether our hair needed washing.'[13] Such responsibilities fell to Seraphine, the Campbells' maid, but when she left to get married, Tess and Anna were left to the less than tender mercies of a series of 'awful girls who read novelettes and hated cooking'.[14]

'Our mother only wanted sons,' Tess explains. 'She never wanted any daughters. And I think she would have been quite happy without children at all.'[15]

'She'd neglect us completely,' says Anna, 'and then suddenly she'd come to life and be very caring. She could be very strict and then terribly casual . . . Our parents were completely wild you know . . . They didn't care. They loved life. Life to them was absolutely wonderful.'[16]

Anna recalls her father's ability to make people laugh, a quality that endeared him to the local children:

> He used to pretend that he was being chased by a bee and pulling off his hat or cap he would pretend to fight it off, making at the same time through his closed lips the noise of loud buzzing – so that he was both bee and victim. He did this until he himself was overcome with laughter. To amuse children, who loved him always, he would paint a face on his bald head and turn his jacket back to front so that he looked terribly odd and very, very funny.[17]

He would also walk backwards into a room and perform 'all sorts of comical stunts'. This was a favourite at the children's birthday parties where Roy was in his element, drawing on an extensive repertoire of party tricks.

> He also played Peter and Jane with cigarette papers which always mystified us. And he managed to get a half-crown through a solid wooden table. How? We never found out. But the best trick was when he blackened the back of a plate with a candle. He would hand this plate to one of the guests and hold an identical one himself – then he would say, 'Do exactly what I do', rubbing the underside of the plate with a finger and stroking it across his face; of course, nothing happened but his victim had moustaches etc. Shown his face in the mirror he was astounded to find it covered with black designs. This made us hysterical . . . He loved children and especially entertaining them.[18]

He entertained his own children by reading to them aloud, particularly Hans Andersen and Edward Lear's nonsense stories. On winter nights he would bring out a large tome of Robert Burns's works and read them hair-raising passages from 'Tam O'Shanter' while the children looked on horrified at the very graphic engravings that illustrated the poem.[19]

At Christmas, Roy took a Dickensian delight in the festivities and always dressed up as Santa Claus on Christmas Eve. He liked to help the children make the crib and Anna recalled delightful moments with her father as they assembled the various figures into their allotted places.

> The Provençal crèche has many figures which do not come into the narration of the gospel, but are part of everyday life in the region. There was one chap called 'le Ravi' to whom Roy was much attached. This man leant out of a window above the stable at Bethlehem, and expressed his joy at the birth of Our Lord, by looking extremely happy. Le Ravi had no legs, but existed only from the waist upwards which was the part exposed at the window. This typically Gallic economy (or parsimony) amused Roy and led to many jokes being made, as he tried to fit the ravished legless one into his window-frame.[20]

Periodically, Tess and Anna would go to stay with their maternal grandmother in Herefordshire, where, in marked contrast to the relative austerity of life in Provence, their days were filled with an exotic opulence. Tess recalled the 'ceremonious meals – the never ending breakfasts and teas'. Grandmother Garman owned a large farm, 'with a stable boy to clean and polish the Wellingtons and shoes, a bull with a ring in its nose, cows, pigs, cart horses and carts, barns full of hay . . . fresh cream milk, butter, eggs, servants and a cook, who cooked all the English puddings'.[21]

It was during the third of these visits to Herefordshire, in 1932, that Tess and Anna learned that their parents had moved to a new, larger house called 'Figuerolles', situated a little further out from Martigues than Tour de Vallier. Roy had sent them an illustrated letter showing the house with a large spreading cedar tree in the garden. The detailed drawing also included the stone ornamental well and the marble table under two huge ilex trees, and, in the distance, Mary under a parasol, painting. Tess and Anna were both excited to have a new home and Tess kept studying her father's drawing with 'pangs of nostalgia . . . it brought back all the flavour of that warm Mediterranean country'.[22]

Tess was not disappointed when she and Anna finally returned to Provence. Figuerolles was 'a dream of a place'. Behind the house were huge cork trees. On one side were olive groves through which a path led to the lake half a mile away. In the spacious garden to the front of the house, which was dominated by the sprawling cedar, were a variety of outbuildings. Tess assembled a menagerie, including rabbits, chickens and a white goat which she named Blanchette.

> Apart from my lessons I used to spend all my day feeding and attending them. I used to milk the goat and we had milk when she didn't put her foot in it and upset it all. With the milk I used to make cheeses and put them in the sun to dry, covered with thyme and rosemary, in the proper Provençal manner.[23]

The move to Figuerolles, however, was destined to mark the beginning of the end of the peaceful existence which the Campbells had enjoyed in Provence. 'It was here at Figuerolles that life seemed abruptly to change for me,' Tess recalls. 'I no longer saw life through a child's eyes.'[24]

Part of the reason for this was the arrival of a governess, named Marie-Louise, whom Tess and Anna both despised. 'What gave her the idea of being a governess is inexplicable,' writes Anna.[25] With obvious lack of enthusiasm she went through the motions of giving the girls their lessons, but was far more concerned with the nightlife of Fos, driving there most nights to dance at the casino. By day, when the chores of teaching had been dispensed with, she sat in the olive trees:

> strumming a guitar and flirting with everyone who passed . . . She even flirted with Roy, a thing we had never seen before and which thoroughly annoyed us and made Mary send her packing . . . She was the first really worldly and materialistic person we had met and sent shivers running down our spines because she was so callous and insensitive, like a tank.[26]

It is not clear what form Marie-Louise's 'flirting' took, nor to what extent Roy responded, but the fact that Mary reacted so angrily suggests that an element of instability had once again crept into the Campbells' marriage following the move to Figuerolles. This would be exacerbated towards the end of 1932 when two beautiful women came to stay with the family. Jeanne Garman, who had married Mary's brother Douglas, arrived with her sister Lisa. Both women were unhappily married and had travelled to Provence to escape their respective husbands. Shortly after their arrival a complicated *ménage à quatre* developed. Roy and Lisa became lovers, as did Mary and Jeanne. Mary's affair with her sister-in-law lacked the intensity of her relationship with Vita and was short-lived, yet Roy's relationship with Lisa, though also short-lived, seems to have been intense while it lasted.

According to Anna, Mary insisted that Roy should sleep with Lisa – 'who was a luscious beauty' – as a means of making up to him for her love for Vita.[27] Mary's complaisance, however, may have had just as much to do with her own fixation with Jeanne. The difficulties arose when her affair with Jeanne ended, while Roy's with Lisa was still very much alive. Roy 'became a bit too involved with Lisa and Mary got jealous', writes Anna.[28] Mary's jealousy was still in evidence more than 40 years later. In a letter to Peter Alexander in July 1976, Mary dismissed both these affairs as 'very light-hearted and frivolous', yet tellingly, she described Lisa as 'fat and yielding', which was surely an indication of the remnants of bitterness that hung on from this sour episode in her marriage.[29]

The extent to which Roy was enamoured with Lisa, at least for a time, is clear from the fact that his love sonnet, 'A Sleeping Woman', was dedicated to her.[30] Mary would accept no rival as Roy's lover or muse and she insisted that he end the affair. He bowed to her ultimatum and wrote apologetically to her after the affair with Lisa had ended.

> I wrote a semi-love letter to Lisa: 'May Venus shower a 1000 blessings on her valiant little soldier' that was the worst I said but I also said I was glad and better that she had gone away (and I only sent her my *spare* love *left over from Mary*. I love only Mary hotly and fiercely).[31]

Once again the Campbells' marriage, apparently so stable in its self-contained security, had blundered into another crisis, and once again it had survived. Yet the infidelities and the jealousies they caused had been a rude awakening. It was not only Tess who sensed that 'life seemed abruptly to change' after the move from Tour de Vallier to Figuerolles. In the following year it would change even more abruptly, catapulting the hapless family from the peace of Provence to the simmering cauldron of Spain.

NOTES

1 Roy Campbell, from 'Wings', *Collected Poems, Volume One*, p. 101.
2 Roy Campbell, unpublished letter to Percy Wyndham Lewis, late 1931.
3 Roy Campbell, unpublished letter to C. J. Sibbett, spring 1931.
4 Teresa Campbell, unpublished memoirs, p. 14.
5 *Ibid.*
6 Anna Campbell Lyle, *Son of Valour*, p. 52.
7 *Ibid.*
8 *Ibid.*
9 *Ibid.*, pp. 52–3.
10 *Ibid.*, pp. 47–8.
11 *Ibid.*, p. 48.
12 *Ibid.*, pp. 48–9.
13 *Ibid.*, p. 51.
14 *Ibid.*, p. 52.
15 Teresa Campbell, interview with the author, Portugal, December 1998.
16 Anna Campbell Lyle, interview with the author, Portugal, December 1998.
17 Anna Campbell Lyle, letter to the author, 5 February 1999.
18 Anna Campbell Lyle, letter to the author, 5 October 1999.
19 Teresa Campbell, unpublished memoirs, p. 18.
20 Anna Campbell Lyle, *Son of Valour*, pp. 72–3.
21 Teresa Campbell, unpublished memoirs, p. 29.
22 *Ibid.*, p. 32.
23 *Ibid.*
24 *Ibid.*, p. 33.
25 Anna Campbell Lyle, *Son of Valour*, p. 71.
26 *Ibid.*
27 Anna Campbell Lyle, letter to the author, 2 April 2000.
28 *Ibid.*
29 Peter Alexander, *Roy Campbell*, pp. 126–7.
30 Anna Campbell Lyle, letter to the author, 2 April 2000.
31 Quoted in Peter Alexander, *Roy Campbell*, p. 126.

CHAPTER SEVENTEEN

FAREWELL TO PROVENCE

> I cannot think (so blue the day)
> That those fair castalies of dreams
> Or the cool naiads of their streams,
> Or I, the willow in whose shade
> Their wandering music was delayed,
> Should pass like ghosts away.[1]

Following the abrupt departure of their children's flirtatious governess, Roy and Mary employed the young Afrikaans poet Uys Krige as tutor to Tess and Anna. Krige proved instantly popular with the girls. According to Anna, they 'really enjoyed' their lessons and 'made rapid progress'.[2]

Krige moved into Figuerolles in October 1932, supplementing his income from the Campbells by playing semi-professional rugby for Marseilles. The combination of athleticism and aestheticism always appealed to Campbell, so it is no surprise that he took an instant liking to this rugby-playing poet from his native land. 'A young Afrikaans poet Uys Krige stays with us nearly all the time here,' Roy wrote to C. J. Sibbett early in 1933. 'We are very fond of him and I think he'll do good work.'[3]

Krige was equally enamoured with Campbell and would later write a memorable account of his time at Figuerolles.

> Roy Campbell had the essential gaiety of the true poet. A man of the sun, life to him was something splendid, something to rejoice over . . . He, more than any poet I have known, had an almost child-like sense of wonder at the beauty and abundance of life and nature . . . Without doubt his character as well as his poetry had a definite Dyonisiac quality. You always felt a little drunk in his company, but it was a mental drunkness without a hangover.
>
> There were times when one asked oneself whether his gaiety wasn't 'a gaiety transfiguring all dread' of which Yeats speaks, whether that spectacular, beautifully executed dive into a shining sky did not come from a spring-board of loneliness of which he never spoke and to

> which there are few references in his poetry . . . For me however Roy's ancient, glittering eyes were always gay . . . But he could be quiet too, and as still and lucid as a mountain pool. Humour he had in plenty. And also wit. Suddenly in the midst of all the ebullient humour he would pause and instantaneously with the sharp edge of his mind, cut a phrase, a sentence, an image or an epigram as clean as a whistle . . .[4]

In the same letter to Sibbett in which he had praised Krige, Campbell wrote of his deep love for Mary, apparently in response to Sibbett's unease at the heartlessness and harshness of *The Georgiad.*

> You asked me in your last letter after reading 'the Georgiad' if I have ever been in love. Yes I am in love with my wife and have been for eleven and a half years. I mean really passionately in love: and it is reciprocated. We are hardly ever separate day or night. We have two really superb children and a healthy farm: and we are very happy indeed apart from occasional economic anxieties as to whether our publishers have gone bankrupt etc.[5]

Even allowing for the less than candid gloss with which Campbell normally shrouded his letters to Sibbett, whose friendship was always decorous and distant, it would appear that Roy and Mary had patched up the differences that arose a few months earlier following the brief *ménage à quatre.*

More ominous was the reference to 'economic anxieties'. *Taurine Provence,* Campbell's impassioned defence of Provençal culture in general and bullfighting in particular, had received some positive reviews but had sold poorly. The proposed follow-up, *Marine Provence,* which Campbell wrote in the early months of 1933, was never published because Desmond Harmsworth, the publisher, ran into financial difficulties. Campbell's study of Wyndham Lewis was withdrawn by the publishers prior to publication early in 1933 and his new volume of poetry, *Flowering Reeds,* was largely ignored by a critical establishment still smarting over *The Georgiad.* Although there were a few exceptions, most notably a review by William Plomer in the *New Statesman* on 18 March, there was none of the widespread interest which had accompanied publication of *Adamastor* three years earlier. Campbell was convinced that the surprising silence was due to a literary boycott. This string of setbacks was exacerbated by the devaluation of the pound, reducing the value of Roy's modest royalty cheques still further. Roy and Mary were now living way beyond their means and were soon deeply in debt with the tradesmen of Martigues.

In the midst of this slide into penury, an alleged indiscretion by Mary placed further strain upon their marriage and finally ended Roy's long and troubled friendship with William Plomer. During one of Mary's irregular visits to England, taking the children to stay with her mother, she had arranged to dine with Plomer in London. This was not unusual since she and Plomer had met up during her previous visits, but on this occasion Plomer alleged that Mary had embraced and kissed him in the taxi after the meal. Alarmed and shocked, Plomer, a confirmed homosexual with puritanical sensibilities, claimed that he had disengaged himself hastily. He recounted the episode to Laurens van der Post, who passed the gossip on to Uys Krige, whereupon Krige informed Campbell. Roy was furious, firing off a bitter letter to Plomer accusing him of fabricating stories and stating that 'my relationship with Mary . . . has stuck in your gizzard like an unforgivable crime'.

> I am not temperamentally equipped to fox out your motives but they smell Freudian enough: and knowing your general hatred of women and marriage in particular coupled with your nancydom it points to a very different triangular predicament which neither of us ever suspected but about which you leave us very little option . . .[6]

Not for the first or the last time, Roy translated his abuse into verse, satirizing Plomer in 'Creeping Jesus'.

> Pale crafty eyes beneath his ginger crop,
> A fox's snout with spectacles on top –
> Eye to the keyhole, kneeling on the stair,
> We often found this latter saint at prayer.

The veiled allusion to the alleged incident that had caused such fury is found in six lines embedded in the midst of the vitriol:

> In him the 'friend' concealed the jealous 'tante'
> Who slandered women he could not supplant,
> Whose faults he would invent and then reveal
> On the pretext of trying to conceal.
> He'd blurt a secret (none so sure as he)
> By hiding it so hard that all could see.

It is implicit from these lines that Mary had denied behaving as Plomer alleged and that, moreover, the allegations were prompted by Plomer's 'Freudian' desire to supplant Mary as Roy's lover – the 'very different triangular predicament' to which Roy referred in his letter. Whatever the roots of this sordid episode, it permanently sullied the friendship between Campbell and Plomer, a severance which both men would later regret. 'It is well known how difficult it is to forgive those whom one has wronged,' Plomer wrote of this quarrel years later, adding that he and Roy had 'wronged one another and neither made enough effort to make amends'.[7]

In August 1933, in the same month that he was firing off his volley of invective against Plomer, Roy was sending a pathetic begging letter to C. J. Sibbett, reminiscent of the one he had written when he and his family had been marooned and penniless in South Africa seven years earlier.

> I . . . have got into a vicious circle of debt. I cannot move from here yet. I am being gradually sucked into the whirlpool. I have not been paid by Harmsworth for my Ms of 'Marine Provence' and am so utterly on the rocks that I don't know what to do, where to turn, and my whole family is threatened with starvation.
>
> Do you think you could be able to help me as before? I write this in an agony of terror for my little family. Such an act would double my everlasting gratitude to you and I should see that it was rewarded in posterity: and I shall repay it as soon as my big book on bullfighting appears . . . Could you manage to lend me £50? Never have I been so desperate as at this minute. If only I could shift out and get to Spain – I could keep the ground under my feet. I know of absolutely nobody who can help me. I despair of going on living. If I were only able to get out of France life could begin again for me . . . if you saw your way to helping me you would be giving a new life to me and to my three girls. I am sending this by airpost. I shall be run in soon if I don't get some cash. If you are able to spare the loan – please wire it, by cable.
>
> If it is in your power, you will be saving my life.[8]

The final, ignominious end to the Campbells' five-year sojourn in Provence came as a result of a tragi-comic incident in the autumn of 1933. Tess's goat broke through a neighbour's fence and in the course of a night destroyed a number of young peach trees. The neighbour demanded compensation, which Campbell was in no position to pay. Left with no other recourse, the irate neighbour successfully sued for a considerable sum. Roy still had no way of paying and faced the prospect of imprisonment.

Roy and Mary planned to evade the imminent intervention of the authorities by making a surreptitious escape across the border into Spain. They travelled by train to Barcelona, where they were joined a few days later by their children, Uys Krige, the French governess Thérèse, their dog Sarah, and whatever luggage they could carry between them. The necessity of leaving quickly and quietly resulted in many of their more bulky possessions, such as books, paintings and furniture, being left behind. It was, therefore, almost as refugees that the poet and his family passed like ghosts from their beloved Provence to face an uncertain future in a country on the brink of civil war.

NOTES

1 Roy Campbell, from 'Canaan', *Collected Poems, Volume One*, p. 95.
2 Anna Campbell Lyle, *Son of Valour*, p. 71.
3 Roy Campbell, unpublished letter to C. J. Sibbett, January or February 1933.
4 Quoted in Anna Campbell Lyle, *Son of Valour*, p. 80.
5 Roy Campbell, unpublished letter to C. J. Sibbett, January or February 1933.
6 Roy Campbell, unpublished draft of a letter to William Plomer, August 1933.
7 Quoted in Peter Alexander, *Roy Campbell*, p. 115.
8 Roy Campbell, unpublished letter to C. J. Sibbett, August 1933.

CHAPTER EIGHTEEN

SPAIN

Outside, it froze. On rocky arms
Sleeping face-upwards to the sun
Lay Spain. Her golden hair was spun
From sky to sky. Her mighty charms
Breathed soft beneath her robe of farms
And gardens: while her snowy breasts,
Sierras white, with crimson crests,
Were stained with sunset.[1]

Daily life in Barcelona in November 1933 was full of surreal uncertainty accentuated by real and threatened violence. The Campbells had arrived in the city at the height of the anarchist strikes that followed the right-wing victory in the recent elections. The abortive 'revolution' was at its most violent in the Barrio Chino, the prostitutes' quarter of the city, where Roy and Mary had found rooms in a tenement. 'The worst part of the "revolution" was in this and the adjoining street,' Campbell reported to Sibbett soon after their arrival. 'Machine guns were posted at every corner and we had to keep indoors after dark.'[2] At the height of the unrest a bomb exploded about 200 yards from where the Campbells were staying, shaking the doors and windows of their apartment. 'The anarchists have made their bombs so badly that they either were duds or when they did go off it was generally during their manufacture – blowing up a posse of anarchists, which discouraged them rather. The only serious tragedy was the derailment of the Seville express by a bomb.'[3]

The turbulence of Barcelona may have been a far cry from the tranquillity of Provence, but Campbell seems to have taken to the city instantly. It was 'a fine place', he wrote to Wyndham Lewis, 'full of pretty dancing girls'.[4] To Sibbett he described it as 'the strangest town I have seen, the most extraordinary clash of modern and ancient'. The city was 'seething with politics and strikes . . . For the Catalonians, as with the Irish, politics is a national industry.'[5]

Roy's relative peace of mind was due in large part to his escape from the debt-ridden mire which had bogged down his spirits during the final months in Martigues. The family were able to live cheaply in Spain, their rooms on the top floor of the large tenement building costing only 130 pesetas a week, and he rejoiced that he had 'got out of the claws of those avaricious Frenchmen'. 'I just stretch my arms and yawn with relief,' he wrote to Sibbett.[6] During the day the children played on the roof in the sun while Roy and Mary enjoyed the fine views of the city which their vantage point afforded them. They had 'all improved vastly in health' and were enjoying the 'brief interlude of town life'.[7] On most days, once the unrest had subsided, Roy and Mary went for long walks in the many parks and gardens, or for even longer walks into the countryside surrounding the city where they strolled among orange groves.

Roy's optimistic view of town life was not shared by his 11-year-old daughter. Tess recalled that the brief sojourn in Barcelona made her 'almost die of nostalgia for the country':

> . . . we who had always stepped from the front door into the woods, felt the harshness of this city life, with all its restrictions and discomforts – I felt as if I was being smothered. I used to drag our poor governess miles across the city to a hill where wild grass grew, not lawn grass like in the parks. I used to pick tufts of it and in ecstasy rub it against my face.

She and the family dog, Sarah, rolled in the long, wild grass and ran about in it 'as if we had gone mad, to the consternation of my sister and governess'.[8]

Anna shared some of Tess's nostalgic sense of loss, but she also retained some happy memories of their new life in Spain. She liked the 'novelty' of Barcelona – the flower stalls, the food, the churches:

> The quantity of churches was a surprise and the fact that they were usually full at least twice a day. Their bells were a delight. Such a variety ringing for so many different services. Such a variety of different tolls and pitches ringing all through the day for Mass, for Benediction, for the dead and for the Angelus. The Angelus ringing every six hours in memory of Our Lady and to venerate her with a short prayer was especially beautiful, especially when heard in the country at some distance from the church when the ringing of the bell was wafted across the fields giving one an ineffable sense of peace and age-old civilisation.[9]

Anna's words, written many years later and coloured by subsequent experience, illustrate nonetheless the real impact that Catholic Christianity exerted on the whole family following their arrival in Spain. The 'sense of peace and of age-old civilisation', exemplified by the Church at prayer and encapsulated most evocatively in Millet's famous painting, *The Angelus*, would emerge as a powerful stimulus to both Roy's and Mary's imagination in the following months. In particular, Mary's enduring love for the figure of St Teresa of Avila had fired her imagination for Spain since her youth. She had passed this imaginative fire on to her husband and this had contributed to their decision to make Spain their destination following their enforced departure from Provence.

Soon after their arrival in Barcelona, Mary enrolled at the local art school. In the evenings she often brought some of her fellow students back to the pension for dinner, many of whom were Jewish refugees from Hitler's Germany. Mary, who spoke German fluently, was a great source of consolation to these pitiful outcasts. 'They were half starved,' remembers Anna, 'and I saw one young lady put a leg of chicken in her handbag.'[10] These young Jews were invited to the Campbells' first Spanish Christmas, which ensured that the festivities had a truly exotic and cosmopolitan flavour. The Jews sang '*Stille Nacht*' and '*O Tannenbaum*', while a Catalonian flavour was provided by Uys Krige's Catalan girlfriend Emilia, whom Anna described as 'an exotic beauty'. No doubt under Emilia's guidance, the seven-year-old Anna danced a paso doble on the table.[11]

This particularly happy Christmas was helped by an unexpected upturn in the family's financial fortunes. 'With my usual luck just when I was bursting for funds I got a Xmas present of £20 which sets me on the rails for good,' Campbell wrote to Wyndham Lewis.[12] In the same letter he reiterated that he was enjoying the spell of town life. 'It is very restful and I find I work better for the change . . . I have at last got rid of my bloody autobiography: and shall stick to poetry for good having caught up my expenses now with plenty to spare.'

The autobiography to which Campbell referred would be published by Boriswood in 1934. Entitled *Broken Record*, it was, Campbell confessed to Lewis, 'stuffed full of lies' and should be taken 'with a pinch of salt'.[13] He had undertaken the task of writing it with extreme reluctance and for purely mercenary reasons under the constraints of financial necessity. Quite literally, he had taken the money and run – writing with little consideration for factual accuracy and in a haste of impatience at the onerous labour it required. 'I am glad, unspeakably glad, to have finished with all this filthy prose which I can't write anyway,' he wrote to Sibbett as soon as the book was finished, expressing his fear that 'my autobiography will be a fiasco'.[14] A year after its publication he would describe *Broken Record* to Laurie Lee as 'largely a spoof to confuse his enemies'.[15]

It would, however, be wrong to consider *Broken Record* merely as the work of a reluctant hack, 'stuffed full of lies'. For all its undoubted flaws, it warrants serious consideration as an exposition of Campbell's intellectual position at the end of 1933. Most notable is his attack on the retrogressive 'progressiveness' of the Bloomsbury group and the fallacious nature of the Freudianism with which its philosophy is underpinned.

> The face of our generation (headed by Strachey) for all its yelling about progress, is turned *backwards* in wrath against the father, and in hunger towards the pre-natal peace of the womb where it left its last vestiges of private property as a self, and where it would have been more dignified to remain.
>
> Freud too is always ready to presuppose any villainy on the part of children; like his master, Charcot, he always loads the dice on the side of the devil; yet he interprets almost every virtue in the terms of a vice – as if evil were the root of all creation: and as if no virtue, not even valour or generosity, were a positive quality compared with cowardice or gluttony, but rather negative, degraded, inverted or decadent forms of them. It is natural that gluttons and cowards should take them up. The modern healer, who has usually more interest in, and sympathy with, the disease than the patient, spreads about ten infections for every one he cures, and invents ten chemical poisons for every cure.[16]

Having stated that the Victorians were 'a lot of cherubs compared with "us" ', Campbell distances himself from the 'moderns' with a flourish of vitriolic contempt: 'I speak as "us" only as English critics classify me, since I don't belong either to their time or way of thinking. My ancestors cleared out of Britain at the first whiff of the nineteenth and twentieth centuries, and I only came back to see what made them clear off in such a hurry, which I soon found out.'[17]

In this latest attack on Anglo-Saxondom, Campbell describes himself for the first time as a 'Catholic', although it seems that he does so as a means of thumbing his nose at English Protestantism rather than as an affirmation of his own belief in Christian orthodoxy.

> Protestantism is a cowardly sort of Atheism, especially in the anglo-Oxfordish-Henry VIII sense. It has even betrayed great minds like Milton's, who in *Comus* attacks female virtue, reducing it to lawcourt, technical terms and destroying the idea of virtue as 'value', charm or valour, in a manner that would make Sappho, Sulpicia, Heloise and the holy Saint Teresa . . . turn somersaults in their graves.
>
> To read a few pages of Saint Teresa and then turn to this unholy

> onslaught makes one regret the wreck of the Armada and the loss of the Inquisition.[18]

As with his satire, the shrillness of tone dulls the sharpness of the point he seeks to make, but Campbell's evident preference for pre-Reformation thought, or what on the following page he terms 'traditional human values', is clear enough.

Particularly memorable is his forthright attack on the cult of youth, which he believed was responsible for much of the malaise afflicting modern thought. Citing Peter Pan, J.M. Barrie's fictional hero, as the symbolic enshrinement of the youth cult, he discusses its implications with a clarity which shines through the often ill-tempered tone.

> 'Youth' as it is in England faces back to the womb, and is an artificially inverted state, entirely retrogressive, in spite of its loud insistence on the contrary; for its two main pre-occupations are with the past, namely, the hatred of the older generation and the home-sickness for the womb, typified in the fear of growing up.[19]

This was the opposite of the concept held by the Greeks, who saw youth as 'a sort of elan, or period of growth, a forward movement' which was eager to grow in order to 'assume manhood and authority'. For the Greeks growing up was growing older, and growing older was growing wiser. Implicit in such a view was a respect for the elders of society and for those traditional values which were the safeguard of inherited wisdom.

> Modern 'youth' with a distaste for knowledge, experience or responsibility as handed out by its elders, begins to creep back to the womb, taking on the very opposite role from that of youth, as elan, acceleration, or impetus: and thereby losing the one and only quality (growth) which distinguishes youth from other states of life . . .
>
> The modern English youth can best be paralleled by the later Roman exoletes who used to castrate themselves in order to prolong the attributes of adolescence. Seneca tells us they had a horror of growing up, so *Peter Pan* is not so new as all that. Though not predisposed to this Peter Panic, I had considerable time to see it at work at first hand: and to watch the petering out of many of my friends who were so predisposed.[20]

Broken Record may have signified more clearly than ever Campbell's break with intellectual modernism, but he still had no ordered or coherent philosophy with which to counter it. Having diagnosed the disease, he was still uncertain of the cure and was left groping, with little more than fragments of a truth only dimly perceived. This groping after truth found expression in the sequence of sonnets entitled *Mithraic Emblems*, which collectively are the most obscure and oblique of all his verse.

Campbell had become interested in Mithraism in Provence, where the earliest of the sonnets were written. Relics of Mithraism, which struggled with Christianity for the hearts and minds of Europeans during the declining centuries of the Roman Empire, are scattered throughout Provence, where Christian churches are often built on the site of previous Mithraic shrines. In many respects, Mithraism, which rated strength and nobility over meekness and humility, was seen as the religion of the soldier, whereas Christianity was the religion of the slave. For Campbell, with his love for Caesar and the martial spirit of Rome Triumphant, Mithraism seemed a more natural home than Christianity. Interwoven with his preference for the faith of the warrior was his attraction to the myth, rooted in tauromachy, which lay at the heart of Mithraism. The forces of life in Mithraism are symbolized by a wild bull, the sacrifice of which by Mithras brought forth all the fruits of the earth. In Campbell's fertile imagination, the courage of the arena took on a mystical transcendence, a ritualistic re-enactment of the sacrificial miracle of life. The bullfight was more than a mere sport: it was a spiritual sacrifice.

This potent imagery, reinforced by the Mithraic worship of the light- and life-giving power of the sun, combined to form the inspiration for the sonnets. The sense of obscurity is heightened by the overlaying of other Mithraic emblems onto the fundamental fabric and design, such as the image of the raven as a messenger of the Sun God, or the snake and the scorpion as images of the hateful designs of the Evil One. Yet this array of mythical images was not enough to satisfy Campbell's mystical quest. He christens his Mithraism by the addition of specifically Catholic imagery, such as the 'seven sorrowful swords' that pierced the heart of the Blessed Virgin following the passion of her Son.

Taken as a whole, *Mithraic Emblems* displays a soul in transit. The earliest sonnets show the poet groping with an uncomprehended and incomprehensible paganism, relishing the irrational, the *obscurum per obscurius* – the obscure by the still more obscure. It is Mithraic 'truth' whispered with masonic secrecy – the affirmation of faith without reason. In the later sonnets, written after Campbell's arrival in Spain, Christianity emerges triumphant, not so much to vanquish Mithraism as to make sense of it. The towering influence of St John of the Cross, the great Spanish poet and mystic who was a friend and ally of St Teresa of Avila, emerges as a herald of divine revelation.

The woods have caught the singing flame
in live bouquets of loveliest hue –
the scarlet fink, the chook, the sprew,
that seem to call me by my name.
Such friendship, understanding, truth,
this morning from its Master took
as if San Juan de la Cruz
had written it in his own book,
and went on reading it aloud
until his voice was half the awe
with which this loneliness is loud,
and every word were what I saw
live, shine, or suffer in the Ray
whose only shadow is our day.

In this sonnet, the sun is no longer a god to be worshipped, but only a symbol of the Son, the true God, who gives the sun its meaning and its purpose. The Mithraic emblem is transfigured into a Christian emblem.

The figure of St John of the Cross emerges in the sonnet sequence as a surrogate St John the Baptist, preparing the way for the coming of Christ. At the end of the sequence Mithras himself speaks, confessing that he, the god identified with the sun, is but a servant of the one true God.

. . . We work for the same Boss
though you are earth and I a star,
and herdsmen both, though my guitar
is strung to strum the world across!

Mithras serves the same God as does the poet, the God who won His victory on the Cross,

under the stretched, terrific wings,
the outspread arms (our soaring King's) –
the man they made an Albatross!

The final sonnet, addressed 'To The Sun', is the poet's unequivocal affirmation of Christian faith.

Oh let your shining orb grow dim,
Of Christ the mirror and the shield,
That I may gaze through you to Him,
See half the miracle revealed . . .

The 23 sonnets which comprise the *Mithraic Emblems* clearly represent the story of a spiritual conversion. Beginning with the seeds of Mithraic uncertainty planted in Provence, the soul's transformation would finally bear

Christian fruit in the fertile, faithful soil of Spain. Indeed, it is likely that their arrival in Spain was crucial to the conversion of both Roy and Mary. 'My parents were romantics,' says Anna. 'They saw life, they saw Spain, through a romance. They saw it through a cloud, a sort of imaginary Spain.'[21]

Roy's intoxication with Spain was evident in a letter to a friend in Provence soon after his arrival in Barcelona.

> This town is quite amazing. What vitality this race has! The cafés, two or three to every street, are always crowded. The town is dominated by the Tibidao mountain on which shelters the ancient monastery of Monserrat which is reached by a terrifying funicular . . .
>
> Besides the noise of the trams, musical bands, church bells, street vendors . . . there is the chatter of machine-guns and an occasional bomb. We appear to have arrived in the middle of a revolution.
>
> Uys and Mary and I went last night to hear the gypsies sing. We fell under the spell of Cante Hondo – I remember you telling me how much you like Flamenco.
>
> How immensely rich Spanish literature is! I am reading Gongora, an extraordinarily modern poet though he lived between 1561 and 1621. He gave rise to the word *Gongorismo* meaning, as far as I can make out, an accentuation of all the characteristics that distinguish Baroque art. He reminds me of Mallarmé but is far greater. And Quevedo, what a satirist! Did you know that Cervantes was also a poet? I always thought he was one of us . . .[22]

'The impact of Spain on Roy was profound,' writes Anna. 'He was quite unprepared for this impact, this deep new experience, and it had a lasting effect. The romantic in his personality was stirred and awakened . . .'[23]

Evidence of this impact was provided many years later by Roy's robust defence of Spanish culture in *Light on a Dark Horse*, his second volume of autobiography.

> Protestants go to these countries for spiritual fresh air, yet . . . they ascribe the attraction, which is really that of the Church and the people who have not been amputated from the Church by force of tyrants like Henry VIII, or crooks like Calvin and Luther – to the climate or the landscape, or to anything else save in the culture and civilization which hold them spellbound. They always consort with the malcontents also. They have not the courage to disown what is wrong in themselves. They would sooner join with atheists and diabolists . . . than with anything straightforwardly European or Roman, though they will hang around a place like Spain for whatever by-products of the Catholic faith they can pick up buckshee, without any responsibilities – the courtesy, hospitality, and nobility of the people.

> From the very beginning my wife and I understood the real issues in Spain. There could be no compromise . . . between the East and the West, between Credulity and Faith, between irresponsible innovation (which catches all 'intellectuals' once they have been hereditarily derailed) and tradition, between the emotions (disguised as Reason) and the intelligence.[24]

It is clear from this uncompromising defence of the Catholic faith that Roy thought he had found in Catholicism the antidote to the 'psychic miasma' which he had sought to confront, somewhat inarticulately, in *Broken Record* and *The Georgiad*. The Church to which he was about to offer his allegiance was very much the Church Militant, waging war on the intellectual modernism which he despised. Until their arrival in Spain, he and Mary had been 'vaguely and vacillatingly Anglo-Catholic . . . but now was the time to decide whether . . . to remain half-apathetic to the great fight which was obviously approaching – or whether we should step into the front ranks of the Regular Army of Christ'.[25]

NOTES

1 Roy Campbell, from 'Posada', *Collected Poems, Volume One*, p. 158.
2 Roy Campbell, unpublished letter to C. J. Sibbett, late 1933.
3 *Ibid.*
4 Roy Campbell, unpublished letter to Percy Wyndham Lewis, late 1933.
5 Roy Campbell, unpublished letter to C. J. Sibbett, late 1933.
6 *Ibid.*
7 *Ibid.*
8 Teresa Campbell, unpublished memoirs, p. 36.
9 Anna Campbell Lyle, *Son of Valour*, p. 75.
10 *Ibid.*, p. 76.
11 *Ibid.*
12 Roy Campbell, unpublished letter to Percy Wyndham Lewis, January 1934.
13 Roy Campbell, unpublished letter to Percy Wyndham Lewis, November or December 1933.
14 Roy Campbell, unpublished letter to C. J. Sibbett, late 1933.
15 Laurie Lee, *As I Walked Out One Midsummer Morning*, London: Andre Deutsch, 1969, p. 154.
16 Roy Campbell, *Broken Record*, pp. 153–4.
17 *Ibid.*, p. 155.
18 *Ibid.*, p. 157.
19 *Ibid.*, p. 157
20 *Ibid.*, pp. 159–60.
21 Anna Campbell Lyle, interview with the author, Portugal, December 1998.
22 Roy Campbell, unpublished letter to Count Frederic de Fremenville, late 1933.
23 Anna Campbell Lyle, *Son of Valour*, p. 77.
24 Roy Campbell, *Light on a Dark Horse*, pp. 316–17.
25 *Ibid.*, p. 317.

CHAPTER NINETEEN

THE SON ASCENDANT

The towers and trees were lifted hymns of praise,
The city was a prayer, the land a nun:
The noonday azure strumming all its rays
Sang that a famous battle had been won,
As signing his white Cross, the very Sun,
The Solar Christ and captain of my days
Zoomed to the zenith; and his will was done.[1]

By the beginning of March 1934 Roy and Mary were growing tired of the 'brief interlude of town life' in Barcelona. The latent threat of political violence and the close proximity of the prostitutes in the brothel quarter of the city forced them to question the suitability of a tenement building in the Barrio Chino as a place to bring up their two daughters. They began to share Tess's desire for a return to the countryside where they could eke out their income, which still consisted primarily of the monthly allowance of £20 a month from South Africa, by growing some of their own food.

Parting company with Thérèse, their children's French governess, and with Uys Krige who had decided to stay on in Barcelona with Emilia, Roy and Mary piled themselves, their daughters, their luggage and their dog into a third-class compartment bound for Valencia. It was in Valencia, having been forced by their dwindling funds to take a squalid room in an even more sordid area than the one they had sought to escape, that Roy and Mary had one of the most violent quarrels of their married life. Anna, who had just celebrated her eighth birthday, recalled this 'terrible row' vividly. She remembered her father 'lying on the bed in a stupor from drink, fully clothed', while her mother 'railed at him to stand up'. Although Anna recalled that there was often tension between her parents at the end of the month if the money from South Africa was late in arriving, she and Tess were taken aback by the sheer verbal violence of this particular quarrel, which culminated in Mary threatening to leave her husband. 'This is the first time that I remember them having a quarrel. It went on for several days.'[2]

Eventually the storm clouds were dispersed by the arrival of the South African money and by Roy winning 1,000 pesetas, then worth about £17, on the national lottery. The family left Valencia and headed south along the coast to look for a home. In May 1934, after days of fruitless searching, they discovered the village of Altea, near Alicante. Squeezed between the mountains and the sea, it was in those days unspoilt by tourists.

The family stayed for a week at the local inn, the Fonda Ronda, before moving into a small peasant house which they rented until they found a larger one, set on a few acres of land about a mile out of the village. Here, surrounded by scrubby olive trees and orange groves, the family once more settled down and began to enjoy the rustic stability that had been lacking since their departure from Provence. They bought a donkey to carry their supplies up the rough and dusty track from the village, and to fetch water from a nearby spring in large containers slung in panniers. Campbell's relief at the rediscovery of this rural idyll was expressed in a postcard to Wyndham Lewis.

> I seem to have got into heaven – with no debts, nothing annoying or troublesome. But I had a fierce time of it for some months. I have had formidable good luck. Now I have got a little farm to myself and I breed pigs and donkeys which I hope to sell to the British public as poets. This place is a bloody paradise and we are all happy.[3]

His contentment was also evident in a letter to John Greenwood, the publisher who had produced *The Georgiad* and *Broken Record*.

> Until today I haven't seen a peseta since April 24th: and I had to give the postman a fowl for my last stamp to you. I live entirely on my farm and what it produces . . . Beyond my rent I have no other expenses and believe I have at last found the way to deal with the crisis – i.e. by living without any cash at all.[4]

The peaceful asceticism of their life in Altea provided the backdrop to Roy's and Mary's conversion to Catholicism. 'I don't think that my family and I were converted by any event at any given moment,' Campbell wrote later. 'We lived for a time on a small farm in the sierras at Altea where the working people were mostly good Catholics, and there was such a fragrance and freshness in their life, in their bravery, in their reverence, that it took hold of us all imperceptibly.'[5]

The final decision to be received into the Church was taken by Mary. Shortly after their arrival in Altea, she announced abruptly, 'I'm going to become a Catholic.'

'Well, kid,' her husband replied without hesitation, 'if you're going to I will too.'[6]

They presented themselves to Father Gregorio, the village priest, and requested instruction. The priest, with disarming simplicity, was delighted that a whole family of 'English' were being won over to the Church.

Initially, Tess was confused by this sudden change of heart on the part of her parents. 'But last year Daddy was calling priests "black beetles" and now we are to revere them!' she complained to her sister.[7] Tess's confusion was rooted in the implicit Protestant prejudices which she and Anna had inherited from their parents and from their protracted visits to Grandmother Garman in England. 'I remember the heated discussions my sister and I had with the French and Spanish children about their sinful priests and superstitious ways. We were champion Protestants against the corrupt Catholic Church. Still, the change came suddenly when our mother led us gently into the Catholic Church, just a few months after our damning and slanging it.'[8]

In practical terms, their parents' decision entailed a great deal of effort on the part of Tess and Anna. Their instruction required them to learn the whole catechism and all the prayers in Spanish. This 'tremendous task' was achieved through their attendance at the village catechism classes for about a year, where they mixed with all the other children of the village. Anna, still only eight years old, was far less confused by developments than her adolescent older sister.

> I took to religion like a duck to water. I liked all its manifestations, dogmas, mysteries and commandments, not realising at that tender age what this entailed. I even liked the catechism, but this was probably due to the fact that I memorised it more quickly than my fellow-catechumens . . . and we had to be word perfect in the question and answer of the catechism:
>
> 'Who made you?'
>
> 'God made me.'
>
> 'Why did he make you?'
>
> 'To love, worship and obey Him in this world and to be happy with Him forever in the next.'
>
> All this seemed to make great sense . . .[9]

Clearly the decision by Roy and Mary to be received into the Church was destined to reverberate through the lives of the whole family. According to Tess, it had 'a profound influence on all our lives and filled an abysmal vacuum'.[10]

For Mary, the decision was the fulfilment of a long-standing but previously subconscious spiritual desire. 'My mother's life was insufficient spiritually,' writes Tess.

> In joining the Catholic Church she found infinite satisfaction and consolation. She had already got the notion of her conversion, years before, when she read St Teresa of Avila's autobiography . . . She had a mystical streak to a high degree – this came naturally to her . . . Her great discovery . . . after her conversion to Catholicism, was the tabernacle in Catholic churches where the Body of Christ remains permanently present. It was there, near the tabernacle, that my mother could spend hours absorbed and it was there that she found satisfaction and consolation.
>
> After my mother's conversion to Catholicism at Altea . . . she started going to Mass every day . . . She walked to the village church about two kilometres away, before breakfast. From then on, all through her life, she went to daily Mass and Communion, unless prevented by illness, or travelling, or some other insurmountable difficulty. Even in difficult circumstances she would nearly always find her way to a church and Mass.[11]

Roy would never be as devout as his wife in terms of Mass attendance, but his conversion of heart and mind was as deep and as genuine, a fact which is expressed clearly in the verse he wrote at this time. Many of the sonnets in *Mithraic Emblems* were written at Altea. During this period he also wrote 'The Fight', one of his finest poems, in which he pours out the fervour of his Christian conversion, and describes the interior struggle which led him to it. In the poem, 'the fight' is being waged for the poet's soul and is depicted as an aerial dogfight.

> One silver-white and one of scarlet hue,
> Storm-hornets humming in the wind of death,
> Two aeroplanes were fighting in the blue
> Above our town: and if I held my breath,
> It was because my youth was in the Red
> While in the White an unknown pilot flew –
> And that the White had risen overhead.

Clearly the struggle is not merely between belief and unbelief, but between the poet's new and previous self. His youth, scarlet with sinfulness and red with the political atheism he had rejected, was at war with a new force in his life – the 'white', symbolic of the Mithraic unity of the spectral colours and also of the dimly discerned purity of Christ, the 'unknown pilot'. The red craft, the former self, is finally shot down so that the white can emerge triumphant, a 'white phoenix' rising from the ashes of 'his scarlet sire'. The final verse is a joyous hymn of thanksgiving for the poet's deliverance, paying homage to the victory of the 'Solar Christ', the Sun and Son Ascendant.

> The towers and trees were lifted hymns of praise,
> The city was a prayer, the land a nun:
> The noonday azure strumming all its rays
> Sang that a famous battle had been won,
> As signing his white Cross, the very Sun,
> The Solar Christ and captain of my days
> Zoomed to the zenith; and his will was done.

Campbell's conversion confirmed him in his love for Spain, which he later described as 'a country to which I owe everything as having saved my soul'.[12] Mary shared his deep-rooted affinity with the Spanish landscape, people and culture and they began to explore the countryside surrounding Altea together. In the autumn of 1934 they began to make long hikes into the mountains where they discovered remote villages, perched precariously on steep hills, which were so inaccessible that it seemed time and changing customs had passed them by. The lives of the villagers were centred solely on the feasts of the Church and the changing seasons of the year, a slow and serene lifestyle which appealed to Roy's Luddite tendencies. Anna believes that her father's natural aversion to rampant industrialism and the worship of science was the underlying reason behind his love for the ordered lives of the Spanish peasants, whose traditions he found 'absorbingly interesting'.

> Spain was the first country he had visited which had not come under Protestant influence and its appeal for him lay in its still being a pastoral society long after most European countries had become industrialised. His dislike of machinery was instinctive – he never learnt to drive a car or use a typewriter. People often argued with him about this – he was not 'progressive' they said; but industrialisation, as he saw it, was inimical to man. People pointed out that without the tractor, for instance, you could never feed the population of the world, to which he answered, 'You are putting the cart before the horse, it is only since the Industrial Revolution that the world has become over-crowded . . .'[13]

Campbell's aversion to industrialization found creative expression in 'Rust' and 'Junction of Rails: Voice of the Steel', two poems written at around this time. The first describes how the omnipotent rust of time shall bring the best-laid schemes of the industrialists to nothing.

> See there, and there it gnaws, the Rust . . .
> Shall grind their pylons into dust.

The same over-riding theme animates the latter poem. The modern city with its artificial, glamorous surface, and its 'smile of golden teeth' masking the smoke and dirt it produces, is compared with the timeless beauty of the moon and stars.

> Cities of cinemas and lighted bars,
> Smokers of tall bituminous cigars,
> Whose evenings are a smile of golden teeth –
> Upon your cenotaphs I lay this wreath
> And so commend you to the moon and stars.

The final verse of 'Junction of Rails' echoes the imagery in 'Rust', prophesying the eventual victory of time over 'progress'.

> A sword is singing and a scythe is reaping
> In those great pylons prostrate in the dust,
> Death has a sword of valour in his keeping
> To arm our souls towards the future leaping:
> And holy holy holy is the rust
> Wherein the blue Excaliburs are sleeping!

This tension between the perennial human spirit and the ravages of 'progress' was not a new theme in Campbell's work. One of his earliest African poems, 'The Serf', had prefigured the climax of 'Junction of Rails'.

> The timeless, surly patience of the serf
> That moves the nearest to the naked earth
> And ploughs down palaces, and thrones, and towers.

Now, however, the prophecy is given a specifically Christian character as Campbell incorporates the *Sanctus* of the Mass – 'holy holy holy' – as a means of sanctifying the rust of post-industrial resurrection. In this he was echoing the similar juxtaposition of Christian prayer motifs which T. S. Eliot, himself a recent Christian convert, had employed in 'The Hollow Men' and 'Ash Wednesday'.

Apart from their love for the lifestyle of the peasants in remote villages, Roy and Mary were also charmed by the warm-hearted friendliness of their neighbours in Altea. From the outset they had been made welcome by the local people, who called on them in relays bringing presents, including vases of geraniums, beautifully woven baskets full of oranges, lemons and tangerines, sacks of almonds, great earthen jars of drinking water from a healing spring called the Fountain of St Ana, newly baked loaves and baskets of artichokes which they taught them to cook in a variety of inventive ways.[14]

It was, therefore, as fully accepted and integrated members of the local community that the Campbell family enjoyed their first Holy Week in Altea in the spring of 1935. 'The whole village and its neighbourhood lived through the Passion of Our Lord,' says Anna. The statue of Our Lady of Sorrows was carried through the streets between rows of barefoot penitents carrying candles. This was followed by the figure of Christ with His great cross. Drums were beating and someone howled a *saeta*, a piercing cry representing the heart being pierced by the arrow of pain. 'It was all incredibly moving and we were transported back through the centuries to the greatest drama of all time.'[15]

'Next came the glorious Saturday of Resurrection – this after forty days of real fasting was indeed a day for rejoicing,' Anna recalls. 'All was music, flowers, bells, sung Masses and the wearing of new dresses for Easter.' Easter week was dedicated to pilgrimages into the surrounding countryside for festivities 'full of song, laughter, the ripple of a guitar' and general merry-making as groups gathered to eat and drink beneath the trees.[16]

In May 1935, shortly after the Easter festivities, Roy's mother came to stay for several weeks. Depicted by Anna as 'stern Granny Campbell', she had taken to touring the world in the years since her husband's death and had recently been to China and America. She was, Tess recalled, very influenced by her stay in the United States and was 'very up-to-date and had gadgets for everything'.[17] Accustomed to wealth and luxury and addicted to modern conveniences, she was shocked by the austerity of her son's existence. 'The simplicity and poverty of our life completely astonished her,' says Tess.[18] She was horrified to find that there was no running water and no roads to the house, so that the water had to be fetched along paths which were just wide enough to lead a donkey. She looked on in disbelief as the donkey was led through the house each night to the stall at the back. Worst of all were the threadbare clothes worn by her son, daughter-in-law and grandchildren. She went on several shopping expeditions to Alicante, where she bought them all new clothes and shoes. She was highly critical that a girl of Tess's age was not suitably attired and promptly bought the 12-year-old her first suspender belt and stockings.

This meddling may have been harmless enough, even praiseworthy, but Grandmother Campbell's insistence that Tess be sent to school in England would have many repercussions, not all of which would be beneficial. 'Tess and I were appalled at the thought of being separated,' says Anna, 'and in fact it was a fateful decision.' Anna is convinced that 'Tess's complexes and traumas', destined to afflict her in later years, were rooted in this period of separation and it is certainly true that Anna, who was very dependent on her older sister, would miss her terribly in her absence. Years later, Anna remained convinced that her grandmother's reasoning had been wrong.

> Granny did not approve of our easy-going way of life; neither was she impressed by our schooling which was profound but unorthodox. Tess and I had been attending the village school where we learnt to write Spanish ... We now knew how to read and write in three languages but, alas, we did not know how much coal England exported every year which to Granny's way of thinking was a necessary part of education.[19]

Roy, however, bowed to his mother's wishes. She was, in Anna's opinion, the great love of his life after Mary, and he loved carrying out her orders. He even gave up red wine during her stay in deference to her wishes. 'He had much respect for her and even a certain amount of awe.'[20] It was decided, therefore, that Tess should accompany her grandmother to England and that Roy and Mary would forsake their rural idyll for a Spanish town, where their younger daughter could get a 'proper education'.

Apart from what she perceived as her son's abject poverty, the other aspect of Roy's lifestyle which frankly shocked and mystified his mother was his conversion to Catholicism. 'Granny Campbell was rather taken aback by our conversion to the Catholic Church,' says Anna, 'and she thought we had been inveigled into taking this step by Roman Machiavellianism.'[21] Unable to believe that anyone could reasonably submit to Rome, she was also mystified by many of the Catholic devotions in the district. One of these was the tradition of taking the Holy Family in a glass case from house to house, where it stayed for a week in each. The household whose turn it was to have this honour would take great pains to prepare an altar for the Family's reception. The best linen and the prettiest flowers were arranged and the whole family gathered there in the evening to say the rosary and sing hymns. Shortly after Granny Campbell's arrival, it was the turn of the Campbell household to receive the Holy Family. Anna innocently told her grandmother that the Holy Family was coming to the house that night. 'What child!' she exclaimed in utter bewilderment. 'What on earth are you saying?'[22]

Early in June 1935 the Campbells departed for Madrid with Roy's mother. In the capital, Roy, Mary and Anna said their farewells to Tess, who left for England with her grandmother. They then proceeded to Toledo to see if it was a suitable place to settle. Roy fell in love with the ancient city with its narrow streets adorned with numerous churches, monasteries and convents, and they decided that this was destined to be their new home. They returned to Altea to pack up.

All this time they had been receiving instruction from Father Gregorio and on 24 June, two days before their departure, all three were finally received into the Church, being rebaptized and remarried in the process. Most of the population of the village turned out for the ceremony and the party which followed it. Father Gregorio, with the same disarming simplicity with which he had expressed his joy at their initial request for instruction, declared that it was the best day of his life. The peasants of the village, all of whom were also their friends, wept openly and embraced the converts.

Significantly, Roy chose St Ignatius Loyola, the militant Spanish soldier who founded the Jesuits, as his patron saint. With equal significance, Mary chose Mary Magdalene, probably the most famous penitent in history.

Roy's delight at his reception into the Church was evident in a letter he wrote to Enslin du Plessis on the following day: 'At last I am in the land of my dreams! . . . Yesterday I had the good fortune to be baptised and married in the Catholic Church. I wish you the same luck.'[23]

Years later, writing in his autobiography, he could look back on the eventful day with undiminished gratitude.

> . . . and the valiant but rather uneducated priest of Altea (who was none the worse for that) gave us a new baptism as Catholics, and re-married us in the Catholic Church, so we started life completely from scratch, all over again, to the envy of all the peasants who lived for miles around: and to our own delight. From then on I went monogamous, and never regret it.[24]

A few months later, when Mary became a Carmelite Tertiary, she destroyed on the advice of her spiritual director all the passionate love letters which Vita Sackville-West had written her between 1927 and 1929.[25] For husband and wife alike, reception into the Catholic Church heralded a fresh start.

NOTES

1 Roy Campbell, from 'The Fight', *Collected Poems, Volume One*, p. 156.
2 Anna Campbell Lyle, *Son of Valour*, p. 81.
3 Roy Campbell, unpublished postcard to Percy Wyndham Lewis, 1934.
4 Roy Campbell, letter to John Greenwood, end May 1934; quoted in Peter Alexander, *Roy Campbell*, p. 151.
5 Quoted in Matthew Hoehn, OSB (ed.), *Catholic Authors: Contemporary Biographical Sketches 1930–1947*, Newark, NJ, USA: publisher?, 1948, p. 104.
6 Peter Alexander, *Roy Campbell*, p. 150.
7 Anna Campbell Lyle, *Son of Valour*, p. 86.
8 Teresa Campbell, unpublished memoirs, pp. 40–41.
9 Anna Campbell Lyle, *Son of Valour*, pp. 86–7.
10 Teresa Campbell, unpublished memoirs, p. 41.
11 *Ibid.*, pp. 41 and 128.
12 Hoehn (ed.), *Catholic Authors*, p. 104.
13 Anna Campbell Lyle, *Son of Valour*, pp. 84–5.
14 *Ibid.*, p. 82.
15 *Ibid.*, p. 87.
16 *Ibid.*
17 Teresa Campbell, unpublished memoirs, p. 41.
18 *Ibid.*

19 Anna Campbell Lyle, *Son of Valour*, p. 88.
20 *Ibid.*
21 *Ibid.*, p. 89.
22 *Ibid.*, pp. 89–90.
23 Roy Campbell, letter to Enslin du Plessis, 25 June 1935; quoted in Peter Alexander, *Roy Campbell*, p. 156.
24 Roy Campbell, *Light on a Dark Horse*, p. 320.
25 Anna Campbell Lyle, *Son of Valour*, p. 37.

CHAPTER TWENTY

SACRED CITY OF THE MIND

> And high above the roaring shells
> I heard the silence of your bells
> Who've left these broken stones behind
> Above the years to make your home,
> And burn, with Athens and with Rome,
> A sacred city of the mind.[1]

Roy's reception into the Catholic Church would confirm his alienation from the secularist ascendancy in British literature which was still centred on Bloomsbury. The reaction of his former friends and present enemies in the Bloomsbury group can be gauged by Virginia Woolf's horrified response to T.S. Eliot's acceptance of Anglo-Catholicism several years earlier. On 11 February 1928 she wrote to a friend:

> I have just had a most shameful and distressing interview with dear Tom Eliot, who may be called dead to us all from this day forward. He has become an Anglo-Catholic believer in God and immortality, and goes to church. I was shocked. A corpse would seem to me more credible than he is. I mean, there's something obscene in a living person sitting by the fire and believing in God.[2]

There is little doubt that Roy's and Mary's submission to Rome would have elicited similar sneers of contempt. Roy, already dead in the eyes of Bloomsbury, could now be considered well and truly buried.

Roy's conversion would also serve to distance him still further from the new generation of young left-wing poets such as Stephen Spender, W.H. Auden, Louis MacNeice and Cecil Day-Lewis. In October 1934 Spender had written dismissively in the *Spectator* that Wyndham Lewis's criticism of Virginia Woolf showed 'a great deal of malice' and that his admiration for Campbell's *The Georgiad* 'does little credit to his taste'.[3] Lewis's reply, published on 2 November, complained that Spender's double standards were 'absurd': 'Anyone has a right to their opinion of the books of Mrs Woolf –

as also of those of Mr Roy Campbell: though both these rights are denied me by Mr Spender. To admire Mr Campbell's books "does little credit to one's taste," I am told: whereas *not* to admire overmuch those of Mrs Woolf is simply "malicious".'

Ironically, Campbell's conversion would alienate him from Lewis, his greatest champion, as well as confirming his 'reactionary' status in the eyes of Woolf, Spender *et al.* He was not, however, alone in his embrace of Christianity. Since the start of the century a host of leading literary figures had accepted the Christian creed, constituting what could legitimately be termed a Christian literary revival. These included G. K. Chesterton, Maurice Baring, R. H. Benson, Ronald Knox, Compton Mackenzie, Alfred Noyes and, more recently, Graham Greene, Evelyn Waugh, T. S. Eliot and C. S. Lewis.

Campbell's own position *vis-à-vis* the rising generation of left-wing poets spearheaded by Spender and Auden was made clear in January 1935 in an article published in South Africa. The arguments he elucidates are particularly significant, not only as a curtain-raiser to the long-running battle he would have with Auden, Spender, Day-Lewis and MacNeice over the next two decades, but also as an exposition of the volatile political cocktail which he was concocting and which would embroil him in new bouts of controversy in the coming years.

> The artist as romantic 'rebel' is the tamest mule imaginable. He dates from the industrial era and has been politicised to play into the hands of the great syndicates and cartels first by dogmatising immorality, breaking up the 'Family', that one defensive unit that has withstood the whole effort of centuries to enslave, dehumanise and mechanise the individual, thereby cheapening and multiplying labour. It is the 'Intellectual' who has been chiefly politicised into selling his fellow mates to capitalism, whether the capitalism be disguised as a vast inhuman 'state' or whether a gang of individuals. Science has also been politicised in this racket. The profound discoveries of Freud, for instance, he has unscrupulously politicised to the same end – popularising, by his bedside manner, what inherited human wisdom discourages with a blast of bawdy laughter. Freud as Pathologist has spread more infection than he has cured: it gives him more power: he is like a doctor in an epidemic (his own epidemic): and he has contributed more to debase the self-respect of the individual and mechanise it than anything else. The last century has seen more class-wars, and wars between generations, than any other period. They have been deliberately fostered by capitalism, of which bolshevism is merely an anonymous form. 'Divide and rule,' said Cato: 'encourage your slaves to quarrel and your authority will be supreme.' A thousand

> artists and reformers with the highest ideals have leaped ignorantly and romantically into these rackets, and by means of carrying hate between man and woman, father and son, class and class, white and black, almost irretrievably embroiled the human individual in profitless, exhausting struggles which leave him at the mercy of the unscrupulous few.[4]

Campbell's words here should be seen in the light, or the darkness, of the political vortex which was stirring Europe into a hate-filled frenzy during the 1930s. This vortex was played out in microcosm in Altea in the months before the Campbells finally left for Toledo when they were befriended by two Norwegians, one a 'communist' and the other a 'Nazi'. Roy recounted the story in his autobiography.

> At this time there turned up two very charming, convivial Norwegian writers, Helge Krog and Erling Winsnes. Helge was a Communist and Erling was a Nazi, but they were both staunchly united in their hate of Christ and Christianity . . . These men were like children; they would argue violently and then totter up, helping each other from side to side, lovingly to bed. Oh! If only people could take their politics as lightly and boozily as Norwegians![5]

One can imagine the many heated discussions between Campbell and these two Scandinavians, in which the newly converted Christian endeavoured to defend Christ and the Church from the attacks of left and right alike.

From the very beginning, Campbell's faith was inextricably linked to politics – and his politics became increasingly linked to and coloured by his love for Spain. Few have understood better than his friend Lawrence Durrell the importance to Campbell of this potent trinity of influences – religious, cultural and political. Durrell explained that he 'was simultaneously happy and saddened' when Roy told him that he had become a Catholic: 'happy for him, sad because I myself could not participate . . . But Roy had taken from Spain the brocades and the dust of the bull-ring and how can anyone penetrate to the heart of Spain without embracing the faith which animates its brutal vivid life? It was totally right for him – "a second motherland".'[6]

Yet Durrell was wrong when he wrote that 'his politics became a faith'. It would be much truer to say that Roy's faith became his politics. In being received into the Church, Campbell had grafted himself onto Catholic Spain and his politics thereafter would be determined by his desire to defend Catholic Spain from its enemies. In fundamental political terms, he perceived the Church as the defender of the integrity of the family against those 'rebels' who sought the family's disintegration. The 'Heart of Rome' and 'hearth and home' were one and indivisible. This axiomatic principle which blossomed in Altea would come to fruition after the Campbells' arrival in Toledo at the end of June 1935.

Roy and Mary had fallen in love with Toledo at first sight. The small city of fewer than 30,000 people, clinging doggedly to the steep sides of the gorge of the Tagus, its houses huddled reassuringly under the walls of the great fortress of the Alcazar, seemed to ooze tradition. It resonated with the spirit of its glorious past when, under the Holy Roman Emperor Charles V, whose arms were still emblazoned in stone on its Visagra gate, the city had been the capital of Spain at a time when Spain was the bulwark of Christendom. The city had changed very little over the centuries, treading warily through present-day realities in its preference for the seclusion of memory over the uncertainties of progress. It was full of hidden plazas that had been Moorish market places, medieval fortifications, fifteenth-century palaces and numerous churches, shrines, seminaries, monasteries and convents, all linked by the narrowest and steepest of streets on which donkeys trudged with timeless nonchalance. It was as though the city had been specially created for souls in self-imposed exile from the modern world – souls such as Roy and Mary Campbell.

Its impact on Roy in particular was both immediate and immense. Toledo may have captivated Mary, but it enraptured Roy, becoming for him 'a sacred city of the mind'. 'Good Lord, kid,' Roy exclaimed to Mary when they first arrived, 'this town is fabulous! I never imagined it would be so marvellous! Let's stay here for the rest of our lives.'[7]

Since Toledo was bulging with religious buildings, including two cathedrals, and since the Alcazar served as one of Spain's leading military academies, every other person seemed to be a monk, nun, priest, seminarian or soldier, of every rank and hierarchy. Anna recalled that her father was 'almost too enthusiastic over the town', soaking up the atmosphere of military and religious discipline that permeated every aspect of its life. 'Its strong, nostalgically evocative historical and literary associations overwhelmed him,' and he went about for the first few months 'in a state of mental and physical intoxication'.[8] Clearly Toledo had cast its spell on Roy as it had on the Austrian lyric poet Rainer Maria Rilke, who had written of the city's mystical beauty in one of his letters from Toledo: 'My God, how many things have I loved because they tried to be like this, because they had a drop of this blood in their hearts . . . Can I bear it?'[9]

'But it was not only Toledo itself that had this effect on my father,' writes Anna, 'it was the whole of Spain – its architecture, its painting, its language.'

> . . . what affected him most profoundly was to find a country where tradition still exercised a civilising force on the population. He was

> deeply affected by the mystery and spiritual strength of this surprising country. Obviously in Toledo he was suffering from culture-shock. Spanish culture had opened up a vast new vein of gold in the fabulous mine of the arts, and he found it intoxicating. His excitable nature was trying to take it all in at one go and it gave him a sort of feverish indigestion. He was immersed in the works of Gongora, Quevedo, Calderón, Lope de Vega, Fray Luis de Leon, Teresa of Avila and John of the Cross; immersed also in the paintings of Goya, Velazquez (his favourite) and El Greco – who lived and died in Toledo.[10]

Anna also believes that her father was fascinated by the Spanish people themselves and their conversation, 'so prolific in proverbs, puns, irony and fatalism'. Then she adds, in words reminiscent of her father's own vitriolic contempt for modern trends, that she is referring to a Spain that existed before the age of mass tourism and 'sameness' – 'when every country had its own personality and variety. Before, in fact, mob rule.'[11]

Mary was similarly, if more mildly, intoxicated by Toledo. In the afterglow of her conversion she was caught up in the passionate embrace of the city's spiritual heritage. It was here that St John of the Cross had been imprisoned by the Inquisition; here also that her heroine, St Teresa, had founded one of her Discalced Carmelite convents. Every morning she attended early Mass at the Carmelite monastery, whose gardens could be seen from the garden of the house the Campbells were renting, and in the evening she went to Benediction at the Carmelite convent, 'where the ever-hidden nuns sang like angels'.[12]

Swept along with enthusiasm for her new-found faith, and with Carmelite spirituality in particular, Mary decided to become a Carmelite Tertiary. In joining the Third Order of the Carmelites she was taking on a rigorous commitment to lengthy daily prayer, as well as other penances and disciplines, which she fulfilled dutifully for the rest of her life. Referring to the little office book which Mary used daily for the next 42 years, her daughter remarked that it was a 'complete mystery how she could say this long prayer every day'.[13] She trained herself to fulfil this daily task by saying it in stages throughout the day, early in the morning and sometimes late at night, 'but it was always said'. When, years later, Tess asked her mother why she subjected herself to this rough treatment, Mary answered that 'the more serious the illness, the more severe the treatment'.[14]

Roy was never tempted to subject himself to anything as harsh in the service of his faith and, as often as not, when Mary was on her knees in front of the Blessed Sacrament in church, he was seated outside a café imbibing wine and conversing with the local people he had befriended. Sunday was the exception. Roy, Mary and Anna would always spend the whole of Sunday together, attending High Mass at the great Gothic cathedral, dressed in their best clothes. Anna retains vivid memories of those High Masses, celebrated in the old Latin rite with three officiating priests in beautiful vestments. Incense and music combined in sensual splendour as the organist filled the vaults of the great building. When the choir sang Palestrina's *Missa de Angelis*, 'we were truly uplifted to a world where, for a time, art and the worship of God were joined in perfect harmony'.[15]

Every evening, Roy, Mary and Anna would make their way to the Plaza de Zocodover, the main square of Toledo, where Anna would invariably be bought a large ice cream while her parents enjoyed their evening aperitifs. At that hour of the day the square came to vivid life for the *paseo*. Girls in their best dresses and immaculate make-up strolled to and fro, arm in arm, receiving elaborate whispered compliments, known as *piropos*, from the youths who walked in the opposite direction, while their parents watched from seats at the café tables. Meanwhile, barefoot gipsy women in voluminous ankle-length skirts strolled about haughtily while their husbands, leaning on tall sticks, watched everything with narrowed eyes.

It was on one such hot summer's evening in 1935, not long after the Campbells had moved to Toledo, that an ostentatious stranger disrupted the regular evening ritual at the Plaza with renditions of Schubert's *Lieder* on his violin. There was a startled silence as the promenading youths stopped to gaze at the young man, who was so sunburnt, Anna remembered, that he looked like 'a blistered lobster' with great streamers of skin hanging from his face.[16] This odd-looking arrival, every inch the Englishman abroad, was Laurie Lee, later to achieve fame as the author of popular volumes of evocative autobiography such as *Cider with Rosie* and *As I Walked Out One Midsummer Morning*. In the latter he offers a memorable account of his meeting with Roy and Mary Campbell in Toledo.

When Mary discovered that the violinist was an Englishman, she invited him to join them at their table. Roy introduced himself to Lee as 'a South African poet . . . reasonably well known in your country' before proceeding to express his derision of England and his opinion that English literature was an unburied corpse. He was living in Spain, he explained, because England no longer had any 'manhood'. Assuring the young Englishman that none of this was intended personally, Roy asked whether Lee was short of funds and whether he needed any help. He then explained that it was his saint's day, which dates the meeting as 31 July, and that he and his wife were dressed in the saint's honour and were drinking his health. He invited Lee to join him in a glass of wine, which the young traveller readily accepted. Lee wrote later:

> I was more than satisfied by this encounter, which had come so unexpectedly out of the evening, pleased to have arrived on foot in

> this foreign city in time to be elected to this poet's table. All things were as they should be – the artist in exile, generous and defiant in mood, his red eyes glittering like broken glass as the phrases came stumbling forth ... I felt the glory of the Word around me, and accepted the stature of the man without surprise, imagining all poets to be made like this.[17]

Mary asked Lee whether he liked risotto and, assuring him that there was more than enough to go around, invited him home for supper. Having eaten alfresco on the patio and being sufficiently mellowed by several bottles of local wine, the two men settled down to talk into the early hours. Roy recited some of his poetry, intoxicating his young admirer with his verse as he had with his wine. Roy's 'thick trembling voice' was 'curiously moving', Lee recalled, 'and nothing could have suited me better at that hour, and at that place and time in my life'.

> I was young, full of wine, and in love with poetry, and was hearing it now from the poet's mouth. It came out in agony, bruised yet alive, and each line seemed to shake his body. He read some of his shorter poems: 'Horses on the Camargue', 'The Sisters', 'Choosing a Mast', and the words seemed to flare at the nostrils, whinny and thunder, and rise like steam in the air.
>
> Half-dazed with sleep, I felt my eyelids falling, printed with succulent images: sisters called to their horses, naked in the dark, and met them with silken thighs; a rich Zulu nipple plugged the mouth of a child; mares went rolling beneath the hooves of stallions ... What had I read till then? – cartloads of Augustan whimsy; this, I felt, was the stuff for me.

As the wine flowed, Roy ended his recital and began to 'talk and gossip ... of his friends and enemies ... boasting of quarrels, feuds and fights'. Famous names were paraded before the wide-eyed 20-year-old as Roy recounted his life as dramatically as he had recited his poetry. T.S. Eliot, A.E. Coppard, Wyndham Lewis, Augustus John, Marie Corelli, Jacob Epstein, T.E. Lawrence, the Sitwells ... One by one they were held up for scrutiny and subjected to exaggerated anecdote.

Lee stayed with the Campbells for a week, sleeping on a mattress propped up by books in a small room off the patio. Roy showed him around Toledo, taking him to the Museo de San Vicente to see El Greco's *Annunciation*, but most of the time was spent in cafés and bars drinking wine or brandy with the locals, who treated Roy 'as a poet and man of their own'. In the evenings, Roy would sometimes sing the Jacobite ballads he had learnt as a child or else converse with humility about his poetry, expressing amusement that

Edith Sitwell had recently suggested he would make a likely Poet Laureate. At other times, especially after the wine had flowed in considerable quantities, his emotions would fluctuate between the loves and hates of his life. He would praise God, the Virgin Mary and Mary his wife, or else he would punch out satirical couplets aimed at his enemies.

During the daylight hours when Roy was either sleeping or lying low, Lee observed Mary and Anna 'in an intimate calm of their own, quietly busy with their spiritual chores'. In the mornings they left for Mass, 'veiled and modest as shadows, and so native in appearance that when I met them in the street I often forgot and addressed them in Spanish'. They returned transformed, 'light-footed and chirpy . . . and their eyes sparkling, as though they'd been to a party'. Anna recalls Lee as 'charming' and 'very good looking', adding that he 'flirted with Mary and me'.[18]

One hot afternoon, after Roy had staggered off for his customary siesta, Lee and Mary talked of religion. Lee, casting his eyes over the crucifixes decorated with knots of jasmine hanging on the walls, spoke with carefree jauntiness of his unbelief.

> But Mary Campbell, soft-voiced and shining-eyed, reproved me with gentle calm. And in her, for the first time, I saw the banked-up voluptuousness of a young and beautiful convert, holding to this single passion in which all hungers were answered and all doubts quietly put away . . .
>
> It may also have been the first, and most dangerous, time – as I sat with the poet's wife through that hushed afternoon, watching her finger her beads in the airless shade – that I felt the pull of that seductive faith.
>
> But I argued against it – at that age I wanted action, not the devout pause before some deferred consummation; I wanted the excitement of doubt, the satisfaction of mortality, the freedom to make love here and now on earth. Beautiful Mary would have none of it; she sat among her pin-up ikons, smiling quietly, unshakeably contained. 'Don't you see?' she kept saying . . . 'You can't imagine the utter peace . . .'

On the day that Lee finally departed from Toledo, Roy accompanied him to the bridge by which he would cross the gorge of the Tagus. They said their farewells and Roy told him to write if he found himself short of money and assured him that he was always welcome to return. Looking back on his stay with the Campbells across the chasm of more than three decades, Lee recalled with fondness and gratitude that he had been treated 'with a matter-of-fact kindness which surprised and charmed me . . . I'd arrived from nowhere, but nobody bothered me with questions; I was simply accepted and given the run of the house.'[19]

Laurie Lee's impressions of the kindness and hospitality he had received from the Campbells were a reflection of the hospitality and kindness that Roy and Mary had discovered among the people of Toledo. Roy's gratitude and love for those who populated the sacred city of his mind was expressed in his poem 'Driving Cattle to Casas Buenas'.

> The church, with storks upon the steeple,
> And scarcely could my cross be signed,
> When round me came those Christian people
> So hospitably clean, and kind.
> Beans and Alfalfa in the manger –
> Alfalfa, there was never such!
> And rice and rabbit for the stranger.
> Thank you very much!

Little could Roy and his wife know in that shimmering summer of 1935 that the peace they were enjoying was the calm which precedes the storm, nor that their gratitude would be turned so quickly and dramatically to grief.

NOTES

1 Roy Campbell, from 'Toledo, July 1936', *Collected Poems, Volume One*, p. 153.
2 Quoted in Walter Hooper, *C. S. Lewis: A Companion and Guide*, London: Fount/HarperCollins, 1996, p. 25.
3 Stephen Spender, review of *Men Without Art* by Percy Wyndham Lewis, *Spectator*, 19 October 1934.
4 Roy Campbell, 'Uys Krige: A Portrait', *The Critic: A South African Quarterly*, Cape Town, Vol. 3, No. 2, January 1935; reprinted in Roy Campbell, *Collected Works IV: Prose*, p. 268.
5 Roy Campbell, *Light on a Dark Horse*, pp. 320–21.
6 Alister Kershaw (ed.), *Salute to Roy Campbell*, p. 26.
7 Anna Campbell Lyle, *Son of Valour*, p. 90.
8 *Ibid.*, p. 93.
9 Quoted *ibid.*
10 *Ibid.*, p. 94.
11 *Ibid.*
12 *Ibid.*, p. 95.
13 Teresa Campbell, unpublished memoirs, p. 127.
14 *Ibid.*, p. 128.
15 Anna Campbell Lyle, *Son of Valour*, p. 101.
16 *Ibid.*, p. 96.
17 Laurie Lee, *As I Walked Out One Midsummer Morning*, pp. 145–6.
18 Anna Campbell Lyle, letter to the author, 7 July 2000.
19 Laurie Lee, *As I Walked Out One Midsummer Morning*, pp. 145–55.

CHAPTER TWENTY-ONE

TERROR IN TOLEDO

Of all that fearful fusillade
I reckoned not the gain or loss
To see (her every forfeit paid)
And grander, though her riches fade,
Toledo, hammered on the Cross,
And in her Master's wounds arrayed.[1]

Late in 1935 Campbell's recurrent spinal injury returned with a vengeance. Recuperating in hospital, he wrote 'The Mocking Bird' and 'Christ in the Hospital'. In the latter poem, describing his body as 'scarcely better than a broken stick', and his spine as running through him 'like a rusty sword / Rasping its meagre scabbard to the quick', he sympathizes with the figure of the 'bloody Christ' hanging from a crucifix in the hospital ward.

Great Albatross, of every storm the Birth! –
His bleeding pinions bracketed a Night
Too small for His embrace; and from his height,
As from an Eagle's, cowered the plaintive Earth!

Campbell's use of the albatross and the eagle to symbolize the outspread arms of Christ in His passionate embrace of a heedless and plaintive humanity is indicative of his contented and untroubled faith during the months in Toledo. His poems from this period are resplendent with images of the Solar Christ as the Son Ascendant or of Christ gliding majestically and ever-watchfully like a bird of prayer. Months later, after Spain had been plunged into bloody civil war, the imagery would emerge again in 'La Mancha in Wartime'. This time it is the shadow of a hovering kestrel that makes the sign of the Cross on the blood-stained landscape.

The kestrel, and the stationary mill
That sail-less hangs upon the tide of war,
Had not this one significance before
With which their merest shadow signs the hill.

The spectre of the approaching war, passing like a silent assassin through cities like Barcelona or Madrid, where political killings and bombings had become commonplace, had thus far ignored sleepy Toledo. This began to change following the electoral victory of the Popular Front, an alliance of various left-wing parties, on 16 February 1936. One of the first acts of the Popular Front government was to release all those who had been imprisoned after the abortive communist and anarchist revolutions in Madrid and Barcelona in October and November 1934.

Within weeks of coming to power the new government meted out repression for repression, banning the Falange, its principal rival. The whole country seemed to be descending into an ever-worsening spiral of political violence, with street fighting between supporters of Right and Left becoming ever more vicious and widespread.

The Church became a target for the socialists and anarchists. Churches were desecrated and burnt all over Spain. Inevitably, the anti-clerical contagion spread to Toledo, where there was a series of violent riots in March 1936 in which churches were burnt and priests and monks attacked in the streets. During these bloody disturbances, Roy and Mary sheltered several of the Carmelite monks, disguised in lay clothes, in their house. 'My parents had become great friends with two of the Carmelite monks who lived in the monastery above our house,' explains Anna. 'We often saw the community of monks walking about in their lemon orchard and they would wave to us, down in the corral, as we set off on our horses.'[2] Roy and Mary grew particularly fond of Father Evaristo and Father Eusebio. 'They were both cultured and intelligent men, but Eusebio, the younger of the two, had such an understanding and angelic nature that he appealed greatly to Roy's heart.'[3]

The anti-clerical riots shattered Roy's perception of Toledo as a pastoral paradise beyond the ravages of time. It seemed that even the sacred city had succumbed to secularism and that he and Mary, refugees from modernity, were once more without refuge.

Roy's relations with many of his former friends among the townsfolk became increasingly strained as those with anti-clerical sympathies learned that he and Mary had sheltered the monks. Even before the elections, Roy had received an ominous warning from a local bar-keeper that he would be shot when the time came, 'if you are still here and haven't been bumped off by anyone else'.[4] The warning almost became reality on 16 March when Roy was accosted by two assault guards, the politically inspired police force established by the new government, while he was out riding. After questioning him belligerently, they beat him severely before parading him through the town *en route* to the police headquarters. Roy recalled the incident in verse:

I never felt such glory
As handcuffs on my wrists.
My body stunned and gory
With toothmarks on my fists:
The triumph through the square,
My horse behind me led,
A pistol at my cutlets
Three rifles at my head:
And four of those Red bastards
To hold one wounded man
To all the staring rabble
Proclaiming thus my clan.[5]

This verse was dedicated to a gipsy friend with whom Roy had been riding that day, 'Mosquito' Bargas, who was murdered by the same assault guards only minutes before Roy's own arrest. It is likely that Roy was only spared the same fate because he was a foreigner.

While Roy was being cross-examined by the police, Mary arrived at the headquarters and, in Roy's words, 'rushed in, lovely, furious, and ready, if need be, to die'.[6] Refusing to leave until she had secured her husband's release from custody, she accompanied him home and helped wash the blood from his battered face. This latest rude awakening to the changing realities in Toledo led Roy to fire off a dramatic letter to his publisher.

> I am rushing this off to you, as I have twice been put against the wall. The handwriting is very bad; I am sorry, but I have been so hit with rifle butts that my hands don't work . . . I am sending this now in case I get bumped off . . .
>
> For some reason I collect more blows than Don Quixote. God knows why! for I am amicable to everybody. But I have been run in twice, for *nothing*! . . . Really bolshies make me laugh. 'Liberty'? It is *death*![7]

In the following weeks the situation worsened. Portraits of Marx and Lenin were posted on every street corner and horrific tales began to filter in from surrounding villages of priests being shot and wealthy men being butchered in front of their families. Toledo's beleaguered Christians braced themselves for the next wave of persecution and the Campbells, in an atmosphere which must have seemed eerily reminiscent of the clandestine gatherings of early Christians in the catacombs of Rome, were confirmed in a secret ceremony, before dawn, by Cardinal Goma, the elderly Archbishop of Toledo and Primate of Spain.

In the midst of the slide into anarchy, and with Tess having recently rejoined the family after her year in England, Roy began to fear for the future safety of his wife and daughters. 'Kid, there's going to be a shemozzle here,' he told Mary. 'Let's get out.' Mary refused. With a bravery bordering on recklessness, she continued to walk ostentatiously to Mass every morning, brandishing her missal and mantilla almost as tokens of defiance. Sometimes she would find herself confronted by grinning *pistoleros* drawing their fingers threateningly across their throats as a promise of what awaited her 'come the revolution'. In his autobiography, Roy wrote that he had forbidden Mary to attend Mass so brazenly, fearing that her life was in danger. 'But she was so kindled and elated by our new faith, that she disobeyed me . . . She was right, I was wrong. Better a broken head than a broken spirit every time! . . . this valiant and beautiful woman walked through the streets in her mantilla with her missal, carrying her life, like a little bird, in her hand.'[8]

Many of those who loitered threateningly around the churches were newcomers to Toledo, drafted in from Madrid or elsewhere, but one was a friend of the Campbells' maid and was known as 'El Ranero', or 'the frogman'. Long before the February election which heralded the onset of anarchy, Anna recalled that El Ranero would visit the maid, normally while Mary was at church and Roy was in one of the local taverns, and would boast of the terrible things he was going to do when the revolution came.

The fear which these words struck into the heart of the nine-year-old Anna was heightened by the grotesqueness of El Ranero's appearance. 'This ill-favoured Frogman carried wherever he went, reeds from the river on which were strung the lower halves of innumerable frogs reminiscent of the buttocks and dimpled legs of naked babies.'[9] These edible frogs were caught by him at night with the aid of an acetylene flare from a punt on the Tagus and would be hawked round the town, flayed and hanging from the reeds, during the day. One morning, as Mary made her way to church, El Ranero pushed a reed full of dangling frogs' legs into her face and said, 'That is what you and your famous daughters will look like after we have raped and killed you.'[10] 'Later,' wrote Anna, 'he was responsible for many terrible murders for which he had a natural aptitude due, no doubt, to his unusual profession.'[11]

As Spain lay parched beneath the summer sun, it was clear that the whole country was like a dry powder keg, requiring only the smallest spark to ignite it into open civil war. That spark was provided by two political assassinations on successive days in Madrid. On 12 July Lieutenant José Castillo, a key figure in the training of communist militia units, was shot dead by four Falangists as he left home. In the early hours of the following morning a group of assault guards seeking revenge arrived at the apartment of the monarchist leader Calvo Sotelo, who was the de facto leader of the parliamentary opposition. On being arrested, he promised his family that he would telephone as soon as he was able, 'if these gentlemen do not blow my brains out'. In fact, the assault guards did just that, shooting him at point-blank range in the back seat of the car before dumping his body at the gates of a cemetery.

The assassination of the leader of the parliamentary opposition seemed to signify the breakdown of any semblance of democracy in Spain. Four days later the military, under General Franco, rose against the Popular Front government. On 17 and 18 July, army garrisons all over Spain and Morocco seized, or attempted to seize, power in the major towns and cities. They were successful in Morocco and Seville, but were defeated in Barcelona and Madrid. In Toledo the presence of the military academy in the Alcazar ensured that the army could assume power with little or no opposition. Apart from isolated skirmishes at night, and occasional sniper fire at the soldiers stationed in the main square, there was comparative calm. On the evening of 20 July, peasants from the surrounding villages who supported the military uprising and who sought the army's protection began to arrive in the city. Whole families, together with all the possessions they could carry, gathered in the shadow of the Alcazar seeking refuge from the coming storm.

On the morning of 21 July, Roy and Tess were watering their horses and mules when the peace was shattered by the rattle of rifle fire. In the distance, a column of government militiamen from Madrid, headed by four armoured cars, was advancing on Toledo. They began engaging in heavy fire with the Toledo garrison, which had declared itself that very morning to be openly in revolt against the Madrid government.

Roy and Tess hastened back to the shelter of the house, remaining there with Mary and Anna as hostilities intensified. The arrival of the column from Madrid had encouraged government supporters inside the city, who began sniping at the men from the garrison. In the afternoon and evening government aircraft carried out bombing raids on the Alcazar. The people of Toledo huddled in their homes, not daring to venture out onto the deserted streets.

After dark, the Carmelite monks called on the Campbells. Once again they were seeking their assistance. This time, however, they were not seeking refuge for themselves but for their priceless archives, which included the personal papers of St John of the Cross. Campbell agreed to take possession of these precious archives and that night a heavy trunk of ancient documents was transported secretly from the Carmelite library to the hallway of the Campbells' house.

The battle for Toledo continued the following morning. Another air raid on the Alcazar was followed by a bombardment of the fortress by a battery of government guns on the hills to the north of the city. Heavily outnumbered and outgunned, the defenders of the city began to fall back towards the

Alcazar. That afternoon, they fought a fierce rearguard action against the advancing Madrid militiamen. Street by street the battle raged, much of it very close to the Campbells' home, but by the following day the Toledo garrison under Colonel Moscardo had been forced to withdraw to the ancient fortress, where they were besieged by the troops from Madrid. The siege of the Alcazar, destined to become known throughout the world in the following weeks and destined to acquire immense symbolic significance to the unfolding of the war, had begun.

Without the soldiers of the garrison to defend them, the priests, monks and nuns fell prey to the hatred of the militiamen. The 17 monks from the Carmelite monastery were rounded up, herded into the street and shot. Their final moments were conveyed to the Campbells by a friend who informed them of the heroism of their friend and confessor, Father Eusebio. 'It was he who kept up the spirits of his fellow-monks when they were all dragged out to be shot,' writes Anna. 'They died heroically. A friend of ours who was with them to the end, said that Father Eusebio was smiling when he fell shouting "Long live Christ! Long live Spain!"'[12]

Campbell discovered the bodies of the murdered Carmelites, left lying where they fell, under a sheet of tarpaulin when he ventured out that evening. His decision to leave the house was taken against the advice of the rest of the family, who were understandably concerned for his safety. 'We felt very apprehensive when we saw him leaving the relative safety of our walled garden,' says Anna. 'I was convinced that we would never see him again.'[13] Their relief when he returned was tempered by the horrific nature of his news. Apart from the murdered Carmelites, Roy informed them that the Maristas, another order of priests, were also still lying in the narrow street where they had been murdered. Swarms of flies surrounded their bodies and scrawled in their blood on the wall was written, 'Thus strikes the Cheka.'[14]

Roy had more shocking news to recount to his family. In the square outside Toledo's town hall, the Madrid militia had lit huge bonfires which were constantly restocked with crucifixes, vestments, missals and any other religious items discovered in looted churches or private houses. Roy then shepherded Mary and his daughters to the back of the house and showed them the Carmelite library which had been set ablaze. By this time Mary, Tess and Anna were in tears, but Roy tried to console them with the thought that, at that very moment, their friends were in heaven, 'something we believed with all our hearts', and that they still had the Carmelite archives and a chance to save them for posterity.

Confronted with such horror, it is little wonder that Roy began to see the conflict in Spain as something which transcended politics. It was deeper than the struggle for temporal power. It was not a fight between fascism and communism, but between Christ and the Antichrist – a fight to the death between good and evil, God and the Devil. The imagery of physical and metaphysical conflict resonates throughout the verse inspired by the terror in Toledo. The great iron cross on the Carmelite monastery roof, which was silhouetted against the flames as the rest of the monastery buildings burned to the ground, became a supernatural symbol of defiant resistance:

> Toledo, when I saw you die
> And heard the roof of Carmel crash,
> A spread-winged phoenix from its ash
> The Cross remained against the sky.[15]

Similarly, in 'Hot Rifles', Toledo's suffering is conjoined with the suffering of Christ. The city is 'hammered on the Cross / And in her Master's wounds arrayed'. In 'Christ in Uniform' Toledo's martyred defenders have welded 'a single heart of fire' with the bleeding heart of 'Christ, our Solar Sire'. In 'The Carmelites of Toledo' the political creed of 'might is right' is countered with the spiritual power of the blood of martyrs:

> And well might Hell feel sick and sorry
> To see the brown monks lying dead,
> Where, as with coarse tarpaulins spread,
> Each seemed a fifty-horsepower lorry
> That to the troops had brought the Bread!
>
> Their wounds were swords – how bravely worth
> The care the angels took to smith them!
> We thought they took their victory with them
> But they had brought it down to earth,
> For it was from their neighbouring spire
> The proud Alcazar caught the fire
> Which gave that splendour phoenix-birth.

At the height of the terror the Campbells were visited by a search party of militiamen who were passing from house to house looking for 'priests, fascists and other enemies of the people'.[16] Fearing such an intrusion, Roy and Mary had previously taken the precaution of removing all crucifixes and religious pictures from the walls. Their main fear was that the trunk containing the Carmelite archives would be discovered. The search, however, was not particularly thorough. At one stage some of the militiamen even leaned their rifles on the trunk without thinking of opening it.

The trickiest moment arose when one of the men noticed a volume of Dante's *Divine Comedy* among Campbell's books. 'Italian,' he announced in disgust to his comrades. 'Fascist!' In different circumstances such ignorance would have been amusing, but in the sadistic climate prevailing in Toledo in July 1936, the moment of misunderstanding could have been deadly. With admirable presence of mind, Roy quickly referred the militiamen to volumes by Gogol, Dostoevsky and Tolstoy. 'All Russians,' he insisted reassuringly. 'Ah Russians . . .' they responded, suitably mollified. Convinced that no 'enemy of the people' would own books by Russians, the comrades passed on to their next hapless victims. The Campbells and the Carmelite archives had survived unscathed.

Roy and Mary were always convinced that their lives had been saved miraculously on this occasion, a belief which would have been reinforced had they been aware of the full extent of the butchery in Toledo during the weeks following the occupation of the city. According to a contemporary commentator, 'practically all the well-to-do were shot . . . The rough rule appears to have been this: that anyone who had employed a servant in the house or more than two workers in his business, merited death. There were exceptions: not many.'[17] Since the Campbells were relatively affluent in Toledo, due in part to the generosity of Roy's mother, and since they employed two housemaids, they could easily have been shot for being 'rich', regardless of the fact that they were known to be Catholics who had earlier sheltered the Carmelites.

Clearly, even though they had survived this time, the Campbells remained in a potentially dangerous predicament. They had little food, apart from cucumbers picked from the garden under cover of darkness, and no means of obtaining the money needed to escape. During the day they were forced to shelter in the gloomy passage of their house as the militias intensified their shelling of the besieged defenders of the Alcazar. Their position was desperate and seemingly insoluble. It was then that fate or providence once again took a hand. Angel Monico, a young communist whom Campbell had befriended some months earlier, arrived at the Campbell house carrying a paper bag containing 3,000 pesetas tied in bundles. Monico explained that he had been the sole witness to the murder of an elderly man, possibly a priest, by a militiaman. The militiaman, seeing that he was being observed by Monico as he searched his victim's pockets, endeavoured to buy Monico's silence by dividing the bundles of banknotes he had taken from the murdered man. Monico had decided to offer the money to Campbell and his family so that they could make their way to the British Embassy in Madrid. Roy and Mary, believing the money to be a godsend and Angel well named, accepted it gratefully.

With Monico's help they managed to procure a safe passage out of Toledo by bribing some militiamen to give them a lift in the back of a lorry used for conveying corpses. Eventually, by long and tedious stages, they made their way to Madrid and then to Valencia. In every village *en route* they saw burnt or burning churches, a grim reminder of the madness gripping the country they had learnt to love but were now being forced to flee. They did not know it then, but a few miles along the coast at Altea the kind and simple parish priest, Father Gregorio, had been murdered by militiamen sent from Valencia, his faithful parishioners powerless to protect him. Spared a similar fate themselves, Roy, Mary, Tess and Anna boarded the HMS *Maine*, bound for Marseilles, on 9 August 1936.

NOTES

1 Roy Campbell, from 'Hot Rifles', *Collected Poems, Volume One*, p. 153.
2 Anna Campbell Lyle, *Son of Valour*, p. 104.
3 *Ibid.*
4 Roy Campbell, *Light on a Dark Horse*, p. 326.
5 From 'In Memoriam of "Mosquito", my partner in the horse-trade, gipsy of the Lozoya Clan', *Collected Poems, Volume Two*, p. 23.
6 Roy Campbell, *Light on a Dark Horse*, p. 344.
7 Roy Campbell, letter to John Greenwood, April 1936; quoted in Peter Alexander, *Roy Campbell*, p. 161.
8 Roy Campbell, *Light on a Dark Horse*, p. 339.
9 Anna Campbell Lyle, *Son of Valour*, p. 95.
10 Roy Campbell, *Light on a Dark Horse*, pp. 339–40.
11 Anna Campbell Lyle, *Son of Valour*, p. 95.
12 *Ibid.*, p. 104.
13 *Ibid.*, p. 111.
14 *Ibid.*
15 From 'Toledo, July 1936', *Collected Poems, Volume One*, p. 153.
16 Anna Campbell Lyle, *Son of Valour*, p. 111.
17 G. McNeill-Moss, *The Epic of the Alcazar*, London: Rich & Cowan, 1937, pp. 150–51.

CHAPTER TWENTY-TWO

'BOLSHEVIK BINSTED'

And, since I was not sent with foreign cash,
Like some, to spread the bolshevistic rash,
Able both to explain the 'Spanish Worker'
From the inside, as to expound the Shirker,
The Communist, whose bungling Left we fight
With this Right hand – in every sense the Right![1]

HMS *Maine* was full of refugees fleeing Spain, among them Robert Graves and Laura Riding, whom Campbell had targeted satirically in *The Georgiad*. Roy was delighted to meet up with two fellow poets, forgetting that he had previously looked upon them as literary enemies, and Graves and Riding seemed happy to accept Roy's apology for his treatment of them. A cordial relationship developed, although Graves recorded privately that Campbell was 'full of coloured lies', describing him as a 'half-crazy schoolboy'.[2] Graves and Riding travelled with the Campbells from Marseilles to London, via Paris, but their friendship apparently did not extend beyond the journey. Ten years later, on the eve of Graves's return to Mallorca, Campbell sent a message, 'God speed', to which Graves replied, 'Tell him to go to hell: I can do without his good wishes.'[3]

During the voyage to Marseilles, Graves had grown fond of Tess and Anna, whose dishevelled appearance elicited his sympathy. 'Fine stuff; poor girls,' he wrote.[4] Others were less sympathetic. Anna recalled that she had tried to make friends with two 'very prim and proper' English girls playing on deck. The younger of the two started to talk to her happily enough until her sister intervened. 'No, Jane,' she said, 'don't talk to her, she is poor.' Anna was devastated. 'My God, how this hurt. It was far worse than the battle of Toledo. I felt a deep, dark pain round my heart.'[5]

Tess's recollections of the voyage were somewhat different from those of her 10-year-old sister. Almost 14 by then, she remembered the Royal Navy officers appearing like 'supermen or angels . . . so serene, tall, fair, in their immaculate white, summer uniforms'. They were 'so blue-eyed, disciplined, beautiful and perfect after all the chaos, poverty, misery we had left behind'.[6]

The Campbells arrived in London on 11 August to a blaze of media interest. The battle of Toledo and the siege of the Alcazar were making international headlines and the fact that the well-known poet and his family had been caught up in the middle of it was too good a story to pass over. Unexpectedly, the level of attention received by her father on his arrival in London enabled Anna to extract sweet revenge on the 'prim and proper' sisters who had snubbed her on the voyage to Marseilles. 'When we steamed into Victoria Station, all the journalists rushed on to the platform shouting, "Is Roy Campbell on this train?" Just then I saw Jane and her sister and I shouted, "Yes, he is my father!" – and I made a hideous face at those embryonic bourgeoises . . . the two girls gazed at us in admiration.'[7]

Over the next few days the newspapers were full of photographs of Campbell, as well as pictures of his daughters riding in the bullring in Toledo, accompanied by lurid stories of their experiences and their final escape under such headlines as 'British Bullfighter Trapped By Rival Armies'.[8]

In spite of Roy's celebrity status, the family were more or less penniless. Having been relatively affluent in Toledo, Roy and Mary found themselves almost destitute in London. Their modest income had been frozen in their bank in Toledo, forcing them to rely on help from friends and relatives. The first week back in England was spent in the hotel in Bloomsbury in which Mary's mother stayed on her rare visits to London. Then, for a fortnight, the family moved to Marsh Farm, the luxurious home of Ernest Wishart, the wealthy publisher who had married Mary's sister Lorna. They were given the run of the house while the Wisharts were away on holiday.

Marsh Farm, a large estate at Binsted, near Arundel in Sussex, seemed to Tess and Anna like a vision of the Garden of Eden after the recent privations of Spain. It was, wrote Anna, 'one of those ancient English houses that do so much to soothe the soul . . . The orchards were laden with apples and plums, the shrubberies with birds, the ponds were full of ducks and geese, the stalls with cows and the garages with Bentleys.'[9]

During this 'heavenly' two weeks in late August, and throughout September, the whole family followed events in Toledo avidly, purchasing five different daily newspapers in an effort to glean every last detail. Day by day they followed what had become known internationally as the 'Siege of the Alcazar', feeling acutely – especially in the light of their present luxury – the sacrifices of the Alcazar's defenders. Besieged within Toledo's ancient fortress were a little over 1,000 combatants and about 700 noncombatants, mostly women and children. Their grim determination to hold out until the bitter end was encapsulated by the officer in command, Colonel Moscardo. When he was informed by telephone that his 24-year-old son Luis would be shot if he did not surrender the Alcazar, he told his son, 'Commend your soul to God, shout *Viva España!* and die like a hero. The Alcazar will never surrender.'[10]

By contrast, some of the besiegers were little more than 'tourists of war', often travelling from Madrid for a few hours of entertainment before returning home. In this category was William Dobby, a visiting British Labour MP, who travelled to Toledo in a chauffeur-driven Rolls-Royce which had been the property of a royalist nobleman before being 'requisitioned'. Dobby was taken to the top of a church tower, now being used as a machine-gun post, which commanded a view across the Alcazar's courtyard. Before leaving, the Labour MP asked if he could be shown how to use the machine-gun because he 'couldn't resist the temptation to fire it at the fascists'.[11] One battalion commander, complaining of the woeful lack of organization among the Republican forces laying siege to the Alcazar, poured particular scorn on the anarchists: 'They were having a holiday, red-and-black scarves everywhere, laughing and chatting with their girlfriends. Occasionally a few shots, that was all.'[12]

Time, however, appeared to be on the side of the besiegers. By 21 September, two months after the siege had begun, the little remaining water was being severely rationed among the Alcazar's defenders and all but one of the 177 horses had been eaten. Meanwhile, in a final effort to break the deadlock, miners from Asturias, summoned by the Madrid government, succeeded in blowing up one of the Alcazar's towers. This had severely weakened the fortress's defences and assault guards from Madrid prepared for the final attack.

Then, on 27 September, just as it looked as though the defence of the Alcazar would end in heroic failure, Nationalist columns led by General Varela reached Toledo. They met with little resistance. The Republican militia fled, with the spectacular exception of 40 drunken anarchists who committed mass suicide by setting fire to a seminary in which they were quartered. The Nationalists proved as brutal in victory as their Republican enemies had been. They took no prisoners in their lust for revenge, and it was reported that wounded militiamen were killed in their hospital beds. Reason, as much as Republicanism, had been routed and hate prevailed.

Roy's delight at the lifting of the siege is evident in his verse, 'The Alcazar Mined', which was written only days after the event.

> This Rock of Faith, the thunder-blasted –
> Eternity will hear it rise
> With those who (Hell itself out-lasted)
> Will lift it with them to the skies!

Till whispered through the depths of Hell
The censored Miracle be known,
And flabbergasted Fiends re-tell
How fiercer tortures than their own
By living faith were overthrown;
How mortals, thinned to ghastly pallor,
Gangrened and rotting to the bone,
With winged souls of Christian valour
Beyond Olympus or Valhalla
Can heave ten thousand tons of stone!

All through the long weeks of the siege, Roy, Mary, Tess and Anna had prayed the rosary together every evening for the Alcazar's defenders. 'During this time our rosary prayer in the evening became fierce with ardour,' remembers Tess. 'We put our mind to prayer, as it was the only means we had of helping the besieged and also the only way we could join in, to help the cause.'[13] This regular evening ritual was kept up by the whole family for the entire three years of the war. More than ever, Campbell's Christian faith was bound up with the fate of Christian Spain, which, like the Alcazar itself, had become for him the very image of the 'Rock of Faith', standing alone against the forces of materialistic modernity. The memory of his martyred friend Father Eusebio, his own feelings of humility in the face of his friend's faith, and the personal importance of the monk's sacrificial example are all in evidence in three successive verses in 'The Carmelites of Toledo'.

His radiant face when last I saw
Eusebio bade me take delight:
His flesh was flame, his blood its light
That sought the fire as fire the straw,
And of his agony so cruel
As ruthlessly devoured the spite
As eager flame devours the fuel.

Small wonder then as trash too earthly
The gunbutts drove me from the pin
They smashed to let such Princes in,
When, too presumptuous, as unworthy,
My carcase for a Crown to barter,
The blows acceding to the Martyr
Rebuffed me for a Harlequin.

In my black mask, with bleeding eyes,
I woke as one for gala dressed,

My scapular beneath my vest
Which only then I learned to prize,
And there, like Romeo, the mad lover,
In the forbidden town, discover
And hold the Loved-One to my breast.

These poignant verses represent the homage of a self-consciously unworthy 'Harlequin' to a saintly man who had won the 'Crown' of heaven. It is as though Campbell's young faith had grown stronger through the terrible experiences he and his family had endured in Toledo. He clearly believed that he had discovered, through grace, a well of gratitude amongst the grief.

Similar sentiments are expressed in 'To Mary after the Red Terror', except that here the homage is paid to his wife as the woman who had brought him to his knees.

Then when we strays were roped and branded
(A burning cross upon the breast)
And in the old Corral were landed
Survivors of the rinderpest –

You led me to the feet of Christ
Who threatened me with lifted quirt:
But by its loving fury sliced
I staggered upright from the dirt . . .

Roy's forthright views on the war in Spain inevitably alienated him from those who took the opposite view. Most people in England in 1936 were more worried by the threat posed by Nazism in Germany than by communism in Russia or elsewhere, and even those who had no time for the communists were uneasy about Hitler's support for Franco. Hitler's troops had just invaded the Rhineland and were noisily demanding territory in Czechoslovakia. War, it seemed, could soon engulf far more than Spain. If it did, Hitler and not Stalin would be Britain's enemy. In such an atmosphere, it was little surprise that most Britons supported the government in Madrid.

This pro-government stance was reflected in a poll of writers taken by Nancy Cunard in 1937 for the *Left Review* and published as *Authors Take Sides on the Spanish War*. Only five writers of the 148 whose replies were published supported Franco, namely Edmund Blunden, Arthur Machen, Geoffrey Moss, Eleanor Smith and Evelyn Waugh. Sixteen declared themselves neutral, including T. S. Eliot, Norman Douglas, Ezra Pound, Alec Waugh, Sean O'Faolain, Vita Sackville-West and H. G. Wells, while the rest, 127 in total, came out in support of the socialist/communist Republic.[14]

Stephen Spender nailed his colours to the mast in more robust fashion, joining the Communist Party and going to Spain to serve the Republican cause. When W.H. Auden travelled to Spain in January 1937 to help the cause in a civilian capacity, the communist *Daily Worker* greeted the news triumphantly under the headline, 'Famous Poet to Drive Ambulance in Spain'. The peril in which Auden was placing himself was made all too apparent by the death of another idealistic young writer who had volunteered to do exactly the same 'civilian' work. Julian Bell, son of Clive and Vanessa Bell, nephew of Virginia Woolf, and one of the leading lights of the new Bloomsbury generation, was killed in 1937 only a month after arriving in Spain, while driving an ambulance for the British Medical Aid Unit.

In his untimely death, Bell was spared the disillusionment which would soon strike at the hearts of many. On the Madrid front,

> [Spender] 'met a young English public schoolboy who said he had joined the International Brigades because he thought they were liberal republican organisations. Then he discovered that they were entirely Communist-run. He told me: "I'm going to spend the rest of my life walking up to that ridge a few hundred yards away and that will be the end of me." A few weeks later he was killed. I think there were many like him.'[15]

In fact, the fatality rate among Britons who joined the International Brigades was horrifically high. Out of a total of around 2,000 volunteers, some 500 were killed and 1,200 wounded.[16]

During the summer and autumn of 1936, however, the disillusionment had still not set in. Hundreds of mildly socialistic youths, wide-eyed in their ignorance, joined the International Brigades to fight for 'freedom' in Spain. This was what Cyril Connolly described as the Spanish war's 'Rupert Brooke period'.[17] During this time there was almost universal support in the nation for the Republican cause, with only the Catholic community raising a dissident voice. Catholics throughout the world were horrified by news of atrocities carried out against priests, monks and nuns by the communists and anarchists in Spain. Priests had their ears cut off, monks had their eardrums perforated by rosary beads being forced into them and the mother of two Jesuits had a rosary forced down her throat. Before the war was over 12 bishops, 4,184 priests, 2,365 monks and about 300 nuns were killed. Churches were systematically destroyed and George Orwell recorded that in Barcelona 'almost every church had been gutted and its images burned'. In *Homage to Catalonia* Orwell wrote,

> Some of the foreign anti-Fascist papers even descended to the pitiful lie of pretending that churches were only attacked when they were used as Fascist fortresses. Actually churches were pillaged everywhere

> and as a matter of course ... In six months in Spain I only saw two undamaged churches, and until about July 1937 no churches were allowed to reopen and hold services, except for one or two Protestant churches in Madrid.[18]

Even though many Catholic writers found the link between Franco and Hitler disquieting, the persecution of the Church in Spain led them to come out in support of the Nationalists. Arnold Lunn, Alfred Noyes, Ronald Knox, Christopher Hollis, Evelyn Waugh, Hilaire Belloc, Douglas Jerrold, Tom Burns, Bernard Wall and Christopher Dawson were all outspoken critics of Republican atrocities and supporters, however reluctantly, of Franco. Waugh's response to Nancy Cunard's poll of writers was indicative of the general view of the Catholic literati. In answer to the weighted question, 'Are you for, or against, the legal government and the people of republican Spain? Are you for, or against, Franco and Fascism?' Waugh replied: 'If I were a Spaniard I should be fighting for General Franco. As an Englishman I am not in the predicament of choosing between two evils. I am not a Fascist nor shall I become one unless it were the only alternative to Marxism. It is mischievous to suggest that a choice is imminent.'[19]

Thirty years later, a British biographer of Franco could look at the Spanish leader's links with Hitler more dispassionately.

> He was inevitably dubbed a fascist for accepting aid from the German and Italian dictators during the civil war ... But he was never particularly fascist, just as he had never been particularly monarchist or republican. Although he accepted help from Hitler, he gave refuge to thousands of Hitler's Jewish victims during the Second World War and revived citizenship rights for the Sephardic Jewish community of Salonika, to save it from Nazi persecution ...[20]

The emerging chasm between the Catholic and secular responses to the war in Spain was nowhere more evident than in an article by Christopher Dawson for the *Catholic Times*:

> It is not merely a conflict of brute force ... it is a battle of will and beliefs, and it is in Spain, which has always been the bulwark of Christian Europe and bore the brunt of the battle with Islam in the past, that the battle with the new enemy of Christendom is being fought out today. It may well be that the issue of the struggle in Spain will decide the fate of Europe.
>
> The victory of Communism in Spain would be a victory of Communism in its most dangerous aspect, for it would not be a victory over capitalism, which is relatively unimportant in Spain, but over Catholicism, which is the very root of the Spanish tradition ...

> If Spain could find herself once more, after the dreary century of disunion and weakness – if she could once more take the place to which her history and her genius entitles her – then it will be a victory not only for Spain but for Europe. It will bring back to the European society an essential element without which European civilisation has become one-sided and incomplete.[21]

Dawson's words were an accurate reflection of the views of Roy Campbell, who wrote plaintively a few years later that his views on the Spanish war were not 'fascist' but simply a reflection of his 'pro-European, anti-Soviet line'. He continued:

> Anyone who was not pro-Red in the Spanish War automatically became a 'fascist' . . . It made no difference that one fought as willingly against Fascism as one had done against Bolshevism previously. So fanatical did the mental goose-stepping of the British Intellectuals become, and so gluttonous their fatuous credulity, that, even if you killed ten times as many fascists as you had previously killed bolsheviks in self-defence, you still remained a 'fascist'.[22]

Lawrence Durrell, who understood Campbell better than most, sprang to his defence over the allegations of 'fascism':

> He made enemies. He was held up as a Fascist by the poets of the Left but since they had already decreed that Plato was a Fascist, this too was something of a compliment. I once heard this wicked Fascist calmly recall that he had to leave South Africa because of the hostility he had aroused by seriously defending the cause of the Blacks in his writings . . .[23]

Perceptively, Durrell explained Roy's 'reactionary' politics in terms of his love for traditional rural realities over transient intellectual fashions. 'His reactions were those of a pastoral world in opposition to the industrial capital – the Tentacular City with its literary intrigues devised by the Intellect.'[24]

Tom Buchanan, lecturer in Modern History and Politics at Oxford University, wrote in his recent book, *Britain and the Spanish Civil War*, that 'Campbell was an isolated (and even hated) figure in literary circles', but in his attitude to the war 'was far from alone amongst Catholic intellectuals'. The war had 'reinforced the distance between Catholics and mainstream intellectual life'.[25] This had created a great deal of division between former friends. Tom Burns, the Catholic publisher, recalled that differences over the war had soured his friendship with W.H. Auden. Burns could not accept Auden's pro-Republican stance, explaining that Campbell spoke 'more for my sympathies'.[26]

These divisions were also striking at the very heart of Roy's and Mary's relations with their own family. As soon as the Wisharts returned from their family holiday at the end of August, the quiet hamlet of Binsted was divided into two factions, the members of which were soon arguing furiously over the rights and wrongs of the Spanish war. On the Republican side were Mary's brother-in-law Ernest Wishart, her brother Douglas Garman, at this time a member of the Communist Party, who was accompanied on his frequent visits to Marsh Farm by Peggy Guggenheim, the millionairess with whom he was having an affair, and a Dr Drury, described by Anna as 'Binsted's atheistic parson'.[27] On the Nationalist side, apart from Roy and Mary, were Ernest's mother Lady Wishart, a somewhat hesitant Lorna Wishart, and their two chauffeurs. 'When these two groups gathered at Marsh Farm the rafters rang with their outraged cries,' remembers Anna. 'Tess and I, lying upstairs trying to sleep, agreed that it was worse than the battle for Toledo and we were heartily relieved when Lady Wishart offered us her Glebe House, at a safe distance from Marsh Farm, though still in Binsted.'[28]

In spite of his anger at his opponents, Roy could still write amusing letters to Wyndham Lewis about the farcical situation in which he and his family found themselves. Their life in the midst of their millionaire communist relatives was 'a real drama . . . of Ben Jonson value':

> We are still in our 'Alcazar' in Bolshevik Binsted, I only wish you were here. My hosts are trying to turf me out (my three brothers in law). I refuse to go – I am abolishing property and practically demonstrating their theories with uplifted fist – they send their ultimatums now by the chauffeur who laughs at them. Because they dare not come near here! . . . And it is a great joke in the village – a Lewis situation!
>
> . . . The wife of Wishart (the only sensible one) is being converted by our objective, classical catholic thinking which simply roots them up like a lot of bloody carrots, and scatters them. Garman who doesn't come in range, says we're a hornets' nest.[29]

Apart from the satirical gibes at his rich relatives, and the allusion to Lorna Wishart's first tentative steps towards eventual reception into the Catholic Church, Roy was full of praise for the 'heroes and saints' of the Alcazar, informing Lewis that he should read either the *Catholic Herald* or the *Universe* for the 'real facts' about the siege. 'The amputations without anaesthetics and the fact that there was not a single case of infection among the besieged Catholics. It makes one think!' The siege's significance was immense. 'From that steel wedge the Christian and classical mind can now drive right into the materialists. It was the victory of the spirit against avoirdupoids [sic]. It shows that spiritual people are even better *as* materialists than materialists, and 50 times braver.'[30]

Sharing in the post-Alcazar triumphalism and rejoicing in Campbell's jocular contempt for his communist in-laws, Lewis replied on 25 October that the 'collective farm hands' of Bolshevik Binsted 'must be feeling extremely dejected, as the tide of Marxist world-revolution recedes, with a sickening hiss!'[31]

Lewis was now dabbling in fascism and, in the autumn of 1936, he arranged a meeting between Campbell and Oswald Mosley, leader of the British Union of Fascists. It was not a success. Campbell returned from London after his meeting with Mosley looking 'wan and tired'. 'It's no good kid,' he replied to Mary's questions, 'he's as bad as the others.'[32] Anna believes that Lewis's efforts to recruit her father to Mosley's cause was evidence that he did not really understand him. 'He thought these two men would be on the same wavelength. I sometimes wonder whether Lewis even began to understand Roy.'[33] As for Mosley himself, it seems that he was more impressed by Campbell than Campbell was with him. In his memoirs, Mosley wrote of this meeting that, while he found Wyndham Lewis 'touchy but agreeable . . . Roy Campbell was an altogether more robust character'.[34]

According to Lawrence Durrell, efforts were also made to recruit Campbell to the cause of British fascism by William Joyce, who would later gain notoriety as 'Lord Haw-Haw' for his propaganda broadcasts on behalf of Nazi Germany during the Second World War. 'And if I loved Roy,' Durrell wrote to Richard Aldington in 1958, 'it was precisely because he turned down Joyce's overtures; he was invited, did you know, to become the official poet of Fascism?'[35]

Campbell read Hitler's *Mein Kampf* at around this time, probably out of little more than curiosity, and found that the book confirmed his worst suspicions about Germany's Führer. Putting the book to one side, he expressed his disdain with characteristic humour. 'Good gracious,' he quipped, 'this man won't do – he's a teetotalitarian vegetarian!'[36]

'Hitler himself had said . . . how much more easy the Protestants were to enslave and bamboozle than the Catholics,' Campbell would write in *Light on a Dark Horse*.[37] For all his contempt for 'Bolshevik Binsted', Campbell was not about to be bamboozled into believing that his enemy's enemy was his friend. His failure to share Lewis's enthusiasm for fascism would serve to estrange him from his old friend and ally, heightening still further his sense of isolation in England. 'Everybody is cynical and fatalistic now,' he wrote to a friend in South Africa, 'it is terrible to see.'[38]

In the letter to Lewis about 'Bolshevik Binsted', Campbell also wrote of the parallels between the strange domestic set-up he was enduring with his rich relatives in Sussex and the uncomfortable domestication on Vita Sackville-West's estate in Kent almost 10 years earlier. 'Here, it is Knole Castle all over again,' he complained.[39]

Although Roy and his family were no longer directly dependent on Ernest Wishart, having left Marsh Farm for Glebe House which was owned by Wishart's mother, it must have irked Roy to feel any sense of indebtedness to his wealthy Marxist brother-in-law. In truth, the two men had nothing in common. Apart from their political differences, Roy must have recalled his earlier impression of Wishart when he and his wife had visited the Campbells in Provence. On that occasion, Roy had been horrified that Wishart had been blind to the beauties of the sunsets and the landscape but instead had complained about the inadequacy of the plumbing. Roy was now pining not only for the southern sunsets and landscape but also for that deficient plumbing. Not for the first time, he was growing uncomfortable with a surfeit of 'domestic comfort'.

This growing feeling of discomfort was exacerbated by the political climate in England. Roy was still living in the psychological shadow of the Alcazar and was developing his own siege mentality in the face of the Republican bias among the English literati. 'My parents began to feel rather lonely among British intellectuals,' writes Anna.

> Except for Yeats, Hilaire Belloc, Blunden, Lewis and a few others, British writers and other artists were all either drunk with enthusiasm for the other side, or carefully sitting on the fence, like Eliot. But what isolated them even more was their newly found faith in God, which passed even Lewis's comprehension. They longed to share with others their wonderful new happiness in the Catholic faith. So gradually the idea of leaving England, where it was so difficult to get to a Catholic church, began to take hold and they decided finally that Portugal being so near to their beloved Spain was the ideal answer.[40]

By January 1937, only five months after their arrival in England, Roy and Mary were making plans to set sail for Lisbon, longing to exchange 'Bolshevik Binsted' for Catholic Iberia.

NOTES

1 Roy Campbell, from 'A Letter from the San Mateo Front', *Collected Poems, Volume Two*, p. 44.
2 Martin Seymour-Smith, *Robert Graves: His Life and Work*, London: Hutchinson, 1982, p. 266.
3 *Ibid.*
4 *Ibid.*
5 Anna Campbell Lyle, *Son of Valour*, pp. 118–19.
6 Teresa Campbell, unpublished memoirs, p. 60.

7 Anna Campbell Lyle, *Son of Valour*, p. 119.
8 *Daily Express*, 12 August 1936.
9 Anna Campbell Lyle, *Son of Valour*, p. 121.
10 David Mitchell, *The Spanish Civil War*, London: Granada, 1982, p. 58.
11 *Ibid.*, p. 59.
12 *Ibid.*
13 Teresa Campbell, unpublished memoirs, p. 64.
14 Louis Aragon and others, *Authors Take Sides on the Spanish War*, London: *Left Review*, 1937; see Hugh D. Ford, *A Poet's War: British Poets in the Spanish Civil War*, Philadelphia: University of Pennsylvania Press, 1965, p. 279.
15 Quoted in David Mitchell, *The Spanish Civil War*, pp. 78–9.
16 *Ibid.*, p. 78.
17 Cyril Connolly, 'Today the Struggle', *New Statesman*, 5 June 1937.
18 George Orwell, *Homage to Catalonia*, in *Collected Works*, London: Secker & Warburg/ Octopus, 1980, p. 260.
19 Louis Aragon and others, *Authors Take Sides on the Spanish War*.
20 Brian Crozier, *Franco: A Biographical History*, London: Eyre & Spottiswoode, 1967, p. 7.
21 Quoted in Christina Scott, *A Historian and His World: A Life of Christopher Dawson*, New Brunswick, USA: Transaction Books, 1992, p. 129.
22 Roy Campbell, *Light on a Dark Horse*, p. 226.
23 Alister Kershaw (ed.), *Salute to Roy Campbell*, p. 25.
24 *Ibid.*
25 Tom Buchanan, *Britain and the Spanish Civil War*, Cambridge University Press, 1997, p. 161.
26 *Ibid.*
27 Anna Campbell Lyle, *Son of Valour*, p. 121.
28 *Ibid.*, pp. 121–2.
29 Roy Campbell, unpublished letter to Percy Wyndham Lewis, early October 1936.
30 *Ibid.*
31 W. K. Rose (ed.), *The Letters of Wyndham Lewis*, pp. 239–40.
32 Anna Campbell Lyle, *Son of Valour*, p. 125.
33 *Ibid.*
34 Quoted *ibid.*
35 Ian S. MacNiven and Harry T. Moore (eds), *Literary Lifelines: The Richard Aldington – Lawrence Durrell Correspondence*, London: Faber & Faber, 1981, p. 54.
36 Anna Campbell Lyle, interview with the author, Portugal, December 1998.
37 Roy Campbell, *Light on a Dark Horse*, p. 317.
38 Roy Campbell, unpublished letter to F. C. Slater, September 1936; quoted in Peter Alexander, *Roy Campbell*, p. 169.
39 Roy Campbell, unpublished letter to Percy Wyndham Lewis, early October 1936.
40 Anna Campbell Lyle, *Son of Valour*, p. 124.

CHAPTER TWENTY-THREE

POET AS PROPAGANDIST

And here the warring principles are shown
Betwixt the male and the rejected drone:
The latter would for safety break their necks
Reducing life to comfort, food, and sex:
The former all-accepting soar above
To triumph over death and die for love.[1]

Campbell's growing sense of alienation in England was exacerbated in October 1936 following the publication of *Mithraic Emblems* by Boriswood. Campbell had high hopes for the book, his largest volume of verse to date, and his overall sense of optimism about its likely reception must have been stimulated by the interest of Faber & Faber in publishing the volume. Geoffrey Faber made every effort to persuade Campbell to let him publish the book and was evidently disappointed when the poet refused his offers. 'It beats me to understand why after the success of *Adamastor* you should have decided to take your poems elsewhere instead of enabling the publishers of *Adamastor* to go on building up your reputation and position as a poet,' he commented.[2]

In the event, *Mithraic Emblems* was largely ignored by the critics, dashing Campbell's hopes and convincing him still further that he was now a pariah as far as the British literati were concerned. Significantly, the only review in the first two months after publication appeared in the *Tablet*, a Catholic paper. Eventually the *New Statesman* and the *Sunday Times* published reviews, on 26 December and 17 January respectively, but they were the only major periodicals to do so. G. W. Stonier, who wrote the review for the *New Statesman*, was far from complimentary.

> Not only do Commando and the Charlies, Christ-Mithras, the garlanded bull, Toledo, become as monotonous as a Southend carnival, but a number of verse-formulae are relentlessly repeated . . . I do not know of any previous volume of Mr Campbell's in which you could find these ineptitudes. For the first time I have found myself reading

> through to find the good ones. They are here, if one looks ... *Mithraic Emblems* might have been cut down to a third of its present size (150 pages). It would still not be on a level with *Adamastor* or *Flowering Reeds*, but it would be real Campbell and not fake cowboy.[3]

It was inevitable that the critics would be baffled by the obscure Mithraic-Christian mysticism of the sonnet sequence that gave the volume its title. Without unravelling the mystical threads which had led to Roy's and Mary's progress towards Christianity in Spain, it was impossible to comprehend the sonnets fully. Critics could not be expected to understand the murky undercurrents, the flow of faith, that had been the poet's inspiration. To the unenlightened, the sonnets must have been perceived as impenetrable, obscurantist self-indulgence. As such, their reception by the critics was always likely to be bemusement at best, irritated impatience at worst. Yet *Mithraic Emblems* contains many other poems which deserve a place beside the finest written by any of Campbell's contemporaries. 'Familiar Daemon', 'Rust', 'Junction of Rails: Voice of the Steel' and 'Posada' are all outstanding, as are the other verses inspired by Roy's conversion and his passionate experiences in Toledo, such as 'The Fight', 'Christ in the Hospital', 'Toledo, July 1936', 'Hot Rifles' and 'The Alcazar Mined'.

Even allowing for the understandable criticism of Campbell's almost monotonous use of certain motifs, and the unease created by the excess of spite in the satirical verses (of which, in any case, there are relatively few in this volume), the deafening critical silence which accompanied publication of *Mithraic Emblems* is a little puzzling. Certainly Campbell had no doubt that the silence was further proof that he was the victim of a continuing literary boycott. He was convinced that the new generation of left-wing poets, such as Auden and Spender, had added their weight to the boycott which had been instigated by the Bloomsbury group following publication of *The Georgiad*. Furthermore, as events in England over the previous few months had demonstrated, his views on the war in Spain were isolating him from mainstream public opinion and from the prevailing literary currents.

It would perhaps be tempting to dismiss Campbell's conviction that he was being systematically victimized as an example of an irrational persecution complex, but there is little doubt that he was being seen as something of a literary untouchable by the end of 1936. Thus Stephen Spender, who secretly admired Campbell's poetry while opposing his politics, felt unable to speak favourably of it for fear of the consequences. After Campbell's death he admitted feeling intimidated by the peer group pressure which existed at the time: '... the main reason why I never wrote about Campbell during the 1930s was Auden's very critical view of him as a poet.'[4]

Crestfallen at the poor reception of *Mithraic Emblems*, and feeling unwanted by and antagonistic towards the dominant political and literary trends in England, Roy sought a return to the rustic simplicity of Catholic Iberia. On 29 January 1937 the family set sail from Southampton, bound for Lisbon on a German boat, the *Niasa*.

It was snowing as they left, but much worse was to come. That night they sailed into a hurricane in the Bay of Biscay and the whole family, with the exception of Roy, were terribly seasick. 'Roy was in his element,' recalled Anna, 'he never suffered from seasickness – the rougher the sea the more he enjoyed it. Every so often he would tear himself away from the wonders of the churning sea to find out how we were getting on.'[5] Tess remembered her father as 'a solitary passenger walking the decks'. At first she had tried to accompany him, staring out across the tempest with him.

> I never believed waves could be so spacious or so high. I had always thought the waves in the *Moby Dick* illustrations exaggerated but these were just as big, if not bigger. I had thought that if my father could, I would manage the deck but when I got there . . . I felt so ill and nearly fainted, while now and then the chilly spray covered me.[6]

She retreated to the cabin, joining her seasick mother and sister.

On the third day, Mary, Tess and Anna emerged tentatively on deck, 'feeling terribly groggy', to join Roy.

> The sea was unrecognisable – gigantic waves like huge walls of water kept sweeping towards us. One felt that each wave that reached the ship would engulf it but, in some wonderful way, it managed to surmount the mass of water with only a huge fountain of spray dashing over the prow, then it would sink sickeningly down into the next valley to be followed by a new wave looming towards us.[7]

The terrifying experience was made worse when it was announced that the ship which had been accompanying the *Niasa* had sunk with no survivors. 'The ugly and strange Nazi flag was at half-mast and this was when we were told that the accompanying ship had gone down.'[8] Eventually the storm abated and the sun shone brightly as the *Niasa* sailed into Lisbon between the masts of sunken boats sticking up out of the flooding waters of the Tagus.

Portugal's capital had still not succumbed to rampant commercialism. Anna remembered it as 'such a romantic town' when they arrived. The fisherwomen still wore their traditional dresses in green and blue with white stockings and leather slippers. 'They ran up and down the steep flights of stairs, carrying shallow baskets of gleaming fresh fish on their heads and shouted their wares in raucous voices.'[9]

The Campbells stayed at a *pension* in the Avenida da Liberdad, but, as in Barcelona three years earlier, they were soon longing for a return to the rural idyll. They made enquiries and were told that they should try Estoril because it was 'where all the English go'. 'God forbid!' Roy exclaimed. 'We shall now travel in the opposite direction.'[10] Thus the family found themselves in the charming fishing village of Sesimbra, where they stayed for the next eight months, first at a *pension* and then in a house by the beach.

Anna and Tess settled into their new lives instantly, picking up Portuguese with ease. Tess, still only 14, was a success with the young men in the village, her waist-length golden-red hair and Celtic blue eyes proving an irresistible lure. She received several proposals of marriage and fell in love with the handsome sacristan at the local church, which made going to Mass a rather self-conscious exercise.[11] As the weather improved, Anna and Tess would join local villagers on excursions to isolated beaches, bays and caves that could only be reached by sea. The fishermen would cook *caldeiradas* (a Portuguese equivalent of *bouillabaisse*) on the beach and, after everyone had eaten, there would be dancing to the accompaniment of a concertina. 'One of the caves we visited was immense,' remembers Tess, 'it made a wonderful ballroom. To us young people, this dancing was wonderfully inspiring as we all had our flirts.'[12]

Mary passed much of her time out of doors painting. She also helped the Sisters of Charity in their ministry to the sick in the local hospital, as well as playing the organ in the local parish church and training the choir. Roy, however, was restless. He became increasingly obsessed with the progress of the war over the border in Spain. He also sought a return to Toledo so that he could check on the safety of the Carmelite archives, which had been reluctantly abandoned in the family's haste to escape almost a year earlier.

Having secured an official letter of accreditation from the Catholic publisher Tom Burns, who had signed him as a special war correspondent for the *Tablet*, Roy set off by train for the Spanish border in June. The war, in the five months since the Campbells had arrived in Portugal, appeared to be hanging in the balance. In February the Nationalists had captured Malaga, but their renewed assault on Madrid had failed. In March, at the battle of Guadalajara, the Popular Army, assisted by the International Brigades, had routed the blackshirt Italian corps, but the end of the month saw a new Nationalist offensive in the Basque province of Vizcaya. In April the unification of the Falange and Carlist-monarchist movements highlighted the Nationalists' growing unity of purpose, whereas the violent street battles in Barcelona between rival communist factions demonstrated the Republicans' disunity. On 17 May, Juan Negrin became the leader of the new communist government of Republican Spain.

'I feel very calm on the train,' Roy wrote to Mary from just outside

Coimbra *en route* to Salamanca, 'not at all as if I were going on an "adventure".' He expressed his regret that he had not brought a map with him so that he could see how he was getting nearer to Spain, as he was 'longing to get there'.[13] Crossing the border, the train reached Salamanca on 24 June. Five days earlier the Nationalists had taken Bilbao, so Roy arrived in Salamanca, the home of the Nationalist head of state, at a time of particularly high morale. 'I have got to Salamanca,' he wrote joyously to Mary, 'it is wonderful. I have never seen such enthusiasm. The troops look splendid.'[14]

The embassies and the Press Service of Nationalist Spain were located at Salamanca, so Roy, armed with his letter from the *Tablet*, spent most of his first day in the city 'chasing about after safe-conducts etc'. He met Merry del Val, chief of the Nationalist Press Service, and was given a safe conduct to the Madrid front, together with letters to authorities in other cities, including a letter of introduction to General Queipo de Llano, the commander-in-chief of the Southern Army who had led the Nationalist forces which captured Seville in July 1936.

Clearly excited, Roy wrote to Mary while he was waiting for his safe conduct to be processed informing her that Merry del Val was 'a charming man' who had been 'very kind'. Roy was determined to see 'as much of Salamanca as possible' before he departed. 'It is very quiet here at night but the central square is extremely lively up till about 11 p.m.' He was staying in a cheap *pension* for 10 pesetas a day, placing a photograph of Mary on his bedside table 'so I am not so lonely as I might be'. At night he was busy putting the finishing touches to 'The Carmelites of Toledo' and he had visited the Carmelite church for Mass.[15]

'If it were not for the wounded soldiers,' he wrote, 'everything is so beautifully run here, that you would not know there was a war on – except for the expression of the soldiers – such a fine mixture of determination & confidence. You can feel Victory tingling in the air!'[16] Roy told Mary that he had tried to enlist as a soldier himself in the ranks of the *requetes*, but that Merry del Val had told him that the Nationalist cause needed 'pens, not swords'. The poet was wanted as a propagandist, not as a soldier.[17] It is, however, significant that Campbell sought to enlist as a monarchist soldier rather than as a member of Franco's regular army. The *requetes* were the least 'fascist' of the Nationalist forces.

With his journalist's pass, Roy travelled by car to Toledo on 28 June. He was recognized by dozens of his old friends and informed Mary that he had 'never done such a lot of handshaking in my life'. He continued:

> You remember how it was when we left it with one tower of the Alcazar in flames. The town is still completely dominated by the Alcazar: it

looks grander if anything . . . Really it is wonderful to tread on this Holy ground again. Tomorrow I will go to Mass at the Carmelites; and then get down to work and show up the English Press.[18]

During the two days he spent in Toledo he spent much time looking for his horse, Moro, but in spite of seeing hundreds of horses he failed to find his beloved stallion.[19] He was, however, greatly relieved to discover that the Carmelite archives were unharmed.

He also found time to write a short postcard to Wyndham Lewis congratulating him on his latest books, *Count Your Dead* and *The Revenge for Love*, describing the former as 'a splendid blow for the cause' in Spain.[20] Lewis was in the midst of writing a volume of memoirs, *Blasting and Bombardiering*, destined to be published later in the year. Somewhat surprisingly, considering his endeavours to convert Campbell to Mosley's cause several months earlier, Lewis appears at pains in this volume to stress that his friend should not be considered a fascist.

> I heard from Campbell this morning . . . and learnt with some surprise that he was at Toledo. The Government Army is only five miles away and that must be rather close quarters; and his house, too, was destroyed by shell-fire last year. I don't know what he's doing there . . .
>
> Campbell has not any regulation political bias, I think. He may incline to Franco because he is a catholic, and to the Old Spain rather than the New Spain because he likes bullfights and all the romantic things. But of politics he has none, unless they are such that go with a great antipathy for the English 'gentleman' in all his clubmanesque varieties; a great attachment to the black-Veldt of his native South Africa; and a constant desire to identify himself with the roughest and simplest of his fellow-creatures in pub, farm, and bullring. Such politics as go with these predilections and antipathies he has, but it would be difficult to give them a name. He certainly is neither a communist nor a fascist.[21]

Leaving Toledo on 30 June, Roy was driven to Talavera where he had a serious fall, twisting his hip painfully. On the following day, the special car travelled southwards down the front, ending its lightning tour in Seville. Although this flying visit appears to have been Roy's only frontline experience of the war, it would not prevent him suggesting that he had witnessed far more of the action than he had. The poet, in his enthusiastic role as a propagandist, would not worry about objective truth. There was, after all, a war to be won.

Over the following months, Roy would write a plethora of poems inspired by the war, most of which were flawed by jingoistic triumphalism and a scarcely controlled shrillness. The verse he wrote after his brief sortie in Spain is bereft of the control which characterized his earlier Spanish work. There is in 'A Letter from the San Mateo Front', the long poem written after his return to Portugal, none of the disarming humility of 'The Carmelites of Toledo', 'La Mancha in Wartime' or 'To Mary after the Red Terror'. Instead, the poet's voice, quivering with near hysteria, sacrifices poetic dexterity for political point-scoring.

'A Letter from the San Mateo Front' was the embryo which, after several months of gestation, would be born as Campbell's 5,000-line would-be epic on the Spanish Civil War, *Flowering Rifle*. Written during a feverish spell of intense creativity in the following summer, *Flowering Rifle* shows Campbell at his least attractive. It overflows with a bullish bombast, tainted by anti-communist and anti-Semitic invective. Many of Campbell's old enemies are dredged up for a fresh attack in the course of the poem's long-drawn-out stream of malevolence. Freud, as author of 'the pervert's Bible', takes another battering, as do poets such as Auden and Spender:

> Who hold by guile the fort of English letters
> Against the final triumph of their betters,
> Muzzle the truth, and keep the Muse in fetters . . .

Flowering Rifle, like *The Georgiad*, is certainly spoilt by spite. Yet, as with *The Georgiad*, there are moments of gem-like brilliance. The comparison between the deep psychological perceptions of the Spanish mystics, such as St John of the Cross and St Teresa of Avila, and the psychoanalytical assumptions of Freudianism reveals the profundity of Campbell's vision – a profundity so often obscured by the abusive and offensive shallowness with which he surrounds it. The Spanish mystics, those 'burning saints on cold and hunger fed', had delved into the subconscious mind to depths that the moderns had not even dreamed existed:

> And, since the pain and sorrow of the world
> Was far too soft a pillow, fiercely hurled
> Their empire to the ends of the Abyss,
> Searching the gulfs of the subconscious mind
> New fiends to conquer, continents to find,
> And ray their thoughts like comets to the blind:
> Who face to face would meet with fiery beams
> The eyeless monsters that molest our dreams
> To show the way they can be faced and routed –
> And Freud, the pervert's Bible, gaily flouted.
> All his worst nightmares they had foxed from earth
> And hunted down – an age before his birth,

When the subhuman dream, to its derision,
Confronted by the clear seraphic vision,
Shrunk like a squid: and left the wakened sprite
To sun its clouds with valour and delight –
All our psychology so damp and dreary,
By practice mastered, where we grope with theory,
By conquest answered, where we pose the query –
Where ours leave off by darkness circled in,
Their terrible discoveries begin,
And far across the line where we draw rein
Their fiery beacons light the fearful plain,
Over the wreck of battles fiercely won,
The vanguard and the outposts of the Sun!
Was this the race that could be tamely fed
On the Utopian blarney of the Red,
Or bribed to trade its devil-daring breath
For slavery, equality, and death:
And, if these lying promises were truth,
For cheaper bread renounce its flaming youth –
Or the religion of the heart and head
For that of the soft belly and its bread?

Unfortunately, these exalted moments are all too rare. For the most part, *Flowering Rifle* fails to flower at all, mired by its own self-consuming anger. It plods about with leaden boots firing scorn-blinded blanks at 'bolshies', anarchists and Jews, offering only an occasional glimpse of the genius which its author possesses. Thus, for instance, in the midst of pages of laboured doggerel, a couplet of rare beauty emerges like an oasis in a desert:

Men without God, the eunuchs of the mind,
Grown embryos, that life has left behind . . .

Such moments are not sufficient to redeem *Flowering Rifle.* It labours its point repetitively, screams its abuse with shrill relentlessness, and hunts down its quarry with a complete lack of empathy or charity. It lacks structure and composure, having been written hurriedly in an uninterrupted stream of consciousness. It is untempered by much needed restraint, so say nothing of much needed revision. Although Campbell defended the poem vociferously in public, he confessed its flaws in private, commenting to a friend shortly before its publication, 'I should have kept it by for revision for a year at least but preferred to strike while the iron's hot . . .'[22]

In *Homage to Catalonia*, George Orwell's account of his experiences in the Spanish war published in 1938, the year in which Campbell wrote *Flowering Rifle*, Orwell lamented the shameless dishonesty of the propaganda on both sides.

> The fighting had barely started when the newspapers of the Right and Left divided simultaneously into the same cesspool of abuse. We all remember the *Daily Mail*'s poster: 'REDS CRUCIFY NUNS', while to the *Daily Worker* Franco's Foreign Legion was 'composed of murderers, white-slavers, dope-fiends and the offal of every European country'. As late as October 1937 the *New Statesman* was treating us to tales of Fascist barricades made of the bodies of living children (a most unhandy thing to make barricades with), and Mr Arthur Bryant was declaring that 'the sawing-off of a Conservative tradesman's legs' was 'a commonplace' in Loyalist Spain. The people who write that kind of stuff never fight; possibly they believe that to write it is a substitute for fighting. It is the same in all wars; the soldiers do the fighting, the journalists do the shouting, and no true patriot ever gets near a front-line trench, except on the briefest of propaganda-tours.[23]

Campbell greatly admired Orwell's *Homage to Catalonia*, but it is difficult to see how he could have read this particular passage without shifting uneasily in his seat. After the briefest of propaganda tours he had wielded his own pen unmercifully, sacrificing objective truth and subjective artistic integrity in the service of the Nationalist cause. In taking up the cudgel of the propagandist, the poet had placed the silver-winged in the service of the worm-tongued.

NOTES

1 Roy Campbell, from 'Flowering Rifle', *Collected Poems, Volume Two*, pp. 175–6.
2 Peter Alexander, *Roy Campbell*, p. 167.
3 *New Statesman and Nation*, 26 December 1936.
4 Stephen Spender, unpublished letter to W. H. Gardner, 26 June 1958; quoted in Peter Alexander, *Roy Campbell*, p. 168.
5 Anna Campbell Lyle, *Son of Valour*, p. 127.
6 Teresa Campbell, unpublished memoirs, p. 66.
7 Anna Campbell Lyle, *Son of Valour*, p. 127.
8 *Ibid.*
9 *Ibid.*, p. 128.
10 *Ibid.*
11 *Ibid.*
12 Teresa Campbell, unpublished memoirs, p. 68.
13 Roy Campbell, unpublished letter to Mary Campbell, late June 1937.
14 *Ibid.*
15 Roy Campbell, unpublished letter to Mary Campbell, late June 1937.
16 Roy Campbell, unpublished postcard to Mary Campbell, 27 June 1937.
17 Peter Alexander, *Roy Campbell*, p. 173.
18 Roy Campbell, unpublished letter to Mary Campbell, 28 June 1937.

19 Anna Campbell Lyle, letter to the author, 15 December 1999.
20 Roy Campbell, unpublished postcard to Percy Wyndham Lewis, end of June 1937.
21 Percy Wyndham Lewis, *Blasting and Bombardiering*, p. 221.
22 Roy Campbell, unpublished letter to F. C. Slater, November/December 1938; quoted in Peter Alexander, *Roy Campbell*, p. 174.
23 George Orwell, *Homage to Catalonia* in *Collected Works*, p. 268.

CHAPTER TWENTY-FOUR

FLOWERING RIFLE

But in their strife, unconscious as they rage on,
Each from the other catches the contagion –
The one by heroism oft inspired,
His foe as oft by desperation fired;
As if his soul into the flesh could strike,
Each in the other conjures up his like;
With rags of flesh upon their nails and teeth
They wrestle now above and now beneath,
And both so foul with blood and soot and dust,
And one by hate, the other by disgust
So unified, by smoke so densely screened,
You scarce can tell the angel from the fiend.[1]

In September 1937, not long after Roy's return from Spain, the Campbells were on the move again. This time they headed south to the picturesque village of Estombar, not far from Portimão, in the Algarve.

'No-one who goes to the Algarve nowadays can imagine what it was like before mass-tourism,' writes Anna. 'It had such strong characteristics that it was like a little country on its own – in fact Portugal used to be called the Kingdom of Portugal and the Algarves.'[2] 'In those days,' Tess concurs, 'there were no tourists and very few foreign residents. It was mostly populated by farmers, peasants and fishermen. Very primitive in every way. The only meat to be had was mutton and even this was scarce.'[3]

Tess and Anna were now fully accustomed to their parents' nomadic lifestyle and they soon settled into life in Estombar as effortlessly as they had in Sesimbra. Once again they went on excursions with groups of young people they had befriended, though this time the trips were not by sea but by land, along miles of donkey tracks. A favourite destination was a farm on the outskirts of Silves, called Matamoros, where the remains of the Moorish settlement were still clearly visible. Here they would enjoy long, leisurely picnics which were supplemented by the fruit picked from the loquat trees.[4]

As well as exploring the local area with their peers, Tess and Anna enjoyed excursions with their parents to Montchique, described by Tess as 'a mountain paradise'. 'We went at the time of the flowering of the mimosa which fell in cascades, all interwoven and clustered with camellias which flowered at the same time. These flowers were a sight and amidst this magnificence we would have our picnic.'[5]

Soon after the family's arrival at Estombar, Roy bought two rather wild horses to serve as transport. Roy used to ride one of them, a coal-black mare called Garrota, into the sea of almond blossom that spread all around the village in every direction. 'The horse's hooves trod delicately on a carpet of small blue iris and every time he brushed a tree they would be showered with pink and white petals.'[6] Although Roy grew very attached to the black mare, the other horse, a small Arab, was less of a success. It was only half broken in and started rolling on its back whenever it got onto sand, regardless of whether it had a rider or not. Nonetheless, with these two horses and some hired donkeys the family explored the whole region in the months following their arrival.

At home in Estombar, Roy would read Shakespeare aloud to Mary, Tess and Anna and this, along with the daily praying of the rosary, was a valued time for the family to be together. Anna recalled that Roy read from Shakespeare's plays regularly over a five-year period between 1936 and 1941. '*Macbeth* moved him terrifically. He shuddered at the Forest marching towards Macbeth's castle. Brutus's stabbing of Caesar filled him with indignation, and as for the ghost in *Hamlet*, he tried, by his acting, to make us feel as deeply as he did the hair-raising experience of Hamlet's seeing his ghostly father.'[7]

In May 1938, Roy and Mary went on pilgrimage to Fatima, the shrine in central Portugal where three peasant children had seen an apparition of the Blessed Virgin in 1917. 'It was just before my father wrote *Flowering Rifle* that my parents went to Fatima,' remembers Tess. 'My father went partly because he was drinking heavily at the time and couldn't give it up. He felt the Virgin would help him (he had a great devotion to the Virgin). I seem to remember he went off half confused, repentant and in a depressed state of mind – in a kind of trance, not at all enthusiastic.'[8]

When Roy and Mary returned, they had a strange story to tell. Shortly before their arrival at the shrine, they stopped at a tavern so that Roy could get his pigskin *bota* filled, half with water and half with wine as was his custom. Later, when he went to drink from it, Roy was astonished to discover that it contained only water. This gave him such a shock that he made a vow to the Virgin that he would not drink again 'until the Catholics win the war in Spain'.[9] He would keep his vow of abstinence 'through every temptation' until the war ended almost a year later. 'He considered it a miracle the

Virgin had worked,' says Tess.[10] Commenting on this belief, Anna declared that it was an example of her father's humble simplicity. 'His religion was like that, it was rather simple. My mother was a great theologian but he wasn't. She read Thomas Aquinas right through. He preferred a simpler sort of faith.'[11]

Anna believes her father was very happy during these months in Estombar. 'The climate and beauty of the Algarve and the gentle, Christian ways of the Portuguese were a respite from the horrors of the political situation.'[12] Yet politics were never far from Roy's thoughts and he continued to follow events in Spain with the ardour of a combatant. It was during these months that his pot-boiling satire *Flowering Rifle* was taking shape in his mind. The 'respite' was merely a period of artistic gestation. When, at last, Roy set about putting his warring emotions onto paper, his labour was brief but intense. The 5,000 lines were written in the space of a few short weeks of obsessive effort.

There is, however, a great deal of confusion with regard to when exactly Roy did settle down to write the poem. Peter Alexander states in his biography of Campbell that it was written in March 1938, but gives no source to verify the statement.[13] In her memoirs, Anna seems to concur with Alexander's chronology, but Tess states specifically that *Flowering Rifle* was not written until the middle of the year.[14] She insists that the poem was not started until after Roy had returned from the pilgrimage to Fatima in May.

It seems that the initial draft was completed by 18 July, because Roy wrote to Wyndham Lewis on that date declaring that he had just sent off the manuscript of the poem, which he had provisionally entitled *Resurgimento*, describing it as 'mostly a poem on the Spanish War but is full of satire about our intellectuals etc and especially about the British International Brigade'.[15] There appears, however, to have been some revision of the poem after that date, according to an account by Armand Guibert, a friend of Roy's who had translated *Adamastor* into French. Guibert visited Estombar in the summer, arriving on the Feast of the Assumption, i.e. 15 August, and remembered distinctly that Roy 'retired after lunch to write the final pages of *Flowering Rifle*'.[16] The bedroom to which Roy retired in order to work on the poem was, in Guibert's words, 'a bare, whitewashed cell with pages of manuscript strewn all round a mattress lying on the floor, a saddle doing duty as a pillow'.

Throughout the duration of Guibert's visit Roy drank only cold tea from a demijohn 'which he poured into his mouth as if using a wine-skin'. He carried this demijohn of tea with him to the cliffs of Praia da Rocha, drinking from it as though it were his customary *bota* of wine. There, beneath the stars and with the phosphorescent sea far below, he sang the 'cosmogonic hymns of the Zulu and Matabele' while accompanying himself on the guitar.

In his letter to Lewis, Roy wrote that he was 'completely cured of booze and have less flies on me than for a long, long time', which suggests that his total abstinence from alcohol was having a beneficial effect. Yet physically he was in poor shape. The injury to his hip sustained on the lightning visit to the Madrid front a year earlier had become increasingly painful and, with the help of financial assistance from his mother, he decided on a trip to Italy to consult a specialist.

In September 1938 the family set out for Rome. *En route*, Roy and Mary took the opportunity to make a brief detour to Toledo while Tess and Anna travelled directly to Seville. Their two days in Toledo proved a disappointment. The front, which had hardly moved in the previous year, was only a few miles away and the city still seemed to be under siege. The streetlamps had been painted blue as a precaution against air raids, and guards were posted outside every prominent building. Roy and Mary were often challenged and searched by security-conscious troops and they were shocked to discover that their house had been occupied by strangers. Many of their possessions had been damaged in the year since Roy's previous visit, though the Carmelite archives were now safe. Deflated by their experience, they journeyed south to Seville to rendezvous with their daughters.

By contrast with Toledo, Seville was relatively relaxed and cheerful. The town was full of soldiers, many in bandages or on crutches, and the cafés were alive with the laughter of troops on leave and their young female acquaintances. After two nights in Seville, the family travelled to Gibraltar, where they boarded the Italian luxury liner *Il Rex*, one of the largest ships in the world and the pride of Mussolini's fascist regime. Campbell, however, was far more impressed by one of the largest British battleships, HMS *Hood*, which sailed majestically into Gibraltar while he and his family were waiting to embark. Overcome with emotion, he pointed it out to his daughters. 'Look at the might of the British Empire,' he whispered. His voice was trembling and Tess and Anna were surprised to see that his eyes were full of tears. 'He was thinking of Trafalgar and the glories of the Royal Navy and his great hero Nelson,' says Anna.[17] This is a poignant example of the contradictions at the heart of Roy's psyche, the confusion of the colonial faced with the imperial might of the motherland. For all his ambivalence towards England and his antagonism towards the 'clubmanesque' gentry of Anglo-Saxondom, Roy remained loyal to the glories and traditions of the Empire.

Arriving in Italy, the Campbells spent a week in Naples, making an expedition to Pompeii to see the frescoes, before proceeding to Rome. They had decided to spend several months in the Italian capital, having arranged to meet up at Christmas with Campbell's mother who was on yet another world tour. With this in mind, they rented a flat on the Via Donatello and set about soaking up Roman society. Roy was both classically and romantically at home in Rome, foundation of the ancient imperial culture he revered and the ancient religious faith he now professed. The family spent much time sightseeing, visiting churches, art galleries, museums, the Colosseum and other ancient sites. At the end of October, Roy wrote contentedly to Wyndham Lewis of his family's situation:

> We have got a nice place here almost in the country and only 5 minutes walk from the hippodrome where they had yesterday the international police championships on horseback and equestrian championships all next week. Now I am here I shall stay on and see as much as I can before going home to Spain. It was very quiet here in the 'crisis' no sign of nervousness at all.[18]

The 'crisis' to which Campbell referred was the diplomatic brinkmanship that culminated in the signing of the Munich Pact on 30 September, when Britain and France acquiesced to the German occupation of the Sudetenland in return for assurances from Hitler that he had no further territorial claims. Neville Chamberlain, the British Prime Minister, returned to London declaring triumphantly that his appeasement had brought peace, whereas, at best, it had only bought time. Over the next 12 months Britain, hopelessly unprepared for war, rearmed frantically in an effort to match the Nazi might. Even as Chamberlain spoke of 'peace in our time', Europe was teetering towards war.

In his note to Lewis, Campbell had written that *Flowering Rifle* would be published by Longman before the end of the year. It would not, in fact, be published until 6 February 1939 and its publication could not have come at a more volatile time. Just over a week earlier, on 26 January, Barcelona had fallen to Franco's troops, precipitating a wave of Republican refugees fleeing towards the French border. On 1 February, Juan Negrin presided over the last meeting of the communist government of Republican Spain. On 27 February, the British and French governments officially recognized the legitimacy of Franco's regime, partly as an acceptance of the inevitability of Nationalist victory, but also in the hope of securing Franco's friendship in the light of the wider storm clouds gathering over Europe. In early March, Negrin's efforts at establishing a communist dictatorship in what was left of Republican Spain sparked yet another Republican civil-war-within-the-civil-war. After heavy fighting in Madrid, the communist forces were defeated and Negrin and his Soviet advisers fled. On 27 March Nationalist forces entered Madrid and five days later Franco announced that the war was over.

On the wider stage, on 15 March Nazi troops marched into Prague in defiance of the Munich Pact. Even as one bloody war ended another loomed ever closer.

Not surprisingly, *Flowering Rifle* provoked a thoroughly uncivil war of words following its publication, a reflection of the deep and bitter political divisions which were ripping Europe apart. Campbell could, however, confidently expect a warm reception for his poem in fascist Italy, where he suddenly became popular in the higher echelons of Roman society. He was introduced to Alfonso XIII, the exiled King of Spain who had been deposed on the establishment of the second Republic in 1931, and his court. 'They had all been reading *Flowering Rifle* which they much admired and the King embraced Roy, who was delighted.'[19] Roy and Mary also became good friends with Prince and Princess Rospigliosi.

Douglas Woodruff, editor of the *Tablet*, visited Rome and through Woodruff's wife, who had connections with the Italian aristocracy, the Campbells widened their circle of influential friends. During February and March, Roy and Mary attended an array of parties which must have stretched to the limit Roy's resolve to abstain from alcohol. At one such party Mary found herself sitting next to Hilaire Belloc, who had just arrived from Spain. He had visited the front and met General Franco, whom he described unequivocally as 'the man who has saved us all'.[20] Mary had brought both her daughters up on Belloc's four-volume *History of England*, published between 1925 and 1931, so she must have had high expectations of her first meeting with him. She was to be bitterly disappointed. Throughout the meal, she was struck by his rudeness. With commendable charity, many years after the event she explained to Peter Alexander that Belloc had been too deaf to hear a word she said, but she was less circumspect in her criticism of him to her daughters. 'What a horrible man, he was so rude. He turned his back on me and he talked to me over his shoulder all the time.'[21]

Roy, however, was very taken with Belloc, who retained considerable energy and fire even at the age of 69. Belloc had read *Flowering Rifle* and told Campbell how much he admired it, declaring with dogmatic bombast and dubious critical judgement that Campbell's other work would not count beside it in the long term. Roy was delighted at Belloc's praise and apparently unconcerned at such a casual dismissal of his other work. In July, after the family had finally returned to Toledo, Roy wrote enthusiastically to his mother, singing Belloc's praises.

> I don't know if I told you that in Rome Hilaire Belloc turned up (a wonderful old man!) . . . He is a very great writer and with Maurras and Daudet in France, and his friend Chesterton, they have all been

> forerunners of the Right movement. He thinks I have done a really good thing with *Flowering Rifle*, and that my other work will not even count beside it in the long run. His word is worth more than the whole of Fleet Street. Even when they were licking my boots I told you that they were a worthless lot so it is not sour grapes if I say so now.[22]

Campbell's plaintive gibes against Fleet Street were an allusion to the hostile reaction which *Flowering Rifle* had provoked from most literary quarters. There were, however, notable exceptions. The *Tablet*, under Woodruff's editorship, was predictably full of praise for the poem, describing it as 'genuine Rabelais' and asking 'why poetry or satire should not be inspired by Fascism as well as by Communism'.[23] Arthur Bryant, in the *Illustrated London News*, declared that it was a 'magnificent epic' and that 'poetry such as this has not been written in English since Julian Grenfell fell in battle'.[24] Yet it was Edmund Blunden's defence of the poem which most pleased Campbell. 'I was highly delighted to see that *Flowering Rifle* had received your fraternal blessing,' he wrote to Blunden at the end of May.

> It was extremely noble and generous of you at a time like this when it is so likely to redound to your unpopularity. I am sure that this spontaneous gesture of yours has helped (more than anything inside the covers) to launch the book so successfully . . . I take it as an excellent omen that you should have been the only English poet to welcome it, as you are the only one who has in your blood that wisdom and those virtues whose victory it celebrates.[25]

Campbell's sense of gratitude towards Blunden was evident in a letter he wrote to his mother in early June.

> It is that Good Samaritan Blunden who has done the most to help *Flowering Rifle* . . . He has the safest and most comfortable reputation in England and he has risked everything to defend my book, and I think that his praise and his lectures about it at Oxford did most to break the boycott. The English Press depended entirely on the boycott, and their bile now is only the result of impotent rage . . .[26]

Informing his mother that *Flowering Rifle* was selling better than anything he had written since *Adamastor*, Roy appeared defiant in the face of media hostility. 'As Byron said, the last poet to be cursed by the Press of his time as much as I am, it doesn't matter *what* they write about you, as long as they *write* about you.'[27]

In the wake of the publication of *Flowering Rifle*, Campbell was certainly being written about. In the May edition of *New Verse* an unsigned, venomous review entitled 'Rum Tum Tum on a Broken Drum' declared that Campbell's poem 'sounds like a hyena, ambitious to be a lion, howling away to itself (and to Mr Blunden, who has crept out of his hole to praise it) in the middle of a lonely and extensive sewage farm'. Stephen Spender, in a review entitled 'The Talking Bronco' published in the *New Statesman* on 11 March, described *Flowering Rifle* as 'an incoherent, biased, unobjective, highly coloured and distorted account of one man's experience of the Spanish War, seen through the eyes of a passionate partisan of Franco'. He continued:

> The poem, as a whole, has no unity of design, no sustained argument, no plot, no single vision. It is a kind of three-decker sandwich consisting of one layer of invective against the intellectuals of the Left, the International Brigade, the Spanish Republican Army, etc; a second layer of autobiography concerning the exploits of Mr Campbell and his flowering rifle; and a top layer of rhapsody about Franco and his colleagues, who are treated as nothing less than angels. The transitions from one motif to another seem to spring from no inner logic in the poem itself, and, particularly when he is being autobiographical, the actual circumstances of the poem are often very obscure.

In spite of the poem's lack of 'a unifying theme', Spender recognized that it contained 'passages of violent and sometimes effective satire, and occasional rhapsodic passages of a certain power, in which Mr Campbell has always excelled ... But these passages are exceptions, they are stones of a certain lustre buried under ignoble sweepings of every kind of anti-Semitic and atrocity propaganda, of boasting and bullying from ... the speeches of dictators.' Alluding to the worst examples of anti-Semitism in the poem, Spender complains that Campbell 'indulges in the degrading abuse of a Julius Streicher', adding that there were several passages 'which make me feel physically sick'.

Contrary to Campbell's claim in the letter to his mother that he did not care what the critics wrote about him as long as they wrote about him, he was both embittered and enraged by Spender's review. His letter to the *New Statesman* replying to Spender's criticism was almost hysterical in its attack on 'Mr Spender and his colleagues' with 'their mouldy day-dreams ... and ... their fungoid proliferations'.

In spite of his protestations, Campbell could not have been surprised by the anger his poem engendered among left-wing poets such as Spender and Auden. The communist poet Hugh MacDiarmid, whose previous work had included two separate *Hymns to Lenin*, was moved by his hatred of Campbell to write a long poem entitled *The Battle Continues* as a reply to *Flowering Rifle*. MacDiarmid's riposte excoriates Campbell for his 'extreme distortion' and accuses him of speaking 'with a voice not only banal / But absolutely anal'.

C. S. Lewis, a writer who could scarcely be termed 'left-wing', was also moved to reply to *Flowering Rifle* in verse. In a poem entitled simply 'To the Author of *Flowering Rifle*', published in *The Cherwell* magazine on 6 May, Lewis condemned Campbell's lack of charity, reminding him that 'the merciful are promised mercy still'. Campbell was a 'loud fool' who had learnt the art of lying from his enemies on the left,

> . . . since it was from them you learned
> How white to black by jargon can be turned . . .

Lewis had retained his early admiration for Campbell's poetic powers, declaring that his verse 'outsoars with eagle pride' the 'nerveless rhythms' of the left-wing poets. Yet his 'shrill covin-politics' and that of his enemies were 'two peas in a single pod':

> – who cares
> Which kind of shirt the murdering Party wears?

A further result of the publication of *Flowering Rifle* was that many of Campbell's former friends became his enemies. Nancy Cunard, frankly bemused that her erstwhile friend could have supported Franco, asked Nina Hamnett why he had sided with the fascists – to which Hamnett replied, 'Catholicism!'[28] Yet many Catholics were repelled by the lack of charity and the glorification of violence in Campbell's poem. *Blackfriars*, a Catholic monthly, complained that the publication of *Flowering Rifle* had 'supplied Marxists with ammunition which they have used with considerable effect'. Campbell was outraged that he should be attacked by fellow Catholics and his angry response was published in the July edition of *Blackfriars*.

> *Blackfriars* may enjoy its immunity while I have yet another cheek to turn. Influenced as I am by the almost perfect union of Spanish Catholics, I will not quarrel with fellow Catholics, however tempting or easy it would be to break their stick on their own pates – even when, to me, they seem to acquiesce, through ignorance, or 'spinelessness', in the wholesale defilement of the Sacrament, the slaughter of half a million unarmed Christians, and the godless imposition of foreign formulas on their fellow Christians in Spain. You may search *Flowering Rifle* in vain for any sort of reciprocal feeling to that which I have aroused unwillingly in your pages by my own special brand of spinelessness, cowardice, etc., etc., to fellow Catholics who have opposed and harmed the cause of Spain.

Blackfriars' literary editor, displaying the restraint that was so evidently lacking in Campbell's letter, replied, 'It should be recalled that our reviewer criticized the "spinelessness" not of Mr Campbell, but of his verse. Our readers must judge for themselves whether the quality of Mr Campbell's "ammunition" is better calculated to serve his own cause or that of his opponents.'[29]

For all Campbell's protestations, the fact that Catholic publications were unsettled by the jingoistic and boastful tone of *Flowering Rifle* indicates a serious flaw at the very heart of the poem. As with his spiteful treatment of the Bloomsbury group in *The Georgiad*, Roy's inability to show charity and restraint in dealing with his enemies had backfired, eliciting sympathy for his intended victims rather than scorn. In his desire to write propaganda rather than poetry, he had inadvertently turned the 'rifle' on himself.

NOTES

1 Roy Campbell, from 'Flowering Rifle', *Collected Poems, Volume Two*, pp. 234–5.
2 Anna Campbell Lyle, *Son of Valour*, p. 133.
3 Teresa Campbell, unpublished memoirs, p. 69.
4 *Ibid.*, p. 69.
5 *Ibid.*
6 Anna Campbell Lyle, *Son of Valour*, p. 133.
7 Anna Campbell Lyle, letter to the author, 10 November 1999.
8 Teresa Campbell, unpublished memoirs, p. 75.
9 Anna Campbell Lyle, interview with the author, Portugal, December 1998.
10 Teresa Campbell, unpublished memoirs, p. 75.
11 Anna Campbell Lyle, interview with the author, Portugal, December 1998.
12 Anna Campbell Lyle, *Son of Valour*, p. 133.
13 Peter Alexander, *Roy Campbell*, p. 174.
14 Anna Campbell Lyle, *Son of Valour*, p. 133; Teresa Campbell, unpublished memoirs, pp. 71 and 75.
15 Roy Campbell, unpublished letter to Percy Wyndham Lewis, 18 July 1938.
16 Alister Kershaw (ed.), *Salute to Roy Campbell*, pp. 27–8.
17 Anna Campbell Lyle, *Son of Valour*, p. 140.
18 Roy Campbell, unpublished postcard to Percy Wyndham Lewis, postmarked 28 October 1938.
19 Anna Campbell Lyle, *Son of Valour*, p. 140.
20 Robert Speaight, *The Life of Hilaire Belloc*, Freeport, New York: Books for Libraries Press, 1970, p. 464.
21 Anna Campbell Lyle, interview with the author, Portugal, December 1998.
22 Roy Campbell, unpublished letter to his mother, received by her 10 July 1939.
23 *Tablet*, 11 February 1939.
24 Quoted in Peter Alexander, *Roy Campbell*, p. 177.
25 Roy Campbell, unpublished letter to Edmund Blunden, 30 May 1939.
26 Roy Campbell, unpublished letter to his mother, 3 June 1939.
27 *Ibid.*
28 Hugh Ford (ed.), *Nancy Cunard*, p. 356.
29 *Blackfriars*, Oxford, Vol. 20, No. 232, July 1939.

CHAPTER TWENTY-FIVE

SURLY FASCISM

Big Ben proclaimed, through mists of grime,
The surly fascism of Time,
And all the small Benitos, then,
Would cuckoo, tinkle, chirp, or chime
Their orders to the race of men.[1]

Safely ensconced in Rome, Roy and Mary were largely shielded from the simmering acrimony which *Flowering Rifle* had caused in England. On 10 February 1939, only four days after the poem was published, Pope Pius XI died. The Campbells made a point of going to see him lying in state, and Roy and Mary attended the coronation of his successor, Pius XII, in St Peter's. Their daughters did not accompany them to the ceremony. 'Tess and I were too busy with our studies to go with them,' remembers Anna. 'We led very independent lives.'[2] In fact, the family's arrival in the Italian capital had opened new vistas for both sisters. Tess, now 16, studied at art school where she sketched models of all descriptions, from wrinkled old peasant women and bearded old men to young male and female nudes. Meanwhile Anna, almost 13, had enrolled with great enthusiasm at a ballet school.

In January the family had travelled to Venice with Campbell's mother, having previously celebrated Christmas with her at the hotel where she was staying in Rome's Piazza del Popolo. After Roy's mother had left to continue her world tour, the family visited Florence where Roy, in the Uffizi Galleries, burst into tears before Botticelli's *Primavera*. 'We left him standing there for about an hour,' writes Anna. 'This habit of bursting into tears whenever he was moved was always strong, but when he was abstaining from wine it happened all the time, which goes to show how intensely sensitive he was and how difficult he found existence without some sort of buffer.'[3]

Roy had lost a lot of weight since taking his vow of abstinence at Fatima and Anna is convinced that his gaunt appearance was evidence that his abstemiousness had been detrimental to his health. It was, therefore, a great relief when the ending of the Spanish Civil War on 1 April 1939 released him from his vow. He was seated with friends at a café table when news of the Nationalist victory reached him. There was a flagon of wine on the table and, according to Anna, it 'disappeared in one impassioned draught, as though it had been the elixir of life'.[4]

With the war in Spain ended, Roy was impatient to return to Toledo and was oblivious of Anna's heartbreak at being forced to leave Rome. The family travelled by train across France, but were delayed at the Spanish border while officials sought to confirm their safe-conduct passes. By a 'lucky chance', as Campbell explained to his mother, they met the Marquess de Merry del Val, 'a very fine old man' who was the father of the Nationalist Press Officer whom Campbell had met in Salamanca two years earlier. The Marquess, who had been the Spanish ambassador to Britain under King Alfonso, asked Roy if he was the author of *Flowering Rifle*. 'As a Spaniard,' he continued after Roy had confirmed his authorship, 'I thank you from the bottom of my heart for the fine work you have done for my country.' Roy was 'very touched indeed', informing his mother that 'it is so little to have done for a country that saved my soul, and I would so willingly have given my carcase for the cause as so many and such much better men than I have done.'[5] At a word from the Marquess, the Campbells were whisked through the border controls without any further formalities and continued their journey towards Toledo.

Anna, dejected at the family's sudden departure from Italy, found her first impressions of war-ravaged Spain 'profoundly depressing'. Exhausted soldiers crowded onto station platforms in the pouring rain and sprawled on their knapsacks seemingly oblivious of the cold and wet. When the train arrived every carriage window was missing and the red velvet seats were greasy with dirt. 'We watched in horror as a sleek procession of bedbugs came and went in the upholstery, like ants.' As the train passed through the landscape, every house that came into view was either burnt or machine-gunned.[6]

Roy, relieved to be back in his beloved Spain, was far more cheerful than his disconsolate daughter. So lifted were his spirits that even the delays in their journey were seen by him as providential acts of kindness. 'We are just on our way back to Toledo but by a stroke of good luck we were held up at Avila the birth place of St Teresa, for Easter Sunday,' he wrote to his mother.[7] Having attended sung Mass at Avila Cathedral, they went out on the ramparts 'in the beautiful freezing air' which was 'very bracing after Rome'.

Roy ended his letter from Avila by stating that the whole family was impatient to reach Toledo – 'we are fairly itching to get home'. Yet on the day of their arrival they discovered that Toledo, along with much of the rest of Spain, was in the grip of a famine. 'We were surprised to see what looked like make-up round the children's eyes,' remembers Anna. 'They were skeletal and stood about outside their houses too apathetic to shoo the flies round their eyes away. They were starving . . .'[8] Many of them had also been orphaned by the war and Anna discovered that Captain Alba, an officer from the Alcazar who was the father of her best friends at school, had died heroically after setting out from the siege disguised as a peasant to get a message to Franco. He was recognized in one of the villages and shot.

Almost at once Mary threw herself into the task of helping the poor of the city. With the aid of Catholic Action and by bullying the Bishop, she managed to start a soup kitchen in the most run-down part of Toledo. She sold all her jewellery to raise funds to refurbish a ruined chapel, and gave away much of her clothing. Roy also gave away many of his clothes, on one occasion handing out three silk shirts which his mother had sent him to people he met in a bar.

On 19 May, Roy and Mary travelled to Madrid for the Victory Parade of Franco's forces. Apart from Spaniards, the parade included Moroccan Muslims, Italian Blackshirts and the German Condor Legion. At this stage, Roy's conscience was not troubled as he watched and presumably cheered the Nazi troops. His love for the Nationalist cause in Spain and his six months in fascist Italy had blurred and distorted his vision of the political situation in Europe. Although he still strenuously denied the charge whenever alarmed friends or outraged enemies accused him of being a fascist, his sympathies were betrayed in his letters. 'I believe in family life and religion and tolerance,' he had written to Enslin du Plessis from Rome at the end of 1938, 'and I find far more tolerance to Britain in Italy than I find tolerance of Fascism in England.'[9] In a letter to his mother in April 1939 he made excuses for Nazi Germany's occupation of Prague, complained that too many Englishmen were 'sat upon or hypnotised by the Jews' and criticized Chamberlain's efforts 'to flirt with Russia which is by far the most dangerous enemy we have'.[10]

Presumably Mrs Campbell was alarmed by her son's apparent sympathy for Hitler and sent him an article from the *Reader's Digest* about Nazi persecution of Catholics. Roy's reply, written on 3 June 1939 only weeks before the outbreak of war, was the nearest he ever came to expressing outright sympathy for Hitler's regime.

> I met many German Catholics in Rome, and know all about what you sent me in the *Reader's Digest*, a paper that has always suppressed any mention of the *real* Persecution of Christians like in Spain, where 500,000 were massacred by hand, including 60,000 children under 15. Catholics are never afraid of the Big Stick and will not change their religion for it as protestants have done in Germany. What catholics

> realise is, that Hitler is a civilised and human adversary, compared to the only alternative, and they suffer cheerfully as they can. That is what bravery is for. It is on the side of the only other alternative that the *Reader's Digest* weeps these crocodile tears for German catholics: to raise up ill-feeling against Hitler who has not persecuted or robbed a tenth of what the IIIrd Republic in France has done, or even what England has done in this XXth century with her black-and-tans in Ireland, burning churches and killings. Yet Ireland and Spain, the two countries that have had the worst persecutions are still the most Christian . . . It is the first thing one expects in being Christened a Catholic, to be persecuted, and it is a very cheap price to pay for being a Christian. What we realise however is that the world is going to become either Bolshevik or Fascist, and we know that with one exception the fascist states are eminently Christian, and allow Christians to live whereas bolshevism simply kills and degrades everything – it is against morality, and against every form of religion.[11]

It is difficult to square this letter with Campbell's previously expressed feelings of antagonism towards both Hitler and his English acolyte Oswald Mosley. Perhaps his drift towards an apparent, if reluctant, acceptance of fascism was due to a genuine belief that the world would inevitably become Bolshevist if it did not become fascist. Certainly his aversion to communism had become so deep-rooted, so psychologically ingrained, that anything would have seemed preferable to Bolshevism – even Hitler.

The simplistic naiveté of Campbell's political position was exposed on 23 August with the signing of the nonaggression pact between Nazi Germany and the Soviet Union. Such an agreement between two apparently sworn enemies forced him to ask fundamental questions about the myopic dichotomy of Left and Right. The straightforward choice between fascism or Bolshevism which had so bewitched and confused him appeared now to be a sham – fascism and Bolshevism had chosen each other. The degree to which the Nazi-Soviet Pact would have unsettled him can be seen from a letter he had written to his mother in July, at a time when it looked as though Britain would enter an agreement with the Soviet Union. 'This alliance with Russia is the last degradation – only evil will come of it as it has come to everybody who ever meddled with Russia. It is like jumping into the river so as not to get wet.'[12] Now that Hitler had jumped into the river with Stalin, Campbell was forced seriously to reconsider his position.

Other factors were also involved in his rapid reappraisal of events. At the time of the Munich Crisis, Franco had made it clear that Spain would remain neutral in the event of a European war. A year later, the Spanish dictator was as determined as ever to keep his country out of any conflict.

Roy's loyalty to Nationalist Spain did not therefore require him to choose sides. On the other hand, his deep emotional attachment to Britain, exhibited by his tears at the sight of HMS *Hood* in Gibraltar a year earlier, forced him to confront his politics with his patriotism. Something had to give.

On 1 September Hitler's troops marched into Poland and bombed Warsaw, in open defiance of the pact signed between Britain and Poland. Two days later a reluctant Britain declared war on Germany. Campbell acted instantly. Taking the train to Madrid on the day after war was declared, he presented himself at the British Consulate to offer his services. He was told that it would be a long time, if ever, before they wanted men of his age – he was nearly 38. Far from requiring his services in Britain, the official at the Consulate advised him that it would be better to keep his family in the safety of Spain. Roy told his mother that when the official discovered he was South African he seemed to think it 'Quixotic' that he had thought of volunteering in the first place.

Roy's instant and dramatic response to the declaration of war, and the official's surprise at his gesture, suggests that his reaction was perhaps an over-reaction. Certainly the immediacy of his decision still causes confusion and disagreement between his daughters more than 60 years after the event, as the following three-way conversation between Tess, Anna and Rob Lyle demonstrates.

ANNA: I think he turned against Hitler when the war started because he suddenly realized what he'd let himself in for by being really so right-wing. And he got a bit frightened because I can remember that summer of 1939 he was very restless and he went straight to the Embassy and said he wanted to join up. I think he was frightened of what his enemies would say if he didn't do that.

TESS: No, no, I don't think so. He just did it.

ROB: It's much more basic than that. He had one fundamental thing: my country, right or wrong.

TESS: That's it. Patriotic. Always. First.

ROB: So whether he liked it or not, he really had no choice.

TESS: He had a great sense of being British.

ROB: Oh yes.

TESS: And we had to join in. You go into the WRNS and you go there. Very patriotic.

ANNA: I'm sorry, but I know that Dad was frightened in 1939 of being thought to be on Hitler's side.

ROB: Both things are correct. He was. I agree with you. He had just taken a few steps too far.[13]

Perhaps the solution to the psychological conundrum is to be found in Roy's own words, expressed in the two poems he wrote at this time, 'The Hoopoe' and particularly 'The Clock in Spain'.

'The Hoopoe', which was begun in 1939 though not finished until after the war, depicts the brightly coloured and crested southern European bird as a harbinger of war. All round the 'desecrated grandeur' of 'Toledo's shattered walls . . . All day the boding hoopoe calls'.

> The fire-bird flits amongst the cattle,
> Pronouncing victory or doom,
> The flashing corposant of battle,
> The torch upon the hero's tomb,
> The feathered tomahawk that waves
> The bonnet of the redskin braves,
> And cries once more his warning cry,
> Before the grass has healed the graves
> Or yet our open wounds be dry.
>
> The comet of approaching war,
> He flashes singing through the land,
> And where his fiery crest is fanned
> The farmyard poultry cluck no more.

In these doom-laden lines, Campbell laments the new war that looms like a shadow over the unhealed wounds of the previous one. Yet the rest of the poem is an effort to justify his position with regard to the war in Spain and to exonerate himself from blame. Significantly, although it is not apologetic in tone, it is more defensive than his previous poems on the Spanish war. In *Flowering Rifle* he had gloated over the killing of communists, whereas in 'The Hoopoe' he sets himself up as a prophet who should have been heeded so that the deaths could have been avoided.

> When long before the bird was singing,
> My cattle-whoop and whip were ringing
> To head them, if I could, from harm . . .
>
> So, when the crazed herds rush the canyon,
> Converging to the fearful jam,
> One rider, their sole sane companion
> May race his warning shots to slam . . .

This is a different, less aggressive, Campbell. Instead of rejoicing over his fellow Britons, the 'Jew and Saxon', who had lost their lives fighting for the International Brigades, he now laments their tragic loss. If only they had listened to his warnings, their lives might have been spared. He no longer wishes to be seen as their enemy but as their estranged friend, 'their sole sane companion'. He is not a fascist ogre, merely a misunderstood prophet who has been stoned for telling the truth.

> Are these the thanks their friends have shown us –
> To have me outlawed, gagged, and tied? –
> When shouldering a thankless onus,
> I blazed the warning far and wide,
> Deserving, rather, of a bonus
> For vigilance, than bards who lied . . .

The real enemy, the 'bards who lied', were the left-wing poets who had eulogized Republican Spain to such a degree that they had lured the innocent youths to their deaths in the International Brigades.

> Did I in Mayfair have my fling
> And traffic in the slaughtered youth
> Who might have lived to serve their King?

These left-wing poets were 'the vultures of the mind', picking over the bones of fallen heroes.

> While birds who fatten on the dead
> And farm the carnage from behind
> For gold or offal – cower in dread . . .

There is little doubt that W.H. Auden, who had emigrated to New York early in 1939, was the 'left-wing poet' Campbell had specifically in mind when he wrote these lines:

> For when the War-Cloud forks their sky,
> They'll seek Utopias oversea,
> To jobs in ministries they'll fly,
> And funk-holes in the B.B.C.

It is also possible that Campbell had Auden's emigration in mind when he made his impulsive decision to volunteer for service at the outbreak of war. There may have been an element of poetic one-upmanship in his gesture. He, at least, would not 'farm the carnage from behind' – although he had done so happily enough from Portugal when writing *Flowering Rifle*.

If 'The Hoopoe' displays a less aggressive Campbell pleading for a little understanding, 'The Clock in Spain' is an exhibition of his profundity and simplicity. Perhaps more than any other poem he ever wrote, it displays both the depths of his psyche and his simple-natured philosophy. It also illustrates his political and emotional volte-face during the summer of 1939. The clock in question was British-made and had been acquired by the Campbells, if the words of the poem are to be believed, after it had been abandoned by a 'panic-shod' member of the International Brigades. On its face was inscribed its place and date of manufacture, 'Birmingham 1922'. The fact that the clock was British but was now in Spain, and the fact that Roy and Mary had been married in the West Midlands in 1922, inspired Roy to employ the clock as a symbol of his own situation and also as a means of celebrating his love for his wife.

Certainly those verses in the poem which evoke his passion for Mary in lines of erotic purity are among the finest she had ever inspired, yet it is much more than a love poem. It is an affirmation of the poet's loyalty to Britain; it is a libertarian protest against the dictates of Time; and, significantly, it is an explicit condemnation of fascism. Thus Time, in one short verse, is policeman, despot and dictator:

> Like a policeman on his beat
> The despot ticked with measured tread,
> Dictating when to sleep, or eat,
> Or drink – for in the darkest street
> No Pub could open till he said.

If these allusions are not obvious enough, Mussolini is derided explicitly a couple of verses later.

> Big Ben proclaimed, through mists of grime,
> The surly fascism of Time,
> And all the small Benitos, then,
> Would cuckoo, tinkle, chirp, or chime
> Their orders to the race of men.

Slow, sleepy Spain is depicted as an antidote to the regimentation of Time, its carefree, timeless culture rebelling against the dictates of the Clock.

> The Sun would pause to hear a song
> And loiter, when he chose to chime,
> Which always put him in the wrong:
> And folk would dance the whole night long
> When he proclaimed it closing time.
> His heart was broken by the trains
> Which left him panting hours ahead:
> And he was liable to sprains,
> For on the wall we knocked his brains
> Each time he shrilled us out of bed.

In a riposte to those who defended fascist Italy by stating that at least Mussolini had made the trains run on time, Campbell is countering the very suggestion that trains should be *expected* to run on time. A train cannot be late, the clock can only be early, 'panting hours ahead'. Here Campbell strikes a note of affinity with Chesterton's statement that the only way of being sure of catching a train is to miss the one before it. Throughout the poem strict punctuality is derided as a Puritan killjoy, which Catholic Spain heartily ignores. Eventually, the Clock is seduced into the same somnambulance as Spain itself, slowing down and stopping as it learns to chime in tune with her Latin charms.

> But when, athwart an open door,
> He smelt the orange-trees in flower,
> And heard the headlong Tagus roar,
> And saw the white sierras soar,
> That moment cost him half an hour.
>
> And when amidst the poplars white
> He heard the nightingales unite
> To drown the torrent's hoarse furore,
> And held his breath from sheer delight –
> It lost him fifty minutes more!
>
> About the time of our Fiesta,
> When gales from the meseta sweep
> To strew the roses fetlock-deep –
> He fell into his first siesta,
> And now he often has a sleep . . .
>
> Today more tractable you'll find him
> And less on edge than was his wont.
> In sprays of lilac we've enshrined him:
> He stops the moment when you wind him,
> Then starts up ticking if you don't.

'The Clock in Spain', having rebelled against 'the surly fascism of Time', is then identified specifically with the poet himself.

> So silent with his rusty bell,
> This ancient veteran of the shelf,
> Whom I can neither pawn nor sell,
> Reminds me somewhat of myself,
> And if you want the reason, well,

Although he may appear to you
To have renounced his race and era,
His steel is British, cold, and blue,
As ever flashed at Waterloo
Or held the line at Talavera.

And if the dreadful hour should chime
For British blood, and steel as grim,
My clock will wake, and tick the time,
And slope his arms and march – and I'm
The one to fall in step with him.

In September 1939, with his country at war, Campbell had pulled himself back from the brink of his own surly fascism to an acceptance that fascism as well as communism was the enemy. He would seek to be reconciled with the race and era he had once renounced. The rebel was ready to fall in step. Time, the despot, was now dictating the terms.

NOTES

1 Roy Campbell, from 'The Clock in Spain', *Collected Poems, Volume Two*, p. 59.
2 Anna Campbell Lyle, *Son of Valour*, p. 141.
3 *Ibid.*
4 *Ibid.*, p. 193.
5 Roy Campbell, unpublished letter to his mother, April 1939.
6 Anna Campbell Lyle, *Son of Valour*, p. 141.
7 Roy Campbell, unpublished letter to his mother, April 1939.
8 Anna Campbell Lyle, *Son of Valour*, p. 142.
9 Peter Alexander, *Roy Campbell*, p. 177.
10 Roy Campbell, unpublished letter to his mother, April 1939.
11 Roy Campbell, unpublished letter to his mother, 3 June 1939.
12 Roy Campbell, unpublished letter to his mother, July 1939.
13 Teresa Campbell, Anna Campbell Lyle and Rob Lyle, interview with the author, Portugal, December 1998.

CHAPTER TWENTY-SIX

ANTI-FASCISM

> And now I see the way. One must be deft
> When liberty's attacked from Right and Left.
> With my left fist the Nazi though I fight
> I've banged the bloody Bolshy with my right . . .[1]

After he had performed his patriotic duty by volunteering for service, Roy seemed relieved that his country did not need him. 'Anyway,' he wrote to his mother on 17 October, 'if I got to England, it is unlikely that I would pass the medical test (though my lameness is better) and we should be stranded there for nothing. So I am delighted to be able to enjoy this glorious Spain for a while.'[2]

Roy's love for Spain was undiminished. In letters to his mother during the summer he had painted an idyllic picture of the family's life in Toledo. The garden was lovely, the roses were in bloom, 'and tonight the nightingales are almost torrential in our trees . . . Toledo looks very majestic with its changed outline – more than ever the impregnable city of God'.[3] He had painted a similar picture when writing to Edmund Blunden:

> We have a really lovely place here. In the garden we have two fountains under huge mulberry trees and two pairs of hoopoes. The craters of the Alcazar are on the hill above us. But from the rhythm of life here you would never think that this had been a front-line town through most of the war. The garden is one battlefield of roses with a twenty horse-power nightingale fusillading overhead . . . To have shared in some of the moments of divine madness of these people was worth having lived for, and it was worth writing about to have aroused the spontaneous sympathy which you have so kindly shown. *Dios se lo pagara* [God will reward you].[4]

Since September Anna had been at a boarding school run by the Teresian nuns in Avila, while Mary and Tess were teaching at the free night school organized by Catholic Action in Toledo. Meanwhile, as the months passed,

Roy grew restless. His initial relief that his services were not required had given way to a sense of frustration that there was nothing he could do to help the war effort. He contacted the Consulate again and was told that he would be informed the moment volunteers were needed. He suggested that he could work as an interpreter in France, but once again his overtures were rebuffed. 'In this war they only seem to want engineers, experts, doctors and aviators outside the young unmarried men,' he complained to his mother, 'though in France everyone has been called up; the same with the Germans.'[5]

During one of his hopeful visits to the Madrid Consulate, Roy met Tom Burns, the friend who had secured him accreditation to the *Tablet* in 1937. Burns suggested that Roy could work for British Intelligence, gathering information from his Spanish acquaintances. Roy accepted, delighted that he could at last feel he was helping the war effort – but in practice his method of gathering information consisted almost entirely of drinking in bars with friends. Not surprisingly, Burns was not impressed by the quality of intelligence which Campbell provided, nor the methods by which he set about acquiring it, and he soon dispensed with his services.

Roy wrote no original poetry at this time, but began instead to translate the poems of St John of the Cross. He was no doubt encouraged to do so by Mary, who greatly admired the saint, not least because St John had been a close associate of her spiritual role model St Teresa of Avila. Roy also felt a great attraction to St John who had close associations with Toledo, having been imprisoned there, and he was well versed in the saint's poetic mysticism, as his evocation of its depth in *Flowering Rifle* had demonstrated. Also, as he revealed during a radio broadcast several years later, he had prayed to St John of the Cross during the search of their house by militiamen at the start of the Civil War, making a vow that he would translate the poems into English if his family's lives were spared.[6] The work on the translations was, therefore, more than a labour of love: it was the fulfilment of an obligation.

The so-called Phoney War, the calm before the impending storm, ended abruptly in April 1940 with the German invasion of Norway. A month later the Nazis invaded Holland, Belgium and France. With the fall of these countries Britain was left to stand alone. The heroism of the RAF during the Battle of Britain in August was followed by the heroic resilience of the civilian population as the Blitz began in London and other cities a month later. The Campbells read about these developments in the Spanish papers with a growing sense of isolation. The people of Toledo were either indifferent to Britain's plight or openly hostile towards her. The latter attitude was demonstrated one afternoon when a peasant passed by their house with two hares he had just shot. '*Inglaterra*!' he grinned, holding the slaughtered animals aloft. 'England!'[7] In an ironic twist of fate, the Campbells once again found themselves passionately following a distant conflict in an environment of open hostility. Four years earlier they had watched events in Spain in the midst of 'Bolshevik Binsted'; now they were watching events in England in the midst of fascist Toledo.

In April 1941 the Germans began their assault on British forces in North Africa, where Campbell's brothers George, Neil and Bruce were on active service. Soon afterwards, heavily outnumbered British troops retreated hastily from Greece. The war was going badly and Roy began to feel that he *had* to go to England to play a part in it, however small. His delay in doing so was due to Mary's objections. She adamantly refused to be left alone in Spain with her two daughters. 'She would neither go with him nor allow him to go without her,' Anna recalls, 'so that a state of tension developed between them which made us all unhappy.'[8]

Eventually Roy's determination prevailed and Mary agreed to accompany him to England. With France under Nazi occupation, the journey would be difficult and dangerous. Through the Consulate in Madrid they made arrangements to travel to Portugal, where it would be easier to organize transit to Britain. On 17 July 1941 they travelled to Lisbon by sea from Valencia. Reluctantly Mary agreed that she would remain in Portugal with Tess and Anna until one of the few remaining clipper flights became available, while Roy left for England by sea, a journey fraught with peril because of the Nazi blockade of Britain and the consequent threat of being torpedoed by U-boats.

On 2 August Roy sailed from Lisbon on a small coaster to Gibraltar, where he would join a convoy to England. In Gibraltar he saw HMS *Ark Royal*, badly hit during a raid against Sardinia, limping into port amid the cheers of the crowds. Roy's first sight of Britain at war affected him with as much emotion as had the sight of HMS *Hood* entering the same harbour three years earlier. With uplifted spirits and tear-filled eyes, the South African of Scottish descent felt the emotive pull of his British roots. In a later poem, 'Autobiography in Fifty Kicks', he recorded this moment as one of the most memorable of his life:

> The kick of my heart, like a punch on the rib
> To see the 'Ark Royal' returning to 'Gib'
> As that great swan of victory rippled the tide
> With a hole in her decks, and a list in her side . . .

During the voyage to England, Roy met many Jewish refugees and several British soldiers who, failing to escape from the Dunkirk beaches, had travelled the length of France and Spain to reach Gibraltar.

Arriving in London on 17 August, he gave an interview to a South African newspaper in which he was at pains to demonstrate his loyalty to the Allied cause. German-occupied Europe was a 'desert' filled with secret police, prison camps and misery, whereas Britain, more than ever, was the bastion of civilized values. In the first glow of war fervour, Roy even managed to praise the Anglo-Saxons: 'This war has made the English greater, nobler, and better than ever before in history.'[9]

Roy had arrived in London penniless, but was rescued from penury by Eve Kirk, an old friend who, like the Campbells, was a Catholic convert. She lent him both money and a room until his mother was able to cable him £100. With this he was able to move into a rented room at 8 Conway Street, just off Fitzroy Square. 'It is so nice to have "a room of one's own" – as Virginia Woolf would say,' he wrote to Mary. Alluding to Woolf's recent suicide, and remembering his previous experience of her 'madness' at Long Barn, he added that she had 'bumped herself off because she was going mad again'.[10]

Eve Kirk was working as an Air Raid Precautions warden and she persuaded Roy to join her post as a full-time warden while he waited to be called up. 'You should have seen the wardens and home-guard trying to march in step,' he wrote to Mary. 'It was grand! When we were told to do right turn half the wardens did left turn and the crowd laughed at us like anything – but it was all good humoured. It reminded me of the Italians trying to do the goose-step.'[11] As a full-time warden he worked 12 hours a day for three pounds and 10 shillings a week. He was taught the shape and function of various types of bomb, how best to deal with them and the damage they caused to sewers, gas mains and electric cables. He was trained to detect the smell of poisonous gas and to divert traffic. Yet he was not content to remain in such a post for long. 'This job helps me out temporarily, and I was lucky to get it,' he wrote.[12] His heart, however, was set on the Royal Navy, into which he was hoping to be accepted for a post in the Naval Intelligence Division.

On 2 October, while Roy was sweeping the floor of the air-raid post, he was astonished to hear Christopher Stone on the radio congratulating him on his fortieth birthday. Writing wryly to his mother of his new-found celebrity status amongst the other wardens, he told her that he had 'taken on the importance of the cat, our mascot'.[13] A few weeks later he heard that his younger brother Neil had been killed in Egypt, at the age of 37. 'It gave me a nasty shock,' he wrote to Mary, '. . . I felt quite dazed.' In his grief, Roy was struck with guilt for the times he had bullied his younger brother when they were children.[14]

When he was not on duty, Roy threw himself headlong into London's social scene, which seemed to be carrying on much as ever, regardless of the

Blitz. In his letters to Mary, marooned in Portugal with their daughters, Roy wrote rather tactlessly of the temptations to adultery that he was fighting to resist.

> You would be very flattered if you could see what I have resisted for your sake in the way of lovely young women etc. I have really got quite a strong will: I have been literally chased all the time and I got a bad flutter from a Mauritian girl but I said Hail Marys to myself and every second one was Hail you! Then I bolted, and everybody has been laughing at me ever since, especially as she waylaid me and bit my hand for turning her down . . . She is a millionairess half Malay and very beautiful indeed – though not spiritually – in that way she is a mere potato.[15]

In similar vein, he wrote on another occasion that 'the young girls are all chucking themselves at my head'. He had not 'encountered any strain in resisting temptation', but added that it would be easier 'when you turn up . . . You better come soon, just in case I break out. (It would only be momentary anyway).'[16] There is no evidence that there were any 'momentary' lapses and Roy insisted in *Light on a Dark Horse* that he 'went monogamous' from the time of his reception into the Church and never regretted it.[17]

There is little doubt, however, that he was keeping less than entirely reputable company. He was spending a lot of time with Nina Hamnett who, now in her early fifties, was as incorrigible as ever. Lawrence Durrell wrote of that 'grubby little English world; the Fitzroy Tavern; Nina Hamnett; Aleister Crowley . . . O dear . . .'[18] Richard Aldington referred to 'poor Nina' as 'a curious mixture of slut and whore, but a very decent chap'.[19] Clearly, even being seen with such a notorious figure would set tongues wagging. Although Roy does not appear to have provided any specific grounds for gossip, the air was thick with innuendoes. Nancy Cunard would merely hint that Nina 'knew him, I think, very well . . .'[20] while Augustus John wrote to Wyndham Lewis that he had seen Roy in a Soho 'speakeasy' in the company of Nina Hamnett, 'who it appeared was affording Roy her boundless hospitality while he awaited the return of his family from Lisbon'.[21]

Lewis replied to John that it was a great pleasure 'to catch a glimpse of you in some smoky den in Soho (for if Nina was there, it must have been a den) exchanging iron fisted he-man salutations with our Vaquero'.[22] In fact, John had greeted Campbell with a degree of hostility. Infuriated with Roy for his authorship of *Flowering Rifle*, John had saluted him with the comment, 'A member of the Axis, I believe.'[23] Within minutes, however, they had forgotten their differences and renewed their friendship. 'Augustus John reconciled himself the minute he saw me – the silly old ass,' Roy wrote to Mary, adding, 'I get on well with everyone here.'[24] His letter failed to make any mention of Nina.

Not everyone was as forgiving as Augustus John. When, in September or October, Campbell arrived at a restaurant in Charlotte Street at which Nancy Cunard was dining with Robert Nichols, whom Campbell had known at Oxford, he was completely cold-shouldered. Nichols hissed into Cunard's ear that it was 'the horrid pro-Fascist', and the couple rose and left. As they walked away into the darkness of the blackout they heard Campbell crying after them, 'I'm not, I'm not a Fascist, Nancy! I am a Requite.'[25]

Roy's defensiveness with regard to his 'fascist' past was in evidence on several other occasions. Laurie Lee recounted a meeting with Roy in a pub in Old Compton Street on 25 August, only days after Roy's arrival in the country. Lee, having failed to seduce Mary in Toledo, had subsequently succeeded in seducing Mary's sister Lorna Wishart, with whom he was having an affair. He and Lorna arrived at the pub to find Campbell seated in a corner. 'Bald, trembling & smiling ... He was delighted to see us, he said, and sat at the table, stuttering, looking from one to the other, smiling & quivering with apologies. He had been f-for F-Franco in the Spanish war and now it was like having backed the wrong horse. "I was wrong Lorna," he said.' His sister-in-law laughed and sought to reassure him, but Roy was inconsolable. 'Yes,' he muttered hoarsely, 'I admit it, I admit being wrong.'[26]

While Campbell made his lamentations, Lee noticed 'a young rather tubby man' swaying at the bar. This was Dylan Thomas, whom Roy had only recently met for the first time. The two men became good friends and insatiable drinking partners. Thomas, 13 years younger than Roy, had admired Campbell's poetry since his youth. As a teenager in the early thirties he had sided with the stance of Campbell and Wyndham Lewis against the Bloomsburys, writing in a long letter to a friend about his contempt for the 'Arty Parties' of the Bloomsbury group.

> The type of party you describe ... is a menace to art, much as I dislike the phrase. Wyndham (Tar) Lewis has struck them hard in 'Apes of God'; D.B. (Blue Moon) Lewis has poked them gently to see if they bite as well as bark; Roy Campbell, in his 'Georgiad', has trampled them down under the feet of his eighteenth-century charger; but still they flourish. Still do seedy things in their mothers' pyjamas, enthuse over some soon-to-be-forgotten lyricist, or some never-to-be-heard-of painter of nature in the raw and angular. Neuter men and lady tenors rub shoulders with 'the shams and shamans, the amateur hobo and homo of Bloomsbury W.C.1' ...[27]

When Campbell arrived in London, Thomas was living in abject poverty with his wife Caitlin, in the same lodging house on Conway Street in which Roy would soon rent a room. Thomas had been judged unfit for active service and was desperately in need of money and a job. Laurie Lee's first impressions of him as he stood swaying at the bar illustrate all too clearly his poverty-stricken plight. 'He was bleak, dead & rather miserable, saying he had a wife & child to keep and no job. He looked about him joylessly with wet subterranean eyes as if the whole world was a wet Monday. I thought him flabby and conceited . . .'[28]

Campbell did not share Lee's contempt for the young poet, and the two men indulged in regular drunken revelries together in the seedier hostelries of Soho in the company of Nina Hamnett and others. On 12 September, presumably before Campbell's money from his mother had arrived, the two friends ran out of cash in the midst of a drinking session. In desperation, Thomas came up with the idea of visiting all the literary people they knew in the hope of borrowing some money. They called on Harold Nicolson, then employed as a senior official at the BBC, and Campbell wisely waited outside while Thomas went into his office. Nicolson gave the Welshman a lecture on the evils of drink, but still gave him a one-pound note. Cecil Day-Lewis was less forthcoming, writing to Stephen Spender in 1946:

> . . . in 1941 Roy Campbell came into my office at the MOI, with Dylan Thomas, both fairly drunk. Campbell was shaking like a leaf. He kept on saying, 'I know you must hate me. I know now that I was wrong. I admit I was wrong' . . . He then asked me if I could get him into the Marines and tried to borrow some money, which I did not lend him. Maybe he thought that, if he said he'd been wrong about Spain, I would fall on his neck and offer him my wallet.[29]

They had better luck with T. S. Eliot, who treated them with considerable kindness and gave them enough money to keep them in beer for several days.[30]

A tantalizing glimpse of Campbell's and Thomas's hedonistic lifestyle in 1941 is offered in *The Death of the King's Canary*, a satirical novel on the writers and painters of Bohemia which Thomas co-authored with John Davenport at around this time. The work is obviously heavily influenced by Campbell's *The Georgiad* and by the novels of Wyndham Lewis. Many of the luminaries of wartime Bohemia are lampooned in the book. Augustus John appears as Hercules Jones, Stephen Spender is Christopher Garvin, and Nina Hamnett makes a transparently obvious appearance as Yvonne Bacon. Particularly intriguing is the identity of the character called Owen Tudor, a 'tough poet' who has a close encounter with Yvonne Bacon.

> Round a corner at the far end of the corridor, two women, one in underclothes, the other Yvonne Bacon, scampered, squealing. From a deep doorway Hilary watched them.
>
> The woman in underclothes was Prudence Whittier, that elegant American who liked her poets to be men. As Owen Tudor rushed the corner after them Prudence giggled to Yvonne who was pretending to escape . . .
>
> 'You're my nymphs, *my* nymphs,' Tudor shouted, 'Phyllida! Amaryllis.' He tried to embrace them both. 'You're *my* goddesses,' he gloated, 'you and you and you and *you.*' At the last shout he threw himself upon Yvonne Bacon and bore her to the ground.
>
> '*Such* fun,' Yvonne said in a muffled voice. It was her titter of anticipation as he stooped above her, crying, 'Amaryllis, Amaryllis,' that brought him to his senses. He rose to his feet and staggered against the wall. He ran his hands through his wild hair. He hiccuped once.
>
> 'Say, what's come over you? Why aren't you doing something? Don't tell me the party's over. You've got hiccups,' Prudence said.
>
> Yvonne lay still. She had, anyway, never expected it to happen.
>
> Tudor closed his eyes, opened them, looked hard at the two women, and closed them again.
>
> 'You'd better come along with us and drink out of a glass the wrong way round . . . Come on, Yvonne. Romeo's got a bellyache.'
>
> The women walked down the corridor, one haughtily, one unsteadily, and Tudor followed them. As he passed the bedroom door, Hilary heard him mutter in amazement: 'Yvonne! Yvonne Bacon! Iessi Crist!' And his voice grew fainter: 'Nymphs! Oh dear! TT now. Ever and ever amen. Yvonne Bacon! What *have* I done?'[31]

The drunken nights with Dylan Thomas, Nina Hamnett and others did not warrant a mention in Roy's letters to Mary. Instead, he concentrated on prosaic descriptions of old friends. 'Old Augustus has got more cordial than ever after the bitterness,' he wrote, and explained that John was busy 'painting Air Marshalls and Admirals and making a lot of money' but had 'aged terribly'. Meanwhile, the octogenarian Walter Sickert was 'having a show at the National Gallery'. 'You see that London is just going on the same in spite of Blitzes etc.,' he wrote reassuringly.[32]

He told her of his new friendship with Aime Tschiffely, the Argentinian horseman and writer whom he had long admired but had only recently met. 'Tschiffely is Cunninghame Graham's friend and biographer who performed the greatest ride in history from Buenos Aires to New York. He is my best friend here. I often told you about him: but I didn't meet him till the other day . . . he has written two wonderful books *Tschiffely's Ride* and *Don Roberto*.'[33]

According to Anna, Roy idolized Tschiffely and saw him as a role model because he was 'very macho' and a hero of the mythical 'equestrian nation'.[34] Her view is buttressed by Roy's description of the Argentinian in *Light on a Dark Horse* as 'that superb rider, in many ways the world's greatest horseman, my friend, Aime Tschiffely, the hero of the ten thousand mile trek from Buenos Aires to Washington, through jungle, deserts, and cordilleras'.[35]

Tschiffely believed that Campbell was being 'wasted' as an air-raid warden and Roy told Mary that he was 'helping me to get a better job'.[36] Yet Roy also confessed that 'this regular work' had been beneficial, a clear allusion to the curtailment of the heavy bouts of drinking which his duties as a warden had necessitated, at least on the days when he was working. 'I am very compos mentis here,' he assured his wife.[37] In another letter he confessed more candidly to his need for Mary's stabilizing influence to counter his more reckless tendencies. 'I only love you and there is too much of the canine element in this free-living pueblicito.'[38]

Mary's replies to Roy's letters do not seem to have survived, but her sense of helpless isolation while she and her daughters were stranded in Portugal can be gauged from Anna's memories of the autumn months of 1941.

> . . . nothing could have equalled the incredible boredom of waiting in Lisbon for a flying clipper to take us back to England. There was a six months' waiting list but we could not settle down to doing anything worthwhile since we had to be on the alert every night in case we were called. It was really very difficult and I think I understood then why boredom is the worst suffering . . . I remember that time as a long, deeply depressing, grey interlude.[39]

The gist of Mary's letters to Roy, her evident sense of neglect and her concerns about Roy's drinking are all apparent from the nature of one of his replies written in November or December 1941.

> I was very sad to get your last two letters . . . both written in an unhappy frame of mind, as if I had neglected you . . .
>
> If you are not well darling just resign yourself, and rest both physically and mentally. I shall never love anybody else and I shall tend you every minute of my spare time. I have seen a million faces since I came here but the combined effect of them is only to make me long for yours to take you in my arms once more and be a good husband to you. If you could see the people here – how they drink and carry on – you will find that I am by comparison a stodgy puritan and a very steady character, and resign yourself better to my faults.[40]

Roy makes little mention of the practice of his faith in any of the letters from this time, although he does say that he was going to confession every week, which would suggest that he was also fulfilling his obligation to attend Mass on Sundays and Holy Days. The weekly confession was no doubt prompted by the danger of sudden death during the Blitz and is not indicative of any new heights of piety. On the contrary, on 8 December, the Feast of the Immaculate Conception, he wrote to Mary, Tess and Anna that he was thinking of them all the time 'and especially today the Annunciation'.[41] His confusion of these two very distinct feasts is further evidence that his Catholicism was more a matter of instinct than instruction.

In the same letter Roy seemed resigned to spending Christmas without his family. 'I wanted us all to be together . . . but I have been everywhere and done everything to try to get you priority and it is of no avail. We just have to put up with things as they are. I don't like them any better than you.'

Roy's enforced separation from his family was fuelling the growing frustration at his failure to get enlisted, exacerbated by his dislike of the depressingly long and cold nights of the first English winter he had endured for years. In the letter to his wife and daughters he reminded them that they had always liked England more than he, 'who was nursed in the African sunshine . . . I would give twenty years of my life to be out in Tobruk with George and Bruce or anywhere there is a spot of daylight or sunshine. Things move incredibly slow here especially with regard to enlistment.' Earlier he had complained that William Plomer, 'a fellow that doesn't know a battleship from a west African canoe', had a job in the Admiralty, while his artist friend Tristram Hillier was an officer in the Royal Navy: 'Hillier, the sea-sick, is a naval officer, though I never saw such a lubber in my life.'[42] While his friends and enemies served their country, it was becoming increasingly difficult to remain sidelined, hoping 'every day to break through the red tape'.

Within days of Roy's dejected letter to his family on 8 December, Mary, Tess and Anna were informed at very short notice that seats were available on a flying boat. They flew at night and arrived at an airfield in the south of Ireland at dawn. They travelled by bus to Dublin, where they stayed overnight in a hotel. On the following morning they flew in a small, uncomfortable plane to Bristol and then caught a train to Paddington Station. 'We had been very prepared for the devastation of the blitz,' writes Anna, 'but not at all for the incredibly efficient black-out. This took quite a lot of getting used to; even the taxis went about in almost total darkness. London was grim and endless.'[43]

Exhausted by their journey, they stumbled through the blackout on a bitingly cold, sleety night to Campbell's lodging house on Conway Street – only to find that he was not at home. There had been no opportunity to wire ahead, so Roy was oblivious of their arrival. In desperation they began to search for him in the local pubs and by a stroke of luck found him drinking in the Windmill with Eve Kirk. Roy had not seen his wife and daughters for over four months and was utterly thrilled when he saw them walk in. The surprise and joy of their reunion eclipsed the blacked-out misery of wartime London, even though they were forced to spend the night in Eve Kirk's bombed and windowless house. Only days earlier they had resigned themselves to spending Christmas apart, but now, quite unexpectedly, they were able to enjoy a family Christmas in the spacious comfort of Mary's mother's house in South Harting, on the border of Sussex and Hampshire.

Early in the New Year, Roy finally received the news for which he had been waiting, with increasing impatience, for almost six months. He had been accepted by the Army Intelligence Corps because of his knowledge of languages and was to begin training, as a private, with the Royal Welsh Fusiliers on 1 April 1942.

With renewed enthusiasm, and with fingers itching to take up arms for his country at last, Roy gave a broadcast for the Overseas Africa Service of the BBC on 2 March. Not for the first time, the poet was taking up the cudgels as a propagandist. This time, however, he had swapped his 'surly fascism' for a jingoistic anti-fascism. With due solemnity, he told his African listeners that when he had arrived from the 'Axis-ridden' continent several months earlier he had 'discovered England'. It was not his first visit, but he had 'never seen the real England before'. Although he had 'secretly revered the British' as his ancestors, he had preferred to do so 'at a respectful distance'.

Campbell's metamorphosis from renegade Spaniard to true son of the British Empire was epitomized in his comparison of the 'dull grey chrysalis' of pre-war England with the 'winged and fiery' butterfly that she had become since the beginning of the war. 'England grew her wings in the first moment of adversity and it's now easy for me to see and admire the emerging strength and beauty,' he said. England was 'a warrior nation', whereas her enemies were merely 'militarized'. 'I had volunteered to come over and share in the privations and misery of the British as represented by Axis propaganda in Spain. But I found I had really come to share the bread and the laughter of the healthiest nation alive.'[44]

The transformation from 'fascist' to anti-fascist appeared to be complete. Many, however, would continue to doubt Roy's veracity, believing that he was protesting his innocence too loudly. The change from enemy to friend seemed too sudden, too abrupt, to be genuine. Roy, for his part, would soon tire of his brief flirtatious affair with the English and would resume his natural antagonism towards all things Anglo-Saxon. Towards the end of the war he would look back wistfully at the oscillating shallowness of his ideological posturing. With disarming honesty he would confess, in lines of self-parody, that the poet was a poseur:

> We change ideas and moods like shirts or singlets,
> Which, having shed, they rise to mock us still:
> And the wind laughs and shakes her golden ringlets
> To set them independent of our will.[45]

NOTES

1 Roy Campbell, from 'Jungle Eclogue', *Collected Poems, Volume Two*, p. 83.
2 Roy Campbell, unpublished letter to his mother, 17 October 1939.
3 Roy Campbell, unpublished letter to his mother, July 1939.
4 Roy Campbell, unpublished letter to Edmund Blunden, 30 May 1939.
5 Roy Campbell, unpublished letter to his mother, November 1939.
6 Teresa Campbell, unpublished memoirs, p. 58.
7 Peter Alexander, *Roy Campbell*, p. 187.
8 Anna Campbell Lyle, *Son of Valour*, p. 146.
9 Natal *Daily News*, 27 August 1941; quoted in Peter Alexander, *Roy Campbell*, p. 188.
10 Roy Campbell, unpublished letter to Mary Campbell, September/October 1941.
11 Roy Campbell, unpublished letter to Mary Campbell, October 1941.
12 *Ibid.*
13 Peter Alexander, *Roy Campbell*, p. 190.
14 Roy Campbell, unpublished letter to Mary Campbell, October 1941; and Mrs Margaret Campbell, unpublished letter to C. J. Sibbett, 9 January 1950.
15 Roy Campbell, unpublished letter to Mary Campbell, October/November 1941.
16 Roy Campbell, unpublished letter to Mary Campbell, October 1941.
17 Roy Campbell, *Light on a Dark Horse*, p. 320.
18 Ian MacNiven and Harry Moore (eds), *Literary Lifelines*, p. 54.
19 *Ibid.*, p. 56.
20 Hugh Ford (ed.), *Nancy Cunard*, p. 356.
21 W. K. Rose (ed.), *The Letters of Wyndham Lewis*, p. 338.
22 *Ibid.*
23 Roy Campbell, *Light on a Dark Horse*, p. 226.
24 Roy Campbell, unpublished letter to Mary Campbell, October 1941.
25 Hugh Ford (ed.), *Nancy Cunard*, p. 355.
26 Valerie Grove, *Laurie Lee: The Well-loved Stranger*, London: Viking, 1999, pp. 149–50.
27 Paul Ferris (ed.), *The Collected Letters of Dylan Thomas*, London: J. M. Dent, 1985, p. 56.
28 Valerie Grove, *Laurie Lee*, p. 149.
29 Sean Day-Lewis, *C. Day-Lewis: An English Literary Life*, London: Weidenfeld & Nicolson, 1980, p. 165.
30 Peter Alexander, *Roy Campbell*, p. 190.
31 Dylan Thomas and John Davenport, *The Death of the King's Canary*, London: Hutchinson, 1976, pp. 120–21.
32 Roy Campbell, unpublished letter to Mary Campbell, October 1941.
33 *Ibid.*
34 Anna Campbell Lyle, interview with the author, Portugal, December 1998.
35 Roy Campbell, *Light on a Dark Horse*, p. 4.
36 Roy Campbell, unpublished letter to Mary Campbell, October 1941.
37 *Ibid.*
38 Roy Campbell, unpublished letter to Mary Campbell, October 1941.
39 Anna Campbell Lyle, *Son of Valour*, p. 147.
40 Roy Campbell, unpublished letter to Mary Campbell, November/December 1941.

41 Roy Campbell, unpublished letter to Mary, Teresa and Anna Campbell, 8 December 1941.
42 Roy Campbell, unpublished letter to Mary Campbell, October 1941.
43 Anna Campbell Lyle, *Son of Valour*, pp. 147–8.
44 Roy Campbell, 'Calling South Africa', transcript of a broadcast for the Overseas Africa Service of the BBC, 2 March 1942; published in Roy Campbell, *Collected Works IV: Prose*, pp. 284–5.
45 From 'Washing Day', *Collected Poems, Volume One*, p. 283.

CHAPTER TWENTY-SEVEN

'I'M FIGHTING FOR NO BETTER WORLD'

I'm fighting for no better world
But for a worse – the blasted pit
Wherein the bones of this were hurled –
And our hegemony of it!
I'm fighting for a funkhole-warren
Of bureaucrats, who've come to stay,
Because I'd rather, than the foreign
Equivalent, it should be they.[1]

On 31 March 1942 Roy set off for Brecon in South Wales to begin his basic training. He was seen off at Harting Station by his wife and mother-in-law on a cold, crisp and bright morning. The day warmed up as his journey continued, reflecting the new recruit's budding optimism at finally being accepted into the ranks of His Majesty's forces. 'It was sweet of you to come with me to the station,' he wrote to Mary on his arrival at the barracks. 'It was a long journey but the weather is a treat – bracing warm and fine. Today might have been a day in Spain.'[2]

As soon as Roy gave his name at Brecon he was greeted with enthusiasm by one of the officers, Andrew Cruikshank, who was a great admirer of his poetry. Campbell was not pleased to be recognized, however, and told Cruikshank that he had given up writing poetry. 'No, no, you mustn't!' Cruikshank exclaimed.[3]

Roy, at 40, was far older than the other recruits and the drunken nights in London had taken their toll. Cruikshank described him as flabby and pale on his arrival, adding that but for his face, the middle-aged poet could have been taken for an unemployed docker. 'I seem to be the Grandfather of our lot here,' Roy wrote to Mary. 'I am very happy though and getting very fit. The air and scenery are both exhilarating and I couldn't be with a better crowd of men though I must seem like an old Fogey among them with my bald head and my limp.'[4] Roy was determined to make a good soldier and worked extremely hard to overcome the obstacles of age and previous injuries.

He informed Mary that he was managing to hold his own with 'the youngsters' in everything but running, 'and even then I don't come last of all, though my hip-joint wobbles atrociously. It is amazing what one's carcase can stand.'[5]

Aware of Mary's concern for his spiritual as much as for his physical fitness, he assured her that there were 50 other Catholics in the camp and that there was a Catholic church in Brecon, 'so I shall be OK from that point of view'.[6]

As his basic training progressed, Roy began to feel a sense of psychological cohesion with his comrades-in-arms. More than ever he felt a sense of duty to the war effort. 'Somehow I don't feel that the British have even started to wake up yet,' he wrote to Mary towards the end of May, 'but it certainly does not pay to try to wake them up . . . What one can do is to volunteer and serve and suffer with the lowest and poorest of them. That is what satisfies me, all other methods having failed.'[7]

In the midst of the rigours of his training, Roy still found time for composition. In May he wrote one of his finest sonnets, 'San Juan de la Cruz', presenting a copy of it to Lieutenant Cruikshank. He had been re-reading and translating the poems of St John of the Cross for the previous two years and the sublime heights reached in his sonnet to the Spanish mystic are almost worthy of the saint himself.

> His voice an iris through its rain of jewels –
> Or are they tears, those embers of desire,
> Whose molten brands each gust of song re-fuels? –
> He crucifies his heart upon his lyre,
> Phoenix of Song, whose deaths are his renewals,
> With pollen for his cinders, bleeding fire!

On 13 June Mary travelled to Brecon to see him, staying for two nights. 'After that lovely two days with you my mind and body and soul were sort of perfumed,' he wrote, 'and I was re-living every day every impression I had and trying to keep it like a flower with the dew on it.'[8] In the afterglow of her visit Roy translated St John's poem '*En Una Nocha Oscura*', which he completed just a few days after Mary's departure.[9]

> O Night that was my guide!
> O Darkness dearer than the morning's pride,
> O Night that joined the lover
> To the beloved bride,
> Transfiguring them each into the other!

Within my flowering breast,
Which only for himself entire I save,
He sank into his rest
And all my gifts I gave . . .

Lost to myself I stayed,
My face upon my lover having laid
From all endeavours ceasing:
And, all my cares releasing,
Threw them amongst the lilies there to fade.

Having completed his basic training, Roy was transferred in July to the Intelligence Corps Depot near Winchester, where he was trained on motor-cycles. He was made to ride across country, over rough terrain, jumping logs and ditches. He complained to Mary that he had 'to concentrate on footgears, magnetos, sprockets, strokes, ignition controls and all sorts of things like that'.[10] For someone who hated anything mechanical, who had never learnt to drive, and who preferred the company of horses to that of cars or machines, the experience was unsettling. Soon after his arrival he wrote in a state of shock to Mary:

> Well: I simply can't even begin to tell you my impressions. I haven't collected my wits yet. I have never even imagined such rigid discipline. For an unmethodical idiot like me it is absolutely *terrifying* . . . Even our weekends are not free, as they were in Brecon. This is Brecon life tightened up with an eight foot spanner. It is just about twice as strenuous too. We creep down the corridors like hunted hares – and shy like horses at the various bellows which are shot at us by the N.C.O.s. Every order sounds the same
>
> Squad Harrrrrrh!!!
> Squad Harrrrrrh!!!
> Squad Harrrrrrh!!!
>
> so you have to decide whether it is stand at ease or quick march or mark time or shunt . . .
>
> But believe me (I may seem to whine for sympathy) this sort of training will do me good, if it does not drive me into an asylum . . .[11]

On 12 August he wrote to his mother that he was 'by some years the grand-father of our platoon', but that he had 'stood the wear and tear pretty well'.[12] At the end of October, Roy was moved to Wentworth, near Rotherham in Yorkshire, for training in map-reading and orienteering. Here, as in Wales and Hampshire, he proved popular with his colleagues. 'I don't know what it is here,' he wrote to Mary, 'but though I was liked in my former Platoon

I seem to have got really extremely popular.' He was surprised 'at the sort of extravagant affection (may it last!)' that he was enjoying. 'It is quite a change for me after being so eminently unpopular as a writer. I only hope it lasts – and spreads!'[13]

He asked Mary to buy a copy of a 'very good' new anthology of modern verse 'with T. S. Eliot and me and Bill Empson and Dylan Thomas and all my friends and enemies in it' as a present for Tess, who was about to celebrate her twentieth birthday. He also assured Mary that he had arranged 'to confess tomorrow before Mass so as to communicate – especially for you my beloved morena', which suggests that Mary had been urging him to practise his faith more devoutly.[14]

Mary was as devout and uncompromising as ever in the practice of her own faith. Tess recalls that she cycled the three miles to church from their rented cottage near Petersfield regardless of the weather: 'In mid-winter, with intense cold, she would cycle through the blizzards and snow to church.'[15] She was also busy proselytizing, endeavouring to persuade her sister Lorna to become a Catholic, much to Laurie Lee's displeasure. Rather disconcertingly, Lee found himself arguing against Lorna's growing attraction to Catholicism as he had argued against Mary seven years earlier. 'Are you an atheist?' Lorna asked him. 'I can't bear you to think otherwise than I do.' Lee responded by dismissing Catholicism as 'the religion of repression'.[16] As with his earlier discussions with Mary, his arguments failed to impress. Lorna was received into the Church soon afterwards, ending the affair with Lee, and remained a fervent Catholic, like her sister, for the rest of her life.

Roy's understanding of the importance of his and Mary's religion, and his own deep dependence on both his wife and his faith, were expressed in a letter he wrote to Mary from Wentworth, a letter which offers a valuable insight into his relationship with her after 20 years of marriage.

> But now . . . is the time that our religion can help us most. Now that the novelty of army has worn off and that most terrible of all my enemies . . . Boredom – is beginning to threaten me at times I find that my Faith is the only thing that keeps me a good comrade so that my temper is even and I don't quarrel or fall into the grooves of grumbling and foul mouthedness. As for women, I am very powerfully armed quite apart from my faith since I love you so very deeply and passionately that I only have to think of you and all other women become spectres and insipid wraiths. You have become a part of me and I converse with you all the time. Whatever I see or do, I wonder what you would think of it or how you would like it. So you are my constant companion in spite of distance and time.
>
> It is Sunday morning. We could not go to mass today as we had

> to do fatigues. I am afraid the nearest church is a long way off from what I hear but there is some sort of bus service. From next Sunday we should be allowed to attend mass as usual.[17]

Mary and Tess were having their own problems during the winter of 1942. The monthly cheques from South Africa had been interrupted by the war, and in desperation they both became domestic servants, working as cook and chambermaid for a wealthy widow near Petersfield. Since Mary had always employed others to do her housework in Provence, Spain and Portugal, the life of domestic service did not come easily to her. Roy felt her predicament acutely.

> You must tell me everything you suffer and not keep it to yourself. Don't be afraid of upsetting me. There is no one else who can share your troubles but me. That is what I am your husband for, and moreover I love you more tenderly and passionately every day of every year . . .
>
> Goodbye for tonight beloved. May God and Our Lady and all his saints watch over you in your trials. I pray for you all the time and if the thought of your suffering does pain me a bit I love that pain because I share it with you. We have grown up well together and there may be a time of great happiness together and a serene old age in peace, when all these trials are over. God bless you.[18]

This was a time of trial for husband as well as wife. Roy was becoming increasingly frustrated by the seemingly endless training and by the absence of any news of his longed-for posting abroad. He had passed at map-reading at the second attempt, but failed in orienteering. His hip, which had held out well during basic training, had finally given under the strain and he was receiving treatment for rheumatism. Although this meant he was excused marching and physical training, he was set to work scrubbing wet stone floors, which hardly helped his recovery. He accepted his own sufferings stoically and kept hoping that he would eventually hear news of the desired posting. 'I have come through it smiling and I refuse to let it get me down whatever happens . . . Anyway I am happy inwardly to have you and the kids always in my mind – and my luck may change any day.'[19]

After spending a depressing Christmas in camp, 200 miles from his family, he finally received the news for which he had been waiting. He was to be posted to East Africa in the spring. In February 1943 he was promoted to sergeant, to his enormous satisfaction, and in March finally set sail on the troopship *Antenor*.

Off the coast of Ireland the convoy sailed into a heavy storm and Campbell's ship began experiencing engine trouble. She lost speed, slipped towards the rear of the convoy and struggled to keep up. Finally she broke down completely, pitching and tossing helplessly. The convoy, with its protective aircraft carrier and destroyers, was forced to abandon her, leaving her defenceless. For five days the *Antenor* wallowed without power, a sitting target for German submarines. The troops, soaked to the skin, lived in their life jackets expecting the worst, while water, thick with vomit, washed through the mess deck. This ordeal became the inspiration for Campbell's poem 'One Transport Lost':

> Where, packed as tight as space can fit them
> The soldiers retch, and snore, and stink,
> It was no bunch of flowers that hit them
> And woke them up, that night, to drink.

Eventually the engineers managed to repair one of the engines and the *Antenor* limped back to the safety of Glasgow. The troops were transferred promptly to another ship and set sail once again. Campbell passed the voyage reading Dante, Samuel Butler and the Portuguese poet Camoëns. He also gave talks to the officers' mess on bullfighting and the Spanish Civil War, for which he was paid in large quantities of whisky and rum, washed down with beer chasers. 'This is a very enjoyable and comfortable voyage,' he reported to Mary. 'I am very well and as happy as either of us can ever be in the absence of the other, after so many years of inseparability.'[20]

For want of room, the padre on the voyage was not able to hear confessions, but general absolution was given to all the Catholic troops because of the imminent danger of death. Campbell attended Mass every morning, communicating daily, and the prospect of danger seems to have channelled his thoughts towards the essentials of his life. He wrote a particularly poignant letter to Mary, putting their lives, past and present, into perspective.

> We must go back together and live for good in Spain after the war. How insipid and unreal most other countries seem by comparison. We should by then be able to settle down for good as our age will excuse us from volunteering in any subsequent world-wars. It is very rough to have to separate now when we both seem to be at our best, and after literally growing up from a boy and girl in each other's arms, and passing such an adventurous and hazardous existence together.
>
> All the delightful comradeship that I have experienced both in the Army in Spain and England (and I have got to love the Britishers very much especially the Yorkshire and Scotch people) cannot make up for being separated from you. But I am far luckier than you since soldiering is a real vocation if one lives it properly and for you, this period is

> one of marking time ... Still, now, if ever is the time for us both to strengthen each other by continual prayer for each other ...
>
> I have a very nice corner of the mess-deck, so that I can get away by myself and study my photos of you and think of you and pray for you and think of all the wonderful crazy and delightful things that you and I have done together in our travels over such a vast tract of time and space together. Why it will not be so very long before we shall have been married a quarter of a century!! and yet we are still so full of beans, it is wonderful. I think with our experience and faith and love we shall be able to make as fine a job of the afternoon of life as we did of the morning – only it is a pity to miss so much of the noon ... For the rest it has been absolutely wonderful, and looking back everything in our lives seems to fall into place and assume the significance of some miraculous design bearing everywhere the signature of Providence – so much so that no accident of death could rob us now of what is between us.[21]

Roy must have sensed the hand of providence when he discovered that the convoy was headed for Durban, sailing into the harbour early in April. He had not seen the city of his birth for over 16 years and his heart must have leapt as the familiar landscape emerged into view. Further good fortune followed because Roy was informed, on disembarkation, that he was being given two weeks' leave. Unexpectedly, he had the opportunity to spend valuable time with his ageing mother, who was now 80, and with his brother George. He passed many happy hours fishing, swimming and sunbathing at his brother's hut in the forest before reporting back for duty.

On 18 April Roy began a marathon trek overland across Africa to Nairobi. From Durban he travelled in a military train to Johannesburg, before proceeding to Beit Bridge and Bulawayo. 'We had the most amazing journey imaginable,' he wrote to Mary from a ship halfway across Lake Victoria Nyanza, 'zig-zagging all the way ... by rail, by road, by rivers, and by lakes, jungle, swamp, mountain, and savannah ...' He had seen the Victoria Falls from a train, 'only ... a passing glimpse but one which I shall never forget', and this was merely 'the beginning of a succession of wonderful sights'.[22] Roy was beginning his active service as a tourist.

The journey ended with the troops' arrival in Nairobi on 5 May. Roy was attached to the King's African Rifles and posted to a camp two miles out of the city. After a demoralizing job as a military censor, he was transferred in June to the 12th Observation Unit of the commando force being trained for jungle warfare against the Japanese. 'I have been transferred to an advanced Recce unit for commando work,' he wrote proudly to Mary. He was 'extremely fit and ... feeling very pleased with myself since I am by far the oldest man selected for the job'. Although he was not at liberty to tell Mary explicitly that he was destined for the Far East, he hinted as much by stating that he would not be in Africa for much longer, 'but very, very far away from here, and still further from you'. Nonetheless, he would be near Mary in his 'prayers and thoughts and poems, for the more I miss you the more acutely I feel you, and think you, and dream you'.[23]

Roy's expectations of seeing real action against the Japanese in the Far East were destined to be short-lived. Late in July he injured his already damaged hip in a fall from a motorcycle during training at the foot of Mount Kilimanjaro. He was sent back to hospital in Nairobi, where the doctors examined an X-ray of his hip and declared him unfit for active service.

During the period of enforced inactivity while his hip was recovering, Roy met up each evening after dinner with a group of young men who were interested in literature. They were mostly young Jewish students from Palestine who were eager to discuss almost anything, from the Talmud and Roman Catholicism to the social purpose of art. They were greatly impressed by Roy's erudition and dubbed him 'Maestro', quite literally sitting at his feet as he expounded his philosophy of life, religion and art.[24]

Now that he was certified unfit, he was employed as a coast-watcher, looking out for enemy submarines on the Kenyan coast north of Mombasa. Between September 1943 and April 1944 Roy's life was divided between the boredom of this sedentary job and the misery of recovering from several bouts of malaria in Mombasa hospital. It was here that he spent the Christmas of 1943, brooding over the future; here too that he spent the whole of February 1944 and much of March. It was difficult in such circumstances to keep believing that his desperate endeavours to fight for Britain had been worth all the sacrifices, yet he did his best to convince both Mary and himself that his labours had not been entirely in vain.

> You will see in the end that it was worth it. There is only one kind of socialism that is not sheer self-seeking claptrap and boloney – and that is voluntarily to share the burdens of the very lowest conscript and all the burdens that are imposed on one's fellow men and women. We could easily have escaped separation if I had accepted the reserved jobs offered me on the BBC and M.O.I. As a South African I was never liable to conscription or enlistment except as a volunteer. But it was the only thing for a Christian soldier to do, in a world where everyone is snarling for his rights . . .[25]

The hints of barely subdued bitterness displayed in this letter would animate much of the verse he wrote at this time. He was alienated by a socialism rooted in the selfish 'snarling' for rights, and saw for post-war Britain only a drab egalitarian future run by bureaucrats in which 'Christian duty' would have no place. This post-war world, the vision of which was so depressing to the romantic poet, had been set out by William Beveridge in the celebrated 'Beveridge Report' published in November 1942. In essence the report called for wider involvement by the apparatus of the state in the lives of the populace, principally through a scheme of 'social insurance' covering the whole population.

Such a vision, hailed in Britain as a blueprint for post-war recovery and renewal, was in Campbell's eyes a further intrusion of the all-powerful bureaucratic state into the lives and liberties of individuals. He derided this report in a terse poem, entitled simply 'The Beveridge Plan', consisting of a solitary quatrain of vitriol in which its underlying principles are attacked as 'Fascidemokshevism'. In this one morosely constructed word, coined in Africa, is to be found the clearest insight into Campbell's political philosophy. Indeed, more can be learnt about his politics from this one word than from the 5,000 lines of *Flowering Rifle*. He was, at heart, a libertarian who believed that modern states, whether they called themselves fascist, democratic or Bolshevist, were exerting too much power over the lives of individuals and families. Against the complex and powerful bureaucracies advocated by Beveridge, Campbell counterposed small, self-supporting communities of freely co-operating families, much as he had seen in Provence, Portugal and Spain.

Bearing in mind his somewhat unorthodox grouping together of fascism, Bolshevism and democracy, Campbell would no doubt have been wryly amused, though perhaps not entirely surprised, to discover that Joseph Goebbels, Hitler's Propaganda Minister, was interested enough in the Beveridge Report to make a close study of it.

Similar disillusionment was present in 'The Moon of Short Rations', in which Campbell lamented that his sacrificial atonement for having backed the 'wrong horse' in Spain was wasted in his service of an Allied cause which championed multinational companies such as Woolworths and left-wing socialism as personified by the Labour MP Tom Driberg.

> Now is the Ramadan of lions,
> When he who fought for Christ in Spain
> Atoning, to remove the blot,
> Crusades for Woolworths and for Lyons,
> Tom Driberg, and the ghostly train
> Whose love will wash away the spot.

This brave new world of creeping centralization, multinational capitalism and international socialism was alien to Campbell. His romantic and oversensitive disdain for modernity and his desire for an uncomplicated life of rustic liberty were out of tune with the times. He was ill-fitted for life in the mechanized and depersonalized society envisaged for Beveridge's Britain, and even as he lay in his hospital bed in Mombasa he was dreaming of an escape to Spain, Portugal or even Latin America where life was simpler. With a growing sense of desolation and isolation, he braced himself for a post-war world ruled by 'bureaucrats, who've come to stay', realizing, as he waited to be invalided home, that he had been 'fighting for no better world / But for a worse'.

NOTES

1 Roy Campbell, from 'Monologue', *Collected Poems, Volume Two*, p. 68.
2 Roy Campbell, unpublished letter to Mary Campbell, 31 March 1942.
3 Peter Alexander, *Roy Campbell*, p. 192.
4 Roy Campbell, unpublished letter to Mary Campbell, April 1942.
5 Roy Campbell, unpublished letter to Mary Campbell, April 1942.
6 *Ibid.*
7 Roy Campbell, unpublished letter to Mary Campbell, late May 1942.
8 Roy Campbell, unpublished letter to Mary Campbell, June/July 1942.
9 Roy Campbell, unpublished letter to Mary Campbell, 18 June 1942.
10 Roy Campbell, unpublished letter to Mary Campbell, July 1942.
11 Roy Campbell, unpublished letter to Mary Campbell, July 1942.
12 Roy Campbell, unpublished letter to his mother, 12 August 1942.
13 Roy Campbell, unpublished letter to Mary Campbell, early November 1942.
14 *Ibid.*
15 Teresa Campbell, unpublished memoirs, p. 128.
16 Valerie Grove, *Laurie Lee*, p. 167.
17 Roy Campbell, unpublished letter to Mary Campbell, early November 1942.
18 Roy Campbell, unpublished letter to Mary Campbell, November 1942.
19 *Ibid.*
20 Roy Campbell, unpublished letter to Mary Campbell, late March/early April 1943.
21 *Ibid.*
22 Roy Campbell, unpublished letter to Mary Campbell, late April/early May 1943.
23 Roy Campbell, unpublished letter to Mary Campbell, June 1943.
24 Peter Alexander, *Roy Campbell*, p. 198.
25 Roy Campbell, unpublished letter to Mary Campbell, 24 August 1943.

CHAPTER TWENTY-EIGHT

BUCKING BRONCO

Then the kick of a bronco that bounced like a ball
And laid me out limp in the mire of the kraal –
And the kick retrospective, the kick, the collective
Accumulative kick one gets out of it all.
For it all totalled up to the kick that is best –
The kick that one gets from enjoying a rest.[1]

During the long months of boredom on the Kenyan coast or in hospital in Mombasa, Campbell began to brood over his predicament. In particular, he began to resent the fact that, in spite of his efforts to fight against Hitler, he was still branded a fascist for having supported Franco. He compared his own position as a volunteer in the armed services with the position of leading left-wing poets such as Louis MacNeice, Stephen Spender, W. H. Auden and Cecil Day-Lewis, who had either settled for 'soft jobs' at home or, in the case of Auden, had emigrated to the United States at the first hint of the coming war. These men, his old adversaries from the previous decade, were perceived by Campbell as the poetic epitome of the vision of Britain set out by Beveridge. He invented a composite word to encompass MacNeice, Spender, Auden and Day-Lewis: they became collectively 'MacSpaunday', the poetic voice of Beveridge's 'Fascidemokshevism'.

. . . joint MacSpaunday shuns the very strife
He barked for loudest, when mere words were rife,
When to proclaim his proletarian loyalties
Paid well, was safe, raked in the heavy royalties,
And made the Mealy Mouth and Bulging Purse
The hallmark of Contemporary verse.
Then joint MacSpaunday, with quadruple bun
Commercially collectivised in one,
A Cerberus-Hyena, could not cease
His fierce Belligerence (in times of peace!)
But plagiarised from Blimp, ten years before,
The most ferocious arguments of war.[2]

Late in February 1944, while he was laid up in hospital, Campbell was incensed to see an issue of *New Writing* in which Day-Lewis had written a poem which began, 'Will it be so again?' Since Day-Lewis was safely employed in a 'soft job' at the Ministry of Information, Campbell was provoked into writing 'The Volunteer's Reply to the Poet'.

> So the Soldier replied to the Poet,
> Oh yes! it will all be the same,
> But a bloody sight worse, and you know it
> Since you have a hand in the game . . .
> You coin us the catchwords and phrases
> For which to be slaughtered; and then,
> While thousands are blasted to blazes,
> Sit picking your nose with your pen . . .
> We can die for our faith by the million
> And laugh at our bruises and scars,
> But hush! for the Poet-Civilian
> Is weeping, between the cigars . . .
> Oh well may he weep for the soldier,
> Who weeps at a guinea a tear,
> For although his invention gets mouldier,
> It keeps him his job in the rear.

Even as Campbell's ill-fated efforts to fight for Britain were coming to an end, he was already picking his next personal fight with his old literary enemies. In peace, if not in war, he would emerge with all guns blazing. For the present, however, he was left tending his 'bruises and scars'. Renewed problems with his hip were added to the bouts of malaria and he wrote to Mary on 12 March to assure her that the bone was not diseased. 'It's more wear & tear through trying to bluff it through route marches etc when it was chipped and twisted and that ground it up.'[3]

Roy's professed disillusionment with the likely political direction of post-war Britain led him to suggest earnestly to Mary that they make their escape to South Africa or Spain. He even suggested Paraguay or Ecuador as possible destinations. The romantic notions he had developed of the latter two countries had been awakened by travel books on South America, the reading of which was probably inspired by his lasting admiration for Aime Tschiffely. Mary, however, had other ideas. The monthly cheques were once more arriving regularly from South Africa and she had managed to find a house at 17 Campden Grove in Kensington. She was determined to settle down to a more conventional life in England.

Roy's injured hip meant that he would never be fit for active service and, on 2 April 1944, he heard that he was to be sent home. Due to an administrative error he was sent by sea to South Africa, so that he found himself unexpectedly reunited with his mother and brothers for the second time in little over a year. He spent four weeks during May hobbling about on two sticks, revisiting old friends and favourite places. Early in June he set sail north again through the Suez Canal on the hospital ship *Oranje*, arriving in Liverpool towards the end of the month.

Convalescing in a hospital in Stockport, Roy discovered from Mary that the house in Campden Grove had been bombed for the second time, making it temporarily uninhabitable. For the time being Mary and Tess were living with the Catholic writers Bernard and Barbara Wall at their home in Oxford. Thus, when Roy was discharged from hospital, he travelled to Oxford to be reunited with his wife for the first time in almost 18 months. By a fortunate coincidence the ballet company with which Anna was touring was also performing in Oxford at that time, so the whole family was temporarily reunited. 'It was wonderful to see darling old Dad again,' Anna recalls.

> He was much subdued. Some of his fire had gone but he had grown in wisdom. Long months of silence and reflection had brought him to a state of mature growth; of spiritual development . . . He was now more tolerant and he had come to the conclusion that in this uncertain world no one person is wholly wrong and bad, or wholly right and good.[4]

Although Roy's bitter battle with Spender, Auden *et al.* would soon demonstrate that, contrary to Anna's assertions, her father was still capable of a good deal of intolerance and vindictiveness, her words are more than mere wishful thinking. There are signs in Roy's letters and his poetry from this time that he had developed a mellower, more sober and sombre approach to life.

In 'Reflections', written soon after his return to England, Roy exhibits an introspective and self-critical judgement of himself:

> Of many selves that meet in me
> The meanest has the most persisted,
> The one that joined the A.R.P
> When half humanity enlisted.
>
> A shifty and insidious ghost,
> Of all my selves he is the one,
> Though it's with him I meet the most,
> I'd go the longest way to shun.

When T. S. Eliot mistook the reference to the ARP as a gibe against Spender, who had served in the National Fire Service during the Blitz, Campbell was quick to assure him that the stanza was meant self-critically. 'As soon as the Blitz was over, I was sorely tempted to remain on in that job. Every man has that side to his nature where the poltroon and the hedonist (and the devil) all pull together against his better Nature.'[5] In fact, Campbell was to show the worse side of his nature a few years later when, possibly in deliberate defiance of Eliot's comments, he amended the stanza in the version that appeared in his first volume of *Collected Poems* so that it was unmistakably levelled at Spender and not at himself:

Of many selves we all possess
My meanest has the most persisted,
The one that joined the N.F.S.
When half humanity enlisted.

The mellower, more introspective Campbell is displayed in two other poems written in the first months after his return to England. In 'Arion', a poem dedicated to Mary, he describes himself as 'limping amongst the prams and bowlers' and dreaming that he 'had coursed in vain'. He is, however, revived by his wife, who emerges, as always, as his muse.

To set the old momentum free,
To launch me into song, and be
My boat of roses, steed of fire,
At once the courser and the shallop,
The dolphin on whose surge I gallop,
The tune, the rapture, and the lyre!

Yet the poem which best displays the mellow Campbell in the depths of humility is 'Rhapsody of the Man in Hospital Blues'. Here Roy attempts to come to terms with his dependence on a walking stick.

From Notting Hill to Prince's Gate
I'd started breaking in my stick
And of my new, three-legged gait
Acquired the quaint arithmetic.

No more to canter, trot or trippel,
Where dandies prance along the Row,
I coaxed the strange unwieldy cripple
I had become yet feared to know . . .

Wistfully, he sees himself among those who have become life's outcasts, unfit for service and unwanted by their fellow men.

Amongst the leafless trees that froze
The wind struck up with flute and fife

> The regimental march of those
> Who've fallen out of step with life.

In such circumstances the poet draws consolation from his faith, asserting that it is the humble who shall be exalted.

> To have one's Cross laid on inside
> Abates no ardour in the strife
> Though something in us might have died
> Yet something more has come to life.

Roy's return to Oxford, a quarter of a century after he had first arrived in the city as a wide-eyed 17-year-old, was a curious experience. Although he was much older, the buildings were unchanged and the streets were as full of American soldiers as they had been in 1919 – 'but this is a thirstier lot and they leave one less beer,' he observed wryly in a letter to Blunden.[6]

It was in Oxford, some time during August, that Roy had a surprise meeting with Nancy Cunard. In the wake of their far from convivial meeting in Soho three years earlier, when Cunard had publicly snubbed Campbell for supporting Franco, the meeting had the potential to be acrimonious. In the event, their shared feelings of mutual apprehension were overcome by a tactful avoidance of any mention of Spain. 'That afternoon it was of the Negroes he talked, and very sympathetically,' Cunard remembered. 'I had not realised that he felt such friendliness towards them . . . I do remember with enthusiasm the way he talked of the African Negroes that day in Oxford while the tact of both of us, in such utterly opposite camps, was equal in not referring to our partisanry in what had been a very serious thing in Spain.'[7] This was the last time they would meet – somewhat appropriately, since their first meeting had also taken place in Oxford all those years earlier, when Cunard had been much impressed by the 'tall, adolescent, strong, loose limbed youth' whom everybody called 'Zulu'.[8] It would not, however, be the last time that the 'very serious thing in Spain' would come between them.

Early in 1950 Cunard wrote an article on Spanish writers in exile, renewing her attack on Franco's regime. 'I was soon, and frequently, being told "Roy Campbell is very angry with you on account of it!"' Cunard recalled.[9] In fact, Campbell's anger led him to new depths of tasteless vitriol. He took his revenge on Cunard in a short but poisonous passage in the volume of autobiography he was writing when her anti-Franco article came to his attention.

> When superannuated English society-tarts take up negro lovers, it is generally a sort of perversion like the exaggerated feeling for dogs and cats. I knew one who went negro in order, as she said, to 'study

> conditions amongst the negroes'. Having selected the negro with the largest 'condition' she could find, she brought him to Europe. I knew this couple and they happened to call on me in a Levantine port where all the inhabitants are partly coloured . . .[10]

This passage, a scarcely disguised allusion to Cunard and her lover Henry Crowder, who had visited the Campbells in Martigues in 1929, is not only offensive but must throw Campbell's much vaunted lack of racial prejudice into question. How could someone who had sided so vocally with the native tribesmen of South Africa hold such an apparently contradictory position?

Perhaps the answer is to be found by examining these words in the context in which they were written. They come in the midst of a lengthy discussion of the race issue in which Campbell defends the record of Spain compared with that of the Anglo-Saxons. The English and Americans were being hypocrites, he maintained, when they condemned the Spanish Inquisition, 'which forbade slavery, and tried to stop it as early as the sixteenth century'.

> Spanish rule conserved millions of the aboriginal Indians of South and Central America, while they were systematically destroyed in North America (all but a few Museum Specimens on Reserves) by Anglo-Saxons of the same race as Charles Kingsley and Prescott who hypocritically indicted the Spaniards of cruelty . . . The destruction of the entire native population in Tasmania, at the hands of Britons, by 'driving' them like pheasants from end to end of the island, has no counterpart in Spanish colonisation.
>
> One thing is certain: Latin and Celtic peoples are not generally attacked by colour-feeling and prejudice in the same way as English, Germans, Dutch, and Norwegians; who appear to be allergic to negroes.[11]

Campbell follows this discussion by stating that he has 'no colour prejudice', although he believes miscegenation to be 'silly', before making the thinly veiled attack on Nancy Cunard. Not for the first time, his efforts at rational debate are strangled by his desire for revenge.

During their stay in Oxford, Roy and Mary visited Campion Hall, home of the city's Jesuit community. They met Father Martin D'Arcy, whose culture and brilliance had won him many friends and admirers among the Catholic literati. Roy was no exception and he and Father D'Arcy became firm friends. It was at Father D'Arcy's suggestion that Roy decided, on 3 October, to seek out J. R. R. Tolkien and C. S. Lewis at the Eagle and Child public house. His meeting with them was recounted by Tolkien in a letter to one of his sons.[12]

Tolkien arrived at noon with Charles Williams, the Christian novelist, and was surprised to find Lewis and his brother Warren 'already ensconced'. The conversation was 'pretty lively' and Tolkien noticed 'a strange tall gaunt man half in khaki half in mufti with a large wide-awake hat, bright eyes and a hooked nose sitting in the corner'. Lewis and his brother had not noticed the stranger because they had their backs to him, but Tolkien saw from his eyes that he was taking an interest in the conversation, 'quite unlike the ordinary pained astonishment of the British (and American) public at the presence of the Lewises (and myself) in a pub'. Intriguingly, Tolkien's first impressions of Campbell reminded him of one of the central characters in *The Lord of the Rings*, the epic fantasy which he was still in the midst of writing. He compared Campbell to Strider, the mysterious stranger who meets the hobbits at the Prancing Pony inn.

> All of a sudden he butted in, in a strange unplaceable accent, taking up some point about Wordsworth. In a few seconds he was revealed as Roy Campbell ... Tableau! Especially as C.S.L. had not long ago violently lampooned him in the Oxford Magazine ... There is a good deal of Ulster still left in C.S.L. if hidden from himself. After that things became fast and furious and I was late for lunch. It was (perhaps) gratifying to find that this powerful poet and soldier desired in Oxford chiefly to see Lewis (and myself).

The 'violent lampoon' to which Tolkien referred was Lewis's poetic riposte to *Flowering Rifle*, published five years earlier. Although Campbell had read Lewis's attack on him, it seems from Tolkien's rendition of events that Campbell, for once, had taken the attack in good spirits and that it was Lewis who became aggressive. The three men arranged to meet again in Lewis's rooms two days later, and again it was Lewis who went on the offensive. According to Tolkien, Lewis 'had taken a fair deal of port and was a little belligerent'. He insisted on reading out his lampoon again, but Campbell laughed the provocation aside. After that Campbell appears to have held court, giving an embellished account of his life while Tolkien and Lewis listened. The combined effect of Campbell's exaggeration and Tolkien's faulty memory is evident in Tolkien's report of the biographical monologue to his son.

> What he has done ... beggars description. Here is a scion of an Ulster prot. Family resident in S. Africa, most of whom fought in both wars, who became a Catholic after sheltering the Carmelite fathers in Barcelona – in vain, they were caught & butchered, and R.C. nearly lost his life. But he got the Carmelite archives from the burning library and took them through the Red country. He speaks Spanish fluently (he has been a professional bullfighter). As you know he then fought

> through the war on Franco's side, and among other things was in the van of the company that chased the Reds out of Malaga . . . But he is a patriotic man, and has fought for the B. Army since . . . I wish I could remember half his picaresque stories, about poets and musicians etc. from Peter Warlock to Aldous Huxley . . . However, it is not possible to convey an impression of such a rare character, both a soldier and a poet, and a Christian convert. How unlike the Left – the 'corduroy panzers' who fled to America (Auden among them who with his friends got R.C.'s works 'banned' . . .).

If Campbell had made a favourable impression on Tolkien, who thought him 'old-looking war-scarred' and 'limping from recent wounds' but 'gentle, modest, and compassionate', Lewis's impressions were somewhat different, to Tolkien's evident consternation.

> C.S.L.'s reactions were odd. Nothing is a greater tribute to Red propaganda than the fact that he (who knows they are in all other subjects liars and traducers) believes all that is said against Franco, and nothing that is said for him . . . But hatred of our church is after all the real only final foundation of the C of E – so deep laid that it remains even when all the superstructure seems removed (C.S.L. for instance reveres the Blessed Sacrament, and admires nuns!). Yet if a Lutheran is put in jail he is up in arms; but if Catholic priests are slaughtered – he disbelieves it (and I daresay really thinks they asked for it). But R.C. shook him a bit . . .

Following the meeting, Lewis stated that '[I] loathed and loathe Roy Campbell's particular blend of Catholicism and Fascism, and told him so'.[13] Yet, however much Lewis had been 'shaken' by the meeting with Campbell and however much he loathed his politics, the three men seem to have parted amicably enough at the end of the evening. It was midnight when Tolkien and Campbell left Lewis's rooms at Magdalen College with all three agreeing to meet again in the future.

Over the following few years Campbell would be an occasional visitor to the Inklings, the informal literary 'club' centred on Lewis and Tolkien which met regularly in Lewis's rooms or in the Eagle and Child. At these gatherings, Campbell and Lewis would continue to cross swords, although it would be their differences on literature rather than religion or politics which would fire the debate. The gist of their differences is encapsulated in one of Lewis's poems, entitled simply 'To Roy Campbell', in which he criticizes Campbell for his negative attitude towards Romanticism. Interestingly, however, Lewis's tone is far more friendly than in his violent lampoon 'To the Author of

Flowering Rifle', suggesting that the two men had warmed to each other at subsequent meetings.

At this time, T. S. Eliot expressed an interest in publishing a new volume of Campbell's verse for Faber & Faber. The two poets saw much of each other during 1945, discussing arrangements for the volume which Campbell had entitled *Talking Bronco*. As this title indicated, the main preoccupation of much of the new poetry was Campbell's obsession with 'MacSpaunday' – 'The Talking Bronco' being the title of Stephen Spender's hostile review of *Flowering Rifle* in the *New Statesman* in 1939. Referring disdainfully to Campbell's eulogizing of 'the bronco Life', Spender had dubbed him the 'Talking Bronco': 'Here we have the Talking Bronco, the Brute Life armed with abusive words . . .'

For six years Campbell had been haunted by Spender's criticism and was now planning his revenge. In 'Talking Bronco', the poem which would lend its title to the whole volume, Campbell defiantly accepts the name that Spender had thrust upon him.

> So History looks the winner in the mouth
> Though but a dark outsider from the South,
> A Talking Bronco, sharked from ear to ear
> With laughter, like a running bandolier,
> With teeth, like bullets fastened in their clips,
> To chew the thunder and to spit the pips,
> Ejecting from the breech, in perfect time,
> The shells of metre and the shucks of rhyme,
> Yet drive the thoughts with perforating aim
> Like tracer-bullets on their threads of flame.

This was Campbell at his most combative and least contrite; the talking bronco transformed into a bucking bronco, kicking out wildly against his enemies.

As though the invective of his verse was not enough, Campbell was also determined to include a violently polemical preface lashing out at MacNeice, Spender, Auden, Day-Lewis and Hugh MacDiarmid. It fell to Eliot to try to dissuade him. Like a skilled horseman endeavouring to bring the bronco under control, Eliot worked all his powers of persuasion to bring Campbell to his senses. He hinted that he agreed with Campbell's hostile opinion of much contemporary verse, but added that he still felt it better to abstain from comment, suggesting that Campbell do likewise. 'So I don't know whether you can abbreviate this preface to what can be left, or prefer to scrap it altogether. I am not sure that it isn't better just to leave the volume to itself: and leave the vipers to be forgotten.'[14]

Campbell agreed to drop the preface entirely, but resisted Eliot's efforts to get him to drop the poems that made vitriolic references to 'MacSpaunday'. He reluctantly agreed to make all but one of the changes which Eliot proposed, softening particularly the attacks on Spender, but what remained was still destined to cause great offence.

Ironically, Campbell's reply to Eliot when he agreed to drop the preface showed that he disagreed with the foundations of his own principal argument against the left-wing poets, namely that they had been cowards in failing to fight during the war. 'Anyway it only shows how hard up we all are if we consider courage or patriotism as a criterion of poetry. (One might as well condemn the paintings of Cézanne because he deserted from the French army in the franco-prussian war!)'[15] Since he had succinctly destroyed his own case in these two short sentences, it seems surprising that he should insist on publishing the poems in the first place. The only possible explanation is that he desired, first and foremost, to inflict a blow, to reap revenge, on his literary adversaries. The truth or otherwise of his arguments against 'MacSpaunday' had little to do with his writing of the poems or his desire for their publication. He sought merely to kick his enemies where it hurt:

> . . . the kick of a bronco that bounced like a ball . . .
> And the kick retrospective, the kick, the collective
> Accumulate kick one gets out of it all.

NOTES

1 Roy Campbell, from 'Autobiography in Fifty Kicks', *Collected Poems, Volume Two*, p. 114.
2 From 'Talking Bronco', *Collected Poems, Volume Two*, p. 87.
3 Roy Campbell, unpublished letter to Mary Campbell, 12 March 1944.
4 Anna Campbell Lyle, *Son of Valour*, p. 161.
5 Roy Campbell, unpublished letter to T. S. Eliot, January 1946; quoted in Peter Alexander, *Roy Campbell*, p. 204.
6 Roy Campbell, unpublished letter to Edmund Blunden, July/August 1944; quoted in Peter Alexander, *ibid.*, p. 203.
7 Hugh Ford (ed.), *Nancy Cunard*, pp. 355–6.
8 *Ibid.*, p. 353.
9 *Ibid.*, p. 355.
10 Roy Campbell, *Light on a Dark Horse*, pp. 152–3.
11 *Ibid.*, p. 152.
12 Humphrey Carpenter and Christopher Tolkien (eds), *The Letters of J. R. R. Tolkien*, London: George Allen & Unwin, 1981, pp. 95–6.
13 Humphrey Carpenter, *The Inklings: C. S. Lewis, J. R. R. Tolkien, Charles Williams, and their friends*, London: George Allen & Unwin, 1978, p. 192.
14 Peter Alexander, *Roy Campbell*, p. 206.
15 *Ibid.*

CHAPTER TWENTY-NINE

OLD ENEMIES AND NEW FRIENDS

For Blacks I've done as much, and risked my life,
As since for Jews or Christians in the strife . . .
Had pity stirred you half as much as greed
We might have had a different tale to heed
When half a million Christians had to bleed . . .
While you with Herod, and the cash, forsooth
Must blink away the evidence of truth.
But truth will ride and race you to your end,
Propitious enemy and baleful friend![1]

In autumn 1944 Mary moved back to the house in Campden Grove, which was now inhabitable again. A few weeks later, after a further spell in a hospital in Oxford, Roy joined her. Their principal worry at this time was Tess, who had suffered a serious nervous breakdown and appeared to be deteriorating. For some time, unbeknown to her parents, Tess had been suffering from what would now be diagnosed as anorexia nervosa. Her eating disorder was the result of deeper psychological problems which had been exacerbated by her deadening experiences in the WRNS. 'I was stationed at Weymouth, a very quiet port,' writes Tess, adding that 'there was very little to do there apart from cleaning sparking plugs'.[2] Weighed down with anxiety and boredom, she began acting eccentrically. When there was nothing else to do she would rummage through the rubbish for discarded spark plugs. She would clean these, knowing that they would never be used, and then throw them away again.[3]

Tess was invalided out of the WRNS while Roy was still in Africa. She returned to live with Mary in London, but the incessant bombing merely added to her problems, precipitating the breakdown. Following an initial spell at Guy's Hospital, she was transferred to a home near Oxford and then to another run by nuns near Epsom. 'When my father came back from Africa I was at my worst. From being his pride and comfort, I became his greatest worry and nightmare. He used to come and see me, already weighed down with troubles, and my heart used to bleed to see him and there was nothing I could do to help my state, I only got worse.'[4]

Tess's treatment was expensive and it was clear that the money from South Africa would not be sufficient for the family's needs. Roy desperately began looking for work and was on the verge of being employed as a lift attendant when he was offered a post as Temporary Assistant on the War Damage Commission, the public body established in 1941 to compensate owners of houses damaged by the war. He began work on 13 November 1944 for an annual salary of less than £300.

'It is the first time I ever worked in an office,' he wrote to his mother on 4 December, 'and it is very different from the Army: though I shall get used to it soon.' He seemed resigned to his fate, informing his mother that he hoped 'to get gradually promoted, and to stay on in the civil service'. He told her that Anna had just returned from touring with her ballet company in Carlisle and Preston and was 'very sturdy and bonny', but confessed his 'anxiety about Tess as to whether her mind would weather the terrible illness which has afflicted her. She is more or less a physical wreck now and makes little progress but she seems to have retained her mental balance.'[5]

In May 1945, having recently returned from a three-month tour of Italy entertaining the Allied Armies, Anna was dancing in a show called *Strike a New Note* at London's Prince of Wales Theatre. Roy saw the show several times. On her way back from one of these performances Anna watched the crowds 'dancing and rejoicing in Piccadilly from the top of a number 9 bus'.[6] It was VE Day. The war in Europe was over.

Within weeks of the Allied victory in Europe, Roy received an invitation to make two broadcast talks for the BBC about his experiences in East Africa. When Desmond MacCarthy, who was then a member of the BBC's Literary Advisory Committee, discovered that Roy was being employed as a government clerk he was horrified. He sent Campbell £40 and arranged for him to be offered the post of Talks Producer at the BBC.[7] Thoroughly delighted at his change of fortune, Roy resigned his position at the War Damage Commission on 21 July and began work amid the 'funk-holes in the BBC'. He entertained his friends with a scarcely believable story of how he reported for work on his first day. Anna reports that he told the story often and Rob Lyle is among those who remembers being entertained by the yarn. Perhaps the most humorous rendition was given by Richard Aldington in a letter to Lawrence Durrell.

> Did Roy ever tell you of how he went to his BBC job the first day? Well, you see, man, after I was demobbed and spent all me blood money, I was working in a Soho restaurant washing up the dirty plates

> to keep Mary and the girls going. Then I got a letter from Desmond MacCarthy, telling me he'd got me a job at the BBC. Being a senior NCO I thought he meant I was to be a Commissionaire. So I put all me gongs up, and went down there, and said to the bloke on duty: 'I believe I'm to relieve you, mate.' 'First I've 'eard of it,' he said. 'What makes you think that?' So I showed him Desmond's letter, and he said: 'You've made a mistake, mate. You got to work with them bastards upstairs.'[8]

Shortly after taking up his new post, Roy was with Mary in the BBC canteen when they ran into Laurie Lee, who had just recorded a talk called 'Journey through Spain'. It was Lee's first meeting with Mary since he had left Toledo 10 years earlier. 'Now she is like an oldish Spanish woman,' he wrote, 'but with extraordinary facial inflexions that are Helen/Lorna.'[9] Lee's reference to Mary's similarity with her sisters is indicative of his continued, almost obsessive, involvement with her remarkable family. After his relationship with Lorna had ended he had switched his romantic attentions to one of Lorna's and Mary's nieces. This was Kitty, the 18-year-old daughter of Mary's sister Kathleen and her long-standing lover Jacob Epstein. Having finished with Kitty, who would later marry the artist Lucien Freud, Lee's attention turned to an even younger niece of Mary's. At a party at the Campden Grove house in August 1945 he noticed Kathleen Polge, the 14-year-old daughter of Mary's sister Helen. Kathleen's father, Marius 'Grandpère' Polge, had been Roy's best friend in Martigues. He was killed on active service in 1942. Although his courtship of the teenage Kathleen continued, eventually leading to marriage, Lee also found time to pursue Anna, now 19 years old. 'Laurie also had a crush on me but this had to be hushed up by all the other female Garmans because of green-eyed jealousy,' Anna recalls.[10]

Campbell settled in surprisingly well at the BBC, enjoying his job and proving very popular with his fellow employees. 'Roy was loved by everybody at the BBC, especially the engineers and all the secretaries,' says Anna, citing a letter from someone who worked with her father at the BBC to verify the claim.[11] Particularly prized by the secretaries were the sketches of animals which Roy would doodle during meetings with directors at which, for the most part, he would remain silent and apparently oblivious of the business being discussed. As soon as the meetings were over the secretaries 'used to rush in to take his drawings . . . they treasured these so much that they rushed in to claim them'.[12]

Contrary to his apprehensiveness about Beveridge's post-war Britain, Campbell seems to have found life in London extremely convivial. 'Strangely enough,' writes Anna, 'I have never seen Roy more contented and peaceful than when he lived in London . . . He loved speaking to his British friends, most of whom were artists of all sorts. He enjoyed the discipline of his job. And it suited him to drink beer instead of cheap wine.'[13]

Campbell's popularity and his relative contentment were conveyed by Mary in August 1946 in a letter to their South African friend C. J. Sibbett. Discussing Roy's first year at the BBC, she spoke of his success with evident satisfaction: '. . . a friend of his there told me he is one of the most popular and respected of all the people working there, and everyone is surprised at how easily he has taken to the job.' Yet, in marked contrast to her husband's success, Mary's letter also discussed the difficulties being experienced by her daughters.

> Tess our eldest daughter has been very ill for a long time now. It was a sudden change from our rather idyllic life in Spain to wartime England . . . She has a complete nervous breakdown from which she does not seem able to recover. This is a very great sorrow to us.
>
> Our other daughter is a ballerina and is in the Anglo-Russian Ballet. She loves her work but like a great many of the young people in England now she is also feeling the strain of the war. These family troubles are the things which touch us most and the other privations and difficulties are small compared to them.[14]

Mary concluded her letter by stating that 'the latest book is a great success and as usual has caused much controversy'. This was a reference to *Talking Bronco* which had been published on 10 May. For the most part it was reviewed positively. *Poetry Review* praised it unreservedly,[15] as did the *New English Review*.[16] In a conspicuous act of charitable forgiveness, Vita Sackville-West, writing in the *Observer*, described Campbell as 'one of our most considerable living poets',[17] a view which was echoed by Desmond MacCarthy in the *Sunday Times*: 'If a man is mainly inspired by a tragic sense of life, and has written beautifully . . . he is a poet of the first consequence. Not a few today put Roy Campbell among the first three living poets, and at his best second to none.'[18] Unlike many of Campbell's critics, MacCarthy looked beyond the vitriol to the deep spirituality which animates his verse:

> His most characteristic sense of beauty as a poet accepts pain, death and, as far as the world goes, despair; indeed, what he values most of all in life seems to be a joy that is wrung from them.
>
> The virtues the glow of which he best transmits are courage and unconscious humility. Of all modern poets I have read he is the most democratic, not – Heavens, no! – not in his politics but in his feeling for the common man and here the common soldier. There is something almost akin to Whitman sometimes, or perhaps it is really Christian, in the passion and pity with which he is on the side of average, coarse,

> faithful, stupid humanity as against the superior sort of man. And yet he adores in pagan wise whatever is grand and glorious.
>
> He is a tragic poet who laughs, and he laughs more often than he grieves. He revels in the pleasures of scorn; he delights in those of pugnacity. He can't stop banging at his enemies after he has knocked them down, and the display of his own zest often mitigates the sting of his satire. He will go raging on until he has worked himself into a kind of angry geniality, when his victim also doubtless begins to feel better. (I know I should.) He loves being angry – sometimes overmuch, and he can't keep his anger on ice as the most formidable satirists of all can do. He sometimes reminds me of Belloc, a poet by the way whose work is likely to be remembered after many who are perpetually praised and discussed today are forgotten or almost forgotten. Like the author of that grand poem 'In Praise of Wine', Roy Campbell writes sound, copious and sonorous English; his images are visible, and to him metre is an inspiration not a hindrance – not something to be wriggled past or through somehow . . .
>
> *Talking Bronco* is the finest poetry which the war has produced, for most of it is war-poetry, or suggested by a soldier's experience. Heroic realism and grimly gay fantastication suit best the theme of modern war – and Roy Campbell can supply them.

MacCarthy singled out the 'rollicking satire' of 'The Clock in Spain' and 'The Moon of Short Rations' for particular praise and described 'The Skull in the Desert' as the 'finest poem of all' in *Talking Bronco* and the 'most contemplative'. He also highlighted 'blemishes' in the volume, 'excesses which are not always fine, impatiences which are far from just', but Campbell must have been overjoyed to read such singular praise from one of the country's most respected critics.

Richard Aldington believed that *Talking Bronco* finally confirmed Campbell as 'a great verse satirist, a difficult and splendid art in which John Dryden was his master and almost his only rival'.

> There was a satirist in Campbell in early days, but he discovered his full strength and eloquence under the stress of his wars and of his return to an England rotten with craven socialism, and lending itself to nothing but derisive laughter with its fatuous illusions of grandeur and pathetic apeing of past grandeur . . . It is in the collection called *Talking Bronco* – a would-be contemptuous epithet of his enemies flung back at them with thousand-fold contempt – that this superb satire is most fully and gloriously represented. Like all great satires it is at once personal and general, fights for a cause while crushing the horde of gadflies which clusters round every great poet . . . In these

> *Talking Bronco* poems Campbell shows a mastery of English verse equal to Dryden himself, while he has taken the racy language of the soldier and the colonial and stamped it with a strength and fitness which makes it classic.[19]

Others, however, failed to share MacCarthy's and Aldington's high estimation of Campbell's work. Many were outraged by his satirical attacks on the left-wing poets. A reviewer in the *Listener* hardly commented on the poems, concentrating instead on a sustained and highly personal attack on the poet. The violent nature of this attack elicited several letters, published in the following edition, protesting at the vindictive nature of the review and defending Campbell. One of these was from the Oxford historian A. L. Rowse.[20]

Clearly Campbell had not lost the ability to create controversy and division among both his critics and his friends. Indeed, the divisions spread even to members of his own family. Anna remains a great admirer of her father's satires and believes that 'in *Talking Bronco* he reached the height of his spiritual strength'.[21] She concurs wholeheartedly with MacCarthy's judgement that 'The Skull in the Desert' was the finest poem in the volume. 'In that poem he puts the importance of the Cross, of the bearing of the Cross, and almost that you have got to love it because, if you don't, you can't get to Christ. What he is talking about is more or less what Christ must have felt in the desert, but also that moment on the Cross which, if we don't share, if we don't cling to, we can't save our soul.'[22] Tess, on the other hand, recalls that she and her mother were uneasy about the lack of charity in much of Campbell's satirical verse.

> My father and I agreed about nearly everything in life. But there was one thing I could not understand and that was the virulence of his satire. He used to read aloud extracts of his work to my mother and where there was satire she was always telling him to take it out or tone it down. I also was shocked by it and said 'poor people, leave them alone', and he would answer 'but they ask for it' or 'they deserve it'. He would not change anything. When not in satire the same topic could be treated differently. Nearly everything he was disturbed about in satire had another side to it when not in satire.[23]

A reviewer in *The Times* appeared to echo Mary's and Tess's view, praising *Talking Bronco* while observing that Campbell would have done better to concentrate on his lyrical verse rather than satire.

Unsurprisingly, those who responded most angrily to *Talking Bronco* were those whom Campbell had singled out for particular attack. Stephen Spender wrote to Campbell accusing him of 'infamous slander' and calling him 'a liar, a gross slanderer, an empty-headed boaster, a coward, a bully and a Fascist'.[24] He sent a copy of this letter to Cecil Day-Lewis whose reply, dated 7 June, illustrates that he shared Spender's anger at the nature of Campbell's attacks.

> Many thanks for your letter, and for the one you sent to Campbell, which seems to me just the thing he needs: I shall be interested to hear what he replies, if anything ... What is Louis' reaction? As he is a colleague of Campbell at the BBC, much seems to depend on his viewpoint, since my own first impulse is that C. should be chucked out of the BBC as a Fascist and an irresponsible calumniator and therefore a person not fitted to direct any civilised form of cultural expression. I agree with you in a dislike of taking such a business into the Courts: a libel action in such a case as this always suggests pique and vindictiveness on the part of those who bring it: it is essential that what we attack and expose in his book should be his vilification, through us, of the Spanish Republicans and all who helped them. And I think you, Louis and I, though we would not pretend to be unhurt by the personal attacks, can honestly say that it was this vilification which we feel most deeply about. I certainly agree that a letter should be sent to the Press: perhaps ... we might compose one with Louis. But I do not think we should necessarily stop there. What we must aim at is a public apology from Campbell, and I think only the most forceful methods are likely to wring an apology from him.[25]

Three weeks later, Day-Lewis had tempered his anger and was taking a lighter view. 'Campbell is so childish and incorrigible that he ought to be made to stand in the corner with a dunce's cap on,' he wrote to Spender on 26 June.[26] Spender, however, was still in no mood to let the matter rest. Clearly in a rage, he wrote several angry letters of protest to Faber & Faber and reviewed *Talking Bronco* for *Time and Tide* under the title 'The Case of Roy Campbell'. In this review, Campbell is described as 'a mixture of pretentiousness, violence, glamour, cruelty and ignobleness'. Quoting Campbell's lines, 'The vultures on the cook-house nest / Like poets on the BBC', Spender noted sardonically that Campbell should feel at home now that he was himself roosting on the BBC.[27]

Spender admitted a couple of years later that he was 'very susceptible' to becoming worried and depressed by criticism, commenting that he had been 'put off from writing for two days by attacks on my public reputation, like one by Roy Campbell which recently appeared in the *Times Literary Supplement*'.[28] Campbell, on the other hand, seemed to be relishing the furore caused by the publication of *Talking Bronco* and was particularly pleased that his attacks on Spender had prompted such an angry response. He sent a long reply to Spender's letter, responding to the accusation that he was a 'coward' and a 'Fascist' by comparing his own war record with Spender's in terms which echoed the attacks levelled at 'MacSpaunday' in *Talking Bronco*.

> For a disabled British Infantry N.C.O., wearing the King's medals for loyal service, and commended on his discharge sheet for 'excellent military conduct' – to be called a 'coward' by a 'chairborne' shock trooper of the Knife-and-Fork Brigade, one who dug himself in with his eating-irons in the rearguard of both wars . . . why to me that seems funny, not annoying![29]

If Campbell and Spender were content merely to exchange angry words, Louis MacNeice (the 'Mac' in 'MacSpaunday') preferred a more direct approach. In May 1946, within days of *Talking Bronco*'s publication, Campbell and MacNeice had a quarrel in the George public house, near the BBC, which culminated in an exchange of blows. MacNeice gave Campbell a bloody nose while Campbell, apparently, gave MacNeice a black eye.[30] Once they had exchanged blows, however, the two poets made it up very amicably and Campbell bought MacNeice a drink. Having satisfied himself that MacNeice was not a coward, Campbell thereafter defended him whenever he heard others criticize him – the old enemy becoming a new friend.

The fact that Campbell's enmity could be turned to friendship with such instant and consummate ease suggests that his attacks, though vicious, were not the product of deeply ingrained personal animosity towards individuals. Four years later, for example, he would praise a new volume of Auden's *Collected Shorter Poems*, admitting that 'of all those who are selling the fort today, Auden keeps the most grace, charm and skill'.[31]

Perhaps the most perceptive insight into the apparent contradictions at the heart of Campbell's ability to make friends and enemies was provided by the South African poet David Wright, who first met Campbell in a crowded London pub in the spring of 1946.

> In the course of the next few years I came to know Campbell well, and to discover that the huge friendly man, with the limp and the unbenevolent-seeming mouth, was almost the exact reverse of the truculent *persona* he loved to project in his writing.
>
> He once said to me: 'I place friendship above art', and, from what I knew of him personally, it was transparent that he also placed it well above those reiterated declarations of intolerance . . . The fact is nobody had a more catholic or contradictory assortment of friends of so many diverse races, colours, creeds, and political tenets, or from so many varying walks of life. In one way, this was no more than a reflection of Campbell's multiple interests and accomplishments, and in another

a consequence of his openhearted, almost childlike, love of human beings, especially those who shared in one form or another his enormous gusto in living . . .

It is true that Campbell hated, but it was usually in the abstract . . . The longer I knew him the stronger the impression I received of a great and fundamental gentleness beneath a superficial truculence, though this may appear absurd to those who take at face value the ferocity of his polemic satire and the violence of his legend. Campbell's ruggedness was theatrical; a thing put on; the apparent vainglory and braggadocio, with which he embroidered his exploits, part of a mask behind which he hid an actual and active humility that touched one more than the assumed modesty or silent pride worn by less naive personalities.[32]

Campbell's beguiling ability to sound pompous in public while exuding genuine and gentle humility in private is the key to understanding his personality. He valued friendship above art, but also made an art of making enemies. On the rare occasions when the two opposing forces collided, it is the gentler, humbler and deeper Campbell who emerges triumphant. Thus, when David Wright made a disparaging remark about one of the poets satirized in *Talking Bronco* whom Campbell had subsequently come to know personally, Campbell gently rebuked his friend for his criticism. Wright does not say which of the 'MacSpaunday' poets he had disparaged, but Campbell defended him as 'a very shy man, not supercilious as you think. I used to hate him and push him out of my way – but I was more at fault than he.'[33] Spender and Day-Lewis may never have obtained the public apology their anger demanded, but there seems little doubt that Campbell had apologized in the contrition of his conscience and in the privacy of his own heart. Even though he was not able to love his enemies, he was equally incapable of hating them.

NOTES

1 Roy Campbell, from 'Talking Bronco', *Collected Poems, Volume Two*, p. 94.
2 Teresa Campbell, unpublished memoirs, p. 86.
3 *Ibid.*
4 *Ibid.*, p. 87.
5 Roy Campbell, unpublished letter to his mother, postmarked 4 December 1944.
6 Anna Campbell Lyle, *Son of Valour*, p. 163.
7 Peter Alexander, *Roy Campbell*, p. 206.
8 Ian MacNiven and Harry Moore (eds), *Literary Lifelines*, pp. 123–4.
9 Valerie Grove, *Laurie Lee*, pp. 222–3.
10 Anna Campbell Lyle, letter to the author, 24 May 2000.
11 Anna Campbell Lyle, interview with the author, Portugal, December 1998.
12 *Ibid.*
13 Anna Campbell Lyle, letter to the author, 20 January 1999.
14 Mary Campbell, unpublished letter to C. J. Sibbett, 20 August 1946.

15 *Poetry Review*, July 1946.
16 *New English Review*, July 1946.
17 *Observer*, 30 June 1946.
18 *Sunday Times*, 7 July 1946.
19 Alister Kershaw (ed.), *Salute to Roy Campbell*, p. 16.
20 *Listener*, 14 and 28 November 1946.
21 Anna Campbell Lyle, interview with the author, Portugal, December 1998.
22 *Ibid.*
23 Teresa Campbell, unpublished memoirs, p. 100.
24 Peter Alexander, *Roy Campbell*, p. 209.
25 Sean Day-Lewis, *C. Day-Lewis*, p. 164.
26 *Ibid.*, p. 165.
27 *Time and Tide*, 8 June 1946.
28 John Goldsmith (ed.), *Stephen Spender: Journals 1939–1983*, London: Faber & Faber, 1985, p. 126.
29 Peter Alexander, *Roy Campbell*, p. 210.
30 *Ibid.*, p. 211; Anna Campbell Lyle, interview with the author, Portugal, December 1998.
31 Humphrey Carpenter, *W. H. Auden: A Biography*, London: George Allen & Unwin, 1981, p. 366.
32 David Wright, *Roy Campbell*, London: Longmans, Green & Co. Ltd, 1961, pp. 38–9.
33 *Ibid.*, p. 39.

CHAPTER THIRTY

COLD COMFORTS

> Whether the chosen agent of Destruction
> Be plague or famine, earthquake or eruption,
> Conquistador, like Cortés or Pizarro,
> Or Commissar, more bigoted and narrow,
> Or, worse than all, a snowy-haired professor,
> Of a neat violin the fond possessor,
> To fiddle when it all goes up in flames,
> The crime is one: the sentence is the same![1]

On 28 November 1946, Campbell renewed his acquaintance with Tolkien and C. S. Lewis when he attended a meeting of the Inklings at Lewis's rooms in Magdalen College. Lewis's brother Warnie recorded in his diary that Campbell was the main attraction of the evening: 'A pretty full meeting of the Inklings to meet Roy Campbell, now with the B.B.C., whom I was glad to see again; he is fatter and tamer than he used to be I think. He read us nothing of his own, except translations of a couple of Spanish poems – none of us understood either of them.'[2]

Lewis appears to have overcome his initial hostility and was finally warming to Campbell. He would no doubt have sympathized with Campbell's attack on the left-wing poets in *Talking Bronco*, since he was himself a staunch critic of the modern trends in poetry which Auden epitomized. '"Poetry" with the Eliots and Audens has become such a horror,' he had written to his brother in July 1940.[3] He had been an admirer of Campbell's early verse and, although they disagreed over some aspects of literature, they shared a love for the Elizabethans and would have respected the depth and catholicity of each other's literary learning. Campbell's respect for Lewis was illustrated by his request for Lewis's advice on which selections from Milton would be best suited for broadcasting on the BBC. Lewis replied that Campbell was 'quite as able as I to choose', but suggested nonetheless 'a good chunk of L'Allegro and Il Penseroso; Sonnet on Deceased Wife; introduction to P.L., III; evening in Paradise from IV; the end from XIII. From Samson the first chorus ("This, this is he") – "But when their hearts are jocund and sublime" (If you can persuade someone to thump it out like Vachell Lindsay, and not moan or murmur!).'

'Oddly enough,' Lewis wrote in the same letter, 'we were all talking about you last night. Next term you must break away and spend a Thursday night with us in College. (I can do dinner, bed, and breakfast.)'[4] Lewis had clearly forgiven Campbell for *Flowering Rifle* and had embraced him as a fellow Inkling. In his poem 'To Roy Campbell' he complained that Campbell was wrong to dismiss Romantic poets such as Coleridge or Wordsworth merely because they were praised by untrustworthy critics. These poets, wrote Lewis, were 'far more ours than theirs',[5] indicating that Campbell was now accepted by Lewis as 'one of us' in the battle against common literary foes. Lewis's friend Walter Hooper confirms that he spoke fondly of Campbell in later years.[6]

Apart from the occasional excursions to Oxford to meet up with Lewis, Tolkien and the other Inklings, Campbell's closest literary association in the autumn of 1946 was with Dylan Thomas. 'My father loved Dylan Thomas,' says Anna. 'He loved him as though he were a child, a slightly lacking child. It's very funny because he had a very, very strong love for him, but at the same time he thought he was very amusing. I think he felt he was a genius . . . He was always at our house but I never could make him out. I could never make him out as a man, he seemed like a fairy, or someone not quite there. He was very sweet but he wasn't real really. No, not completely real.'[7]

Campbell's critical estimation of Thomas's genius was expressed in *Vandag*, a South African journal, in December 1946.[8] 'More than any other poet writing today in English,' Campbell began, Dylan Thomas was 'a verbal magician':

> . . . one who electrifies words, clashes them into new combinations and intensifies both their meaning and their sound, by means of an almost primitive intuition . . . In an age of hesitant and furtive experiment, Thomas achieves a complete finality of utterance which baffles analysis. He not only writes with a conscious assurance which is almost hypnotic; he criticises, too, with the same conscious authority; and when he reads aloud he is equally impressive, sweeping his audience away with him . . .
>
> Thomas has nothing exotic or perverse in his make-up. In strength and growth he resembles . . . one of those European forests, thrilling with sap and energy, but with paths which have been made by many generations of civilised human beings, and all those paths leading to a real destination from a real starting-point – rather than a jungle traversed by the tracks of wild animals. For this the deeply ingrained

> Christian sense of the Welsh people is partly responsible, and for the rest, Thomas's own sense of balance. As a human being he may suffer like most of us do from being personally an ordinary sensual human, but wherever his conscious creativeness leads us in his poetry it is in the direction of Charity, to which Faith and Hope are mere tributary sidelines.

In this critical appraisal of his friend and drinking companion, Campbell also provided a clue to his own devotion to Thomas. The wayward Welshman was 'one of the people'. As the son of a schoolmaster 'in a grimy mining town', he remained 'always in close contact with the class that works the hardest, suffers the worst, sings the most, and laughs the loudest – in fact the class that lives the most intensely'. He had 'no genteel accent or bogus appearance to act as a barrier between himself and the humblest of his fellow men. He can drink, laugh, and fool with them.' The warmth of this description displays both Campbell's love for Thomas and the reason why he found him such convivial company with whom to 'drink, laugh and fool'.

David Wright, so often a perceptive judge of Campbell's character, wrote that 'he and his friend Dylan Thomas were much alike; they shared the same magnanimity of spirit, plus a rustic mistrust of the urban and the urbane'.[9] Constantine Fitzgibbon, Thomas's biographer, suggests that Thomas looked on Campbell as a 'tough' role model whom he sought to imitate.

> Like most of Dylan's qualities his 'toughness' was, I think, largely cerebral and defensive. With one part of his mind he had no wish whatsoever to be the sickly boy his parents and his appearance told him he was. He would then pose as a tough schoolboy, a tough journalist, a tough poet in the manner of his friends Roy Campbell or John Davenport.[10]

Campbell's friendship with the hard-drinking Thomas inevitably led to many nights in London's pubs and clubs, after which the poets would stagger home together, hopelessly drunk. Watching Thomas light his first cigarette on the morning after was so terrifying that Roy told Anna he had to leave the room. Such was the stench of alcohol on Thomas's breath that Roy was convinced he would blow himself up.[11]

Their wives also became good friends, and Anna recalls several amusing episodes relating to Caitlin Thomas. On one occasion Mary left for Mass, informing Anna that she was expecting a cleaning woman and if she arrived before her return Anna was to sit her down in the kitchen and make her a cup of tea. When a bedraggled-looking woman turned up soon after Mary's departure, Anna mistook her for the cleaning woman and ushered her towards the kitchen. 'I'm Caitlin Thomas!' the woman exclaimed indignantly. 'Would you give me a glass of wine at once!'[12]

Another time, the peace was shattered by 'a tremendous rumpus' outside the Campbells' house, culminating in a shrill scream: 'Mary Campbell!' Mary looked out of the upper-storey window, to be confronted by the sight of Caitlin, evidently drunk and staggering around in the street below. 'Mary Campbell,' she shouted, 'give me a cup of tea at once. I'm the wife of the greatest poet in the world.'

Mary was unimpressed. 'Caitlin,' she replied, 'you go home and stop drinking!'[13]

In spite of his reputation as a hardened drinker, Thomas remained in huge demand as an actor and speaker on the radio. In July 1946 he and Campbell dined with John Arlott, a young producer responsible for many of Thomas's verse-reading programmes for the BBC, although he would be better known in later years as an author and cricket commentator.[14] Campbell was also directly responsible for many of Thomas's radio appearances, the frequency of which increased dramatically following the launch of the BBC's high-culture network, the 'Third Programme', in the autumn of 1946. Campbell organized many of the network's readings, ensuring that Thomas was a regular feature as both actor and speaker. He appeared as an actor in Milton's *Comus*, the first drama production on the fledgling Third Programme; he played Aristophanes in a 'panorama of Aristophanic comedy' written by Louis MacNeice, Campbell's enemy-turned-friend; and in November 1946 he played the part of Private Dai Evans in a radio version of *In Parenthesis*, the strange prose-poem by the enigmatic writer David Jones, in which a minor part was taken by the young Richard Burton.

Apart from acting, Thomas read the works of Blake and Edith Sitwell, and talked about the work of Walter de la Mare. Campbell described Thomas as 'the best all-round reader of verse that I ever produced', particularly when he was reading the works of 'wild and woolly poets' which brought out the best of his voice – 'it was with Blake and Manley Hopkins that Dylan became almost Superman'. In Campbell's opinion, Thomas was not as good with 'correct' poets like Pope and Dryden.[15]

Inevitably, perhaps, Campbell eventually found himself in an embarrassing situation when Thomas arrived drunk for a live reading on the Third Programme. Roy was horrified to find his friend 'snoring in front of the mike with only twenty seconds left' before he went on air. He slurred his first title, 'Ode on Saint Sheshilia's Day', and struggled desperately to pronounce '*Religio Laici*' correctly. He 'had about three shots at it, bungled it, gave it up,' wrote Campbell.[16]

Not surprisingly, Campbell's superiors at the BBC were not amused. He was sent for by the Third Programme Controller, George Barnes, and was at pains to reassure him that the unacceptable incident would not be repeated. Thomas was apologetic, promising Campbell that he would be better behaved in the future.

Barnes had made it clear that he would hold Roy personally responsible for Thomas's behaviour from then on, and, although Roy kept faith with Thomas, he would not let him out of his sight in the hours before he was due on air. 'My father used to keep Dylan Thomas company all afternoon patiently, patiently, patiently,' says Anna, 'because if he didn't he'd be off to the pub and by the time he got to the microphone he was completely plastered. The people at the BBC were so terrified that he wouldn't be able to be coherent enough to read that they told my father that it was his responsibility.'[17]

Roy's resolute support for Thomas in the face of the scepticism of his BBC superiors was, in the opinion of one of his colleagues, 'primarily responsible for Dylan's public acclaim at the end of his life, through broadcasting'.

> I can remember Roy, at a Talks Department meeting coming down with both feet, like a two-legged literary elephant, in favour of Dylan's verse and for Dylan speaking it himself into the microphone. With their minds full of the still dominant Reithian hypocrisy and a vision of a vinous Dylan drunk and incoherent at the microphone, all the little talks producers with literary pretensions ran like rabbits – nothing but white scuts in all directions. The upshot was that Roy was left with the production on the 3rd Programme. What would happen was awaited with curiosity; and, I guess, not without a touch of malice by some. Well it emerged as a triumph, with what is called 'critical acclaim', with the enigmatic Roy skilfully avoiding the limelight of success which everyone was anxious to share.[18]

If Roy was at pains to keep Thomas sober before broadcasts, he was more than willing to get drunk with him in the evenings. A favourite venue for these drinking bouts was the Catherine Wheel, the nearest pub to the Campbells' house in Campden Grove. More than 30 years afterwards, elderly locals could remember the two poets eating a whole bunch of daffodils – flowers, leaves and stems – for a bet on St David's Day.[19]

The Catherine Wheel became a favourite meeting place at which Roy would play host to the many new literary friends he had met through his work for the BBC. In 1947 he made the acquaintance of Alister Kershaw and Geoffrey Dutton, two young Australian writers. He met Dutton in May at a lecture given to a poetry society in Oxford. Seizing his hand, Roy exclaimed, 'Man, thank God to see another colonial amongst all these bloody Pommies!

Come and let's have a drink, quick, before the pubs close.'[20] Another colonial writer he met at this time was the South African Alan Paton, to whom he was introduced by Laurens van der Post and Uys Krige. Roy was delighted to meet up with his two old friends and Paton recalled the animated discussion which ensued. 'Campbell's solar presence set Krige on fire, and van der Post and I witnessed a pyrotechnical display in the gloom of Sloane Square, so dazzling that the pale faces of the waitresses seemed to catch alight, if not with comprehension, then with admiration and envy that human beings could still explode and crackle in such a dreary world.'[21]

Armand Guibert, the old friend who many years earlier had translated *Adamastor* into French, visited Roy at Campden Grove to discover him translating the poems of Lorca and St John of the Cross, in order 'to maintain some contact with the Iberian countries', while in the basement Mary 'cooked *paellas* in the Valencian style'. Guibert noticed how Londoners in pubs or on bus platforms 'would turn to stare' at Roy's somewhat eccentric appearance, including 'his cowboy hat and great studded walking-stick'.[22]

Through Alister Kershaw, Roy began to correspond with Richard Aldington, who was living in Paris. The two poets, who had admired each other's work for years, struck up an instant and enduring friendship. In December 1947 Aldington sent the Campbells a huge Christmas turkey, by airmail, a gift which was most appreciated at a time of extensive food rationing in England.

The most important friendship to be instigated during this period was with the young poet Rob Lyle, who was destined to be Roy's closest friend for the remainder of his life. Roy would become Lyle's mentor, while Lyle became Roy's patron. They first met in the Catherine Wheel in February 1947 and Lyle's account of his first impressions offer an interesting insight into the younger poet's perception of his new-found friend.

> My first general impression was neither 'poetic' nor military; still less colonial: it was pastoral. Roy looked like the shepherd or herdsman whose type he so much admired and of whom he wrote so eloquently – the eternal horseman who was there before civilisation arose from the plain, and who will be there when it has brought itself down by over-reaching itself in its own pride and presumption: the herdsman who calmly and philosophically astride his horse and chewing a flower between his teeth, once watched Babel rise – and fall. It was one aspect of Roy that Augustus John caught so well in his portrait. Roy, of course, was never a shepherd in practice: but in a deeper sense he was such, lonely and contemplative, proud and conservative, a poet among shepherds, a shepherd among poets: and that independence of spirit and solitude of soul were reflected in his appearance and in many of his ways.[23]

Roy's sense that he had found in Lyle a kindred spirit, a soul who understood his own poetic psyche, is clear from the immediacy and depth of their friendship. Throughout the coming years they met almost daily, discussing poetry, politics and the dire predicament in which post-war civilization had found itself. In October 1948, Roy made a beguiling confession of his personal political creed to Lyle:

> I don't believe in anything. At heart I'm a complete anarchist. I fought in the Spanish War because I was disgusted with the crimes of the Reds and the humbug of the liberals. I joined the British Army ... because I couldn't sit at home while my comrades went out to fight. I didn't believe in democracy or in any of the 'causes' for which we were supposed to be fighting: but I believe in comradeship and in standing shoulder to shoulder with my fellow-men.[24]

Lyle stresses that Campbell's concept of anarchism must be distinguished from the nihilistic aspects of its philosophy or its political manifestation in Spain and elsewhere. He was speaking of anarchism in a far broader libertarian context, 'as a free spirit who objects to any kind of coercion'.[25] Anna explains that, although anarchism 'means different things to different people',

> in his case he meant that any institutionalised faction was anathema to him. He did not mean a bomb-throwing fanatic. But rather a cosmopolitan admirer of every form of *ethnic* civilisation. Every country had its own charm and character. Africa was still Darkest and China was excitingly unique. Since Marxism and globalisation everywhere is boring – the coca-cola, Macdonald, Monsanto civilisation. Yes, the anarchism of my father was the horror of everything becoming the same. He would have been horrified by what the world has become now.[26]

Perhaps Campbell summed up his own libertarian political philosophy most accurately in two succinct sentences in *Light on a Dark Horse*: 'I hate "Humanity" and all such abstracts: but I love *people*. Lovers of "Humanity" generally hate *people and children*, and keep parrots or puppy dogs.'[27] There is an enigmatic similarity in such a statement with the politics of G. K. Chesterton, who had argued that the philanthropists' love for *Man* was blind to the deeper needs of *men*. For Campbell, as for Chesterton and Belloc, the creeping omnipotence of the welfare state was turning people into servile conformists who were increasingly reliant on impersonal bureaucracies for their economic wellbeing. Campbell expressed his contempt for Beveridge's Britain in an epigrammatic verse entitled 'How it Works'.

> Salute the free Utopian State
> We fought for. Feed, but do not look.
> For each free tuppence-worth of Bait,
> They charge a dollar on the Hook!

Campbell's sense of alienation from the welfare state in Britain was heightened by his dismay at the international situation. He was horrified that the Allied victory had placed half of Europe under Soviet communist control, and he was equally horrified that the remainder of the world appeared to be falling under the domination of multinational capitalism and its creed of global consumerism. The world had entered a political ice age as the two internationalist systems, communist and capitalist, Moscow and Washington, carved up the world between them in what would become known as the Cold War.

The advent of nuclear weapons had filled Campbell with a deep sense of foreboding. It signified the destructive power of science and he now added Einstein, whose theories had paved the way for nuclear technology, alongside the figures of Marx and Freud as being responsible for the modern miasma. Marx signified the triumph of inhuman abstract humanity over the lives of people; Freud the triumph of lust over love; and now Einstein symbolized the triumph of destructive science over civilization. In his 'Dedicatory Epilogue to Rob Lyle' for the revised version of *Flowering Rifle*, Campbell foretold

> . . . Annihilation from Above,
> The fate of all who play the fool with Love!
> As Sodom and Gomorrah proved too true,
> The Incas and the Aztecs lived to rue,
> And Rome and Babylon can witness too.
> Whether the chosen agent of Destruction
> Be plague or famine, earthquake or eruption,
> Conquistador, like Cortés or Pizarro,
> Or Commissar, more bigoted and narrow,
> Or, worse than all, a snowy-haired professor,
> Of a neat violin the fond possessor,
> To fiddle when it all goes up in flames,
> The crime is one: the sentence is the same!

As though to leave no doubt that Einstein was the 'snowy-haired professor' who was the author of the worst of all the 'agents of Destruction', Campbell appended a footnote to this part of the poem: '"I pressed the button." (Einstein, on hearing of Hiroshima.)'[28]

The extent to which Mary shared her husband's post-war pessimism and his horror at the advent of the nuclear age was clear in a letter she wrote to C. J. Sibbett on the subject of modern art on 13 September 1947:

> . . . the whole thing is very much of a racket, and everyone concerned makes a good living out of it, and of course the more startling and obscene it is the more it is considered smart to buy it. Even the honest painters seem to get contaminated by the age they live in which is not surprising when one hears quite harmless people talking with equanimity about using the atom bomb. In the time of Michael Angelo and Dante at least people *recognised* the difference between right and wrong, but now they do not want to.[29]

Roy and Mary were far from unique, of course, in their abhorrence of nuclear weapons. Neither was Roy the only person to write portentous and doom-laden poetry in the wake of the dropping of the atom bombs on Hiroshima and Nagasaki. Siegfried Sassoon wrote 'Litany of the Lost', bewailing the 'breaking of belief in human good', the 'slavedom of mankind to the machine', and the 'terror of atomic doom foreseen'. At around the same time, Edith Sitwell wrote 'The Shadow of Cain', the first of her 'three poems of the Atomic Age', after reading a chilling eyewitness description of the immediate effect of the atomic bomb on Hiroshima. In words with which Campbell would have concurred, Sitwell described 'The Shadow of Cain' as being about 'the fission of the world into warring particles, destroying and self-destructive. It is about the gradual migration of mankind, after that Second Fall of Man . . . into the desert of the Cold, towards the final disaster, the first symbol of which fell on Hiroshima.'[30] Her poem was 'partly a physical description of the highest degree of cold, partly a spiritual description of this.'[31] Sitwell, it seemed, was feeling the same sense of alienation as Roy and Mary as the world lurched uncertainly from World War to Cold War. *Après le déluge* . . . the Cold.

NOTES

1 Roy Campbell, from 'Dedicatory Epilogue to Rob Lyle', *Collected Poems, Volume Two*, p. 133.
2 Clyde S. Kilby and Marjorie Lamp Mead (eds), *Brothers and Friends: The Diaries of Major Warren Hamilton Lewis*, San Francisco: Harper & Row, 1982, p. 197.
3 Walter Hooper, *C. S. Lewis*, p. 174.
4 C. S. Lewis, unpublished letter to Roy Campbell in the Bodleian Library, undated, *c.* 1946–7.
5 C. S. Lewis (ed. Walter Hooper), *Poems*, London: Geoffrey Bles, 1964, p. 66.
6 Walter Hooper, letter to the author, 22 February 2000.
7 Anna Campbell Lyle, interview with the author, Portugal, December 1998.
8 Roy Campbell, 'Dylan Thomas', *Vandag*, Johannesburg, Vol. 1, No. 7 (December 1946); reprinted in Roy Campbell, *Collected Works IV: Prose*, pp. 295–7.
9 David Wright, *Roy Campbell*, p. 40.

10 Constantine Fitzgibbon, *The Life of Dylan Thomas*, London: J. M. Dent, 1965, p. 51.
11 Anna Campbell Lyle, interview with the author, Portugal, December 1998.
12 *Ibid.*
13 *Ibid.*
14 Paul Ferris (ed.), *The Collected Letters of Dylan Thomas*, p. 596.
15 Roy Campbell, 'Memories of Dylan Thomas at the BBC', *Poetry* (Chicago), November 1955; quoted in Paul Ferris, *Dylan Thomas*, London: Hodder & Stoughton, 1977, pp. 206–7.
16 *Ibid.*, p. 207.
17 Anna Campbell Lyle, interview with the author, Portugal, December 1998.
18 Quoted in Anna Campbell Lyle, *Son of Valour*, pp. 187–8.
19 Peter Alexander, *Roy Campbell*, pp. 210–11.
20 *Ibid.*, p. 210.
21 Alister Kershaw (ed.), *Salute to Roy Campbell*, p. 82.
22 *Ibid.*, p. 29.
23 Anna Campbell Lyle, *Son of Valour*, p. 179.
24 Peter Alexander, *Roy Campbell*, p. 21.
25 Rob Lyle, letter to the author, February 2000.
26 Anna Campbell Lyle, letter to the author, 9 June 1999.
27 Roy Campbell, *Light on a Dark Horse*, p. 183.
28 Roy Campbell, *Collected Poems, Volume Two*, p. 133.
29 Mary Campbell, unpublished letter to C. J. Sibbett, 13 September 1947.
30 Edith Sitwell, *Taken Care Of: An Autobiography*, London: Hutchinson, 1965, p. 153.
31 Victoria Glendinning, *Edith Sitwell*, p. 260.

CHAPTER THIRTY-ONE

TO CATACOMBS RETURNING

To catacombs returning
Where faith and kindness hold.
And keep an altar burning
To other gods than Gold.[1]

The Campbells were plagued by ill health during much of 1948. Roy suffered from recurring bouts of the malaria he had contracted in Africa five years earlier. For weeks on end he was forced to retreat to his bed, sweating and shaking. In June, Anna had a minor breakdown as the pressure of her dancing roles took their toll. Mary took her to Italy, leaving Roy at home to struggle with the family finances. His letters to Mary during her absence display a practical ineptitude which must have added to her worries as she struggled to nurse Anna back to health. 'Things are getting pretty desperate,' he wrote, complaining of the cost of everything from Tess's hospital bills to 'various tons of coal etc. etc.', adding that he would 'manage somehow even if I have to mortgage the house'.[2] The following letter detailed how he had paid the bills 'which I was not prepared for . . . by selling a book of Van Gogh and Bellini . . . There is still the wireless if anything terrible happens – but I should only pawn it. I think that everything is all right now.'[3]

Mary wrote to say that Anna was recovering well and feeling the benefits of the Italian sun. 'How lovely to hear that our little flower has got so bronzed and healthy,' Roy replied.[4] Yet it was their elder daughter's mental state which continued to cause the greatest anxiety. When Mary returned from Italy, she decided to bring Tess home to Campden Grove where Mary herself would take on the responsibility of nursing her. Tess appeared to be improving and had been asking to be allowed to come home for some time. In fulfilling her daughter's wishes Mary would also be relieving the pressure on the family's finances. Yet her decision, however much it appeared to make sense, would have near disastrous consequences.

Tess showed little sign of progress after her return home. 'Through these years I had become a wreck,' she writes. 'So weak I could hardly stand up. Every sound confused me. I got up and tried to dress, I got so confused and felt so weak I just went back to bed and lay there.' Her problems were exacerbated by a deep sense of guilt at the amount of worry she was causing her family. She watched helplessly as Mary, who was suffering from a stomach ulcer caused by the stress of her daughters' illnesses, worked tirelessly around the house. She did all the cooking, shopping and housework and brought Tess her food in bed. 'My mother had the power, the uncanny power, which made her do things other people couldn't do. After all, it was not for nothing she went to Mass and Communion every morning. It was her faith which gave her the necessary courage.' Mary arranged for one of the Carmelite fathers from the nearby church to come to the house to give Tess Holy Communion, all apparently to no avail.

> Even communicating I did it in the depths of depression. Then to cap the situation, the suicidal state occurred. One afternoon when the house was silent, my mother was absent, I gave a few paces to the kitchen, got hold of the sharpest knife I could find, took it back to bed with me and started with the sharp blade to cut the veins on the inside part of my elbows. First one and then the other, then I lay – the blood flowing slowly. In a kind of a maze, I heard my mother enter the house and come down to me. I was lying in a pool of blood. She phoned the ambulance and I was taken urgently to Queen's Hospital, where I was operated on, saved and interned.[5]

After two weeks convalescing, Tess returned home. The suicide attempt was to prove the turning point on her slow road to recovery. It was a 'crisis, but the crisis was the end of the trouble as very often is the case'.

On 6 October 1948 Campbell enjoyed a brief respite from the domestic tribulations besetting his family when he travelled to Spain with Rob Lyle to give a lecture on modern English writers at the Ateneo in Barcelona. Although his Spanish was rusty (he had been absent from the country for seven years), his talk was well received and he was paid a generous honorarium of 2,000 pesetas. 'I lived like a king,' he wrote to his friend, the Provençal writer Charles de Richter, 'and when I wanted to pay my hotel bill, I was told that I was the guest of the government.'[6]

Back in England, Roy found a new friend and ally in Hamish Fraser, who, as a committed communist, had fought for the International Brigades in Spain but had subsequently renounced Marxism and been received into the Catholic Church. Anna described him as 'one of the heroes of the International Brigades' who became 'a much-loved friend' of the whole family.

> Until the Russo-German treaty he had been a starry-eyed communist and had worked and fought hard for the cause, but after that he became disillusioned and gradually began to see that he was on the wrong path. He was converted to the Church and worked just as hard for his new faith as he had for the old. Another hero who fought on the Red side and later became a lifelong friend was Hugh Oloff de Wet. He joined up in the Republican Air Force and was one of the pilots who bombed Toledo while we were there. He recorded his experiences in a very moving book, *The Cardboard Crucifix.*[7]

Roy paid tribute to both these friends by dedicating the third book of the revised version of *Flowering Rifle*, 'To my heroic Ex-Enemies, Hamish Fraser, ex-Communist Kommissar of one of the toughest Units in the Whole International Brigade, now a Christian, and to Hugh Oloff de Wet who flew for the Reds as a fighter pilot, and realised the truth before he finished.'[8]

Campbell and Fraser had much in common. Both men displayed a harsh and sometimes humourless public persona which concealed a warm rumbustiousness in private. Rob Lyle remembers staying with Fraser at his home in Glasgow and spending most of the time 'rolling on the floor' with laughter because of the Glaswegian's sense of humour. 'He was completely different from his writing in *Approaches*. He was a completely different person.'[9] *Approaches*, the Catholic and anti-communist periodical that Fraser edited for many years, was, says Anna, 'very, very serious' and 'too polemical'.[10] Lyle recalls with amusement that Roy found Fraser very difficult to understand because of his heavy, working-class Glasgow accent. 'Roy loved him but he couldn't understand him!'[11]

Lyle was also present late in 1948 when an extremely drunk Evelyn Waugh visited the Campbells at Campden Grove. 'He came to the house one day and he was so completely stunned with drink,' recalls Anna, adding that, on this occasion, 'my father was sober'. Waugh had been brought to the house by a friend. 'He was plastered. He could just walk.' Waugh's inebriated state made conversation difficult. He slumped in the corner and appeared to pay little attention to what the others in the room were discussing. He 'only came to life once', says Anna, and that was when someone alluded to someone as 'Lady somebody or other's sister'. 'No it's not,' Waugh interjected. 'No it's not, it's her niece.' Having clarified the point, he relapsed into his coma. 'It was just his snobbery,' says Anna.

An incident as Waugh was about to leave illustrates both Campbell's innate generosity and Waugh's legendary rudeness. During his recent visit to Spain, Roy had been presented with a *traje de luces* – a 'robe of lights', the sequined costume that a bullfighter wears. Roy was delighted with the gift and was so proud of it that he kept it hanging in the hall, but as Waugh was leaving he offered it to him as a gift. 'Evelyn would you like this? It's just been given to me in Spain.' Waugh looked the costume up and down indifferently, said 'I don't think that would interest me', and staggered off into the street. 'It wasn't the most successful meeting,' says Anna, 'but it was amusing all round and we laughed about it for a long time afterwards. Father thought it was terribly funny.'[12]

Anna says that her father did not allow this anticlimactic meeting to dent his admiration for Waugh, believing him to have 'a great talent'. Waugh was certainly as popular as ever in 1948. *Brideshead Revisited*, published three years earlier, had secured his position as one of the century's most prodigious authors and his latest novel, *The Loved One*, would serve to enhance his reputation still further.

Roy's own star was also once more in the ascendant. The first volume of his *Collected Poems* was being prepared for publication and would subsequently receive good reviews, including a full page in the *Times Literary Supplement*.[13] Earlier in the year his translation of Federico García Lorca's play, *Bodas de Sangre* (*Blood Wedding*), was staged in London and enjoyed a successful run. At the opening night Anna had attended with her father because Mary was nursing Tess at a small country cottage at Winchelsea in Sussex.[14] A week or two earlier Campbell's poem 'Tristan da Cunha' was broadcast on the BBC, read by Dylan Thomas.

Campbell's literary reputation in the United States was also enjoying a considerable revival and he was flattered to be added to the Gallery of Living Catholic Authors, a project which was being co-ordinated by an American nun, Sister Mary Joseph. 'I should be very highly honoured indeed to be put in the Gallery of Living Catholic Authors,' he wrote to her in August 1949.[15]

The depth of Campbell's Christianity had a profound influence on Rob Lyle, who converted to Catholicism largely under his mentor's influence. On the occasion of his reception into the Church, Lyle asked Campbell to be his godfather. With all the fervour of a recent convert, Lyle launched a new magazine in April 1949 called *The Catacomb*, intended as the voice of tradition, Catholic and classical, which had been driven underground by the forces of socialism and secularism, but which was surviving defiantly in the midst of adversity.

Lyle paid Campbell for contributing to *The Catacomb* and after a few issues he asked him to take over as its full-time salaried editor. Roy jumped at the opportunity and in September he resigned his post as BBC Talks Producer. He had grown tired of life as a BBC employee, its novelty having long since faded, and was happy to escape from the regimentation implicit in regular working hours. Now he could once more live the undisciplined life of a poet. 'Roy is most relieved to have left the B.B.C.,' Mary wrote to Sibbett on 16 October.[16]

'Some criticism has been made of our title,' Campbell wrote in the November 1949 issue of *The Catacomb*. 'Since underground movements have become so popular, we hesitate to remind our critics that our special movement is 2,000 years older (and younger!) than any of theirs.' Over the following months, *The Catacomb* would contain many of the verse translations of Lorca, Rimbaud, Baudelaire, Apollinaire and Aurelio Valls that Campbell had been working on in recent years. Not surprisingly, he also used the freedom he enjoyed as editor of his own journal to renew his attack on old enemies such as Stephen Spender.

On 14 April 1949 Campbell had continued his war of attrition against Spender by publicly denouncing him at a meeting of the Poetry Society in Bayswater. Hearing that Spender was due to address the meeting, Roy arrived with Mary, Anna, Lyle, Tschiffely and a couple of other friends. When Spender stepped up to the podium, Campbell bellowed at the top of his voice from the back of the hall that he wished to 'protest on behalf of the Sergeants' Mess of the King's African Rifles'. He then began to stomp down the aisle as the audience stared at him in disbelief. Climbing onto the stage, he limped purposefully across to Spender and swung a right-handed blow which connected with Spender's nose, causing it to bleed. Pandemonium broke loose and Roy was bundled from the stage. Lyle and several others ushered him from the premises. Wet handkerchiefs were applied to Spender's nose, but when it was suggested that the police be called, Spender called for restraint. 'He is a great poet; he is a great poet. We must try to understand.' Spender declined to press charges and insisted on continuing with his poetry reading.[17]

In a letter to Ross Nichols, the organizer of the event, Roy sought to justify his actions in forthright terms that illustrate his ongoing grudge for the angry letter Spender had despatched to him following the publication of *Talking Bronco* three years earlier.

> No doubt you will wonder at my reason for disturbing your session the other night. There was no option left me by the speaker's own announcement that he was going to denounce me from every public platform as 'a fascist, a coward, and a liar' – merely because I had called attention to his war record. As I volunteered when over-age and while my own country (S. Africa) was still neutral, to fight against fascism which is merely another form of communism . . . I could not allow myself to be called a coward by one who during the struggle against fascism had employed no weapon more formidable to the adversary than his own knife and fork and his highly lucrative but

> innocuous pen – while I was on rankers pay suffering malaria in the jungle. By a couple of wide passes in the direction of your speaker I was forced to demonstrate the unmanliness of my accuser. And having caused him to cower, I required no further chastisement of his person, and am now quite satisfied. I am only sorry to have deranged the comfort of your audience though some have thanked me for providing a mild diversion. To those who were not diverted I offer my sincere apologies for this unfortunate but necessary demonstration. I can show you the letter wherein he promises to denounce me and impugn my patriotism. It no more constitutes fascism to have helped drive the communists out of Spain than it constitutes communism to have fought the Nazis. Both are equally unsympathetic to me. I hope you will tender my explanation along with my apology, the latter being strictly conditional to the former.[18]

Campbell's combative spirit was again on display in the May 1949 edition of the *Poetry Review*. This time his quarry was the critic, minor poet and former editor of *New Verse*, Geoffrey Grigson. Campbell condemned Grigson for being responsible, as editor of *New Verse*, for promoting the worst poetry of the previous decade: 'It was under his presidency that the poetry of "the thirties" became synonymous with cynical hypocrisy, poltroonery, greed, self-seeking, and the cowardly double-facedness of fire-eating egalitarians and peace-time belligerents.' Even worse, Grigson had either attacked or had failed to appreciate 'many of his elders and betters . . . such as Graves, Eliot, Lewis, Sassoon, the Sitwells, Aldington, Rickword, Plomer, and so on . . . Mr Grigson has a great deal to answer for to posterity, for it was under his somewhat tetchy dictatorship that English poetry sank to the lowest level of pusillanimity in its whole history – morally, technically and intellectually.'

Campbell was angered by Grigson's attack on Desmond MacCarthy during a radio broadcast and was further incensed by his published criticism of Edith Sitwell for writing about childbirth even though she was childless: 'yet he is always writing about the War: and his own War-record is about as virginal as Miss Sitwell's contribution to the birth-rate. Anyway, amongst civilised communities virginity has always been venerated as being associated with sanctity, heroism, and creative powers – sufficient reason for Mr Grigson to take offence at it.'

Clearly Campbell had added Grigson to his list of enemies and when he came across him in a London street soon afterwards he advanced towards him threateningly. No doubt aware of Campbell's recent assault on Spender, Grigson was understandably worried. According to Campbell he fled into a cake shop, although Grigson maintained that he stood his ground.[19]

Inevitably, stories abounded of Campbell's latest physical attack on a 'left-wing poet', adding to his notoriety.

Although Roy had not met the Sitwells for many years, his defence of Edith in the *Poetry Review* elicited the gratitude of Osbert Sitwell. The two men met in London in June, rekindling their old friendship. 'Just a line – long overdue – to say how much I appreciated your kindness and enthusiasm the other day, and what a pleasure it was to see you again,' Osbert wrote from Renishaw Hall on 28 June.[20] In August Edith wrote to Campbell, inviting him and Mary to lunch with herself and William Walton, another friend whom Roy had not met since his Oxford days. From that moment, Edith and the Campbells saw each other regularly.

At a party at Rob Lyle's house at the end of 1949, Roy knelt at Edith's feet, kissed her hand and announced solemnly, 'Edith my darling, you are a great lady! I will be your knight and fight your battles for you!'[21] Sitwell was delighted to accept Campbell's chivalrous gesture and seems to have considered him her literary champion from this time onwards. As for Campbell's view of Sitwell, even allowing for an element of alcohol-induced exuberance in his melodramatic placing of himself at her service, there is no doubt that he had always been a great admirer of her verse. In at least one letter he expressed, in a rare display of poetic humility, that he could not 'even hope to be as good as Edith Sitwell'.[22]

Over the next couple of years, Roy and Mary were regular luncheon guests of Edith at her club, although she was careful to ensure that they were not invited on the same day as some of her other friends, such as Stephen Spender. Edith also attended parties at Campden Grove where Mary, ever watchful for possible converts, began to proselytize. Anna remembers that her parents and Edith 'became great friends'. 'I think they began talking about the soul and God and things which I don't think the Sitwells had thought about much at all.' It was through these discussions that Edith became interested in Catholicism. 'I know that my mother had a very strong effect on Edith. I think that Edith was finding that life had nothing left. When you get to a certain age, if you haven't got God what have you got? She was a very sensitive woman and very intelligent. I think she was fascinated when my mother started telling her about the joys of Catholicism. My mother could talk very, very beautifully about those things and Edith became fascinated.'[23]

It would, however, be surprising if Roy had been content to remain a passive spectator in this theological dialogue. His own faith, its crucial importance to him and the importance he perceived it to have on developments in the post-war world, were all in evidence in a short article, possibly the finest piece of prose he ever wrote, which appeared in *Enquiry* in September 1949.[24]

> Descriptions of imaginary states, civilisations, and modes of life are by no means a novelty as we see from Plato's *Republic*, More's *Utopia*, and the voyages of Pantagruel and Gulliver: but they have become increasingly popular during the last century, during which time they have generally taken the form of voyages into the future. The father of all the sciences, theology, had been crowded out of the scene by an upstart progeny of petty sciences each of whose practitioners or quacks would have substituted it for the original science as the infallible regenerator of human society. Utopian futurists such as Marx and Nietzsche believed that by such simple expedients as suppressing the top-dog or the underdog, a state of superhumanity could be obtained, original sin domesticated, and a perfect social equilibrium obtained throughout the world. Meanwhile more people have been imprisoned in the name of liberty: more people degraded and ill-used in the name of equality: and more people tortured and murdered in the name of fraternity, in the last thirty years, than there have been for many centuries under the more straightforward forms of despotism.

Having named theology as the father of all sciences, the rejection of which had led to the Nietzschean utopia of Nazi Germany or the Marxist utopia of the Soviet Union, Campbell launched into a blistering attack on concepts of 'progress' which would have resonated with Sitwell's chilling vision in 'The Shadow of Cain' and still resonates with ecological foreboding more than half a century later.

> The orgy of irresponsible innovations and inventions – which originating as a sort of drunken procession of detribalised nomads, without a spiritual home or destination, or even a roadway in the shape of a tradition, now threatens to become a Gadarene stampede of headlong and irresistible impetus – was regarded as something beneficial and called 'progress', which it certainly *is*, being downhill and completely without brakes: the most rapid and disastrous 'progress' ever witnessed.

This 'Gadarene stampede', headed by Shaw and Wells and other 'progressive optimists', was only possible because of the lack of a living faith:

> We have seen how the despots of police states always attack first of all the traditional Faith of the people: who are inevitably forced to substitute the loss of this priceless gift with the inferior makeshift of mere *credulity* which places them completely at the mercy of their new masters . . . instead of Faith, humanity was reduced to living on that hopeless fatalistic credulity which for want of anything better, has to subsist in the future on promises and plans – five year plans superseded by ten year plans, and so on, ad infinitum.

Turning his attention to the 'theologically unscientific' utopias of Shaw and Wells, Campbell employed the weapons of wit and wisdom normally associated with the literary criticism of Chesterton. Wells's *Men Like Gods* was 'a sort of glorified nudist camp of professors, pedants, and bluestockings', while Shaw's *Back to Methuselah* presented a glum utopia 'where semi-immortal vegetarians vegetate for centuries before they die'. Faced with these atheistic visions of 'paradise', Campbell preferred the honesty of a Catholic Hell. 'There is no corner of Dante's Hell where one would not meet livelier and better company, more variety, and less boredom.' He went on: 'The irresponsible day-dreamings of such writers as Wells and Shaw have now had their crushing answer, not only in the final confessions of Wells himself, who lived to see many of his dreams come true, and was completely disillusioned by them, but by the world they have helped to bring about.'

On the literary level, the 'crushing answer' had been provided by Aldous Huxley and George Orwell. Like Wells and Shaw, Huxley had started out 'as one of the prophets of modern progress but became more and more bewildered and exasperated as it realised itself'. The disillusionment of *Brave New World* had been followed by the 'rage and hatred' of Huxley's *Ape and Essence*, published in 1948, in which the survivors of a nuclear holocaust are depicted as degenerating into bestial individualism. The weakness of *Ape and Essence*, wrote Campbell, was 'the weakness of the old Hellfire Sermons, in which one felt that the preacher exulted rather in the punishment he predicted than in any possible redemption that might result from his preaching'. Huxley 'not only lacked pity or sympathy with his fellow-men', but his book was actually 'an example of the very same destructive hatred which it set out to expose'.

George Orwell's recently published *Nineteen Eighty-Four* was, in Campbell's judgement, 'a far more important and terrible book' than Huxley's *Ape and Essence*, 'a book which seems to have been inspired by the same didactic purpose as Huxley's but one which holds us spell-bound because of its tragic grandeur, its pity, and its deep feeling for humanity'.

> This is a book written in the heart's blood of a great and valiant fighter who has always mixed with his fellow men – not a dehydrated scholar sneering from the supercilious eminence of an ivory tower . . . In the case of Orwell the man of action has always enriched the creative intellect throughout a stormy and uncompromising career . . . In *Animal Farm* he expressed his disillusionment with Communism so forcibly that if today the Soviet Culture-Police were to take over English literature, George Orwell would be 'liquidated' long before any of the most die-hard reactionaries.

Presumably it was after publication of Campbell's positive comments about Orwell's new novel that the two writers became friends. Campbell's daughter testifies to the fact that there was considerable correspondence between them, now sadly lost,[25] and Campbell describes Orwell in *Light on a Dark Horse* as 'that valiant and fine writer, my friend, the late George Orwell'.[26]

Their correspondence appears to have centred largely on their respective memories of the Spanish Civil War. Campbell expressed his admiration for Orwell's *Homage to Catalonia*, but it is a little surprising that Orwell also seems to have written positively about Campbell's *Flowering Rifle*. 'Orwell and Roy admired each other and corresponded about *Homage to Catalonia* and *Flowering Rifle*,' writes Anna,[27] and Campbell wrote that Orwell was 'a great admirer of *Flowering Rifle* and wished that the Reds had had a poet on their side "with the same verve and fire"'.[28] The use of quotation marks suggests that Roy was quoting verbatim from one of Orwell's letters, although the fact that his claim to Orwell's endorsement of his most controversial poem was not published until four months after the latter's death in January 1950, removing the possibility of any rebuttal, leaves the lingering suspicion that Campbell may have exaggerated Orwell's praise of the poem. On the other hand, Orwell's undoubted disillusionment with his erstwhile socialist sympathies, and his recent defence of Waugh's *Brideshead Revisited* against charges of being 'reactionary', may have indicated a radical shift in his sympathies sufficient to embrace at least the finer aspects of Campbell's poem.

Either way, there is little doubt that their friendship was genuine. Alister Kershaw recalls meeting Orwell at Campden Grove, describing him as 'singularly self-effacing', and quotes Roy's effusive praise of him: 'Orwell's all right, let me tell you. He fought for his beliefs with rifle and bayonet, not with eating-irons. He may have believed in something rotten, but he wasn't one of those well-paid poltroons like Auden and Spender who pushed better men into the fight while they sat back and banquetted for Marxism . . .'[29]

Ultimately, Campbell's admiration for Orwell transcended conventional notions of Left and Right. He saw in Orwell what he had already seen in Hamish Fraser and Hugh Oloff de Wet. These new friends, his former foes, were admired by Campbell as men of action who had never ceased to love their fellow men even as they were fighting them. In the bleakness of a cold war between communism and consumerism they now found themselves as outcasts, alienated by both sides. In the past they had manned the barricades for a faded vision of an illusory utopia, but now they were embraced by Campbell as fellow denizens of the catacombs, waging an underground war against the uncomfortable future offered by an equally illusory 'progress'.

NOTES

1 Roy Campbell, from 'Auguries', *Collected Poems, Volume Two*, p. 96.
2 Roy Campbell, unpublished letter to Mary Campbell, summer 1948.
3 Roy Campbell, unpublished letter to Mary Campbell, summer 1948.
4 *Ibid.*
5 Teresa Campbell, unpublished memoirs, pp. 87–8.
6 Alister Kershaw (ed.), *Salute to Roy Campbell*, p. 110.
7 Anna Campbell Lyle, *Son of Valour*, p. 129.
8 Roy Campbell, *Collected Poems, Volume Two*, p. 209.
9 Rob Lyle, interview with the author, Portugal, December 1998.
10 Anna Campbell Lyle, interview with the author, Portugal, December 1998.
11 Rob Lyle, interview with the author, Portugal, December 1998.
12 Anna Campbell Lyle, interview with the author, Portugal, December 1998.
13 *Times Literary Supplement*, 24 March 1950.
14 Roy Campbell, unpublished letter to Mary and Teresa Campbell, early 1948.
15 Roy Campbell, unpublished letter to Sister Mary Joseph, postmarked 16 August 1949.
16 Mary Campbell, unpublished letter to C. J. Sibbett, 16 October 1949.
17 Peter Alexander, *Roy Campbell*, p. 214.
18 Roy Campbell, unpublished letter to Ross Nichols, 2 May 1949.
19 Peter Alexander, *Roy Campbell*, p. 215.
20 Osbert Sitwell, unpublished letter to Roy Campbell, 28 June 1949.
21 Peter Alexander, *Roy Campbell*, p. 215.
22 Roy Campbell, unpublished letter to an unspecified relative, referred to by Anna Campbell Lyle, interview with the author, Portugal, December 1998.
23 Anna Campbell Lyle, interview with the author, Portugal, December 1998.
24 Roy Campbell, 'Books in Britain', *Enquiry*, London, Vol. 2, No. 3 (September 1949); reprinted in *Collected Works IV: Prose*, pp. 346–8.
25 Anna Campbell Lyle, letter to the author, 5 February 1999.
26 Roy Campbell, *Light on a Dark Horse*, p. 11.
27 Anna Campbell Lyle, letter to the author, 5 February 1999.
28 Roy Campbell, 'A Decade in Retrospect', *The Month*, New Series Vol. 3, No. 5, May 1950, p. 327.
29 Alister Kershaw (ed.), *Salute to Roy Campbell*, p. 43.

CHAPTER THIRTY-TWO

HUMOUR AND HUMILITY

> The steeper upward that I flew
> On so vertiginous a quest
> The humbler and more lowly grew
> My spirit, fainting in my breast.
> I said 'None yet can find the way'
> But as my spirit bowed more low,
> Higher and higher did I go . . .[1]

Campbell's preoccupation with the infernal utopias of Huxley, Orwell, Wells and Shaw was already in evidence in July 1949 in another blistering attack on 'scientific optimism' and its blind faith in inexorable 'progress'. He warned that the Cold War reality could be far worse than the imaginary 'nightmares' of Huxley or Orwell, or the fanciful 'day-dreams' of Wells and Shaw.

> As a follow-on from *Brave New World*, this 'cautionary nightmare' *Ape and Essence* reverses even more drastically than the former prophecy, the scientific optimism of such prophets as Shaw, Wells and Jules Verne, most of whose day-dreams no less fantastic than Huxley's nightmare, have come true to the detriment of human culture and civilisation. It does not require much imagination, following the Gadarene stampede of 'Progress' for the last couple of centuries, to foresee that even worse hells than Huxley's nightmare (or Orwell's *1984* which is written in a very different spirit) may be realised in our own life-time. He foresees . . . the 'squalid disintegration of the very substance of our species' when human love will be penalised: and when demons will laugh round the whipping posts: with eunuch priests impaling deformed babies on their knives: and flogging mothers in the presence of their children, etc . . . there is nothing so very prophetic about that. The equivalent happened in Spain, in Nazi Germany, and is happening in Russia. Worse happened at Hiroshima and Nagasaki. It will not be long, perhaps, before it is universal.[2]

The same preoccupation with 'progress' was also in evidence in May 1950 in an essay entitled 'A Decade in Retrospect' which Campbell wrote for an issue of the Jesuit journal *The Month*, which also contained articles by Ronald Knox, Angus Wilson and Campbell's old friend Augustus John. In his appraisal of the previous decade, Campbell linked the credulous belief in a benevolent progress with the decline in religious faith, reiterating the Gadarene imagery which appears in each of these articles with monotonous regularity.

> Now it is the intellectuals of this world, and Britain in particular, who have by far the least faith: and once faith is removed, credulity is its inevitable substitute. Man is a believing animal. If he is not allowed to believe *sense* – he believes any *rubbish* . . .
>
> That is why, during the last forty or fifty years, coincident with the decline in Faith, 'progress' has assumed the momentum of an almost vertical Gadarene stampede: the most rapid and disastrous 'progress' ever witnessed: and all for the want of those two sensible stand-bys (a brake and a steering wheel) *Tradition* and *Reaction*. A body without reactions is a corpse. So is a Society without Tradition.[3]

Campbell's reasoning would have struck a sympathetic chord with his fellow Inklings, C. S. Lewis and J. R. R. Tolkien, who were addressing similar concerns in their own work. Lewis's novel *That Hideous Strength*, published five years earlier, and Tolkien's *The Lord of the Rings*, published four years later, would encompass the antithetical themes of tradition against 'progress' and of faith against scientism, i.e. the idolatry of science. Campbell's view was also being echoed in the work of Eliot, Sassoon and Sitwell, all of whom shared his sense of alienation at the way in which the post-war world was regressing in the name of progress. In many crucial respects, these writers were kindred spirits, sharing a common aversion to the modern malaise. More surprising was the attitude of Edward Sackville-West, Vita's cousin and a prominent member of the Bloomsbury group whom Campbell had met more than 20 years earlier during those interminable dinner parties at Long Barn.

Like Campbell, Sackville-West had been profoundly impressed by Orwell's *Nineteen Eighty-Four*, which had convinced him that 'the Devil's agents, recently associated with the conquered Nazis, were still very much with us' and that it was 'high time to declare myself – to take the side of Christ against the gospel of materialism'.[4] His decision to seek instruction in the Catholic faith had also been influenced by Graham Greene's novel *The Heart of the Matter*, and by correspondence with Evelyn Waugh, in the course of which Sackville-West had admitted to Waugh that 'theologically speaking, your position is unassailable'.[5]

Waugh was thrilled to learn that his friend was receiving instruction. Expressing his 'intense delight', he wrote to him in early August 1949: 'Conversion is like stepping across the chimney piece out of a Looking-glass-World, where everything is an absurd caricature, into the real world God made; and then begins the delicious process of exploring it limitlessly.'[6] Waugh's delight at Sackville-West's reception into the Church on 17 August 1949 was not shared by Edward's friends in the Bloomsbury group, many of whom were as outraged by his conversion as Virginia Woolf had been by Eliot's conversion two decades earlier. 'Eddie Sackville-West turned Roman Catholic and the others were very indignant,' recalled fellow Bloomsbury member Frances Partridge, who objected to the crucifixes in Sackville-West's room. 'I remember being slightly disquieted by the crucifixes beside his bed.'[7] Like Campbell, Sackville-West had experienced Bloomsbury from the inside and had passed beyond its atheistic precepts to an acceptance of traditional Christianity.

Campbell's faith was not merely evident in his progress-defying prose, but also in the mysticism of his verse translations, particularly those of St John of the Cross which he had almost completed. His own acceptance of suffering, still present in his life through the problems with his hip, the recurring bouts of malaria and his concerns for the psychological suffering of his daughters, was expressed in 'Counsel', a sonnet which he freely translated from a Portuguese original by Manuel Bandeira.

> The world is pitiless and lewdly jeers
> All tragedy. Anticipate your loss.
> Weep silently, in secret. Hide your tears,
> So to become accustomed to your cross.

There was also a good deal of jollity amidst the suffering, tears of laughter mingling with those of pain, as three of Campbell's finest and funniest satirical verses testify. In the April 1949 issue of *The Catacomb* he published 'Ska-hawtch Wha Hae!', described as 'A Likkle wee wee poom i' th' Ye Aulde Teashoppe Pidgin-Brogue, Lallands or Butter-Scotch (Wi' apooligies to MockDiarmid)'. The spirit of the satire harks back to 'Georgian Spring', Campbell's attack on Vita Sackville-West's idolization of a 'chocolate box' England. This time, however, the butt of the joke is not the poetic pose of an English aristocrat but the poetic posturing of a Scottish communist – Campbell's old enemy Hugh MacDiarmid – who was as guilty, in Campbell's eyes, of falsifying the true spirit of Scotland as Vita was of falsifying the spirit of England. Whereas Vita had written of pastoral streams under a silver moon and country wenches tumbling in the hay, MacDiarmid – with equal artificiality – had concocted a hotchpotch of real and imagined Scottish regional colloquialisms to convey his own singular blend of communism and nationalism. In both cases art had surrendered to artifice.

For once, Campbell succeeds in keeping his satire under control, refraining from spitting venom by keeping his tongue firmly in his cheek. The result is that 'Ska-hawtch Wha Hae!' gains in humour what it lacks in spite.

Skwawtch wha hieland clanship braggis
Yet rides himsel' for want o' naggis
Whiles frae his chin a sporran waggis
O' new-mown hay!
Skwawtch wha heehaw! Skwawtch wha haggis!
Skwawtch wha hae!
Skwawtch wha heehaw-heehaw-hae!
Skwawtch wha heehaw doon the brae!

Funnier still, and perhaps the most ingenious of all Campbell's satirical verses, were two parodies of Gerard Manley Hopkins. Campbell considered Hopkins 'quite unnecessarily complex', recalls Rob Lyle. 'He had a principle which he tended to apply rather wickedly that complexity disguised a lack of thought, so he tended to dismiss Hopkins for that reason.'[8] It seems strange that Campbell should lack sympathy for Hopkins's concept of *inscape*, the metaphysical design at the heart of all beauty, which the Jesuit poet had developed from his reading of scholastic philosophy, particularly the writings of the medieval Franciscan philosopher Duns Scotus. Yet his apparent inability (or unwillingness) to comprehend Hopkins's philosophical depth did not prevent him imitating Hopkins's style with hilarious effectiveness. Roy's first lampoon of Hopkins, published in *The Catacomb* in autumn 1951, was entitled 'The Drummer Boy's Catechism' and subtitled 'An Essay in Hopkinese'.

Wagwanton man-chick, soldier-budlet, boyling
's soul needs grace more than his boots need oiling.
So comes he to the cleric (an
Orphan he is, whose sole aunt turned American).

Comes he to learn. Ah! visit now the tenth this is
To me, unworth. But in the mean parenthesis
Ah how ecstatic is m-
-y waiting soul with gust to hear his catechism!

The other lampoon of Hopkins, published in April 1952, was entitled 'Inscape of Skytehawks on the Cookhouse Roof'.

> See! see the skytehawks perch, smelling the cookery, all in a rosary-rookery
> Ranged, ranged in order, in file ranged, and, Ah! Oh! in rank ranged, on the topmost
> Ridge o' the cookhouse roof. See, too, Rihambo, the cookboy, desist from his cookery
> To fling a half-brick at them, fling a half-brick . . .
> And all in a rosary-rookery, bead-bird-busted, those skytehawks scatter for shelter –
> Skytehawks scram in a scramble up-sky, scram in a scramble. A scramble. You said it!
> Raucous the caucus of the whole skytehawkery – and helter they go in a skelter, helter-a-skelter.

These playful parodies signal a subtle change in Campbell's temperament as he approached his fiftieth year. They are full of the raucous, rumbustious humour with which he had always entertained and delighted his friends, yet they lack the uncharitable savagery that had so often distressed both friends and enemies alike. In acquiring an element of tact while retaining his humour, a mellower man and a more restrained poet emerges.

Early in 1950, Roy delivered several books to his publishers almost simultaneously. These were his translations of the poems of St John of the Cross, on which he had been working for over a decade; the manuscript of *Light on a Dark Horse*, his second autobiography (or 'my autobuggeroffery', as he described it dismissively in private correspondence) which was as factually inaccurate and as outrageously entertaining as his earlier volume, *Broken Record*; and four volumes of translations of Lorca, which Eliot wanted for Faber & Faber. With the advances for these, and with additional financial help from Lyle, Campbell departed with Tess on 11 May for the south of France.

Ostensibly, the visit had been planned to assist Tess in her slow but steady recovery, yet Roy was as anxious as his daughter to return to the southern sun and the Latin culture. They stayed in Bormes, a village overlooking the Côte d'Azur, which was only six miles from the villa of Richard Aldington, with whom Campbell had corresponded but never met. The two poets were soon meeting every day. Roy's early impressions of Aldington provide further evidence of his mellowing attitude. 'He seems a bit like W.L. [Wyndham Lewis] in the way that most of his reactions are hostile. He is a recluse and seems anti-everything. For him everybody is a "Jew" – including

Eliot, Lewis and Pound. He is unlike Lewis however in that he is good-naturedly "anti" – there is no real rancour in what he says . . ."[9]

Roy's own good nature was remembered by Aldington's 10-year-old daughter Catherine, who retained fond memories of his sense of fun. He had taken her to a small circus in the village, explaining that small circuses were far better than larger ones because those in the audience were able to see the performers at close quarters. The circus was run by gipsies and Roy, typically, succeeded in befriending the whole company so that the 'boss', to Catherine's delight, invited them back to his caravan for coffee.

> As we left, Roy stumbled over a wild boar which was tethered outside. Instantaneously he gave a wonderful imitation of a man overcome with terror. Needless to say, he wasn't in the least perturbed, but it gave him the material for a wonderful story about the terrible danger from which we had miraculously escaped.
>
> On another occasion we were together in a café in Bormes. Suddenly he whispered that he was going to talk to me in Zulu and that I had to pretend to understand so that the other customers would wonder what on earth was going on. After a minute or two of listening to the strange clicks in his throat, I began to laugh so hard that he had to give up the joke.[10]

Roy's delight at the sun, scenery and simple life of the Mediterranean was shared by Tess, who began to make a remarkable recovery. She smiled for the first time in several years and began gaining weight. Roy's sense of nostalgia for the long-lost days in Martigues must also have been heightened by regular meetings with Augustus John, who was spending the summer in a nearby village while he finished work on an autobiography, *Chiaroscuro*.

Mary and Anna had gone on pilgrimage to Rome for the Holy Year, during which they had an audience with Pope Pius XII, before they eventually joined Roy and Tess in France in July. For the next two months the family enjoyed a renewal of their old Mediterranean lifestyle and visited many of their old haunts in Provence, accentuating Roy's nostalgia for the paradise lost. It was, therefore, with a degree of reluctance that he returned with the rest of the family to London in late September. Almost immediately his health suffered, as his hip deteriorated with the onset of the damp English autumn. He was confined to bed for over a month in November and December. He spent that time correcting proofs of his translations of St John of the Cross and finishing a children's story, *The Mamba's Precipice*, a powerful evocation of his own childhood in Natal. Increasingly, as the world headed into a future filled with foreboding, Roy felt more and more attracted to memories of his past, wallowing in its wonder-filled moments.

Artistically, his standing was healthier than ever. The publication of the first volume of his *Collected Poems* in 1949 had helped secure his reputation. He could write with confidence and satisfaction in the preface to a new South African edition of *Adamastor* that 'poets and critics as different as T. S. Eliot, Dylan Thomas, Desmond MacCarthy, William Empson, Wyndham Lewis, C. S. Lewis, Edith, Osbert and Sacheverall [sic] Sitwell, Graham Greene, and John Betjeman' had praised his recent work. He was also in great demand with student literary groups, receiving invitations to speak at Oxford, Cambridge and several Scottish universities, including St Andrews. Typically, he would commence these talks by reading some of his own poems before launching off on an opinionated tour of modern literature, praising Eliot, Dylan Thomas and Edith Sitwell and damning those who dared attack them.

In May 1951 he made another trip to Spain to lecture at the Ateneo in Madrid, and a month later his translations of the Spanish mystic St John of the Cross were finally published, fully 15 years after his prayerful promise that he would translate the poems if his family was spared during the fighting in Toledo. The book, published by Harvill, was received more favourably by the critics than anything he had written since *Adamastor*. The wider public must have been equally impressed, because it quickly surpassed all his other books in terms of sales.

The reviews were almost universally enthusiastic. An anonymous reviewer, writing in the *Times Literary Supplement* on 15 June, echoed the general view of most critics that the translations were fine poems in their own right: 'The translations from St John of the Cross are . . . among the most pure and lucid of English mystical poems.' Edwin Muir called the work 'a triumph',[11] and Kathleen Raine, writing in the *New Statesman*, encapsulated the general consensus that Campbell's translations represented a superlative achievement in English verse. 'Of all living English poets Roy Campbell is the most masterly in his use of rhyme, and he is able to use metre so as to convey a sense of intense passion. He has reproduced the Spanish rhymes and metres as closely as possible, and yet his English versions have the freshness of original poems.'[12]

Raine's words were echoed by Edith Sitwell, who wrote that Campbell's use of rhyme was 'masterly' and that he was 'one of the very few great poets of our time'. Specifically, his 'ineffable translation' of St John of the Cross's 'Upon a Gloomy Night' was 'certainly among the great poems of our time'.[13] Martin D'Arcy commented, 'Roy Campbell carries us with him to Spain and into the presence of a Saint singing of the love of God. He proves, also . . . that translation can be a stimulus and an original pleasure to a genuine poet.'[14]

Perhaps the most perceptive insight into the profundity of the relationship between Roy Campbell and St John of the Cross was given by Mary several years after the translations were published. The key to understanding the two poets, she wrote, and to understanding the love of her poet husband for the poet saint, was to be found in their shared experience of Toledo. Quoting those who had written about Toledo, Mary stressed that the impact which the ancient city had exerted on both her husband and on St John of the Cross was far deeper than words could convey.

> St John of the Cross did not write of it, he wrote in it, in the miserable cell so small that he could hardly turn round, and where he was all through the burning summer of 1567 and where, as he said, through suffering came to him the experiences which he could only express through purest poetry . . .
>
> [Toledo had] hardly changed in essentials since the sixteenth century, or had not when we lived there twenty years ago . . . It is indeed very much the Toledo of St John of the Cross, and when we became Catholics it was his successors and sons who taught us all we wanted to know. [Roy] found that his Carmelite friends resembled very closely a type he often wrote of, as in the 'Horses on the Camargue':
>
> Still out of hardship bred
> Spirits of power and beauty and delight,
> Have ever on such frugal pastures fed
> And loved to course with tempests through the night.

Roy, Mary said, had known the Carmelite writers in Toledo who had researched so thoroughly the lives and texts of St John and St Teresa, but he was most attached to Father Eusebio, 'his chief friend and his confessor . . . who was not a writer but a saint and martyr, and whom Roy mentions several times in his poetry'. After Father Eusebio was murdered in cold blood in Toledo in July 1936, 'his white bloodstained cloak was cut up into relics for the many penitents who had venerated him'.

> Among them was Roy. He loved him as a friend and revered him as a father. Through him and his death he came to understand the spirit, not only of St John, but of the Cross, which then became for him as never before the central feature of Christianity . . .
>
> Roy would have laughed if anyone had called him a mystic; but it is significant that his first great enthusiasm was for Rimbaud and his last for St John of the Cross, and it would have been impossible for him to make such translations as he did of them both if he had not understood them perfectly. For although they do not at first sight appear alike, there are many things in their work to show that they

> set out on the same voyage of discovery ... But whereas St John reached his goal, Rimbaud foundered miserably. Roy was too humble even to think of embarking, but he knew their secret ...
>
> Roy could not have translated these most delicate and deeply theological poems unless he had known well what they were about; this knowledge he acquired from Father Eusebio in Toledo, and from studying theology in the works of Calderón and other poets of the Golden Age. All of them, poets and dramatists, were full of theology, and Calderón de la Barca was the most subtle and imaginative theologian. Roy would not study this science from books of theology, but when it was poured from the mouths of the characters in *La Colmena, El Magico Prodigioso, La Vida es Sueño* he imbibed it with ease.[15]

The creative trinity of humility, mysticism and theology which Mary had singled out as the essential ingredients of Roy's ability to translate the poems so successfully were all present in a broadcast talk on St John of the Cross which Roy gave for the BBC in 1952. In a disarming example of self-effacement, he stated that the success of the poems was due more to the grace obtained by the saint's supernatural intervention than by any innate ability of his own. 'Were I superstitious I should say that San Juan brought me luck,' he said. 'Not being superstitious, I say that he wrought a miracle.'[16]

A similar instance arose after Roy had just finished delivering a lecture at the Ateneo in Madrid in 1954. A member of the audience, a well known priest and writer, asked him to what he attributed the extraordinary success of his verse translations of St John of the Cross. 'But the good saint helped me Father,' Roy replied. 'You see, when I got tired, or my spirit flagged, or I got stuck, I would just look over my shoulder and there St John would be, sitting against the sky, smiling down at me. He would call out *Arre burrico!* ['Go, little donkey!'] And I just went on trotting ...'[17] This charming mixture of mischievous humour and mystical humility delighted his Spanish audience, who erupted in spontaneous laughter and applause. Never before had the controversial poet enjoyed such popularity. In humility he was being exalted.

NOTES

1 Roy Campbell, from 'Other verses with a divine meaning by the same author', *Collected Poems, Volume Three*, London: The Bodley Head, 1960, p. 52.
2 Roy Campbell, 'The Mahatma of Misanthropy', *Enquiry*, London, Vol. 2, No. 1 (July 1949); reprinted in Roy Campbell, *Collected Works IV: Prose*, pp. 338–41.
3 Roy Campbell, 'A Decade in Retrospect', *The Month*, May 1950, p. 329.
4 Michael de-la-Noy, *Eddy: The Life of Edward Sackville-West*, London: Hutchinson, 1988, p. 237.
5 *Ibid.*, p. 230.
6 *Ibid.*, pp. 237–8.

7 *Sunday Telegraph*, 12 July 1998.
8 Rob Lyle, interview with the author, Portugal, December 1998.
9 Peter Alexander, *Roy Campbell*, p. 219.
10 Alister Kershaw (ed.), *Salute to Roy Campbell*, p. 10.
11 *Observer*, 2 June 1951.
12 *New Statesman*, 16 June 1951.
13 Edith Sitwell, Foreword to Roy Campbell, *Collected Poems, Volume Three*, pp. 5–7.
14 Martin D'Arcy, Introduction to Roy Campbell, *St John of the Cross: Poems*, Harmondsworth, Middlesex: Penguin Classics edition, 1960, p. 24.
15 Mary Campbell, Preface in *ibid.*, pp. 9–15.
16 Peter Alexander, *Roy Campbell*, p. 221.
17 Anna Campbell Lyle, *Son of Valour*, pp. 80–81.

CHAPTER THIRTY-THREE

TROOPERS OF THE SUN

While you and I with no more luggage pass
Than springbok bounding over plains of grass –
Free as the air, responsible to none,
Soldiers of chance, and troopers of the Sun.
Luck on our side, we play at pitch and toss
Christ for our king and Mithras for our boss . . .[1]

On 17 January 1952, at a literary luncheon at the Dorchester Hotel in London, Roy was awarded the Foyle Prize for Poetry for his translation of the poems of St John of the Cross. Anna, who attended the luncheon and was seated beside Lord David Cecil, remembered it as 'a great day' for her father. 'I felt such a deep pride and happiness for him. Many of the hurts he had received were mended that day. We spent the night with our best friends, talking until the dawn came up. It was wonderful to see my father so fulfilled and happy.'[2]

Campbell was highly amused to discover that Stephen Spender had been selected to present the prize. According to Campbell's version of events, recounted in a letter to a friend, Spender had not known until shortly beforehand who the recipient was to be. Nonetheless, the two poets shook hands with the utmost cordiality, in marked contrast to their previous encounter.[3]

Although Anna recalled that the prestigious luncheon was 'attended by all the literary lights of the day', one particular guest of honour was conspicuous by her absence. Vita Sackville-West had received an anxious phone call from Mary, the first time they had made contact in more than 20 years, pleading with her not to attend, 'lest Roy should make a scene'. Vita, wishing as much as Mary to avoid any unpleasantness or embarrassment, stayed away.[4] The bad blood between Campbell and the Bloomsburys had been resurrected with the publication a few weeks earlier, on 7 December 1951, of Roy's new autobiography, *Light on a Dark Horse*. Before its publication Harold Nicolson had written threateningly, no doubt with veiled hints of libel proceedings, to protest his fears about Campbell's account of his stay at Long Barn. The publishers, Hollis & Carter, bowed to pressure and agreed to tone down all references to Campbell's brief encounter with Bloomsbury.

In truth, although Campbell complained bitterly about the editing, there was much else in *Light on a Dark Horse* which would also have benefited from toning down, particularly in the latter parts of the book where Campbell's prejudices occasionally surface with embarrassing shrillness. Half a century after its publication, Anna still seems embarrassed by its excesses. 'You must not take *Light on a Dark Horse* seriously,' she insists, 'because he didn't. Only the parts about South Africa he took seriously. All the rest is nonsense. The second part of *Light on a Dark Horse* is just complete nonsense.'[5]

Anna's view was shared by Dylan Thomas, who reviewed *Light on a Dark Horse* for the *Observer* on 16 December 1951. Thomas praised 'the first half of this often beautiful and always bee-loud autobiography', relishing the 'fantastic world' of his friend's African childhood. 'But in the second half of the book, especially in the chapters about Bohemian London and his private life, those prejudiced dogs come snarling from their kennels and worry the marrow out of every bone in sight.' The concluding sentences of Thomas's review captured the book's strengths and weaknesses succinctly: 'I acclaim the first twelve chapters, written by a poet of genius. But, for much of the rest, I think it throws rather a bad light on an old war-horse.'

The only writer of stature who sought to shed a positive light on Campbell's dark prejudices was Laurie Lee. In a foreword to a new edition of *Light on a Dark Horse* published in 1969, Lee described Campbell as 'a romantic idealist'. He was 'one of our last pre-technocratic, big action poets who, like D'Annuncio and Byron, were not only the writers of exquisite lyrics but whose poetry was part of a physical engagement with life . . .' Lee even found an excuse for Campbell's exaggerations and falsehoods. 'Personally,' he wrote, 'I much preferred his style to the English passion for understatement, which is only boasting stood on its head.' Campbell was 'somewhat larger than the life of his day', and his vivaciously flamboyant poetry was a verse parallel to Hemingway's prose. Lee described Campbell as a 'wounded hunter bound to his cave . . . whose daggered epigrams could strike instant death'. While Lee's foreword was full of genuine warmth for an old friend, however, even he felt constrained to distance himself from Campbell's 'dottier prejudices'.[6]

If those dottier prejudices still emerged occasionally to tarnish Campbell's reascendent reputation, the gratitude and humility which had been the foundation for his new-found popularity was clear from the closing paragraph of his introduction to *Light on a Dark Horse*:

> Ever since that first night out at sea and my last view of Durban, my memories have become clearer and clearer until I have at last been

> literally forced to write them out in this book so as to repay my debt both to Almighty God and to my parents, for letting me loose in such a world, to plunder its miraculous literatures, and languages, and wines: to savour its sights, forms, colours, perfumes, and sounds: to see so many superb cities, oceans, lakes, forests, rivers, sierras, pampas, and plains, with their beasts, birds, trees, crops, and flowers – and above all their men and women, who are by far the most interesting of all.[7]

In December 1951, just as *Light on a Dark Horse* was being published, Campbell's editorship of *The Catacomb* was coming to an end. He and Lyle had fought valiantly to keep the journal alive, in spite of a small and declining circulation. In the summer of 1950 it had ceased to be published monthly, appearing only quarterly thereafter. The first quarterly edition had included an encouraging letter from T. S. Eliot, and other issues could boast contributions by Richard Church, Peter Russell, John Heath-Stubbs, Bernard Bergonzi, Charles Causley, Charles Tomlinson and Sacheverell Sitwell. Significantly, Campbell's old friend Wyndham Lewis had refused to contribute, presumably because of his suspicion of *The Catacomb*'s Catholicism, even though Ezra Pound wrote to Campbell praising the magazine and urging him to persuade Lewis to write for it. (Campbell and Lewis remained on cordial terms, as was demonstrated by Campbell's article praising Lewis in *Time and Tide* on 7 July 1951 and Lewis's letter thanking him for it in which he expressed the hope that 'we shall always remain comrades-in-arms'.[8] Cordiality aside, however, the two men now had far less in common than in the past.)

In spite of its impressive array of contributors, *The Catacomb* was failing to win new readers and Lyle, who had always heavily subsidized the journal, decided to suspend publication at the end of 1951. Although this meant that Campbell could no longer rely on the salary he had received as editor, Lyle, by then Campbell's greatest benefactor as well as his closest friend, ensured his financial independence by making him a gift of a house in London which guaranteed an annual income in rent of £1,000. Informing C. J. Sibbett of his good fortune, Campbell wrote that 'for the first time in my life I start being a plutocrat. Lyle found that a house belonging to him was more of a liability than an asset as it piled up his 99% income tax – so he gave it to me and it brings in £1,000 a year (keep this under your hat).'[9] Roy was also earning more money through his writing than ever before, following the publication in swift succession of his *Collected Poems*, his autobiography and his translations of St John of the Cross.

Freed from their obligations to *The Catacomb*, and after consultation with their respective wives, Lyle and Campbell decided to seek an escape from the stifling dreariness of post-war England. Roy's desire to return to the Latin culture which had been the inspiration for so much of his finest poetry had been growing insistently for some time. His recent extended trip to the south of France and a succession of visits to Spain to give lectures had only served to heighten his determination to seek the sun and sanity of southern France or Iberia. He had tired of London – not, *pace* Dr Johnson, because he had tired of life, but because he sought it more fully.

He and Mary had been happy and relatively settled in London. The parties they held in the basement of their Campden Grove house were popular social events at which all classes seemed to mix with ease. At a typical party the local butcher and various ex-servicemen Roy had befriended in the local pubs would rub shoulders with the Spanish Ambassador or the South African High Commissioner. These in turn would mingle with the illustrissimi of English letters, such as T. S. Eliot, Edith, Osbert and Sacheverell Sitwell, Dylan and Caitlin Thomas, Evelyn Waugh and Laurie Lee, and sundry others such as Augustus John, Father D'Arcy, the bullfighter Mario Cabre, the Provençal writer Charles de Richter, the Australian horseman and film actor Chips Rafferty, and the sculptor Oloff de Wet.

Yet, in spite of his popularity and the gregarious ease with which he mixed with friends, Roy was determined to seek a simpler life, at a slower pace, and in sunnier climes. He prevailed upon Mary to consider a move back to Spain or Portugal and she, it seems, having perhaps grown tired of the experiment in English urban domesticity, agreed to uproot once again in pursuit of her husband's dreams. 'None of us wants to grow old and die in a Protestant country,' Roy told his friend Armand Guibert. 'I'd rather be a beggar in Spain than a bureaucrat here.'[10]

Campbell and Lyle started to look into the possibility of renting a small farm in Portugal. In March 1952 they discovered a beautiful smallholding called Quinta dos Bochechos ('Gurgling Farm') in the hills at Galamares, near Sintra, northwest of Lisbon. Roy was delighted at the prospect of living once again in his beloved Iberia. He relished the slower pace of life, the sunshine, the culture, the food and the wine. In a haze of contentment he wandered aimlessly through the streets of Lisbon, limping along under a Spanish sombrero, watching the crowds, eating snacks of olives, nuts and salted cod's tongues, and visiting the bars. His sense of liberation was almost tangible and was reminiscent of the lines dedicated to Mary in his *Collected Poems*, published three years earlier. He and Mary were

> Free as the air, responsible to none,
> Soldiers of chance, and troopers of the Sun.

On 24 March, Campbell and Lyle returned to London to make the final arrangements for the move to Portugal.

Roy took the opportunity to meet up with as many friends as possible during his last few weeks in England. On 1 May he dined with Evelyn Waugh, their relationship having warmed since their less than successful first meeting. 'I dined tonight with Roy Campbell (Dark Horse) a great beautiful simple sweet natured savage,' Waugh wrote to Nancy Mitford, adding that he felt 'quite dizzy from his talking to me'.[11] A few days later Roy had lunch with his fellow South Africans, Laurens van der Post, Enslin du Plessis, Uys Krige and Alan Paton, the last of whom had become internationally famous following the publication of his best-selling anti-apartheid novel *Cry the Beloved Country* four years earlier. During lunch the five men composed and signed an open letter to the South African government, protesting against the plans to remove voters of mixed race from the electoral roll. The letter, which was subsequently published in several South African newspapers, indicates Campbell's continuing concerns over the plight of his native land. His views on the subject had been expressed in *Light on a Dark Horse*:

> The present disqualification of the native from so many aids to his own betterment is exactly on a par with the natives' treatment of each other. We are behaving about a quarter as badly as the Zulus and Matabeles did to their fellow Bantu, and it will do us little more good than it did them . . . and we may end by ranking the majority of the population in violent opposition to the white minority, which happened in the mad revolution of Haiti, when the black Emperor, Jean Christophe, out-Caesared Nero and Caligula in the name of Liberty and Equality.
>
> We must never forget that theoretical Bolshevism is the most attractive dream-bait that was ever invented. Though practical Bolshevism may be the most diabolical and cruel hook that was ever inserted into bait . . . you can expect a rustic Zulu to be proof against the seductive blarney which completely seduced the 'knowing and sophisticated' intellectuals of England and Western Europe for so many years.[12]

Campbell's preference for the perennial wisdom of the rustic, whether he be a Portuguese peasant or a Zulu warrior, over the sophisticated knowledge of liberal or Marxist intellectuals was at the heart of his opposition to developments in South Africa as well as being at the heart of his desire to leave England for Portugal. It also illustrated his fundamental differences with Alan Paton and other liberal South Africans who wished to see South Africa transformed into a complex 'democratic' state similar to the monolithic bureaucracies emerging in post-war Europe and America. Contrary to the liberal dream of a universal welfare state, governed by the same liberal democratic principles throughout the world, Campbell believed in the power and integrity of indigenous cultures to govern their own destinies, irrespective of global master plans. This had been a recurring motif in his work from the earliest days. In 'The Serf', written 25 years earlier, he had written respectfully of the Zulu ploughman, predicting that he would remain long after the liberal democracies had passed away.

> The timeless, surly patience of the serf
> That moves the nearest to the naked earth
> And ploughs down palaces, and thrones, and towers.

Campbell's respect for the Zulus was undiminished. He had recently translated a Zulu war song which conveyed not only his prodigious abilities as poet and translator, but also his deep sense of affinity with the people of whom he wrote.

> Great must be this people that,
> one strong purpose binding,
> Is like a great black snake along
> the valleys winding,
> Whose scales are shields, whose
> teeth are spears, who thunders
> as he goes,
> Whose crests of feathers flutter
> like the faint hearts of his foes,
> Who rises in the daybreak from
> the forest dark and cool,
> And goes to drink at sunset from
> the crimson coloured pool.[13]

During those last weeks in England before departing for Portugal, Roy worked furiously on a translation of the poems of Baudelaire. 'I determined to translate a fellow sinner, who was hardly less a Catholic Christian and a believer, even in his blasphemous and rebellious moments,' he wrote. 'I have been reading Baudelaire since I was seventeen, carried him in my haversack in two wars and loved him longer and more deeply than any other poet.' Above all, he had decided to translate Baudelaire because both poet and translator had much in common, 'with similar sins, remorses, ostracisms and poverty and the same desperate hope of reconciliation'.[14] No doubt he had also been encouraged to attempt a translation of Baudelaire by the great success of his translation of St John of the Cross. Yet he was not satisfied with the results, expressing his frustration in words that he would later regurgitate in the Spanish lectures. 'I have not made such a good translation of Baudelaire as St John, not so much from lack of striving but want of

Supernatural aid, for in the latter case the Saint only needed to raise his stick and say *Arre Burro!* ('Gee up Donkey') to me – and the donkey trotted.'[15]

On 9 May 1952 Campbell, Tess and Rob Lyle's wife Felicia departed for their new home in Portugal. Rob and Mary joined them a month later after they had secured tenants for the house in Campden Grove. With the help of a handful of local peasants hired by Lyle, tomatoes and potatoes were planted and the rearing of pigs began. Roy, thoroughly at home in his new environment, fished for eels in the stream that ran beneath the house and worked at leisure in his study. In the evenings he drank wine and discussed literature with Lyle. Occasionally, as the wine flowed, he would sing the songs of his youth to the accompaniment of Mary's guitar. It was all so reminiscent of the long nights on the terrace in Martigues 20 years earlier.

After a year, the abundance of fruit which grew on the farm was supplemented by a bumper harvest of various vegetables grown from seeds that Mary had been planting assiduously. Bread was baked from home-grown wheat which was ground at the local mill. In time the farm became almost self-sufficient. Although it was a far cry from the parties at Campden Grove, this simpler life seemed ideally suited to Roy and Mary, rekindling memories of previous halcyon days when they had hewn a personal paradise from the sun, soil and simplicity of Provence, Portugal and Spain.

'After all these years my father had not changed much although he was older,' remembers Tess. 'All through his life he had a natural simplicity in his possessions and habits. He only possessed the bare necessities of life. He had no wardrobe except a suit my mother kept in a cupboard for interviews, lectures or important occasions. It was a natural disposition, in this way he was freer to concentrate on the only thing that mattered to him, poetry.'[16]

In 'Twin Reflections', a poem written around this time, Roy celebrates the only thing that mattered to him even more than poetry – Mary, his lifelong companion and muse. As with so many of the other poems directly inspired by his wife, 'Twin Reflections' resonates with erotic imagery, an affirmation of the beauty of spiritual love fused with sexual passion.

> Like an Atlantic roller, steep and strong,
> She hit me, broke on me, and hid the sun.
> I surfed a foam of roses all night long.
> Day broke with two auroras. She was one.
>
> White Pegasus, with jet-blue mane astream,
> Her girlhood reared and bolted me astray,
> The jockey to a thunderbolt of cream
> Galloping headlong up the Milky Way.

The poem's purpose, however, is not principally to celebrate Mary's youthful 'girlhood' but her mature womanhood. Their youthful passions spent, the poet now looks forward to the comforting afterglow of their final peaceful years together, far from the madding crowds.

> Such is her wrestling whiteness, even yet,
> Where beauty strives with age, as art with time,
> But it was with her eyes, that scorn to set,
> She made herself immortal and my rhyme.
>
> In their dark fire I saw myself made younger
> Star-twinned, with Castor, in the night to shine.
> Far into their huge depths, with mystic hunger,
> Two breathless Muses gazed at her from mine.

NOTES

1 Roy Campbell, from 'Dedication to Mary Campbell', *Collected Poems, Volume One*, p. 176.
2 Anna Campbell Lyle, *Son of Valour*, p. 184.
3 Peter Alexander, *Roy Campbell*, p. 221.
4 Victoria Glendinning, *Vita: The Life of V. Sackville-West*, pp. 371–2.
5 Anna Campbell Lyle, interview with the author, Portugal, December 1998.
6 Quoted in Valerie Grove, *Laurie Lee*, p. 387; and in Barbara Hooper, *Cider with Laurie: Laurie Lee Remembered*, London: Peter Owen Publishers, 1999, p. 155.
7 Roy Campbell, *Light on a Dark Horse*, p. 9.
8 W. K. Rose (ed.), *The Letters of Wyndham Lewis*, pp. 542–3.
9 Roy Campbell, unpublished letter to C. J. Sibbett, early 1952.
10 Alister Kershaw (ed.), *Salute to Roy Campbell*, p. 30.
11 Mark Amory (ed.), *The Letters of Evelyn Waugh*, London: Weidenfeld & Nicolson, 1980, p. 373.
12 Roy Campbell, *Light on a Dark Horse*, p. 154.
13 Roy Campbell, 'Zulu Song', *Collected Works I*, Johannesburg: Ad Donker, 1985, p. 616.
14 Quoted in Anna Campbell Lyle, *Son of Valour*, p. 9.
15 Quoted in Teresa Campbell, unpublished memoirs, p. 108.
16 *Ibid.*, p. 107.

CHAPTER THIRTY-FOUR

NOVEMBER NIGHTS

Now peasants shun the muddy fields, and fisherfolk the shores.
It is the time the weather finds the wounds of bygone wars,
And never to a charger did I take as I have done
To cantering the rocking-chair, my Pegasus, indoors,
For my olives have been gathered and my grapes are in the tun . . .

But for the firelight on your face I would not change the sun,
Nor would I change a moment of our winter-season, no,
For our springtime with its orioles and roses long ago.

Roy and Mary became grandparents on 13 May 1953 when Anna, who had recently married a Spanish nobleman, Viscount Jaime Cavero de Carondelet, gave birth to a daughter. Roy was delighted by little Francesca, whom he called 'Impi' or 'Cooky', and the child was soon equally taken by her grandfather. 'When I had bad dreams,' she remembers, 'I went and climbed into his bed with him and he never complained. He'd sit me on his lap and draw monkeys in trees and tell me stories about all the animals in South Africa.'[1]

Roy also took her with him when he made his regular visits to the local bar, 'where he would buy sweets for all the barefooted children of the village'.[2] Anna described her father toddling off to the village with his grand-daughter, who was 'the great joy and pride of his last years'.

> It was enchanting to watch them walking slowly through the orchards of Quinta dos Bochechos, over the river-bridge hand-in-hand down to the village of Galamares; Roy limping badly and Cooky toddling sedately beside him asking innumerable questions. She only reached up to his knees so when she got tired he would hitch her onto his shoulder, just as he had done when I was a little girl.[3]

Francesca also had fond memories of her grandmother, leaping to her defence when Anna discussed the times when Mary had been neglectful in her younger days. 'She might have been a bad mother but she certainly made up for it as a grandmother. I think she recognised that she had failed a bit as a mother, but then as a grandmother she made up for it, she really did.'[4]

Apart from fulfilling their grandparental duties, Roy and Mary were also struggling to continue running the farm by themselves. In April 1953 Lyle had been forced to return to England after his wife became homesick. 'The Lyles are going back to England this month,' Roy informed his mother, 'so we are taking on the farm alone. We shall miss them very much but Mrs Lyle is a town girl and, though she tried hard, could not get used to life on a farm.'[5] In practice, most of the extra burden of work fell on Mary's shoulders because Roy was either busy translating poetry and novels from Portuguese or else was away lecturing in Spain.

In October 1953 his lecturing took him further afield when he undertook a two-month lecture tour of the United States and Canada, organized by the Canadian poet John Sutherland who was editor of the Montreal literary magazine *Northern Review*. 'I have heard from John Sutherland,' Campbell wrote to Lyle. 'He has a list already of about 23 colleges and universities which will be paying about 2,500 dollars . . . That means about 2,200 for me plus expenses if all goes well.'[6] The offer was simply too good to refuse and Roy sailed from Lisbon on the *Vulcania*, arriving in Halifax, Nova Scotia, on 20 October.

The lecturing engagements commenced immediately. On 21 October he lectured at St Francis Xavier, a Roman Catholic university in Antigonish, Nova Scotia, before travelling by train to Sackville, New Brunswick, where he lectured at Mount Allison University on the following day. From there he wrote enthusiastically to Lyle about his first impressions of the Canadian audiences.

> I am well launched on my tour now . . . and find I am able to take it. These audiences are more in my line than Oxford & Cambridge. They stimulate one to all kinds of real *flights* of extempore rhetoric and I feel myself letting myself go (as I never did before) with things like Tristan da Cunha and carrying everybody with me.[7]

Shortly before giving the twelfth of his lectures in Canada, at Assumption College in Windsor, Ontario, he wrote again to Lyle, his enthusiasm undiminished. The audiences had been 'most sympathetic and stimulating . . . Easily the kindest and most appreciative I've ever had.' Referring to the press coverage of the previous 11 lectures, he reported that his reception had been 'all "ovations" except one and that was reported as "prolonged applause"'. From the guest room at Assumption College he could see Detroit just over the border in the United States, 'with the hugest bridge and skyscrapers I've yet seen – quite an amazing sight – about three miles off though the bridge goes overhead'. There were also the first signs that the hectic schedule was beginning to take its toll. 'I am not too tired . . . but on the whole it is a *hell* of a rush.'[8]

In Toronto on 4 November he met Marshall McLuhan, the Catholic convert writer who was Professor of English at St Michael's College. The two men took an instant liking to each other. McLuhan had befriended Wyndham Lewis in Canada during the war and he and Campbell shared memories of their mutual friend. Campbell also proved very popular with McLuhan's sons, who were fascinated by his endless stories about Africa and his haunting renditions of Zulu songs. McLuhan was impressed by Campbell's 'stage-craft' and told him that with a professional agent he could 'clear easily 20,000 dollars' and that, with this in mind, he should try to return to the US and Canada during the following year.[9]

On 9 November, while Roy was in Seattle where he was to give a lecture at the University of Washington, he was shocked to hear that Dylan Thomas had just died in New York. He wrote at once to Caitlin, who had been left destitute, offering to adopt one of her children. 'You heard of poor Dylan,' he wrote to Lyle. 'He had DTs so they gave him a shot of Morphia which proved too strong for his heart.'[10] Roy reacted to Thomas's death by getting drunk on bourbon whiskey with the poet Theodore Roethke. 'Dylan was killed by American hospitality,' he muttered grimly, pouring himself another liberal measure.[11]

Once he had recovered from the initial shock of Dylan's death, Roy began once again to enthuse about America. 'I am having a *formidable* success (touch wood),' he wrote to Lyle from the University of Iowa.

> America is *absolutely marvellous*, especially Chicago and Milwaukee the corn and cattle lands where the wealth consists in real values – meat, bread, and beer. The affability and true kindness of the people is remarkable, especially in Chicago which is a magnificent spectacle, especially at night; with the statue of Ceres (like Our Lady) with her foot on the moon. I have never heard anything so stupid as the propaganda that makes out that Americans are undeveloped – I get student audiences of hundreds (for tens in Oxford and Cambridge) sometimes 1200 – and their responses are more intelligent than in England.[12]

Beneath the optimism, and his claim that 'this country gives me new faith', there was a re-emergence of the crudest reactionary politics. Senator McCarthy and General MacArthur were described as 'the two greatest Yanks', and he had nothing but contempt for Adlai Stevenson, who had been the unsuccessful Democratic presidential candidate in the previous year's election. Campbell was staying with Stevenson's former wife, whom he described in the letter to Lyle as 'a leading anti-left'. 'Mrs Adlai is anti her husband's politics and a great girl,' he declared to Mary.[13] To Lyle he reported that Stevenson's former wife had said, 'How can those mugs, grown up men, listen to Adlai – I was only seventeen when I met him and I found him out before I was 19.'[14] In the same letter he referred to New York, rather tastelessly, as 'J(N)ew York', an indication of his lingering anti-Semitism. Even as he mellowed emotionally and spiritually, he still remained embittered politically.

Flying down to California, Roy found himself sitting next to Eleanor Roosevelt and thought her delightful. During his lecture at Santa Barbara College on 13 November, he spotted his old friend Iris Tree in the audience. They had not seen each other for a quarter of a century. When they met after the lecture, Roy embarrassed Iris by kneeling at her feet to kiss her hand.

As the weeks drew on, and the number of cities at which he had lectured mounted, Roy began to feel the strain. 'Forgive me for not writing oftener,' he wrote apologetically to Mary, 'it is a hellfire rush from pillar to post, without a pillar box or post box in sight between railways and planes. My letters stay in my pockets till they are unsendable and unreadable because I have to fumble so much after tickets.'[15]

The gruelling tour ended in New York, where Roy was delighted to meet up with Gene Tunney, the former world heavyweight boxing champion. Tunney knew Campbell's great friend Aime Tschiffely, and Tschiffely had asked Campbell to pass on his regards should they meet in America. Campbell and Tunney talked affectionately about their mutual acquaintance as they waited on a station platform, blissfully unaware that, even as they spoke, Tschiffely was seriously ill in a London hospital. He was to die within a fortnight. Several months later, when Campbell wrote 'In Memoriam A. F. Tschiffely', his meeting with Tunney in New York was still branded on his mind.

> Only a week before you died, we stood,
> Gene Tunney and myself, on Stamford station
> And voted it was worth a celebration
> To drink the health of one so great and good:
> We did not know how near to death you lay,
> And as the train rolled onward through New York,
> Each from his memories drew forth the cork
> To which you are the vintage and bouquet.[16]

On 10 December 1953, both exhausted and exhilarated by his experiences, Campbell set sail aboard the American liner *Constitution*, bound for Gibraltar.

He hitched a ride in a cattle-truck to Lisbon, and Mary drove him home from there. He had barely settled back into the somnambulant lifestyle on the Portuguese farm, however, when he heard that the University of Natal intended to confer an honorary doctorate on him. Delighted at this belated recognition from his native land, he began making plans to travel to South Africa. On 10 March he travelled by air to Rome, where he stayed for three days before catching the South African Airways flight to Johannesburg. *En route*, the plane flew into Khartoum just after dawn, affording the poet a spectacular view of 'a magnificent sunrise over the windings of the Nile'.[17]

Roy was greeted on his arrival in Durban on 18 March by his brother George, his old schoolmaster Bill Payn and a host of other old friends and relations who carried him off at once to a rowdy party. In the days preceding and immediately following the degree ceremony he stayed with his mother, then 92 years old, and was swept away by the beautiful views of the Valley of a Thousand Hills which could be seen from her house. 'I'm sitting on my mother's stoep looking over Pietermaritzburg, Table Mountain and the Valley of a Thousand Hills,' he wrote to Lyle. 'From her back stoep you can see Drakensburg range, cobalt and indigo taking up the whole horizon with incredible rock formations . . . like ramping dragons and saw-toothed dinosaurs. Nearer, bright green and yellow, forest and crags, are the Kaarkloof and Inthloraan ranges.'[18]

Intoxicated by the rekindling of his love for South Africa, Roy gave an ill-advised and highly controversial address at the degree ceremony, which was held at Pietermaritzburg City Hall on 20 March. Abandoning his carefully prepared notes, he careered off on a tangent, giving free rein to his reactionary politics. His defence of South Africa and his vigorous attack on England led many to assume, quite wrongly, that Roy was defending Prime Minister Malan's racial policies. Later in the speech he condemned such policies, referring to 'the dangerous and suicidal plight of our country', but by that time the venom of the rest of his speech had led many to the false assumption that Campbell's defence of South Africa indicated a defence of apartheid. As his audience listened with a growing sense of unease and astonishment, Campbell dismissed Churchill as 'a valiant but superannuated Beefeater', denounced Roosevelt as 'a tittering zombie' and condemned the part they had both played in 'the Yalta booby trap' which had consigned half of Europe to Stalin's dictatorship.[19] Adding a final insult to the liberal sensibilities of many in the audience, he made a point of praising Franco's Spain. When he sat down, the applause was markedly muted. 'The inspiring crash of dropping bricks echoed through Pietermaritzburg City Hall,' reported the *Natal Witness* on 22 March.

In spite of the cool reception, Roy was unrepentant. On the following day he wrote defiantly to Rob Lyle. 'I made a shock-speech mostly about the fuss being kicked up about our ten million natives by people guilty of the sale of two hundred million *natives* of Europe to a far worse slavery, that tittering zombie Roosevelt and his henchman, the once valiant but senile Beefeater, Winston, sold half Christendom for a bottle of vodka at Yalta etc.'[20] In his anger he almost appeared to be condoning Malan's racist regime while simultaneously condemning American hypocrisy on the issue of apartheid.

> Catholics aren't too popular with Malan but the whole of the set-up out here has been criminally exaggerated – Zulus and Indians who got their MA's and BSc's and BA's kneeling on the same cushion as me got uproarious applause from the whites. Throughout half the USA they wouldn't even have been allowed in the same Hall. The natives here in Natal are a picture of contentment and well-being: though it's far different in the Transvaal.[21]

Not for the first time, Campbell's sense of logic had been betrayed by his sense of anger.

Roy's sweeping and simplistic generalizations were also in evidence in a letter he wrote soon afterwards to Edith Sitwell. Churchill was once more dubbed a 'valiant but stupid Beefeater' and Roosevelt was again a 'tittering zombie', although the latter, for good measure, was also 'a criminal moron if ever there was one!' Both of them were compared unfavourably to Franco. 'Franco, the only man that ever fooled Stalin and Hitler has been called a "puppet",' yet in reality Churchill and Roosevelt 'were the "puppets" when they walked into their own self-set booby trap at Yalta to sell Christendom for a bottle of Vodka!' He also claimed, in an amazing example of selective and wishful thinking, that Spain, Portugal and Ireland were all 'run on papal encyclicals by kindly people'.[22]

While Roy was busy stirring up a political hornets' nest in South Africa, Mary, alone in Portugal, was writing anxiously beseeching his early return. 'All I know is that I have had enough of being quite alone here, and I am *longing* for you to come back,' she wrote.[23] Roy's reply, giving his reasons for wishing to tarry in South Africa a while longer, was prophetic. 'I am longing to see you my beloved – but this is the last time I will ever set eyes on my beloved country (How I love it!) so let me take in all I can before I finish with it.'[24]

Having extended his leave of absence from Portugal, Roy spent a week fishing with his brother on the coast south of Port Edward. He attended his sister Ethel's funeral after she died in April following a long illness, and then set off north in a Land-Rover to the Hluhluwe game reserve. His attempts to secure a photograph of himself 'toreadoring' a black rhinoceros with his dufflecoat almost ended disastrously when the infuriated animal charged their vehicle. He alluded to this incident in a letter he wrote later to his friend Charles Ley. 'We had a lot of fun in Mocambique and Zululand: a rhino went for our jeep, smashed the bonnet, and removed the number plate. We took wonderful photos of Rhino, elephants, giraffes, buffaloes, gnus, hippos, crocs and hundreds of different antelopes and zebras.'[25]

Roy eventually arrived back home in Portugal on 14 May to find that Tess had fallen in love with a young man, Ignatius Custodio, and had fallen pregnant by him. Plans were hastened for a wedding, but from the start there was angry disagreement between Tess and her fiancé. Ignatius was bitterly anticlerical and resented Tess's insistence that they should be married in a Catholic church. He eventually succumbed to her wishes and they were duly married in a religious ceremony on 7 August. Within two weeks he had deserted her for a wealthy Swiss woman, although he resumed contact following the birth of their son early the following year. 'Tess's baby is doing fine,' Roy wrote to Charles Ley in February 1955. 'His name – Francisco. The father called him after Frank Sinatra: but we say we called him after the Caudillo.'[26]

Roy's return to Portugal was accompanied by a recurrence of malaria. He spent weeks in bed during the summer of 1954 making translations of the plays of Lope de Vega, Calderón de la Barca, Federico García Lorca and Tirso de Molina for the BBC. He also translated Eca de Queiro's novel *The City and the Mountains*. He was too ill to accept an invitation to be crowned a 'Soci' of the Felibrige, a society of Provençal poets in Avignon, but his delight at being honoured in this way was evident in a poem he wrote at the time.

> I've had my share of solitudes and caverns.
> What mountain-tops could teach I learned of old,
> But got the true Provençal in the taverns
> By which I sailed into the 'Isles of Gold'.
>
> To sit with Mistral under the green laurels
> From which his children gathered me my crown,
> While the deep wine that is the end of quarrels
> Glows through me like the sunset going down.

There is little doubt that Campbell received a great deal of consolation from the belated honours being bestowed on him by his literary peers. Since the Anglo-Saxons he had so often berated had honoured him with the Foyle Prize for Poetry at the beginning of 1952, he had been honoured by his native

South Africa, by his Provençal peers, and by enthusiastic audiences the length and breadth of Canada and the United States. Yet the same period had seen the passing of two of his closest friends, Dylan Thomas and Aime Tschiffely, adding to Roy's belief that his own life, having waxed so eloquent, was on the wane. His late poems meander with the slow serenity so often absent from the impatient surge of his earlier verse. Instead of the roar of battle there is only 'the deep wine that is the end of quarrels', which glows with the lingering but dying warmth of the setting sun.

A similar sense of serenity tinged with melancholy was the dominant feature of one of Roy's last poems, 'November Nights'. In long lines and tranquil rhythms, the poem displays a contented acceptance of imminent old age. He and Mary, so long the 'troopers of the Sun', were now fugitives from the cold. 'November Nights' was a reaffirmation of Roy's lifelong love for Mary and for life itself. It was also a powerful and evocative poetic swansong.

> But for the firelight on your face I would not change the sun,
> Nor would I change a moment of our winter season, no,
> For our springtime with its orioles and roses long ago.

NOTES

1 Francesca de Carondelet, letter to the author, 18 April 2000.
2 *Ibid.*
3 Anna Campbell Lyle, *Son of Valour*, p. 212.
4 Francesca de Carondelet, interview with the author, Portugal, December 1998.
5 Roy Campbell, unpublished letter to his mother, postmarked 15 April 1953.
6 Roy Campbell, unpublished letter to Rob Lyle, summer 1953.
7 Roy Campbell, unpublished letter to Rob Lyle, 22 October 1953.
8 Roy Campbell, unpublished letter to Rob Lyle, early November 1953.
9 *Ibid.*
10 Roy Campbell, unpublished letter to Rob Lyle, mid-November 1953.
11 Peter Alexander, *Roy Campbell*, p. 230.
12 Roy Campbell, unpublished letter to Rob Lyle, mid-November 1953.
13 Roy Campbell, unpublished letter to Mary Campbell, mid-November 1953.
14 Roy Campbell, unpublished letter to Rob Lyle, mid-November 1953.
15 Roy Campbell, unpublished letter to Mary Campbell, mid-November 1953.
16 Roy Campbell, 'In Memoriam A. F. Tschiffely', *Collected Works I*, p. 626.
17 Roy Campbell, unpublished letter to Rob Lyle, March 1954.
18 *Ibid.*
19 Peter Alexander, *Roy Campbell*, pp. 231–2.
20 Roy Campbell, unpublished letter to Rob Lyle, 21 March 1954.
21 *Ibid.*
22 Roy Campbell, unpublished letter to Edith Sitwell, *c.* April/May 1954.
23 Peter Alexander, *Roy Campbell*, p. 232.
24 *Ibid.*
25 Roy Campbell, unpublished letter to Charles Ley, July 1954.
26 Roy Campbell, unpublished letter to Charles Ley, postmarked 22 February 1955.

CHAPTER THIRTY-FIVE

TEARING THE VEIL

For when that final rosary is told,
He who is still new-born (though none so old)
The still-unchanging Present, fold from fold
Tearing the veil, will prove to us at last
That there was never Future time nor Past,
But that, a mere illusion in each tense,
Time was the mere reflection of events,
To fill up gaps between them in our sense . . .[1]

Roy and Mary returned to England in October 1954, remaining until the New Year. They invited David Wright and his wife to spend Christmas with them, and Wright recalled that Campbell appeared to be his old vivacious self. Over Christmas dinner he kept his guests entertained with 'gargantuan stories of disgraceful mishaps'. He also astounded Wright and his wife with what appeared to be a feat of superhuman strength. Wright had been struggling to crack a walnut when Campbell took it from him, placed it in 'the massive crook of his elbow' and set his biceps to work to split it in two.

> He went through a formidable pantomime of effort, veins bulging from his forehead and the sweat pouring down, while the rest of us watched appalled, wondering if he was going to burst a blood-vessel. After thirty excruciating seconds of terrifying exertion, he produced the nut neatly cracked. Overwhelmed by his spectacular demonstration I thought 'My word, the old man's even stronger than he says he is'. But, later, he took me aside and, after swearing me to secrecy, explained it was a parlour trick (you hold the nut in a certain way so that the slightest pressure cracks it). Then it struck me that Campbell's most grandiose feats of physical prowess, of which he loved to boast, had about them the same element – part bluff, part illusion, and part joke – which is not to say that they were phoney, but that for him these feats did not have the importance he pretended to attach to them.[2]

It may have been during this Christmas that Campbell wrote 'Nativity', one of his most overtly religious poems. Infused throughout with a spirit of humility, the poem shows the poet in penitential mood, his 'Cloven heart' a 'hoofprint in the mire'. His sorrow, like his sin, is overpowered by the unfathomable joy of the Incarnation.

> Never so joyfully the brave cocks crew –
> No more by turns, but all with one accord.
> Never so early woke the mule and ox
> Since it was day before the east was blue:
> Mary was dawn, the Sunrise was Our Lord,
> And Joseph was the watchtower on the rocks.
>
> . . . Love filled with fierce delight the humblest creature
> As heaven fills an eye, or as the Holy
> Infinitude the wafer and the cup.

Roy's health continued to arouse concern amongst his friends and family, and in January 1955 Rob Lyle persuaded him to consult a doctor. It was discovered that, apart from his other problems, he was also suffering from diabetes. Soon after their return to Portugal early in 1955, financial anxieties were added to the problems surrounding Roy's health. The labourer who helped Mary run the smallholding, José Mel, fell from a ladder, breaking his right leg and ankle. Under Portuguese law, having failed to insure him against accidents Roy and Mary were responsible for his hospital bills. These were considerable because three operations were carried out in an effort to reset his fractured bones. The operations proved unsuccessful, leaving the labourer permanently disabled. In these circumstances the law stipulated that Roy and Mary were responsible for paying an amount equal to two-thirds of his monthly salary for the rest of his life.

This was a savage blow, wiping out the Campbells' financial security in one devastating stroke. In June they were forced to sell the lease on their house in Campden Grove and they abandoned any hope of buying Quinta dos Bochechos outright. In desperation, Roy revived plans to write a book on Portugal and began making plans for a further tour of North America in the autumn, no doubt hoping that Marshall McLuhan's predictions about its lucrative potential would be fulfilled.

In the midst of the financial gloom, the Campbells' spirits were lifted by news that Edith Sitwell was about to be received into the Catholic Church. On 14 July 1955 Edith had written to Roy, informing him of her decision and requesting that he and Mary be her godparents. It was a graphic illustration of her high regard for Roy and Mary and her sense of gratitude to them for helping to bring her to the threshold of conversion. 'Roy Campbell represented a great deal to her,' wrote Elizabeth Salter, the Australian novelist and biographer who served as Sitwell's secretary.

> Not only was he a poet whom she greatly admired, but he was that rare thing in her life, a champion. Perhaps because she had proved herself to be so formidable, it was not often that she was defended by her admirers and seldom, if ever, defended physically. She had an Elizabethan appreciation of a man who could use his hands as well as his head and she responded to Roy Campbell's championship with an entirely feminine gratitude.[3]

'It's great news from Edith,' Campbell wrote delightedly to Charles Ley, 'she sent us a wire "my dearest godparents I am to be received on August 4".'[4] Roy told Ley that somebody else had deputized for him and Mary because ill health had prevented him travelling to London for the occasion.

Edith was received at noon on 4 August at the fashionable Jesuit church in Farm Street in the heart of Mayfair. Evelyn Waugh, her other godfather, was in attendance and described Edith's appearance on the day with a novelist's eye for detail. She was 'swathed in black like a sixteenth-century infanta'.[5] On the day of her reception, Edith wrote to Edward Sackville-West, evidently eager to share the day's joys with an old friend who was also a fellow convert.

> Today is that on which I shall be received into the Church, and I do, in a way, tremble at the thought . . . You say it took twelve years to bring you to your resolution. It must have taken about the same time to bring me to mine. I could not at first. Because Osbert is so ghastly ill, and I felt, so to speak, that I could not leave him. Then one day in New York this winter, he told me that I must become a Catholic. And he said, 'How do you know that I may not become one too.' So I hope he will.[6]

'Is Alec Guinness a friend of yours?' Sitwell asked Sackville-West as a postscript. 'He is a friend of mine. He, too, is becoming a Catholic.'

On 9 October 1955, having barely recovered from the bout of diabetes which had prevented him travelling to Sitwell's reception, Roy set sail for his second lecture tour of Canada and the United States. He was not really fit enough to undertake another demanding tour and poor health dogged his efforts to fulfil his obligations. Nonetheless, he could still write lively letters to Mary overflowing with infectious enthusiasm.

> I am staying 40 miles out of Louisville Kentucky at one of the most beautiful convents I've seen. (I spoke and read for 2 hours last night

> without feeling the worse for wear). This convent is next to Gethsemane Trappists where Thos Merton ('Still Waters') hangs out: it is in beautiful woods, with very intelligent sisters who teach Literature, Classics, Music (including the Harp) and very lively girl students – many of them Spanish speaking . . . Today is Sunday, I went to Mass at the Convent Church: a beautiful affair.[7]

He had flown to Kentucky from his previous engagement in New York and the day after this letter was written he flew to Cleveland for the next scheduled lecture. Roy's enfeebled constitution was no longer able to take such a rigorous regime, however, and inevitably he buckled under the strain. After only 15 lectures it became clear that he could not continue. Cutting short the tour, he returned to Portugal aboard the *Andrea Doria* on 19 December. Arriving home utterly exhausted, he was put to bed by Mary and remained there for several weeks.

In January 1956, while Roy was still bedridden, news arrived from South Africa that Mrs Campbell had died at the age of 93 after a protracted illness. Two months later, Roy discovered that she had left him £6,000 in her will, a windfall that solved his and Mary's financial problems as unexpectedly as the labourer's accident had created them. They persuaded the disabled José Mel to accept a lump sum in lieu of the lifetime monthly payments, but it was too late to abort the plans they had set in motion to leave Bochechos, a move forced upon them by the previous year's financial crisis.

On 29 April they moved into a small rented modern house in the nearby village of Linho. It was barely large enough to hold Roy's books and problems were caused by the close proximity of neighbours, one of whom owned a large dog which barked incessantly while Roy was writing his book, *Portugal*. 'Still it's an ill wind that blows no good,' he wrote resignedly to Edith Sitwell, 'the climate here is so dry and bracing that I do not suffer a tenth what I did on our misty, damp farm which racked us both with rheumatism.'[8]

In the months following her reception into the Church, Edith's relationship with Roy seemed to grow closer than ever. In particular, Roy was delighted to see that Edith now saw herself as his champion and protector in much the same way that he had seen himself as hers. 'My god-daughter Edith has put up a terrific battle and wiped the floor with the American critics who were pitching into me as a fascist on all sides,' he informed Charles Ley. 'She also wrote the most magnificent review of my *Collected Poems* in the *Saturday Review*.'[9]

Roy's unease and anger at the lingering allegations, particularly in America, that he was a 'fascist' were evident in several letters he wrote at this time. Typical of these was a long, indignant letter to Harvey Brit, whom

Roy had met in New York during his recent visit, in which his justifiable frustration at being misrepresented was combined with a far from justifiable embellishment and fabrication of the truth.

> Apparently the systematic misrepresentation of your reviewers ... is due to the fact that Mrs Rebecca West in her best selling 'Meaning of Treason' falsely says that I once belonged to the Fascist Party ... but she was forced abjectly and publicly to apologise in the London *Times*. I was approached by Percy Wyndham Lewis in 1936 to lunch with Mosley when I had been badly wounded in Spain and had been decorated for saving life (not for 'storm-trooping') under fire, fourteen times, with the Spanish Purple Heart (Cruz de San Fernando). That was when the English Fascist Party was at its zenith and I was regarded as a hero of the Right. I not only refused Mosley's and Lewis's offer of a very high and lucrative position in the Fascist party but explained that I was going back into the ranks to fight Red Fascism, the worst and most virulent variety, and that when the time came I was ready to fight brown or black fascism and that I could (although badly disabled) knock out both their brains with my crutches there and then! I explained that I was only fighting as a Christian for the right to pray in my own churches, all of which (save 3) had been destroyed in Red Spain ... I then asked for my coat and hat: Lewis has never forgiven it. I have been 2 times 'severely' and once dangerously wounded in fighting as a volunteer against fascism, Red, Brown and Black, and now I may be dying of my wounds which have sprouted tumours – possibly malignant ... How is it conceivable that I can still be accused of fascism? ...
>
> My good natured, not malicious, digs at the Jews come from the very opposite of the Fascist attitude, which treated them as inferiors – the envy of a Celt for a *superior* race in favour of whom 150,000,000 of my fellow Christians were sold for a bottle of vodka at Yalta to a worse form of tyrannous baboonery than that from which we declared was to save them: I always stick up for the underdog. Yours is a Christian-baiting paper as witness all the fantastic lies about me to which Edith Sitwell, Eliot, Dylan Thomas, and Bill Empson have all indignantly referred. My digs are only defensive. Eliot wrote to me 'You will find yourself misrepresented in the U.S. for considerations that have nothing to do with literature' ...
>
> And I am an exile deported from my country because I stood up for fair play for the blacks – is that Fascism?[10]

In August 1956 Sitwell sang Campbell's praises when she was televised at the Edinburgh Festival. She had befriended Sir Kenneth Clarke, the celebrated art historian, who was currently the head of Independent Television, and she reported to Campbell that Clarke had enthused about a passage from *Flowering Rifle* which had been published in a literary journal, describing it as 'the most transcendental splendour he had seen since he could remember'. Edith asked Roy if she could show Clarke a copy 'of that glorious work, just discovered, the poem to Mary, that you sent me'.[11] This was presumably the surviving fragment of 'The Golden Shower', the long love poem to Mary on which Roy had spent months of painstaking effort before it was lost when the cabin was flooded during the return voyage to England from South Africa in January 1927. With the assistance of his old friend C. J. Sibbett, Roy had recently discovered the only section of the poem which had been printed in South Africa and had reworked it for inclusion in the second volume of his *Collected Poems*, which was almost ready for publication.

Clearly greatly impressed with the poem, Sitwell was equally impressed with the love it celebrated. 'It is, I may say, one of the great things in my life, this lasting love between you and Mary, in an age of little, fireless unreal would-be emotions, gone in a moment, everything turned to ashes, to know that such greatness and undying love exists, unquenchable. You deserve, and she deserves, your poetry.'[12]

The closeness of Roy's relationship with the Sitwells placed a further strain on his fading friendship with Wyndham Lewis. His more critical attitude towards his old 'comrade-in-arms', already expressed in the letter to Harvey Brit, was reiterated in another letter written in 1956.

> Lewis is as mad as a hatter – but a genius. (He makes up anything he likes about me). He puts me in about 5 of his books as the hero or villain. I come into 'Revenge for Love' as Victor Stamp: in 'Snooty Baronet' as Rob McPhail: in the 'Apes of God' as Zulu Blades and Blackshirt: Hyperides in the Childermass: and Enemy No. 2 in One Way Song. I hear he has put me in some of his later novels etc (but not 'Condemned to Live'). He has always suffered from a terrible persecution mania and he never forgives any one who does him a good turn. I never lent him money or helped him in any way – so I remained a friend of his for many years, about thirty: but he didn't like it when I became Edith Sitwell's Godfather. The Sitwells generously supported him for about 20 years and he never forgave them. On the surface we are friends and I always go to see him when I'm in London – but he suspects me of 'spying on him for the Church' (!!!). He has a mania about people 'spying' on him.[13]

Apart from Sitwell's continuing vociferous support, other friends also sprang to Campbell's defence whenever they heard him attacked. Richard Aldington, writing to his friend Alan Bird in June 1956, beseeched him to adopt 'a more cheerful view of Roy' – 'I no more accept his Catholicism than his bull-killing, but I can tell you that he is one of the most warm-hearted and generous men I ever met, keeps the table in a roar. And he is a very great poet, certainly our greatest satirist since Byron.'[14] Muriel Spark, meeting up with Edith Sitwell at the Sesame Club in 1957, was delighted to discover that they shared a deep affection for Campbell, 'whom I greatly admired, both as a person and a poet'.[15]

A particularly fond reminiscence of Roy, as he appeared in the final months before his death, was given by David Wright.

> The last time I saw Campbell was some months before his death. He was to fly to Portugal the next day and I had gone to 'The Catherine Wheel' to say goodbye. When I arrived at the pub he was not there, but his wife and daughter and a dozen or more friends sat waiting for him in an alcove in the saloon bar. Everyone was worried about Campbell's health . . . We were wondering if he was going to appear at all when the swing door opened and the old man came in, huge and rolling, his black Cordoba at an angle over his whitening sideburns, and great torso wrapped in a magnificent cape. He was leaning on a silver-headed malacca, his whole appearance flamboyant and fabulous, a shark among goldfish; ex-sergeant, poet, and toreador, grinning like a schoolboy. Before we could get up to welcome him, an extraordinary thing happened: everyone in the pub spontaneously rose to his feet, though only those who were waiting in the alcove may have known to who or for what the involuntary ovation had been given.[16]

Having left London for what would be the last time, Roy and Mary settled down to what they hoped would be a new chapter in their life together. They had found a plot of land for sale on a hillside, a mile out of Linho, with superb views across the coastal plain to Cascais seven miles away and the Atlantic beyond. With the money remaining from Campbell's inheritance they began building a house – the first they had ever owned in 35 years of marriage. A local man was hired to divine water, a well was sunk, and a rocky path was smoothed to allow their little Fiat access to the building site.

As their new home took shape, Roy and Mary settled down to some of the most peaceful and serene months of their married life. The restless wanderlust appears to have departed, so that Roy could write reflectively in 'November Nights' of 'cantering the rocking-chair' contentedly – 'For my olives have been gathered and my grapes are in the tun.'

By the end of 1956 Roy seemed to have surrendered the violent inconsistencies in his character to the tranquillity of age. Each morning he and Mary went to Mass at the nearby convent and each evening they prayed the rosary together. 'We have to say one-fifth for the bolshies' conversion,' he wrote to Edith Sitwell. 'I would sooner be fighting them – but the Holy Father knows best.'[17] The words were rhetorical, designed to play up to Sitwell's view of him as a champion on a charger, but the bombast belied his increasing inability to fight anyone. He was now suffering from sciatica, so that a walk of more than a hundred yards was a severe struggle. Although he was still only in his mid-fifties, he looked much older.

Roy and Mary spent a quiet religious Christmas in Portugal with their daughters and grandchildren, discarding their usual practice of returning to England for the festivities. Increasingly haunted by premonitions of his own death, Roy's Christmas letters to old friends conveyed a peacefully resigned and prophetic note. To Daphne Collins, his BBC secretary with whom he had corresponded since 1950, he wrote, 'I am rather ill; maybe I shall not write to you again, but I send my respectful affection, as from the first day that you so kindly worked with me.'[18]

In January 1957 he finished correcting the proofs of the second volume of his *Collected Poems*, but he had little energy for new work. He made half-hearted efforts to finish his history of the Spanish Civil War, a project undertaken 'to correct the Kremlin-crazy liars in England'[19] as early as 1939 and to which he had returned intermittently ever since. 'I'm having a neck-and-neck race to finish my Military history of the Spanish War, before I go to Purgatory,' he wrote to a priest friend, Father Jones.[20] His obsession with impending death resurfaced in February in a letter to Max Reinhardt, who was publishing Campbell's book on Portugal.[21] It seemed as though Roy was ready to sign off and was simply awaiting the graceful glide towards death.

On 5 April he and Mary set off in their tiny Fiat 600 for Spain, destined for the Holy Week celebrations in Seville. *En route* they stopped off for several days in Toledo, 'this heavenly place which means more than all the world to me', as Campbell described it in a postcard to Vernon Watkins.[22] Throughout the week of processions in Seville, Mary noticed that her husband was unusually quiet and particularly serious in his devotions.

On 23 April they set off back to Portugal, crossing the border in the early afternoon. By four o'clock they were near Setúbal in southern Portugal and looking forward to arriving home in time for tea. Suddenly a front tyre burst, and the car swerved out of control into a tree at the side of the road. Mary was dragged unconscious from the wreckage, her foot crushed and her arm, ribs and front teeth broken. Roy's injuries were more serious. He had a broken neck. After breathing for a short time, he sighed twice before life slipped away.

Roy was buried in the cemetery of São Pedro, near Sintra, four days later.

Mary, recovering in hospital, could not attend. She would live for a further 22 years in the new house, still unfinished in April 1957, in which her husband was never destined to reside.

In the void created by his absence, Roy's presence could still be felt in the final lines of the poem he had written to Mary more than 30 years earlier when their love was young.

> When all that was, or shall be, merely *is*
> And all existence is self-known in His,
> That which we feel today in either sprite,
> And which we know in moments of delight
> Will then be fixed. If into you I burn
> Or both into that All, or each return
> Singly into ourselves – all shall be one.
> And in our love some part of this is done,
> For though He shines by us, it's not to dim
> The least existence that exists in Him.[23]

NOTES

1 Roy Campbell, from 'Fragment from "The Golden Shower" ', *Collected Poems, Volume Two*, pp. 21–2.
2 David Wright, *Roy Campbell*, pp. 40–41.
3 Elizabeth Salter, *The Last Years of a Rebel: A Memoir of Edith Sitwell*, London: The Bodley Head, 1967, p. 19.
4 Roy Campbell, unpublished letter to Charles Ley, July/August 1955.
5 Michael Davie (ed.), *The Diaries of Evelyn Waugh*, London: Phoenix, 1978, p. 735.
6 Richard Greene (ed.), *Selected Letters of Edith Sitwell*, London: Virago, 1997, pp. 366–7.
7 Roy Campbell, unpublished letter to Mary Campbell, November 1955.
8 Peter Alexander, *Roy Campbell*, p. 238.
9 Roy Campbell, unpublished letter to Charles Ley, early 1956.
10 Roy Campbell, unpublished letter to Harvey Brit, early 1956.
11 Richard Greene (ed.), *Selected Letters of Edith Sitwell*, pp. 372–3.
12 *Ibid.*, p. 372.
13 Roy Campbell, unpublished letter to an unidentified recipient, 1956.
14 Miriam J. Benkovitz (ed.), *A Passionate Prodigality: Letters to Alan Bird from Richard Aldington*, New York: New York Public Library and Readex Books, 1975, p. 235.
15 Muriel Spark, 'A Drink with Dame Edith', essay posted on the Internet at litrev.dircon.co.uk/0297/spark.html, dated 3 February 1999.
16 David Wright, *Roy Campbell*, pp. 41–2.
17 Peter Alexander, *Roy Campbell*, p. 239.
18 *Ibid.*, pp. 239–40.
19 *Ibid.*, p. 240.
20 Roy Campbell, unpublished letter to Father Jones, January/February 1957.
21 Peter Alexander, *Roy Campbell*, p. 270.
22 *Ibid.*
23 From 'Fragment from "The Golden Shower" ', *Collected Poems, Volume Two*, p. 22.

CHAPTER THIRTY-SIX

POSTMORTEM

For only out of solitude or strife
Are born the sons of valour and delight;
And lastly for her rich, exulting life,
That with the wind stopped not its singing breath
But carolled on, the louder for its death.[1]

There was something symbolic about the violent nature of Campbell's death. Ever a man of action, real and imagined, he had endured, and even on occasions enjoyed, the violent aspects of life. He died, it seemed, as he had lived. Not for him the slow subsidence into sickness and a protracted exit. The self-styled 'soldier-poet' had died with his boots on. The symbolism was not lost on Edith Sitwell, who was shocked and horrified when news of Campbell's death reached her in the middle of a press conference during a visit to New York:

> This simple giant, with 'devocioun in his heart', was the true Knight of Our Lady, and if he had to be taken by death, it was suitable that this should have been when he was returning from the celebration of Her Son's Resurrection.
>
> I think, too, that he, who was all energy, all fire, would have hated to die slowly and helplessly, in bed. He died, as he had lived, like a flash of lightning.[2]

One wonders whether Sitwell had also noticed that her champion, the knight who had defended her reputation against the attacks of various literary dragons, had been killed on the feast of St George. She was the most prominent of the literati to attend Roy's requiem, celebrated by their mutual friend Father Martin D'Arcy, at Farm Street on 21 May, and her words of comfort to Mary 'in your greatest grief, desolation, and loneliness' were a true testament to the depth of her love for him. Roy, she said, was 'one of the only really great poets of our time – such fire, such a holy spirit, such ineffable beauty'.[3]

From the moment of Campbell's death, Sitwell clearly saw herself as his literary champion, repaying a perceived debt to him. As he had defended her while he was alive, she would defend him now that he was dead and unable to defend himself. She reviewed the second volume of his *Collected Poems* for the *Sunday Times* and wrote the foreword to the third volume which was published in 1960, describing his poems as being 'of great stature' and having 'a giant's strength and power of movement, without a giant's heaviness' as well as 'an extraordinary sensuous beauty – a sensuousness that is extremely rare in our time'. In her autobiography, *Taken Care Of*, published shortly after her own death in 1964, she repeated her adoration of his poetry and expressed her admiration for the man behind the poetry.

> One would have noticed him anywhere, towering above the crowd, not only because of his height, and certainly not because of any flaunting characteristics – he was utterly lacking in affectation, in appearance or manner – but because of his extraordinary personality.
>
> He had a great simplicity, and his courtesy and sweetness to his friends could not have been greater. Fantastically brave and chivalrous, he had the simple heart and faith of a child . . . He has been accused of being a fascist. He was never a fascist. But, a deeply religious man, he fought against the Reds in Spain. He believed, as I believe, that it is equally infamous to massacre priests, nuns, Jews, peasants, and aristocrats.[4]

Many others shared Sitwell's love for Campbell and her grief at his passing. Richard Aldington wept openly when he heard the news, one of the few occasions that his daughter had ever seen him cry,[5] and Lawrence Durrell's warm words of tribute summed up the feelings of many who had known Roy intimately.

> A man of honour, a simple man devoid of affectation and egotism: riding a horse and writing poetry went together. He loved to wage his battles in the open. He was also a tremendous jester and he was a splendid enemy and an unforgettable friend. Modern poetry has lost a great huntsman who never spared the stupid, the complacent and the pompous, whose satire sang like a lasso. He loved wine and laughter. He is dead.
>
> Salutations, Roy! Something of the *real* world has died with you![6]

In the end, when all the tributes have been paid, one wonders whether the real Roy has emerged from the praise of his friends and admirers or whether he has been obscured by it. Certainly Roy's enemies – and there were many – would not have shared Durrell's view that his enmity was in any way 'splendid'. One cannot imagine Auden, Spender, Grigson, Day-Lewis or MacDiarmid concurring with such an opinion. Similarly, Sitwell's and Durrell's claim that Roy was 'utterly lacking in' or 'devoid of' affectation seems at variance with his fabrications and fantasizing about his exploits in the bullring and on the battlefield. When all the dust of claim and counterclaim has settled, the enigma remains.

Perhaps the only reliable way of getting to the heart of this enigma is through the person who was nearer to the enigma's heart than anyone. Nobody knew Roy better than the woman with whom he shared the greater part of his life and Mary's words, written in September 1957 only five months after her husband's death, throw invaluable light on the shadowy recesses of his character. Mary admitted that Roy was 'in some ways a violent poet', but she was at pains to point out that the 'apparent violence in his life or work was not the most characteristic side of him ... The violent side of his character was used as a cloak for a vulnerable contemplative soul. The tough soldier, the crack shot, the jouster, the convivial storyteller were all so many masks covering the retiring, gentle, creative spirit from a too brutal contact with everyday life.'[7]

Mary's life still seemed to revolve around Roy years after the sudden and violent severance of their physical relationship, as though she was refusing to be parted from him even in death. She loved to talk about him to visitors, laughing at the memory of his exploits, real and imagined. 'Oh, old Roy,' she would say, chuckling, 'you never stopped laughing when he was around, never.'[8] Eventually, after more than two decades of widowhood, Mary's enforced separation from her husband was ended. She died suddenly of a stroke on 27 February 1979, a few days before her eighty-first birthday, and was reunited with Roy, being buried with him in the same grave.

> For all the freight of Stygian ferries,
> Roll on the days of halcyon weather,
> The oriole fluting in the cherries,
> The sunlight sleeping on the farms,
> To say the Rosary together
> And sleep in one another's arms![9]

NOTES

1 Roy Campbell, from 'Choosing a Mast', *Collected Poems, Volume One*, p. 104.
2 Edith Sitwell, *Taken Care Of*, p. 166.
3 John Lehmann and Derek Parker (eds), *Edith Sitwell: Selected Letters 1919–1964*, New York: Macmillan, 1970, pp. 216–17.
4 Edith Sitwell, *Taken Care Of*, p. 164.
5 Alister Kershaw (ed.), *Salute to Roy Campbell*, p. 9.
6 *Ibid.*, p. 26.

7 Mary Campbell, preface to Roy Campbell, *St John of the Cross: Poems*, p. 13.
8 Peter Alexander, *Roy Campbell*, p. 241.
9 From 'The Skull in the Desert', *Collected Poems, Volume One*, p. 163.

BIBLIOGRAPHY
OF CAMPBELL'S PRINCIPAL WORKS

POETRY

The Flaming Terrapin, London: Jonathan Cape, 1924
The Wayzgoose, London: Jonathan Cape, 1928
Poems, Paris: The Hours Press, 1930
Adamastor, London: Faber & Faber, 1930
The Gum Trees, London: Faber & Faber, 1930
The Georgiad, London: Boriswood, 1931
Nineteen Poems, London: Ernest Benn, 1931
Choosing a Mast, London: Faber & Faber, 1931
Pomegranates, London: Boriswood, 1932
Flowering Reeds, London: Boriswood, 1933
Mithraic Emblems, London: Boriswood, 1936
Flowering Rifle, London: Longman, 1939
Sons of the Mistral, London: Faber & Faber, 1941
Talking Bronco, London: Faber & Faber, 1946
Nativity, London: Faber & Faber, 1954
Collected Poems, 3 vols., London: The Bodley Head, 1949, 1957, 1960

TRANSLATIONS

Helge Krog, *Three Plays*, London: Boriswood, 1934
The Poems of St John of the Cross, London: Harvill Press, 1951
Baudelaire, *Poems: A Translation of Les Fleurs du Mal*, London: Harvill Press, 1952
Eça de Queirós, *Cousin Basilio*, London: Max Reinhardt, 1953
Eça de Queirós, *The City and the Mountains*, London: Max Reinhardt, 1955
Paco d'Arcos, *Nostalgia, a Collection of Poems*, London: Sylvan Press, 1960

PROSE

Taurine Provence, London: Desmond Harmsworth, 1932
Broken Record, London: Boriswood, 1934
Light on a Dark Horse, London: Hollis & Carter, 1951
Lorca, Cambridge: Bowes & Bowes, 1952
The Mamba's Precipice, London: Frederick Muller, 1953
Portugal, London: Max Reinhardt, 1957

INDEX